ESG Investing and Analysis: A Practitioner's Guide

ESG Investing and Analysis: A Practitioner's Guide

How to Incorporate ESG Considerations in the Investment Process

Marie Lehmann, Martina Macpherson and Daniel Ung

Risk books

Published by Risk Books

Infopro Digital
133 Houndsditch
London EC3A 7BX
Tel: +44(0) 20 7316 9000
Sites: www.riskbooks.com

ISBN 978 1 78272 444 5

Commissioning Editors: Sarah Hastings and Victoria Nightingale
Managing Editor: Lewis O'Sullivan
Designer: Lisa Ling
Copyeditor: Laurie Donaldson

Typeset by Mark Heslington Ltd, Scarborough, North Yorkshire
Printed and bound in the UK by PrintonDemand-Worldwide

Contents

About the Editors

Marie Lehmann is Head of Global Partnerships – Banking Solutions at Moody's Analytics, where she is responsible for defining and delivering the global partner strategy for the banking division of Moody's Analytics. She has extensive experience in relationship and partnership management within the investment banking, asset management and insurance sectors. Previously, Marie worked as Advisor – Capital Markets for HRH The Prince of Wales's Accounting for Sustainability Project at St. James's Palace, a charitable organisation that aims to inspire action by finance leaders to drive a fundamental shift towards resilient business models and a sustainable economy. She also held senior relationship and managerial roles for Thomson Reuters and Dow Jones, and contributed to the Handbook on Species Extinction Accounting and Biodiversity. Marie holds an MBA from Warwick Business School with a specialisation in corporate citizenship, as well as an MBA from Montpellier Business School in France. She has also completed an MSt in sustainability leadership at the University of Cambridge Institute for Sustainability Leadership.

Martina Macpherson is a board and senior management level financial services strategy, product and engagement expert, with a track record and passion for developing ESG and fintech solutions across segments and asset classes. She has held several global leadership roles in ESG strategy, product development and innovation, and is head of product management at SIX, Swiss Exchanges Group and a board member of the Network of Sustainable Financial Markets. Martina was previously head of ESG strategy and on the executive management team at ODDO BHF Asset Management, senior vice president ESG and engagement strategy at Moody's, global head of ESG index products and research at S&P DJI and managing director of Sustainable Investments Partners, among other roles. She is a visiting fellow at University of Zurich and

Henley Business School. Martina has an MBA certificate in finance and business from LSBF/UK, and an MA in law and human sciences from University of Frankfurt. She is a fellow member of the Institute for Corporate Responsibility and Sustainability UK, a honorary doctoral fellow of the Institute for Certified Risk Management Professionals UK, and an alumnus of the German National Academic Foundation. Martina is a public speaker in sustainable investing and has co-authored a range of ESG and fintech books.

Daniel Ung is the head of quantitative research and analysis, ETF model portfolio solutions at one of the world's largest global asset managers, where he is responsible for research on asset allocation using ETFs. Previously, he was a senior smart beta strategist and in charge of conducting product research and analysis of ETFs, with a particular focus on smart beta. Before joining his current employer, Daniel was a director of global research and design at S&P Dow Jones Indices, and worked in the Structured Products Group at Barclays Wealth and Investment Management and the Commodities Investor Derivatives Group at BNP Paribas Fortis Bank. He has published extensively in journals, is an associate editor of the Journal of Beta Investment Strategies and has co-authored books on ESG and smart beta investing. In addition, Daniel is also active in academia, and was a guest lecturer at the Imperial College Business School and an examiner of the Chartered Alternative Investment Association (CAIA) exams. He holds a masters from the Ecole Supérieure de Commerce de Paris and is a CFA, CAIA and FRM charterholder.

About the Authors

Jill Atkins is a Professor in Accounting at Cardiff Business School and a visiting professor at the University of the Witwatersrand, South Africa. Her research focuses on corporate governance, responsible investment, sustainability, integrated reporting and extinction accounting. Jill is series editor for the *de Gruyter Studies in Corporate Governance*, and edited *The Business of Bees: An Integrated Approach to Bee Decline and Corporate Responsibility*. She also wrote and edited *Around the World in 80 Species: Exploring the Business Case for Extinction Prevention*, co-edited *Extinction Governance, Accounting and Finance* and co-authored *Chief Value Officer: Accountants Can Save the Planet*. Jill's leading textbook, *Corporate Governance and Accountability*, is now in its 5th edition. She has a BA hons (first class) in European economics with a Licence ès Sciences Economiques from the University of Nantes, an MSc in corporate and international finance from the University of Durham, and a PhD in finance from the University of Manchester.

Arthur Carabia is Director, ESG Policy Research, at Morningstar Sustainalytics, where he is in charge of identifying, analysing and engaging on proposed laws, rules, regulations and prescribed practices applicable to the company and its clients. He previously worked for the International Capital Market Association (ICMA), Aviva, the French Asset Management Association (AFG), and the European Parliament. Arthur holds a master's degree in European affairs from Sciences Po Lyon and an advanced master's degree in financial markets from Solvay Brussels School.

Lucy Carmody helps institutional investors allocate capital at scale to global carbon projects for Climate Impact Partners, a leading player in the global voluntary carbon market. She has over two decades of operational, communications, strategy and board experience in public and private equity investment, has been involved in launches of funds in impact and emerging market ESG, and has curated and hosted events on sustainability themes for investors. In 2012 Lucy sold her business, Responsible Research, to Sustainalytics and exited in 2020 when Sustainalytics was bought by Morningstar. She has published research on topics as wide ranging as the future of fish, green building in Asia and palm oil in Asia. Lucy is Chair of the Friends of Grantham Institute, and holds a masters in climate change management and finance from Imperial College Business School and the Grantham Institute, and an MSc in geography from St John's College, University of Cambridge.

Kartik Chawla is a senior quantitative research analyst within the model portfolio solutions at one of the biggest global asset manager, where he is responsible for providing research on asset allocation using ETFs in investment portfolios. Previously, he worked at Credit Suisse's Delta One, Prime Services desk, where he worked on quantitative index and ETF trading, market making, replication and rebalance strategies across EMEA and APAC equity product line. Before that, Kartik led the Index Research and Design functions of Nasdaq and S&P Dow Jones Indexes, where he worked extensively on smart beta, ESG and new generation thematic strategies across different client segments. He has also worked at a proprietary high frequency trading firm in India, and holds a bachelor's of technology degree in computer science and engineering from Kurukshetra University, India.

Christine Chow is the global head of stewardship at HSBC Asset Management and a board member of HSBC Asset Management UK. Christine is a board member of the International Corporate Governance Network, an honorary adviser to the Financial Reporting Council Hong Kong, and the convenor of the FRC Sustainability and Climate Action Task Force. She is also an emeritus governor of the LSE, was a member in the Data Governance Task Force of the UK All Party Parliamentary Group on artificial intelligence, and an adjunct professor in finance at the Hong Kong University of Science and Technology. Christine was named as in the top 30 Inspirational Women in the City of London, and has won the *Finance Monthly* "Women in Finance" award. She is a graduate of the LSE and the University of Melbourne, and has completed an executive education course on financial engineering at Stanford University.

Marc Olivier Dines is the Head of Listed Investments at the Velux Foundations in Denmark. He previously served in various roles as a senior portfolio manager at PensionDanmark, where he worked on implementing a Paris Agreement-aligned investment portfolio, and as Senior Treasury Manager in FIH, a Danish bank, covering most listed asset classes. Marc has increasingly worked with integrating ESG considerations into the investment process. He holds an MSc in economics from the University of Copenhagen, where he has also lectured as External Associate Professor. Marc is a CFA charterholder and also holds the Certificate in ESG Investing.

Carol Nolan Drake is the CEO and founder of Carlow Consulting, is the Governance and Stewardship Policy Manager for the International Corporate Governance Network, and a facilitator for training programmes. She previously represented the School Employees Retirement System of Ohio as its federal liaison in Washington, D.C. Carol's career began as an assistant county prosecutor and assistant city attorney, and she has served as a cabinet director of the Department of Administrative Services and as chair/vice chair on several boards and commissions. She was the co-chair of the ICGN Shareholder Responsibilities Committee, is a licensed attorney, and has authored many articles on governance and ESG best practices, and regularly speaks on corporate governance, ESG and investor issues. Carol is a *cum laude* graduate of Ohio Wesleyan University and the Claude W. Pettit College of Law, Ohio Northern University.

Caroline Escott leads Railpen's global stewardship and corporate governance activities across £37 billion of assets under management and on behalf of 350,000 members of the UK railways pension schemes. She was previously in charge of the investment, stewardship and collective engagement programme at the Pensions and Lifetime Savings Association (PLSA) and Head of Public Policy at the UK Sustainable Investment and Finance Association (UKSIF). Caroline is an accredited professional trustee at the Standard Life Master Trust, winner of Investment Week's "Investment Woman of the Year 2019" award and was one of Financial News' 2020 "Top 25 Rising Stars of Asset Management in Europe". She is chair of pensions industry organisation NextGen and a trustee at the Social Market Foundation (SMF).

Jens Güldner is Head of Wealth and Foundation Management at Johannesstift Diakonie. He previously held the same role at Paul Gerhardt Diakonie, and has also been chairman of the board, and before that CFO, at the Werner and Maren Otto Foundation. Jens has also been Head of Wealth Management and Head of Treasury at Evangelisches Johannesstift, and Head of Finance/Controlling at Erinnerung, Verantwortung und Zukunft. He also previously worked in the Corporate Clients Department at Commerzbank and in the Private Clients Department at Berliner Commerzbank. Jens also had the role of Foundation Advisor at Universität für Wirtschaft und Recht, worked in marketing at Martin-Luther Universität Halle-Wittenberg, and has won numerous industry awards, and been published in a range of industry magazines and books.

Lydia Harvey is an executive director, ESG specialist, Global Index Research at JP Morgan Chase. Born in Sydney, Australia, she developed her passion for the environment and sustainability by exploring the extraordinary, diverse and often remote natural landscapes of her country. Lydia completed a bachelor of resource economics (hons) from Sydney University and a master's degree in environmental management from the University of New South Wales. Initially focusing on environmental issues as a senior consultant for S&P Trucost, she later worked as a risk manager for Merian Global Investors with a strong focus on ESG. Lydia has extensive experience in assisting financial institutions to meaningfully integrate ESG.

Andreas G. F. Hoepner is Full Professor of Operational Risk, Banking & Finance at the Michael Smurfit Graduate Business School and the University College Dublin Lochlann Quinn School of Business. He also serves on the schools' management team, and is a named supervisor for UCD's SFI Centre for Research Training in Machine Learning. Andreas works on the EU's Platform on

Sustainable Finance and was previously an independent member of their Technical Expert Group on Sustainable Finance. He is on independent advisory/assessment committees for many organisations, is co-founder and chair of two socially motivated enterprises, and has consulted for international organisations. Andreas has also been published in many journals, his research has won several awards and been covered in international media, and he co-organises conferences with policy makers such as the EU Science Hub Summer Schools on Sustainable Finance. He received his PhD from the University of St Andrews.

Christian Kjær is Senior Vice President and ATP's Head of Liquid Markets, an in-house risk balanced multi-asset investment team with overall responsibility for the liquid part of ATP's investment portfolio. He is a member of the investment committee, the committee for social responsibility and the corporate governance forum within ATP. Christian has previously held responsibility for global equities, inflation and volatility in ATP, which he joined in 2015 as portfolio manager. Prior to joining ATP, he was Head of Inflation Trading in Nordea Markets, and before that held positions in the Insurance and Pension Solutions Group at Credit Suisse, the Institutional Solutions group at Nordea Markets, and McKinsey & Company. Christian holds a MSc in economics and a PhD in economics (game theory) from the University of Aarhus, Denmark.

Karl Lange is ESG and Risk Analyst for EFG Asset Management, where he works with the ESG and quant team and assists in risk assessments and portfolio optimisations from an ESG, climate and traditional risk perspective. He is also responsible for development of the in-house ESG rating software. Prior to joining EFG Asset Management, Karl worked in investment banking with a focus on developing ESG analysis for research teams, and he has also worked on ESG assessments and risk modelling for a large pension fund in Sweden. He holds a master's degree in financial mathematics and an engineering diploma in industrial economics from the Royal Institute of Technology in Sweden. As a master's thesis project, Karl developed a quantitative risk measure for sustainable portfolios taking into account the slightly different risk structures in the ESG portfolios.

Michael Leithead is Head of Fixed Income and Senior Portfolio Manager at EFG Asset Management, which he joined in 2007. He manages the New Capital Wealthy Nations Bond Fund and the New Capital Global Value Credit Fund. Michael focuses primarily on global fixed income fund management, credit research, fixed income strategy and trading. He previously worked at Fidelity International, where he held a number of roles within risk management and both equity and fixed income derivative valuations. Michael holds a BSc in economics from Birmingham University, the IMC, the CFA UK certificate in ESG investing and is a CFA charterholder.

Callum Macpherson is Head of Commodities at Investec Bank in London, where he has built up a commodity hedging capability to help clients manage their commodity exposures with a particular focus on energy markets. He is also Chair of Investec's Sustainable Business Forum, whose purpose is to help support business areas across the bank to increase their sustainability-related revenues. Callum has been in the financial services industry since 1999, having previously worked with commodity derivatives at Nomura and Lehman Brothers. He graduated from the University of Cambridge with an MA in computer science.

Joachim Merten is an experienced finance professional. He has worked for the last 15 years in private investment, holding various roles such as COO and CFO in venture capital and private equity. Joachim has been a strong advocate of ESG compliance and integration into the investment process since 2008. He developed an ESG reporting tool internally and has since kept his interest on how digitalisation can drive the ESG efforts of the industry. Joachim holds a master's degree in economics from Goethe university, and he is a CFA and CAIA charterholder.

Stefano Montobbio is Research Director and Global Head of Investment Governance and ESG for EFG Asset Management, where he oversees the ESG analysis and integration processes. Previously, he was Head of Investment Coordination and ESG for BSI Bank, and before that built the advisory business for Credit Agricole (Suisse) in Ticino and was fund manager for a S&P 4 stars

European equity fund. Stefano has also developed an ESG rating system to assess companies and sovereigns sustainability performance, and lectures on sustainable finance at Centro Studi Villa Negroni. He is Chairman at cenpro, a Swiss foundation contributing to the promotion and development of the non-profit sector and philanthropy in Italian-speaking Switzerland. Stefano holds a master in economics from the University of Genova, a CAS in asset management from the University of Bern/Rochester and an ESRA certificate from INCAE Business School/UNEP.

Jens-Jakob Kratmann Nissen is a senior portfolio manager in ATP's Liquid Markets team. Prior to joining Liquid Markets, he worked in ATP's risk department, which he joined in 2014. Jens-Jakob holds a MSc and a PhD in mathematics from the University of Aarhus, Denmark.

Alexis Royer is a quantitative analyst specialising in high yield, credit strategies and ESG. Prior to joining a global asset manager in 2017, he was a financial engineering assistant at Lyxor ETF, where he was heavily involved in the development of fixed income, short and leveraged ETFs. Prior to that, Alexis was a financial engineering assistant at Amundi ETF, where he worked in the product development process of equity and smart beta ETFs. He holds a master's degree in capital markets and asset management from Neoma Business School. Alexis has passed all three levels of the CFA programme and is a CFA charterholder.

Carlos Sanchez is Executive Director for the Coalition for Climate Resilient Investment, and also the Climate Resilience Investment Director at Willis Towers Watson, where he focuses on the integration of physical climate risks in asset valuation and investment decision-making processes. Additionally, he is a member of California's Climate-Related Risk Disclosure Advisory Group, and vice-Chair of CFA UK's Climate and Investing Certification Panel. Carlos was previously a climate resilience finance facility at the Multilateral Investment Fund, and has worked at the Economic Office of the Spanish Embassy in Angola as Foreign Direct Investment Advisor and later as Business Development Manager for a project finance advisory firm. He holds a masters in finance from the London Business School, where he contributed to the drafting of the ESG chapter within their private equity textbook, and a masters in global affairs from Georgetown University.

Anne Schoemaker is Director of ESG products and oversees a number of compliance and regulatory-driven ESG research products at Morningstar Sustainalytics. She has also been spearheading the product strategy and development of EU Sustainable Finance Action Plan related solutions for Sustainalytics' investor clients. Anne is a member of the ESMA Consultative Working Group on Sustainable Finance, providing technical advice on ESMA sustainable finance work streams and expertise on ESG topics. She was also a member of the EUROSIF Advisory Group, creating policy recommendations for SFDR. Anne previously worked in ESG in development finance, after having started her career in the asset management industry. She holds a master's degree in business mathematics and informatics.

Michael Sheren is a fellow at the Cambridge Institute for Sustainability Leadership, Cambridge University and a senior advisor at the United Nations Development Programme Sustainable Finance Hub. Michael was previously a senior advisor at the Bank of England, where he led their green finance and fintech work. He was the co-chair of the G20 Sustainable Finance Study Group and member of G20 Infrastructure Group, as well as being delegate to the NGFS market dynamics committee and advisor to the BIS Innovation Hub. He is a governor emeritus at the LSE, a non-executive director on various boards, and has spent over 25 years in the debt capital markets in New York and London. He has master degrees from Harvard University, the London School of Economics and New York University, and a BA from the George Washington University.

Edmund Shing is the CIO of BNP Paribas Wealth Management, and has over 25 years of experience in financial markets in a wide variety of positions, ranging from proprietary trading to portfolio manager in a number of financial institutions in London and Paris. Since 2015, he has held the role of Global Head of Equity and Derivative Strategy at BNP Paribas in London, where he is responsible for piloting investment strategy and continues to rollout recommendations and themes with actionable advice. Edmund is an EFFAS-certified financial analyst, and authored the book *The Idle Investor*, published in 2015, which proposed three simple investment strategies that take only a few minutes to execute per month. He has a PhD in cognitive and computing science from the University of Birmingham, and has done advanced studies in knowledge-based systems and in experimental psychology.

Beate van Loo-Born is Global Head of Business Management at SIX Financial Information, and is a seasoned C-Level executive in the financial services and data space. She spent 15 years at UBS, where her last role was Head of Strategic Programs. With a background in risk, compliance and capital markets, Beate manages geopolitical change for the organisations she serves, and is an ESG thought leader with particular expertise in sustainable investing and ESG disclosure, She also leads the European chapter of Women Data Professionals and the global Enterprise Data Management Council ESG Regulatory Group. Beate is a member of the board of trustees at First Light, and is a published author and keynote speaker and panelist on various financial services and data topics, with a focus on regulatory developments and the effects of ESG paradigm shifts. She has a master's degree from Cambridge at the Institute for Sustainability Leadership.

Pei-Shan Yu is the data scientist at Smart Data Foundry (previously known as GOFCoE), where she is responsible for data analytics in the data Safe Haven, mainly for Covid-19 impacts on citizen and SME projects. She was previously post-doctoral research fellow at Smurfit Graduate Business School, University College Dublin, and worked on an anti-money laundering project at a top global asset manager, conducting research on a rule-based suspicious activity detection system, and analysing real transaction data, to establish a predictive model with machine-learning techniques. Pei has a PhD in finance, and is a keen and experienced researcher, with a focus on most financial data-related topics and econometrics, with particular emphasis on carbon finance, carbon data science and the integration of ESG aspects into investment decision-making.

Abbreviations

A4S	Accounting for Sustainability
ACCF	American Council for Capital Formation
AI	Artificial intelligence
APT	Arbitrage pricing theory
AUM	Assets under management
BAT	Best available technology
BIS	Bank for International Settlements
BLM	Black Lives Matter
BNPP WM	BNP Paribas Wealth Management
CA100+	Climate Action 100+
CCUS	Carbon capture, utilisation and storage
CDP	Carbon Disclosure Project
CDSB	Climate Disclosure Standards Board
CEE	Carbon emissions
CEO	Chief executive officer
CF	Carbon footprint
CI	Carbon intensity
CII	Council of Institutional Investors
CIO	Chief investment officer
COP	Communication on Progress
CRA	Credit rating agency
CRDP	Climate-resilient development pathway
CSRD	Corporate Sustainability Reporting Directive
D&I	Diversity and inclusion
DCF	Discounted cashflow
DWP	Department for Work and Pensions
EBIT	Earnings before interest and taxes
EET	European ESG Template
EFRAG	European Financial Reporting Advisory Group
ESG	Environmental, social and governance
ESMA	European Securities and Markets Authority
ETF	Exchange-traded fund

EUGBS	EU Green Bond Standard
EV	Electric vehicle
EV	Enterprise value
EVIC	Enterprise value including cash
FCA	Financial Conduct Authority
FPIC	Free, prior and informed consent
FRC	Financial Reporting Council
GFANZ	Glasgow Financial Alliance for Net Zero
GHG	Greenhouse gas
GIGN	Global Investment Governance Network
GIIN	Global Impact Investor Network
GRI	Global Reporting Initiative
GSG	Global Steering Group for Impact Investment
GSIA	Global Sustainable Investment Alliance
HML	High minus low
IAMC	Integrated Assessment Modelling Consortium
IASB	International Accounting Standards Board
ICMA	International Capital Market Association
IEA	International Energy Agency
IFRS	International Financial Reporting Standards
IIF	Institute of International Finance
IIGCC	Institutional Investors Group on Climate Change
IIRC	International Integrated Reporting Council
IOSCO	International Organization of Securities Commissions
IPCC	Intergovernmental Panel on Climate Change
IRIS	Impact Reporting and Investment Standards
IRSG	International Regulatory Strategy Group
ISSB	International Sustainability Standards Board
ITR	Implied temperature rise
KPI	Key performance indicator
LSEG	London Stock Exchange Group
LTIP	Long-term incentive plan
M&A	Mergers and acquisitions
MPT	Modern portfolio theory
NEST	National Employment Savings Trust
NET	Negative emissions technology
NFRD	Non-Financial Reporting Directive
NGFS	Network for Greening the Financial System

NGO	Non-governmental organisation
NGSS	Next Generation Science Standards
NZAM	Net Zero Asset Managers Initiative
NZAOA	Net Zero Asset Owner Alliance
NZBA	Net Zero Banking Alliance
NZFSPA	Net Zero Financial Service Providers Alliance
NZIA	Net Zero Insurance Alliance
NZICI	Net Zero Investment Consultants Initiative
OECD	Organisation for Economic Co-operation and Development
PACTA	Paris Agreement Capital Transition Assessment
PAI	Principal Adverse Impact
PAII	Paris Aligned Investment Initiative
PCAF	Partnership for Carbon Accounting Financials
PCRIG	Pensions Climate Risk Industry Group
PLSA	Pensions and Lifetime Savings Association
PPE	Personal protective equipment
PRI	Principles for Responsible Investment
PTF-NFRS	Project Task Force on Non-Financial Reporting Standards
R&D	Research and development
RLAM	Royal London Asset Management
RPS	Railways Pension Scheme
RSPO	Roundtable on Sustainable Palm Oi
SAA	Strategic asset allocation
SAMOA	SIDS Accelerated Modalities of Action
SASB	Sustainability Accounting Standards Board
SBP	Social Bond Principles
SBTi	Science Based Targets initiative
SDA	Sectoral Decarbonization Approach
SDG	Sustainable Development Goal
SEC	Securities and Exchange Commission
SFDR	Sustainable Finance Disclosure Regulation
SI	Sustainability investing
SICM	Sustainable Insight Capital Management
SIDS	Small Island Developing States
SIP	Statement of Investment Principles
SLB	Sustainability-linked bond
SMB	Small minus big

SME	Small and medium-sized enterprise
SOCF	Sustainable Ownership Client Forum
SPO	Second party opinion
SRI	Socially responsible investing
2DII	2 Degrees Investing Initiative
TCFD	Task Force on Climate-Related Disclosures
tCO2e	Tonne of carbon dioxide equivalent
TNFD	Taskforce on Nature-related Financial Disclosures
TPI	Transition Pathway Initiative
TR	Temperature rating
UCITS	Undertakings for the Collective Investment in Transferable Securities
UKSIF	UK Sustainable Investment and Finance Association
UN	United Nations
UNEP	United Nations Environment Programme
UNFCCC	United Nations Framework Convention on Climate Change
UNGC	UN Global Compact
UNGPFR	UN Guiding Principles Reporting Framework
UNPRI	United Nations Principles for Responsible Investment
USS	Universities Superannuation Scheme
VaR	Value-at-risk
VRF	Value Reporting Foundation
WACI	Weighted average carbon intensity
WBA	World Benchmarking Alliance
WBCSD	World Business Council for Sustainable Development
WEF	World Economic Forum
WEF-IBC	World Economic Forum International Business Council
WMO	World Meteorological Organization
WRI	World Resources Institute
WWF	World Wide Fund for Nature

Foreword

Linking ESG scenarios to real economy outcomes

Michael Sheren

Former co-chairman, G20 Sustainable Finance Study Group

Climate change is the biggest risk multiplier facing the financial markets and the real economy today. Our response to this inter-generational challenge will require unprecedented collaboration, and the window for action is closing fast. However, making sense of where we are on the path to a more sustainable world and what we need to do next is not always straightforward – which is why the insights provided in this book could not be timelier or more valuable.

Over the following chapters, the contributing authors deliver a smart and practical guide that helps us to identify, understand and manage climate risks. The transition to a greener economy will also create opportunities for those who innovate and enhance resilience. The title of the book, *Climate Change: Managing the Financial Risk and Financing the Transition*, references two of the key ways that the finance sector can help in the move to net zero. From creating the tools and analytics to quantify climate risk to helping channel financing for resilience and adaptation projects, the financial sector has a critical role to play.

As the authors make clear, the response to the climate challenge must be a collective one. The private and public sectors need to work together as we navigate these rapidly evolving risks. Climate data, tools and analytics – discussed in the first part of this book – are emerging and advancing at an unprecedented rate. Nevertheless, understanding sustainability and net-zero plans remains a challenge. Data gaps, comparability issues and uncertainty around environmental disclosures are some of the obstacles to reaching informed decisions that inspire confidence.

Although progress has been made, change must come in three key areas: first, we need a robust definition of what makes a credible carbon transition plan and identify any gaps; second, we must unlock finance to fund resilience and adaptation measures; and third, we must adopt economy-wide transparency and accountability on climate risk.

A key element to achieving these goals is consistency. Standardisation and harmonisation in areas such as climate regulation, financial reporting and data disclosures will help us to make the transition. Proper accounting and disclosure of greenhouse gas emissions is also fundamental. Financial institutions need the tools to assess climate-related claims and the credibility of borrowers' transition plans. While companies are disclosing more about environmental impact than before, it can be hard to separate the signal from the noise. A more transparent, 360-degree view of risk will accelerate climate action.

In the second part of the book, the authors explore the crucial topics of frameworks, methodologies and analytical tools. Embedding climate risk analytics into mainstream risk management tools and platforms will help financial institutions manage risk in a more holistic and integrated fashion. A final chapter is dedicated to private sector funding for climate transition, with huge investments needed into green businesses and technologies.

As this book demonstrates, knowledge-sharing, collaboration and innovative thinking will be essential as the finance sector helps channel investments to address the climate crisis. The insights presented clearly set out the risks and opportunities faced by the financial industry. We are grateful to the authors for their important contribution to the debate.

We won't reach our climate goals unless the entire system plays its part and takes on shared challenges. What we do together, from today and over the next decade, will be critical to the well-being and prosperity of future generations.

PART I

INTRODUCTION TO ESG IN PORTFOLIO CONSTRUCTION

1

Analysing ESG policy, market and portfolio construction considerations

Kartik Chawla, Martina Macpherson, Alexis Royer and Daniel Ung

Since the early 2000s, investors have increasingly considered environmental, social and governance (ESG) criteria within their investment decisions to meet their varying expectations, such as using ESG as an expression of personal ethics and values, as a means of downside risk protection in the investment portfolio, or as a new source of investment alpha. Since the launch of the European Union Sustainable Finance Disclosure Regulation (SFDR), regulators are demanding that investment managers classify and disclose their sustainability risks. This chapter will evaluate the developments in sustainable investing, both in terms of the size of the sustainable investment market and the approaches that investors commonly adopt. It will also examine how ESG can be incorporated into the portfolio construction process, and look at how controversies can potentially negatively impact investment performance.

OVERVIEW OF SUSTAINABLE INVESTMENT MARKET AND STRATEGIES

Market and regulatory developments in brief

A study by the CFA Institute (Fender *et al*, 2020) that surveyed its global members base highlighted that sustainable investing has entered the mainstream, and is now increasingly being adopted across institutional retail segments and markets. In fact, more than 85% of CFA Institute members are taking E, S and/or G factors into consideration in their investing, up from 73% in 2017.

Figure 1.1 The spectrum of financial and extra-financial investment strategies

	Philanthropy		**Social impact investing**		**Sustainable and responsible investing**	**Conventional financial investing**
	Traditional philanthropy	Venture philanthropy	Social investing	Impact investment	ESG investing	Fully commercial investment
Focus	Address societal challenges through the provision of grants	Address societal challenges with venture investment approaches	Investment with a focus on social and/or environmental outcome and some expected financial return	Investment with an intent to have a measurable environment and/or social return	Enhance long-term value by using ESG factors to mitigate risks and identify growth opportunities	Limited or no regard for environmental, social or governance practices
			Use of ESG metrics and methodologies			
Return expectation	Social return only	Social return focused	Social return and sub-market financial return	Social return and adequate financial market rate	Financial market return focused on long-term value	Financial market return only
	Social impact ⟷		Social and financial ⟷		Financial returns	

Source: Boffo and Patalano (2020)

Meanwhile, sustainable investing, continues to exist within a broad spectrum that aims to generate financial and extra-financial returns. On one end of the spectrum, investors adopting this approach may only wish to invest in companies that seek to maximise shareholder value, and will principally focus on absolute or risk-adjusted measures of financial return. Inherent in this approach is the belief that capital markets are efficient and will effectively allocate resources to areas of the economy that maximise economic benefits. On the opposite end of the spectrum, philanthropy and social impact investing aim to enhance the welfare of certain, or all, segments of society, particularly in relation to human and worker rights, gender equality and climate change, among other social considerations (see Figure 1.1).

According to the Global Sustainable Investment Alliance (GSIA, 2020), figures for the overall sustainable investment market size vary between US$35.3 trillion and US$ 40.5 trillion, according to an ESG market study (Baker, 2020). Whichever study one uses, one trend is clear: the adoption of ESG funds continues to grow unabated (see Table 1.1). In 2020, global sustainable investment assets made up about 36% of total assets under management, an increase from 28% in 2016 (GSIA, 2020; Diab and Adams, 2021), and some estimate that the sustainable investment market may even reach US$53 trillion by 2025.

Table 1.1 Total sustainable investment assets across regions

Total assets across regions

Regions	**2016**	**2018**	**2020**
Total AUM of regions	81,948	91,828	98,416
Total sustainable investments	22,872	30,683	35,301
% sustainable investments	27.9%	33.4%	35.9%

SRI assets

Region	**2016**	**2018**	**2020**
Europe	12,040	14,075	12,017
United States	8,723	11,995	17,081
Canada	1,086	1,699	2,423
Australia	516	734	906
Japan	474	2,180	2,874
Total (USD billions)	22,839	30,683	35,301

Source: GSIA (2020)

Much of the growth in ESG-focused funds has emanated from North America and Europe, driven by investor demand and increasing regulatory efforts around the world. In Europe, €4 trillion, or 40% of all assets managed in European Union-domiciled funds (Wilkes, 2022), are already invested in ESG-focused funds. Outside of Europe and North America, Japan has also witnessed solid growth. Sustainable assets only represented 3.4% of total assets under management in the country in 2016, but skyrocketed to 24.3% in 2020 (Kerber and Jessop, 2021).

One of the reasons why ESG-focused funds have seen more adoption can be attributed to a change in investor mindset. A report by Natixis (Bloomberg, 2021) suggests that 60% of investors around the world expect ESG issues to be considered in their investments, and reject the idea that companies are responsible only for creating shareholder value. Through an increase in awareness of social issues, evolving expectations and a changing regulatory landscape, investors are committing increasing amounts of money into investments where ESG considerations are accounted for.

In choosing an investment, the prioritisation of extra-financial versus financial returns depends on the extent to which investors are prepared to balance one with the other in the pursuit of their overall objectives. One approach is social impact investing, which aims to generate a social or environmental outcome and impact. This contrasts with sustainable and responsible investing, which focuses mainly on improving (extra-)financial returns by using ESG factors to assess longer-term risks and opportunities. This is achieved through an evaluation of factors beyond a company's short-term financial performance to incorporate the assessment of its longer-term environmental, social and governance challenges and developments.

Another reason for the impressive growth in ESG investments can be ascribed to increasing demand from retail investors. Historically, ESG investing was always the preserve of institutional investors, but according to a report by GlobeScan (2021), 82% of retail investors globally expressed an interest in investing in socially and environmentally responsible companies, while 72% of them would like to avoid industries that contribute to climate change. There is also a notable difference in attitude towards sustainable investments based on age. The baby boomer generation is much less informed about sustainable investments than younger generations, such as millennials and Generation Z.

The increased emphasis on ESG considerations in investments is not limited to the amount of assets that ESG-themed funds managed to attract, but also extends to the ongoing monitoring of such investments. An example of this is active ownership, where investors use their rights and position of ownership to influence the behaviour of investee companies (PRI, 2018). Indeed, active ownership is closely aligned with the ambitions set out in global corporate governance and stewardship codes, and is what shareholder and investor groups are using to put pressure on companies to further tighten their ESG objectives and positive change trajectories. In 2021, we saw a record-breaking 34 shareholder proposals on environmental and social matters receiving majority support, up from 21 in 2020 (Quinson, 2021).

This happened against the backdrop of the Covid-19 pandemic when investors opted to focus their attention on how longer-term themes, such as public health, racial justice, as well as environmental matters (Morgan Stanley, 2021), might impact corporate performance. Alongside the growing interest in ESG, we have seen a vast array of ESG regulations initiated around the world. The Principles for Responsible Investing (PRI, 2021) reports that there are now more than 750 policy tools and guidance frameworks globally, including 159 new or revised ESG policy instruments.[1]

Meanwhile, there has been increasing regulatory scrutiny in relation to ESG data quality and rating methodologies, especially since the publication of the International Organization of Securities Commissions (IOSCO) report on "ESG Ratings and Data Products Providers" (IOSCO, 2021). This development has contributed to the announcement by the European Securities and Markets Authority (ESMA) that "tackling greenwashing and promoting transparency in ESG ratings is its number one priority" (ESMA, 2022).

There is also a growing push by regulatory authorities to develop "universal" ESG reporting and disclosure standards for both corporates and investors.

Table 1.2 Comparing approaches of 12 European ESG labels

	Screen: norms-based	**Screen: controversial weapons**	**Screen: conventional weapons**	**Screen: military equipment**	**Screen: tobacco**	**Screen: nuclear power**	**Screen: thermal coal**	**Screen: unconventional coal & gas**	**Screen: oil & gas**	**Screen: power generation**	**Screen: other**	**Portfolio construction: ESG integration**	**Portfolio construction: best-in-class**	**Portfolio construction: thematic**	**Portfolio construction: impact**
EU PAB	Yes	Yes	NA	NA	NA	NA	Yes	NA	Yes	Yes	NA	NA	Yes	NA	NA
EU CTB	Yes	Yes	NA	NA	NA	NA	NA	NA	NA	NA	NA	NA	Yes	NA	NA
EU Ecolabel*	Yes	Yes	Yes	Yes	Yes	Yes	Yes	Yes	Yes	Yes	Yes	NA	NA	Yes	Yes
FNG-Label	Yes	Yes	Yes	NA	NA	Yes	Yes	Yes	NA	NA	NA	NA	Yes	Yes	NA
Verbändekonzept*	Yes	Yes	NA	Yes	Yes	NA	Yes	NA	NA	NA	NA	Yes	Yes	NA	Yes
Ecolabel UZ 49	Yes	Yes	Yes	NA	NA	Yes	Yes	NA	Yes	Yes	Yes	NA	NA	NA	NA
Towards Sustainability	Yes	Yes	Yes	Yes	Yes	Yes	Yes	Yes	Yes	Yes	Yes	Yes	Yes	Yes	Yes
SRI Label	NA	NA	NA	NA	NA	NA	NA	NA	NA	NA	NA	NA	Yes	NA	NA
AMF Doctrine	NA	NA	NA	NA	NA	NA	NA	NA	NA	NA	NA	NA	Yes	NA	NA
Greenfin Label	NA	NA	NA	NA	NA	Yes	Yes	Yes	Yes	Yes	Yes	Yes	NA	Yes	NA
LuxFLAG ESG Label	Yes	Yes	NA	NA	Yes	Yes	NA	NA	NA	NA	NA	NA	NA	NA	NA
Nordic Swan Ecolabel	Yes	Yes	Yes	NA	Yes	Yes	Yes	Yes	Yes	Yes	NA	NA	NA	NA	NA

Source: Qontigo (2022)

- On the corporate side, efforts are underway to unify a variety of reporting standards, as evidenced by the "dual materiality"[2] frameworks championed by the European Financial Reporting Advisory Group (EFRAG) and the Global Reporting Initiative (GRI), as well as the financial materiality frameworks as introduced by the International Accounting Standards Board (IASB)/ International Sustainability Standards Board (ISSB), among others.[3] In March 2022, the GRI and ISSB announced a closer collaboration (IFRS, 2022).
- As for investors, FinDatEx proposes a "European ESG Template" (EET) for fund reporting that covers a broad spectrum of separate ESG investment frameworks and standards, such as the EU Sustainable Finance Disclosure Regulation (SFDR)'s "Principal Adverse Impact" (PAI) criteria, the EU taxonomy's alignment criteria, as well as other national ESG disclosure requirements, stewardship codes and common ESG labels.

With the increasing efforts related to the harmonisation and standardisation of ESG frameworks, there is hope that there will be more clarity, comparability and consistency around ESG convictions, narratives and definitions. Until now, the sheer pluralism of normative and regulatory ESG standards, methodologies, frameworks and labels has led to widespread confusion (Berg, Kölbel and Rigobon, 2019), and has made investor compliance, such as with ESG fund labels (see Table 1.2), very difficult.

ESG approaches for sustainable investing

The GSIA has highlighted seven main ESG approaches for sustainable investing into which most sustainable investment funds fit. These are: ESG integration; negative screening; norms-based screening; positive and best-in-class screening; corporate engagement and shareholder action; sustainable-themed investing; and impact and community investing (see Table 1.3).

In terms of assets under management, the three most significant sustainable investment approaches are as follows (GSIA, 2020).

- Integration = Assets under management US$25 trillion: The explicit integration by asset managers of ESG risks and opportunities into investment decision-making through a systematic

Table 1.3 Common ESG approaches for sustainable investing

AUM in Billions USD	2020	2018	2016	Growth (2016–2020)
ESG integration	25,195	17,544	10,353	143%
Negative/exclusionary screening	15,030	19,771	15,064	0%
Corporate engagement and shareholder action	10,504	9,835	8,385	25%
Norms-based screening	4,140	4,679	6,195	-33%
Sustainable-themed investing	1,948	1,018	276	606%
Positive/best-in-class screening	1,384	1,842	818	69%
Impact/community investing	352	444	248	42%

Source: GSIA (2020)

process of ESG research. This investment approach considers ESG factors alongside financial factors in the analysis of future investments, and considers the potential impact of ESG issues on company fundamentals that may affect its future valuation.

- Exclusions and screening = Assets under management US$14 trillion: An approach that excludes specific investments or classes of investment from the investible universe (such as companies, sectors or countries) based on their involvement in certain predefined activities. Common exclusion criteria include weapons, pornography, tobacco and animal testing. Exclusions can be applied at individual fund or mandate level, but are also increasingly applied at the individual asset manager or asset owner level. As exclusions are often based on the choices made by asset managers or asset owners, this approach is also commonly referred to as "ethical- or values-based exclusions".
- Corporate engagement and shareholder action = Assets under management US$10 trillion: This approach represents engagement activities and active ownership activities through voting and engagement with companies on ESG topics. This is typically a long-term process that seeks to positively influence corporate behaviour. Engagement and voting on corporate governance only, while necessary, is not sufficient to be counted separately as part of this strategy.

Emerging and growing investment categories are thematic and impact investment approaches. Thematic ESG investing seeks to reap an attractive financial return through contributing to a specific environmental or social theme. This approach differs from impact investing, which aims to generate social and environmental impacts, commonly defined intentionally *ex ante*, alongside a financial return. The level of return targeted depends on the investment in question and can range from below market to market level, and are often project-specific. This style of investment is distinct from philanthropy, as investors retain ownership of the investment asset and expect a positive financial return. Examples of impact investment include microfinance, community investing, social business/entrepreneurship funds and the "*fonds solidaires*" in France.

Among the ESG-themed asset allocation approaches discussed, purely exclusionary approaches are gradually becoming less popular. In fact, 81% of asset managers and 72% of asset owners (BNP Paribas, 2021) are actively including ESG factors in their analysis to better manage the risk and return dynamics in their portfolios, rather than merely excluding companies and certain sectors from their investment strategies. However, in most regions (such as Europe and Australasia) investors often combine and blend several sustainable investment approaches, and exclusionary screening may well form part of the overall mix of strategies, as outlined in Table 1.4.

Table 1.4 ESG approaches, drivers and assets by region

Region	SRI assets	Top SRI approach (in order of AUM and growth in AUM)	Key drivers
US	\$17T	ESG integration Negative/exclusionary screening Sustainability themed investing	Socially responsible and inclusive investing
Europe	\$12T	Negative/exclusionary screening Corporate engagement and shareholder action ESG integration	Sustainable Finance Disclosure Regulation (SFDR) Industry collaboration
JP	\$2.8T	ESG integration Sustainability themed investing	Corporate engagement Shareholder action
AU+NZ	\$0.9T	ESG integration Negative/exclusionary screening	Task force on Climate-related Financial Disclosures (TCFD) Industry collaboration

Source: GSIA (2020)

In terms of asset classes, equites remain the primary asset class used to deploy ESG considerations (69%), followed by fixed income and green instruments, according to the GSIA (2020). It is equally noteworthy that ESG considerations are also increasingly being accounted for in non-listed assets, such as infrastructure, real estate, and private equity and debt. A prime motivation for this is that investors aim to align their investments with their ESG values and beliefs to minimise reputational risks and satisfy external stakeholder requirements, according to BNP's ESG global survey (BNP Paribas, 2021).

Negative screening and exclusions in focus

The UN-backed Principles for Responsible Investment is an international organisation launched in April 2006. Its objective is to work on the promotion of including ESG factors into the decision-making process. According to the PRI's report "An Introduction to Responsible Investment" (PRI, 2020), one of the first forms of (ethical) investment screening, against slavery, was developed and implemented by the Quaker community as early as 1758 (Quakers, n.d.). However, there were also divergences of opinion on the topic and in relation to its approach within the Quaker community until 1774.

The formal definition, of screening-based investing provided by the PRI is as follows.

- Screening uses a set of filters to determine which companies, sectors or activities are eligible or ineligible to be included in a specific portfolio.
- These criteria might be based on an investor's preferences, values and ethics.
- For example, a screen might be used to exclude the highest emitters of greenhouse gases from a portfolio ("negative screening") or to target only the lowest emitters ("positive screening").
- It can be based on the policy of an asset manager or asset owner.

There are three common screening approaches: negative screening; norms-based (values-based); and positive/best-in-class screening (see Table 1.5).

Table 1.5 ESG screening approaches in sustainable investing

NEGATIVE SCREENING Avoid the worst performers	NORMS-BASED SCREENING Use an existing framework	POSITIVE SCREENING Include the best performers
❏ Excluding certain sectors, issuers or securities for poor ESG performance relative to industry peers, or based on specific ESG criteria (eg, avoiding particular products/ services, regions or business practices) ❏ Absolute avoidance of activities such as alcohol, tobacco, gambling, adult entertainment, military weapons, fossil fuels and nuclear energy ❏ Sets a materiality threshold (eg, 10%) based on revenue exposure or business activity/ operation ❏ Avoidance of worst-in-class investments using quantitative ESG measurements ❏ Faith-based/Shariah-compliant screening, as guided by Islamic finance principles, is a subcategory of negative screening	❏ Screening issuers against minimum standards of business practice based on international norms. Typical frameworks include UN treaties, Security Council sanctions, UN Global Compact, UN Human Rights Declaration and OECD guidelines. ❏ A subcategory of negative screening that excludes companies or government debt on account of any failure by the issuer to meet internationally accepted norms such as the UN Global Compact, Kyoto Protocol, UN Declaration of Human Rights, International Labour Organization standards, UN Convention Against Corruption, OECD Guidelines for Multinational Enterprises ❏ Can be called "controversy screening" or negative business/ product involvement screening when companies engage in unethical behaviours or practices	❏ Investing in sectors, issuers or projects selected for positive ESG performance relative to industry peers ❏ Active inclusion of companies within an investment universe because of the social or environmental benefits of their products, services and/or processes ❏ Endorsing best-in-class or "leaders" in best practice using quantitative ESG measurements ❏ Positive thematic development such as: companies transitioning to "carbon neutrality", renewable/clean tech, social enterprises, or initiatives

Source: PRI (2020)

ESG risk and opportunities management and portfolio performance

The impact of ESG-focused strategies on portfolio performance has been at the forefront of the academic and industry literature debate for some time.[4] More recent studies, such as the meta studies by Harvard Business School (2015), found "a positive correlation between sustainability and superior market performance".

The focus of many studies had been traditionally on the quality and management of corporate governance (G) and how this "factor" can positively or negatively influence stock price performance (Clark, Feiner and Viehs, 2015). In line with the surge in interest in climate change mitigation and adaptation, circular economy and biodiversity issues, research has also documented a direct link between the environmental (E) performance of firms and stock price performance.[5] Linked to the Covid-19 pandemic and global health crisis, changing demographics and the impact of globalisation, there is also increasing investor focus on the impact of social issues and stock returns, with a particular emphasis on health, safety and well-being,[6] as well as on human capital management issues such as employee satisfaction,[7] and diversity and inclusion.[8]

There are a range of ESG risks at the macro and micro level that can influence portfolio performance. These are commonly summarised in at least three categories (Allianz, 2019).

- Macro and economic risks: These originate from (geo)political, or long-run systemic events linked to negative ESG characteristics, which can have a widespread, cross-sectoral impact.
- Sectoral risks: These refer to risks of adverse movements in a sector's overall performance due to its systematic ESG characteristics or long-run ESG trends.
- Company and issuer risks: These are essentially the downside risks to a company's financial health (for example, increased cost to capital) as a result of its poor ESG performance compared to the rest of the sector. At the portfolio level, company/issuer ESG risk can be more easily managed through diversification and should be assessed from a risk/return perspective.

Nevertheless, it is important to note that some studies still question the positive performance value of ESG strategies. Some acknowledge the extra-financial benefits of ESG investing, and highlight that "ESG strategies shall be considered more for their unique benefits that they can provide, such as hedging climate or litigation

Table 1.6 Evaluating ESG factors in portfolio construction and for active ownership (selection)

	ESG management expectations	Potential ESG impacts for portfolio management
ESG risks and opportunities management in portfolio management and active ownership	ESG risk/return management	ESG factors may protect from portfolio downside risk, but do not necessarily generate additional upside (Scientific Beta, 2021)
		Active management of tail risks through ESG may deliver positive performance over a market cycle (Allianz, 2019)
		Avoiding portfolio drawdowns linked to ESG risks and controversies may contribute to risk-adjusted returns over the longer term (Allianz, 2019) for active[10] and passive portfolios[11]
		There may be a relationship between ESG quality and sovereign risk as measured by credit spreads,[12] principally driven by developed markets[13]
	ESG alpha and opportunities management	Active management of ESG may enhance alpha opportunities (Allianz, 2019) across asset classes[14]
		Portfolios with higher ESG ratings may generally beat their style-specific index more often than funds with lower ESG ratings[15]
		Increased ESG disclosures may contribute to portfolio stability over time[16]
		ESG strategies may show positive effects on the financial markets during crises[17]
	Active ownership	Active ownership may help to minimise intertemporal losses of profits and negative externalities[18]
		Active ownership may provide a positive performance contribution at the portfolio level over the medium[19] to longer term

risk, aligning investments with norms, and making a positive impact for society".[9]

Referring to key findings from across industry and academic research, Table 1.6 summarises some of the key investor considerations for ESG, highlighting how ESG, or aspects of ESG – such as active ownership, can contribute to: (i) downside protection from a risk perspective; and (ii) potential alpha opportunities at the portfolio level.

Controversies and their impact on stock price performance

Academic and industry research outlines that unethical business practices, involving a range of material ESG issues (so-called "controversies"), can have a material impact on corporates' cost of capital as well as on their share price performance.

One of the criteria that the asset management industry uses to assess the adequacy of ESG controversy management is whether a company has signed and submitted annual updates to the "UN Global Compact Annual Communication on Progress" (UNGC COP), an environmental, social and governance progress report.[20]

However, this approach has an inherent size bias: Judging by the market capitalisation of the UNGC signatories, it seems that the larger the market capitalisation of a company, the greater the likelihood that it will be a UNGC signatory as this accountability and reporting commitment can be a barrier to membership for smaller companies, even if the "Ten Principles"[21] of the UNGC – which focus on human rights, labour, environment and anti-corruption – are often already incorporated into national practices and European laws in which small caps operate. Analysis by ODDO BHF AM (2021, and Figure 1.2) found that 81.3% of companies with an average market capitalisation of more than €19 billion (MSCI EMU (Eurozone) Index) are signatories to the UNGC, versus 37.7% of companies with an average market capitalisation of less than €1.5 billion (MSCI Europe Small Cap Index).

Figure 1.2 UN global compact signatories by corporate market capitalisation

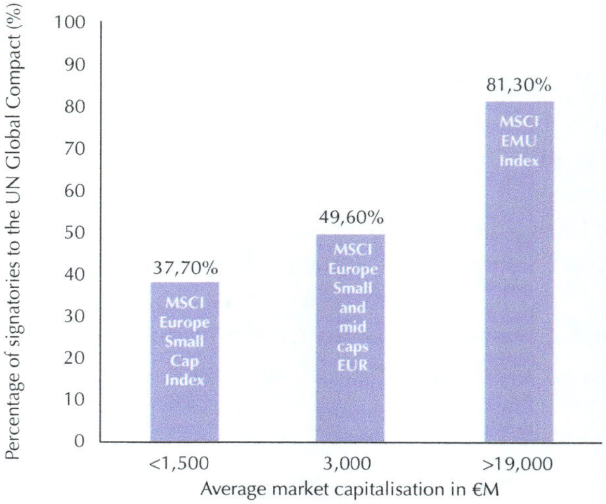

Source: ODDO BHF AM SAS, Sustainable Investment Reports (data as of March 31, 2021)

Figure 1.3 Impact of Controversies on portfolio performance

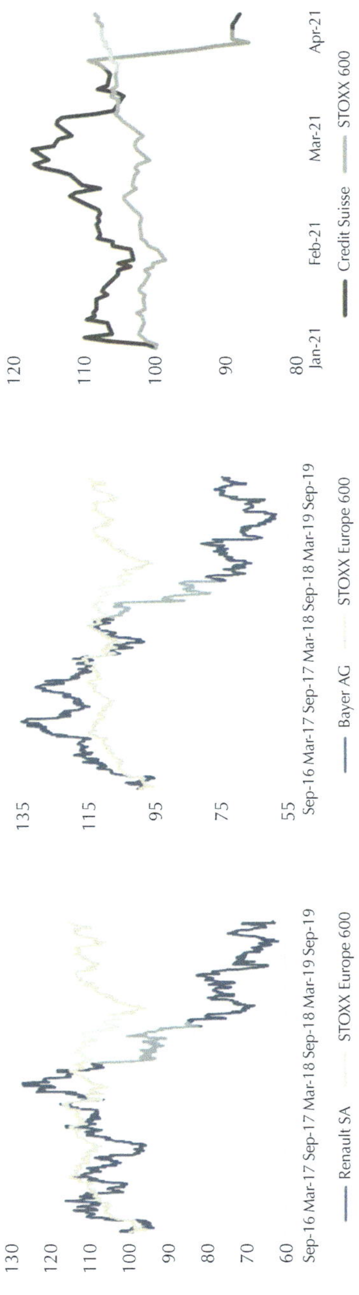

Source: ODDO BHF Asset Management (2019)

Meanwhile, controversies can have an immediate and substantial negative impact on stock price performance, as highlighted by various examples across sectors (see Figure 1.3). This impact can mean a material loss of financial value. According to research by Bank of America (2019),[22] controversies wiped more than US$500 billion off the value of large US stock/listed companies since the mid to late 2010s, as outlined in Figure 1.4.

The research examines the impact on stock prices of companies in the S&P 500 index implicated in 24 types of controversies related to accounting scandals, data breaches, sexual harassment cases and other ESG issues. It found these companies together experienced peak to trough market value losses of US$534 billion as their share prices sank relative to the S&P 500 over the 12 months after the controversies were uncovered.

Meanwhile, research from Société Générale (Stevens, 2020) found that "two-thirds of companies hit by a major controversy saw their stock price underperform the MSCI World Index by an average 12% in each of the following two years and underperform their regional benchmark by 4%". The research, based on 80 historic ESG controversies incidents dating back to 2005 and spanning

Figure 1.4 Controversies impact on share price performance

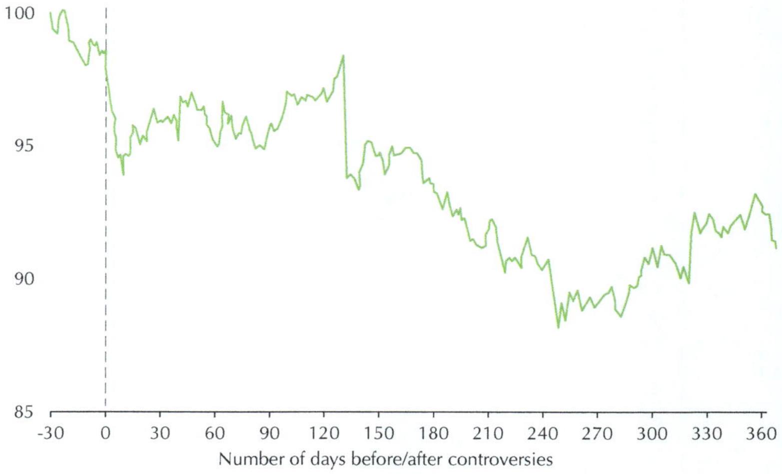

Source: Bank of America Merrill Lynch (2019) (data time series: 2014–19)

various regions and sectors, identified 12 companies that experienced a "high" ESG controversy in the previous year, all of which had underperformed since.

Furthermore, research by Cui and Docherty (2019, see Figure 1.5), which focuses on the S&P Composite 1500 index, found that:

- market reactions are much more pronounced for "bad" than "good" news flow, as investors overweight the possibility that the impact of the controversy could be prolonged or recur;
- firms that are subject to bad news achieve abnormal losses (but there is no clear pattern around positive news); and
- negative returns are substantially larger in magnitude for smaller cap stocks and those held by more transient investors.

Another paper from the University of Virginia (Glossner, 2021) expands the dataset by examining more minor ESG incidents such as "environmental damage", "discrimination", "occupational health and safety issues", "fractious relations with local

Figure 1.5 News flow impact linked to controversies on share price performance

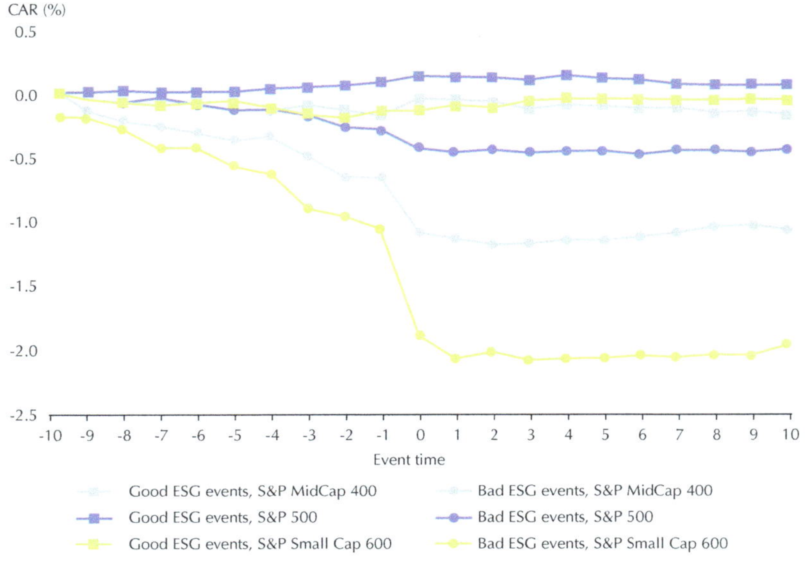

Source: Cui and Docherty (2019) (data time series: 2000–18)

communities", and "anti-competitive practices". They found as many as 80,000 incidents among listed US companies over the decade 2007–17, and concluded:

- there appears to be a clear relationship between the number of past incidents and future financial and stock performance; and
- a portfolio of stocks with high rates of ESG "breaches" had lower profits and underperformed the wider market by about 3.5% per year, even after taking into account sector exposure and other risk factors.

Aviva Investors (2021) concludes that material impact of controversies on companies and stock prices are strongly dependent on the nature of companies' businesses, and their products and services models. Meanwhile, not all issues are being detected and disclosed, and hence priced-in appropriately. They also see the necessity for human judgement in the process, which in turn carries inherent risks and biases.

FROM THEORY TO PRACTICE: ESG IN PORTFOLIO CONSTRUCTION

Aligning investor portfolio objectives with ESG strategies

Before delving into the implications of how ESG considerations can have an impact on the portfolio construction and management process, it is worth revisiting and defining briefly "what" portfolio management is and the various "stages" that make up the portfolio management process.

Broadly speaking, portfolio management is an integrated series of steps undertaken to assemble and maintain a suitable combination of assets to meet the end clients' goals. It often consists of three steps: planning; execution; and feedback.

- Step 1 – portfolio planning: The first step involves planning and necessitates the definition of investment objectives and the formulation of investment policies. At this stage, capital expectations are also formed, and strategic asset allocations established.
- Step 2 – portfolio construction: After careful planning, the next phase is execution. For this step, the investment portfolio is constructed.

- Step 3 – portfolio monitoring: The final step is feedback, which is when the manager monitors and evaluates the portfolio compared with the initial plan set out in the planning stage.

While ESG considerations permeate all three steps of the portfolio management process, we will focus our attention on the ESG implications within the first step, and look at how and when the investors' goals are being set, their constraints are being defined and their beliefs are being considered. For many investors, ESG considerations are mainly considered as investors' beliefs that can inform the guiding principles governing their investment decisions and activities. Sure enough, there is an increasing amount of research touting the return-enhancing benefits of integrating ESG into the investment process, but there is still much debate about whether ESG can genuinely generate alpha.[23]

The lack of consensus over the alpha-generating abilities of ESG does not necessarily undermine the worth of incorporating such considerations into the investment portfolios as they may be incorporated for reasons other than purely financial (see previous section). A case in point is that investors may simply wish to align their investments with their values and norms, make a positive social impact, and reduce climate or reputational risks, beyond just seeking to maximise financial return. Against this backdrop, a conflict may arise between maximising financial return and satisfying investors' non-pecuniary objectives, and a compromise to resolve this conflict should be struck that will also likely influence the ESG investment approaches investors opt for.

Running a tracking error is inevitable in ESG strategies

Regardless of the ESG investment approach that investors aim to ultimately adopt, it will, to a greater or lesser extent, tilt away from the market cap-weighted benchmark, an inevitable consequence of either excluding companies that do not meet a particular threshold or including companies that demonstrate superior ESG characteristics.

Put differently, all ESG approaches involve some degree of tracking error. Of course, it is possible to attempt to control this by means of an optimisation technique through which tilts away from the benchmark are constrained. However, as the strategy excludes

Table 1.7 Trade-off in typical ESG strategies

Technical goal	Data granularity	Risk aversion	Strategy	Trade-off
Exclude unwanted securities	Binary	Low	Cap-weighted exclusion	Excess tracking error
		High	Optimised exclusion	Risk of unwanted exposure
Tilt on a theme	Scored	Low	Maximum score	Excess tracking error
		High	Minimum risk	Risk of unwanted exposure
Excluded and tilt	Binary and scored	Low	Custom tilt exclusion	Excess tracking error
		High	Tilt exclusion	Risk of unwanted exposure

Source: Branch, Goldberg and Hand (2020)

more stocks or targets a narrower subset of stocks with a strong ESG profile, it must deviate materially from the benchmark and run a significant level of tracking error. Strategies that claim to deliver a high level of ESG improvement at no cost should be treated with due scepticism. Table 1.7 shows the trade-offs of different ESG strategies.

This is not to say that a strategy cannot deploy portfolio management techniques to optimise the amount of tracking error it runs against the amount of ESG improvement it can attain. However, it often comes at a cost through higher transaction costs, more portfolio turnover, risks of unwanted exposures and/or substantial concentration in certain names and/or certain sectors.

Different ESG approaches are likely to lead to different costs, compromises and outcomes. Investors should be fully cognisant of this trade-off before deciding which approach is most appropriate for their portfolios.

Understanding different ESG strategies involving different portfolio trade-offs

As outlined in the previous section, there are a variety of approaches[24] that consider ESG issues when building a portfolio. To recap, these include:

- integration, where the strategy explicitly and systematically includes ESG issues in the analysis;

- screening, where the strategy applies filters to rule in or out companies based on investors' ethics, preferences or values; and
- thematics, where the strategy seeks an attractive risk/return profile with an intention to contribute to a specific environment or social outcome.

Regarding thematic investments, their investment approach tends to involve a "top-down" stock selection, and seeks to capitalise on opportunities created by macroeconomic, geopolitical and technological trends. They often hold very concentrated portfolios and target niche businesses. Because of this, investment capacity is often restricted, and they are also likely to run a very high tracking error if measured against broad-based market cap benchmarks.

Running a high tracking error *per se* is not necessarily a matter of concern, but where that tracking error comes from has major implications on the portfolio construction process, especially if the investment portfolio is measured against a broad-based benchmark.

Taking ESG exclusionary approaches as an example, Alessandri and Jondeau (2020) examined portfolios that exclude firms with the 50% lowest ESG scores from different regions.

- Their findings show that these portfolios substantially increase the *ex post* ESG scores, but also incur significant sector biases.
- Tech firms are substantially overweighted in all regions, particularly in the US and emerging countries.
- Financials are severely underweighted in all regions but for different reasons.
- Their findings show that the underweighting was as large as 5.8% in Europe for the governance score and as large as 9.6% in emerging countries for the environmental score.
- Besides sector biases, these portfolios are also exposed to certain risk factors that might not have been anticipated and, while the portfolios did not incur higher market beta, they tended to tilt towards larger cap and more expensive companies in the US and Europe, and towards smaller cap and cheaper companies in the Pacific and emerging countries.[25]
- When ESG portfolios were formed using a worldwide rather than regional investment set, persistent tilts away from the US in

favour of Europe were found. Overall, the analysis shows that a purely exclusionary ESG approach gave rise to significant and persistent regional, sectoral and risk factor exposures of the portfolios.

To deal with persistent biases in screening approaches, strategies can explicitly include ESG scores into the portfolio construction process by maximising the portfolio ESG portfolio score or achieving some baseline ESG improvement. Both objectives can easily be achieved via an optimisation procedure to avoid constant biases and unwanted exposures through the imposition of appropriate constraints. While an optimisation procedure can help optimise the "efficiency" of the trade-off between the various ESG and financial objectives, it is still the case that investors must be prepared to run a tracking error if the objectives are to create portfolios with strong ESG characteristics.

Uncovering the sources of tracking errors

Instead of choosing between a purely exclusionary approach or an ESG integration approach, most investors may adopt a "mixed" strategy that combines both approaches where they first exclude some "undesirable" securities and then target others with a strong ESG profile via optimisation.

In this set-up, it is important to understand the sources of the tracking error that the final strategy incorporates. If most of the tracking error comes from the exclusion of a large number of stocks in the first stage, the strategy will already be running a huge amount of tracking error even before the optimisation stage, thereby limiting its manoeuvrability to target strong ESG securities and achieve other objectives in the optimisation stage of the portfolio construction process. This is because most of the tracking error budget will already be "exhausted" by that point.

For this reason, it is advisable to limit the number of exclusions at the initial phase to ensure that sufficient securities are available in the subsequent phase of the portfolio construction process. Limiting the number of exclusions at the initial phase means that the strategy does not automatically exclude poor ESG stocks, but may instead hold an underweight position in them to maintain overall diversification.

Another issue that may arise from this combined exclusion and integration approach is when too many stocks that share the same characteristics are removed at the exclusionary phase of the process. In this scenario, the strategy may be forced to look for and substantially overweight securities that strongly correlate with the excluded securities to remain within a specific tracking error budget, and this inevitably leads to concentration risks on a select number of individual names. For this reason, not only must investors understand the importance of running a sufficient tracking error if their objective is to see strong ESG improvement, but they must also appreciate the source of that tracking error. These portfolio considerations hold true, regardless of whether the objective of the investor is to exclude undesirable "controversial" securities, maximise their portfolio ESG score or create climate portfolios that are in line with "Paris-aligned" standards.

Balancing the multiple portfolio objectives in ESG investments: Doing good versus doing well?

Integrating ESG considerations in the portfolio construction process inevitably means balancing multiple investment objectives. No longer is the focus purely on selecting the "best" portfolio that optimises the risk/return trade-off based on Harry Markowitz's modern portfolio theory,[26] but it is also about incorporating non-financial considerations, such as ESG information. To address the increasingly multi-faceted and complex objectives investors have, various authors have posited different ways in which these sometimes-competing objectives can be resolved.

One such approach is to seek to concurrently trade-off between the various objectives. A case in point is the "tri-criterion" portfolio selection approach as proposed by Hirschberger *et al* (2013). This involves adapting Markowitz's classic efficient frontier framework in such a way that an additional consideration, beyond simply risk and return, can be considered.

The effect of this is that we now have a "three-dimensional" efficient "surface" that balances risk, return and the additional objective (see Figure 1.6), rather than just a "two-dimensional" efficient frontier. Hilario-Caballero *et al* (2020) also made use of the tri-criterion approach to select portfolios that consider risk, return as well as investors' climate change-related preferences.

Figure 1.6 Tri-criterion portfolio selection approach that seeks to balance risk, return and an additional criterion (criterion X)

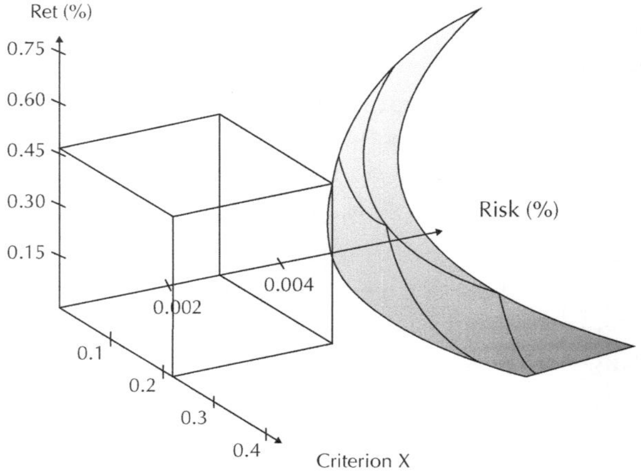

Source: Adapted from Hirschberger et al (2013)

Besides the tri-criterion approach, other authors suggest simply to trade-off between risk and return for a targeted level of ESG. Said differently, they treat ESG considerations in the portfolio as a classic constrained portfolio optimisation problem, with ESG representing the constraints. For instance, Drut (2010) created different efficient frontiers to demonstrate risk/return trade-offs for various ESG targets, and concluded that the efficient frontier is likely to move to the right, reflecting a cost in responsible investing (see Figure 1.7).

Another approach is to directly integrate ESG into the objective rather than treat it as a mere constraint in the optimisation process, and explicitly specifies how risk/return efficiency should be traded off with ESG risk efficiency.

Chen and Mussali (2020) and Alessandrini and Jondeau (2020) suggest combining both risk/return efficiency and ESG risk efficiency into a single measure, and treat that as the portfolio objective. This efficiency measure combines financial performance through the excess return per unit of risk ("Sharpe Ratio") and ESG quality through the ESG score per unit of risk ("ESG Ratio").

Whether investors prefer more risk/return efficiency over ESG risk efficiency, or vice versa, is controlled via gamma (γ):

Figure 1.7 ESG considerations as a constrained portfolio optimisation problem

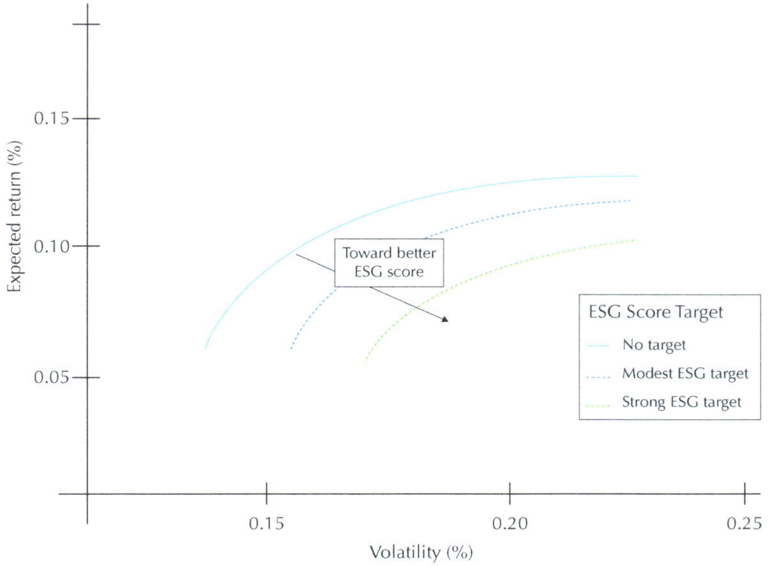

Source: Drut (2010)

$$Eff_p = (1-\gamma)\left(\frac{R_p - R_f}{\sigma_p}\right) + \gamma\left(\frac{Score_p}{\sigma_p}\right) = (1-\gamma)SR_p + \gamma ESGR_p;$$

where R_p, $Score_p$, σ_p denotes the average annualised return, the ESG score and average annualised volatility of a portfolio p, and R_f, the annualised average risk-free rate.

In this portfolio construction set-up, the ESG scores must be expressed roughly on the same scale as an annual return to have two ratios of comparable magnitude. The main advantage of this approach is to allow investors to define trade-offs between risk/return efficiency and ESG risk efficiency.

The final approach that is commonly used to integrate ESG considerations into the portfolio construction process is where ESG information is treated as alpha signals. For example, Henriksson *et al* (2019) advocate including ESG considerations by adjusting the expected return of individual securities. Depending on the importance of the ESG issue in question, it is then appropriately scaled as either a penalty or reward in the optimisation process that seeks to equilibrate active returns (alpha) and active risk (tracking error).

Overall, this approach is simple and can be readily incorporated into existing portfolio construction frameworks. However, it should be highlighted that investors adopting this approach are explicitly expressing the view that ESG information is an alpha signal, something that is not universally accepted by practitioners.

Is active ownership the next frontier in unlocking further ESG alpha?

The issues highlighted above mainly deal with the portfolio construction decisions prior to investments. However, the relevance of ESG considerations permeate the investment management process, and there is a belief that active ownership may also lead to investment alpha, once an investment in a company is made. For clarity, active engagement involves the use of rights and position of ownership to influence activities or behaviour of investee companies, and can include engagement and voting activities.

Whether and how active ownership can impact investment performance is still an ongoing research theme. However, authors such as Dimson, Karakaş and Li (2015) suggested that corporate engagement can be a return driver over the longer term. In a later study, they highlighted the return-generating potential by companies that successfully improved their ESG practices by virtue of their engagement with activist investors (Dimson, Karakaş and Li, 2018).

HOW DO BUSINESS "CONTROVERSIES" AND SOVEREIGN RISK IMPACT ON INVESTMENT PORTFOLIO PERFORMANCE?

Business and product involvement risks in investment portfolios

Defining ESG "controversies" remains a continuous challenge because of the lack of market consensus on its definition. For some investors, ESG controversies are linked to a company's business area and/or involvement – ie, the business activities where companies generate their revenue. For this reason, companies in industries such as tobacco, brewing and distilling, gambling, defence, or certain biotechnology industries are seen as "controversial" and are excluded from the investment universe. In truth, they represent a very small proportion of the benchmark weight as outlined in Table 1.8. Meanwhile, some studies have pointed out how these

Table 1.8 Total weight of companies involved in controversial business activities (exposure in MSCI World)

Business involvement category	**Exposure (%)**
Controversial weapons	0.59
UN Global Compact violators	0.99
Nuclear weapons	0.53
Thermal coal	0.14
Civilian firearms	0.23
Oil sands	0.29
Tobacco	0.66
Total	**3.43**

Source: Author's estimates based on iShares website information (as of March 31, 2022)

stocks, sometimes classified as "sin stocks", in Europe and the US have delivered strong performances over time.

Other investors and research studies[27] define "controversies" as specific weaknesses of a company that can potentially have a significantly negative impact on its business and, by extension, on its financial performance. In many instances, these incident-related controversies are so severe that they create strongly adverse reactions in the market and can create "bad" news flow. These types of controversies can expose the company to severe short- and long-term consequences, such as reputational, legal and litigation risks, or a loss of business opportunities (see also the stock price impacts of bad news flow in the previous section). Contrary to ESG ratings, which commonly apply a sector materiality focus, incident-related controversies do not depend on a sector, and are most likely when and where a company does not have the right mechanisms, policies and procedures in place to prevent them. What matters here is the severity level and sector-specific E, S and G implications[28] of these incidents.

According to research by Schroders (2017), ESG ratings are directly impacted by controversies, and can fall by a full ESG rating downgrade in the few months after a controversy becomes public as most ESG ratings include corporate controversies in their calculations. However, past controversies are not indicative of future controversies. ESG ratings that rely heavily on past controversies are therefore at risk of being ineffective.

Business controversies' impacts on portfolio performance

While studies show that ESG ratings can fall following a controversy, what is interesting is how controversies can impact on the portfolio performance and whether this varies across geographies. One academic study (de Franco, 2020) examined the controversies associated with a sample of companies in the US, Europe and Asia–Pacific between 2010 and 2018. Specifically, it looked at the performance of companies grouped by their controversy rating, which is defined based on 10 Sustainalytics "incident-related" indicators (operational incidents, environmental supply chain incidents, product and service incidents, business ethics incidents, etc).[29]

Overall, the study shows that "no-controversy", "low controversy" and, to some extent, the "moderate-controversy" portfolios outperform the market cap-weighted benchmarks in Europe and in the US ,while the "high controversy" portfolio severely underperforms. In addition, the authors found that unexpected downgrades in the controversy rating in Europe are usually associated with persistent negative excess returns up to 12 months after the downgrade. This is different from the US where the effect is less noticeable, but progressive downgrades are also gradually penalised by the market and the portfolio performance deteriorates over time. Interestingly, controversial stocks in Asia–Pacific do not seem to suffer the same negative effects upon a controversy downgrade as the market there historically might not put as much emphasis on these issues as the US and Europe.

Corporate lobbying, portfolio management and active ownership impacts

Traditionally, business controversies rarely deal with corporate lobbying efforts, but investors are now increasingly focusing on such activities and including them in investment guidelines. One of the reasons for this increased focus is to ensure that the lobbying efforts conducted on behalf of investee companies do not contradict the interests of their shareholders, particularly in relation to their ESG policies.

For instance, a group of investors led by Sjunde AP-fonden, AP7, BNP Paribas Asset Management and the Church of England Pensions Board, launched the first "Global Standard for Responsible

Corporate Climate Lobbying",[30] a standard backed by members that collectively manages over US$130 trillion. The 14-points standard calls on companies to make formal commitments to responsible climate lobbying, to disclose the funding and other support they provide to all trade associations involved in climate change-related lobbying, and to act if lobbying activity undertaken by them, or their trade associations, runs counter to the goals of the Paris Agreement. The standard is influencing the latest revision of climate risk assessment tools such as the Climate Action 100+ (CA100+) benchmark and the Transition Pathway Initiative (TPI).[31]

Interestingly, the standard also encourages positive lobbying efforts that help them to deliver on their carbon transition plans. Through working with non-governmental organisations (NGOs), companies can continue to promote climate change mitigation initiatives and start to close the gap between the climate change commitments they make and the actions they have taken thus far. It is expected that the development of this anti-lobbying standard will strengthen the position of investors' active ownership and engagement activities, and set a precedence for other anti-lobbying standards that are being developed by different sectors.

Lastly, investors are also highlighting through shareholder actions[32] that diversified financial services groups should better align their investment and banking efforts when it comes to climate and sustainability risks and controversies. Sustainability ambitions, from an entity and business unit level, are often not aligned when it comes to ESG governance frameworks and due diligence scrutiny. A case in point is fossil fuel financing where banks made commitments towards the Paris Agreement and the phasing out of coal within the 2020s. However, since then coal financing almost doubled between 2016 to 2017, and has remained elevated ever since (see Figure 1.8).[33]

Portfolio management impact from sovereign risk

Beyond business controversies, there has also been increasing investor focus on controversies committed by governments. There is much interconnectedness between corporate and sovereign controversies as together they can cause substantial systemic ESG risks. An example of this is the Russian invasion of Ukraine when investors were concerned about their exposure to Russian

Figure 1.8 Coal financing of leading banks (aggregated data by Bloomberg Green, March 30, 2022)

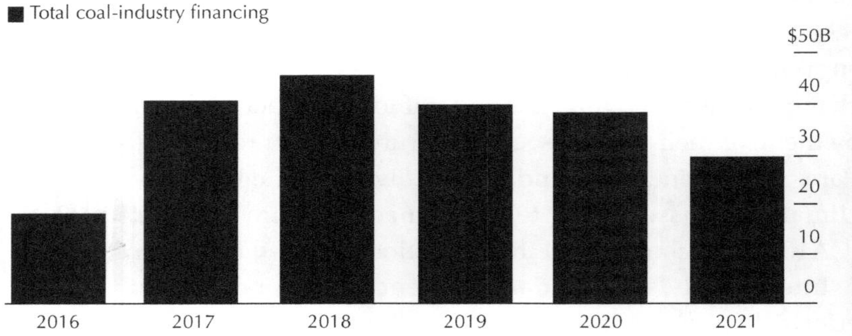

Source: Quinson (2022)

companies because of their desire to dissociate themselves from the behaviour of the Russian government. According to Morningstar Direct, as of January 31, 2022, Russian equities made up just 0.27% of long-term European assets in funds and exchange-traded funds (ETFs), or €32.8 billion of the €12 trillion in total assets (Gard, 2022).

Before the invasion, it was customary and unpolemical to have significant exposure to Russian assets, especially in emerging Europe-focused funds. However, the conflict demonstrated how ethical dilemmas can suddenly arise from holding a specific country's assets, as well as the purpose of responsible investment.

- According to a report by Capital Monitor (Bindman, 2022), 210 individual investors held a total of US$870 million in Russian sovereign bond exposure in their ESG funds as of January 31, 2022.
- On average, these holdings made up just 0.28% of ESG fixed income funds exposed to Russia, compared with 1.2% of regular fixed income funds.
- Meanwhile, total exposure in ESG funds to Russian debt fell in January 2022 by an average of 15%, to its lowest level in just under three years (see Figure 1.9).

From policy commitments to portfolio management actions?

While the commitment to remove controversy-stricken companies from the investment universe has become more of a mainstream

Figure 1.9 Exposure to Russian government debt in ESG funds falls to three-year low

Source: Morningstar; Capital Monitor (January 31, 2022)

financial risk management topic, the same level of commitment has not yet been extended to governments involved in questionable practices. This is illustrated in the report compiled by ShareAction (2020),[34] which found that only 16% of the world's largest 75 asset managers had made firm commitments to exclude sovereign bonds issued by countries that were under international sanctions or involved in human rights violations (see Figure 1.10). Indeed, Russia was already under international sanctions for past violations before the Ukraine war in 2022, and yet its bonds were often held in most mainstream sovereign bond funds and emerging market debt portfolios.

Figure 1.10 Lack of investor actions to exclude human rights violations in investment portfolios

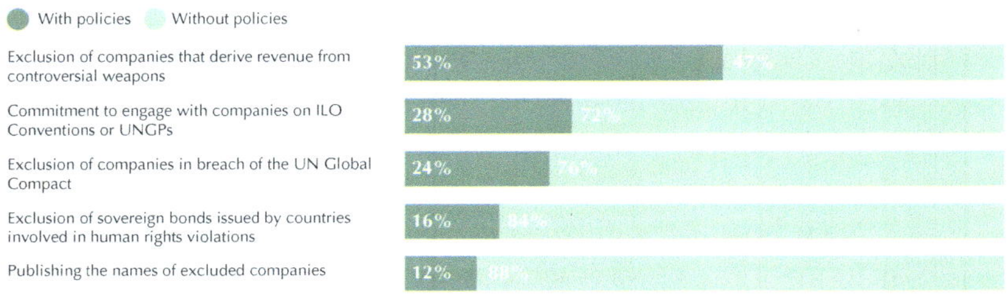

Source: ShareAction (2020)

That being said, it would be inaccurate to suggest that only asset managers did not fully reflect sovereign risks in their investment processes. ESG ratings, on which many institutional investors depend in their asset allocation processes, do not appear to have appropriately accounted for the Russian sovereign risks either.

- For instance, MSCI only decided on March 8, 2022, to downgrade its ESG rating for the Russian government from "B" to "CCC".
- Sustainalytics only stated on March 11, 2022, that it was still "reviewing its ESG risk ratings and country risk ratings in light of the conflict in Ukraine", according to an assessment conducted by the *Financial Times* (Moisson, 2022).

CONCLUSION

A report by Blackrock (2021) has aptly highlighted the ESG investing trends. It states that investors use both systematic and fundamental (ESG) approaches to generate excess returns, and found that sustainability can continue to affect investment returns through three interrelated channels:

- the "tectonic shift" in investor preferences that drives investment flows into sustainable assets and reduces sustainable firms' cost of capital;
- the use of innovative data sources and fundamental research to help identify sustainable business practices and business models that could lead to excess returns compared with the broader market; and
- the evolving relationship between sustainability and traditional style factor investing.

It is without doubt that ESG's place in investor portfolios is assured in the longer term. However, the role that ESG plays in investor portfolios remains a topic that generates huge debate. Some believe that ESG simply reflects investors' preferences and ethics, while others believe that ESG can by itself generate alpha signals. Related to this is how mitigating controversies can impact future portfolio performance, and whether they can really be identified in advance through ESG analysis or are only noticed with the benefit of hindsight.

1 From the PRI Regulation Database (see https://www.unpri.org/policy/regulation-database).
2 In financial reporting, "dual materiality" means that companies have to report about how sustainability issues affect their business and about their own impact on people and the environment. This approach is supported by EFRAG and the GRI.
3 Other "financial materiality" reporting efforts by the IFRS and the Value Reporting Foundation (SASB/IIRC), CDP and CDSB are already setting the scene for harmonisation and standardisation.
4 See, for example, Cesarone, Martino and Carleo (2022).
5 See, for example, Klassen and McLaughlin (1996); for a broader summary, see Clark, Feiner and Viehs (2015).
6 See, for example, Fabius and Phares (2021).
7 See, for example, Edmans (2011; 2012).
8 For a summary, see, for example, Harvard Kennedy Business School (n.d.).
9 For a summary of the debate, see, for example, Scientific Beta (2021).
10 See, for example, Amato and Dyot (2019).
11 See, for example, Konqui, Millet and Darolles (2019).
12 See, for example, Reznick *et al* (2019).
13 See, for example, Hermes Investment Management (2020).
14 See, for example, Lester and He (2018).
15 See, for example, the study of 4,300 funds in Ptak (2021).
16 See, for example, Climent *et al* (2021).
17 See, for example, Nofsinger and Varma (2014).
18 See, for example, Dimson, Karakaş and Li (2015).
19 See, for example, Allianz (2019).
20 A UN Global Compact Corporate Signatory is required to submit an annual "communication on progress" (COP) report regarding their sustainability efforts and has to undertake material ESG commitments.
21 The Ten Principles of the UN Global Compact (see https://www.unglobalcompact.org/what-is-gc/mission/principles) include four categories: human rights; labour; environment; and anti-corruption. These Ten Principles are derived from: the Universal Declaration of Human Rights; the International Labour Organization's Declaration on Fundamental Principles and Rights at Work; the Rio Declaration on Environment and Development; and the United Nations Convention Against Corruption.
22 See Bank of America Merrill Lynch (2019); for further references, see also Flood (2019).
23 See, for example, Scientific Beta (2021).
24 The focus here is on ESG approaches that can be applied prior to initial portfolio construction. Improving trustee's ESG performance after investment is beyond the scope of this section.
25 On the basis of Fama–French's "three factor decomposition model", which includes the market portfolio, the "small minus big" (SMB) factor and the "high minus low" (HML) factor.
26 See Markowitz (1952). The modern portfolio theory (MPT) is a practical method for selecting investments to maximise their overall returns within an acceptable level of risk.
27 See, for example, de Franco (2020).
28 Note that some sectors are more likely to suffer from pernicious incidents on the environmental side (eg, utilities or energy), others on the governance side (eg, financials) and others on the social side (eg, information technology or healthcare).
29 This is based on Sustainalytics Product Involvement Screening: "Product Involvement Screening by Sustainalytics helps identify companies involved in a range of products, services and business activities for screening purposes. Each activity is accompanied with a concise summary of the way the company is involved in the relevant product or activity." (See https://connect.sustainalytics.com/product-involvement#:~:text=Sustainalytics'%20Product%20Involvement%20research,the%20relevant%20product%20or%20activity).

30 Global Standard for Responsible Corporate Climate Lobbying (see https://climate-lobbying.com).

31 See https://www.transitionpathwayinitiative.org.

32 See, for example, ShareAction (2021).

33 For a summary on remaining issues linking to coal fuel financing, see, for example, Quinson (2022).

34 ShareAction (2020) ranks 75 of the world's largest asset managers, and analyses their performance on stewardship, transparency and governance.

REFERENCES

Alessandri, F. and E. Jondeau, 2020, "Optimal Strategies for ESG Portfolios", Swiss Finance Institute Research Paper No. 20–21, April 20 (available at https://papers.ssrn.com/sol3/papers.cfm?abstract_id=3578830).

Allianz, 2019, "Active is: Managing Tail Risks through Active Integrated ESG Investing", June (available at https://ap.allianzgi.com/-/media/AllianzGI/AP/AP/ESG/sustainability-092020/pdf/Tail-Risks-in-ESG.pdf).

Amato, J. V. and I. S. Dyot, 2019, "ESG Investing: An Active Approach to Long-term Value Creation", white paper, Neuberger Berman, January (available at https://www.nb.com/documents/public/global/t0349_0119_wp_esg_investing_an_active_approach.pdf).

Aviva Investors, 2021, "Living in the Past: Why are Controversy Scores so Controversial?", April 8 (available at https://www.avivainvestors.com/en-gb/views/aiq-investment-thinking/2021/04/controversy-scores/).

Baker, S., 2020, "Global ESG-data Driven Assets Hit $40.5 Trillion", *Pensions & Investments*, July 2 (available at https://www.pionline.com/esg/global-esg-data-driven-assets-hit-405-trillion).

Bank of America Merrill Lynch, 2019, "ESG Matters", September 23.

Berg, F., J. F. Kölbel and R. Rigobon, 2019, "The Aggregate Confusion: The Divergence of ESG Ratings", MIT Sloan Business School, August (available at https://papers.ssrn.com/sol3/papers.cfm?abstract_id=3438533).

Bermejo Climent, R., I. Figuerola-Ferretti Garrigues, I. Paraskevopoulos and A. Santos, 2021, "ESG Disclosure and Portfolio Performance", *Risks,* 9(10), p. 172 (available at https://www.mdpi.com/2227-9091/9/10/172).

Bindman, P., 2022, "What Russia's War Means for Responsible Investment", Capital Monitor, March 8 (available at https://capitalmonitor.ai/strategy/responsilbe/what-russias-war-means-for-responsible-investment/).

BlackRock, 2021, "Seeking Outperformance through Sustainable Insights", October 8 (available at https://www.blackrock.com/corporate/literature/investor-education/sustainable-data-insights-research.pdf).

Bloomberg, 2021, "Natixis Investment Managers Survey Finds that Environmental, Social and Governance (ESG) Investing Momentum Builds as 60% of Investors Say Companies are Accountable to More Than Just Shareholders", November 9 (available at https://www.bloomberg.com/press-releases/2021-11-09/natixis-investment-managers-survey-finds-that-environmental-social-and-governance-esg-investing-momentum-builds-as-60-of).

BNP Paribas, 2021, "The ESG Global Survey 2021", September 13 (available at https://securities.cib.bnpparibas/esg-global-survey-2021/).

Boffo, R. and R. Patalano, 2020, "ESG Investing: Practices, Progress and Challenges", OECD Paris (available at https://www.oecd.org/finance/ESG-Investing-Practices-Progress-Challenges.pdf).

Branch, M., L. Goldberg and P. Hand, 2020, "A Guide to ESG Portfolio Construction", Mission Investors (available at https://missioninvestors.org/sites/default/files/resources/Download%20the%20Guide.pdf).

Cesarone, F., M. L. Martino and A. Carleo, 2022, "Does ESG Impact Really Enhance Portfolio Profitability?", working paper, Roma Tre University, January.

Chen, M. and G. Mussali, 2020, "An Integrated Approach to Quantitative ESG Investing", *The Journal of Portfolio Management: Ethical Investing,* 46(3), February (available at https://www.panagora.com/wp-content/uploads/JPM-An-Integrated-Approach-to-Quantitative-ESG-Investing.pdf).

Clark, G. L., A. Feiner and M. Viehs, 2015, "From the Stockholder to the Stakeholder: How Sustainability Can Drive Financial Outperformance", Arabesque Partners, March, updated version (available at https://arabesque.com/research/From_the_stockholder_to_the_stakeholder_web.pdf).

Cui, B. and P. Docherty, 2019, "Stock Price Overreaction to ESG Controversies", Monash University (available at https://papers.ssrn.com/sol3/papers.cfm?abstract_id=3559915).

de Franco, C., 2020, "ESG Controversies and Their Impact on Performance", *Journal of Investing,* ESG Special Issue, 29(2), pp 33-45 (available at https://joi.pm-research.com/content/29/2/33.short).

Diab, A. and G. M. Adams, 2021, "ESG Assets May Hit $53 Trillion by 2025, a Third of Global AUM", Bloomberg Intelligence, February 23 (available at https://www.bloomberg.com/professional/blog/esg-assets-may-hit-53-trillion-by-2025-a-third-of-global-aum/).

Dimson, E. O. Karakaş and X. Li, 2015, "Active Ownership", *The Review of Financial Studies,* 28(12), December, pp. 3,225-68 (available at https://academic.oup.com/rfs/article/28/12/3225/1573572).

Dimson, E., O. Karakaşand X. Li, 2018, "Coordinated Engagements", European Corporate Governance Institute - Finance Working Paper No. 721/2021, July 26 (available at https://papers.ssrn.com/sol3/papers.cfm?abstract_id=3209072).

Drut, B., 2010, "Social Responsibility and Mean-variance Portfolio Selection", Working Papers CEB 10-002,RS (available at https://econpapers.repec.org/paper/solwpaper/10-002.htm).

Edmans, A., 2011, "Does the Stock Market Fully Value Intangibles? Employee Satisfaction and Equity Prices", *Journal of Financial Economics,* 101, pp. 621-40.

Edmans, A., 2012, "The Link Between Job Satisfaction and Firm Value, with Implications for Corporate Social Responsibility", *Academy of Management Perspectives,* 26(4), pp. 1-19.

ESMA, 2022, "Sustainable Finance Roadmap 2022-24", February 10 (available at https://www.esma.europa.eu/sites/default/files/library/esma30-379-1051_sustainable_finance_roadmap.pdf).

Fabius, R. and S. Phares, 2021, "Companies that Promote a Culture of Health, Safety, and Wellbeing Outperform in the Marketplace", *Journal of Occupational and Environmental Medicine*, **63**(6), June, pp. 456-61.

Fender, R., R. Stammers, R. Unwin and R. Preece, 2020, "Future of Sustainability in Investment Management: From Ideas to Reality", CFA Institute (available at https://www.cfainstitute.org/-/media/documents/survey/future-of-sustainability.pdf).

Flood, C., 2019, "ESG Controversies Wipe $500bn off Value of US Companies", *Financial Times*, December 14 (available at https://www.ft.com/content/3f1d44d9-094f-4700-989f-616e27c89599).

Gard, J., 2022, "How Exposed are European Funds to Russia?", Morningstar Direct, February 25 (available at https://www.morningstar.co.uk/uk/news/219189/how-exposed-are-european-funds-to-russia.aspx).

GlobeScan, 2021, "Investors Views on ESG", December (available at https://3ng5l43rk-kzc34ep72kj9as1-wpengine.netdna-ssl.com/wp-content/uploads/2021/12/GlobeScan-Radar-2021-Retail_Investors_Views_of_ESG-Full-Report.pdf).

Glossner, S., 2021, "ESG Incidents and Shareholder Value", University of Virginia, Darden School of Business, February 17.

GSIA, 2020, "Global Sustainable Investment Review" (available at http://www.gsi-alliance.org/wp-content/uploads/2021/08/GSIR-20201.pdf).

Harvard Kennedy Business School, n.d., "Diversity and Inclusion: The Business Case for Investors", presentation (available at https://iri.hks.harvard.edu/files/iri/files/tlf-diversity-and-inclusion-the-business-case-for-investors-slides.pdf).

Harvard Kennedy Business School, 2015, Corporate Sustainability: First Evidence on Materiality written by Khan, Serafeim and Yoon, available at https://dash.harvard.edu/bitstream/handle/1/14369106/15-073.pdf

Henriksson, R., J. Livnat, P. Pfeifer and M. Stumpp, 2019, "Integrating ESG in Portfolio Construction", *Journal of Portfolio Management* (available at https://cdn.pficdn.com/cms/pgimquantsolutions/sites/default/files/static_files/pdf/QMA_Integrating_ESG_in_Portfolio_Construction.pdf).

Hermes Investment Management, 2020, "Pricing ESG Risk in Sovereign Credit: An Emerging Divergence", March 2.

Hilario-Caballero, A., A. Garcia-Bernabeau, J. V. Salcedo and M. Vercher, 2020, "Tri-criterion Model for Constructing Low-carbon Mutual Fund Portfolios: A Preference-based Multi-objective Genetic Algorithm Approach", *International Journal of Environmental Research and Public Health,* 17(17), 6324 (available at https://www.mdpi.com/1660-4601/17/17/6324).

Hirschberger, M., R. Steuer, S. Utz, M. Wimmer and Y. Qi, 2013, "Computing the Nondominated Surface in Tri-criterion Portfolio Selection", *Operations Research,* 61(1), pp. 169-83.

IFRS, 2022, "IFRS Foundation and GRI to Align Capital Market and Multi-stakeholder Standards to Create an Interconnected Approach for Sustainability Disclosures", March 24 (available at https://www.ifrs.org/news-and-events/news/2022/03/ifrs-foundation-signs-agreement-with-gri/).

IOSCO, 2021, "Environmental, Social and Governance (ESG) Ratings and Data Products Providers", Final Report, November available at https://www.iosco.org/library/pubdocs/pdf/IOSCOPD690.pdf).

Kerber, R. and S. Jessop, 2021, "Analysis: How 2021 Became the Year of ESG Investing", Reuters, December 23 (available at https://www.reuters.com/markets/us/how-2021-became-year-esg-investing-2021-12-23/).

Klassen, R.D. and C. P. McLaughlin, 1996, "The Impact of Environmental Management on Firm Performance", *Management Science*, 42(8), pp. 1,199-214;

Konqui, M. H., F. Millet and S. Darolles, 2019, "Why Using ESG Helps You Build Better Portfolios", Lyxor Dauphine Research Academy, July (available at https://www.lyxor.com/why-using-esg-helps-you-build-better).

Lester, A. and C. He, 2018, "Harnessing ESG as an Alpha Source in Active Quantitative Equities", IQ Insights, State Street Global Advisors (available at https://www.ssga.com/investment-topics/environmental-social-governance/2018/07/harnessing-esg-as-an-alpha-source.pdf).

Markowitz, H., 1952, "Portfolio Selection", *The Journal of Finance*, 7(1), pp. 77-91.

Moisson, E., 2022, "ESG Investors Accused of 'Failing' Over Russia", *Financial Times*, March 11 (available at https://www.ft.com/content/fad3e241-08fa-47fc-bdbd-32dd5b72403d).

Morgan Stanley, 2021, Sustainable Signals: Individual Investors and the COVID-19 Pandemic", October 27 (available at https://www.morganstanley.com/assets/pdfs/2021-Sustainable_Signals_Individual_Investor.pdf).

Nofsinger J. and A. Varma, 2014, "Socially Responsible Funds and Market Crises", *Journal of Banking & Finance*, **48**, pp 180-93.

ODDO BHF Asset Management, 2019, "Sustainable Investment Report".

ODDO BHF Asset Management, 2021, "Sustainable Investment Report".

PRI, 2018, "A Practical Guide to Active Ownership in Listed Equity" (available at https://www.unpri.org/download?ac=4151).

PRI, 2020, "An Introduction to Responsible Investment Screening" (available at https://www.unpri.org/download?ac=10608).

PRI, 2021, "88 new policies added to PRI's regulation database" (available at https://www.unpri.org/pri-blog/88-new-policies-added-to-pris-regulation-database/8532.article)

Ptak, J., 2021, "Did ESG Pay Off for Fund Investors Last Year? Yes and No", Morningstar, January 5 (available at https://www.morningstar.com/articles/1016714/did-esg-pay-off-for-fund-investors-last-year-yes-and-no).

Qontigo, 2022, "An 'Impossible Product'? Comparing Europe's Dissonant ESG Fund Labels", blogpost, January 10 (available at https://qontigo.com/an-impossible-product-comparing-europes-dissonant-esg-fund-labels/).

Quakers, n.d., "Eliminating Slavery Amongst Quakers" (available at https://www.quakersintheworld.org/quakers-in-action/58/Eliminating-Slavery-amongst-Quakers).

Quinson, T., 2021, "The World's Biggest Investors Get Louder About ESG", Bloomberg Green, June 9 (available at https://www.bloomberg.com/news/articles/2021-06-09/the-world-s-biggest-investors-get-louder-about-esg-green-insight).

Quinson, T., 2022, "Banks Still Stand Behind Dirtiest Fossil Fuel", Bloomberg Green, March 30 (available at https://www.bloomberg.com/news/articles/2022-03-30/bankers-still-stand-behind-dirtiest-fossil-fuel-green-insight).

Reznick, M., M. Viehs, N. Chockalingam, T. Panesar, G. A. Lizarazu and J. Moussavi, 2019, "Pricing ESG Risk in Sovereign Credit, Research Paper, Hermes Investment Management, Q3 (available at https://www.hermes-investment.com/ukw/wp-content/uploads/2019/07/bd03720-credit-research-paper-pricing-esg-in-sovereign-credit-q3-2019.pdf).

Schroders, 2017, "Managing Corporate Controversies: The Role of Environmental, Social and Governance (ESG) Ratings" (available at https://www.schroders.com/pl/insights/economics/managing-corporate-controversies-the-role-of-esg-ratings/).

Scientific Beta, 2021, "'Honey, I Shrunk the ESG Alpha': Risk-adjusting ESG Portfolio Returns", April (available at https://cdn.ihsmarkit.com/www/pdf/0521/Honey-I-Shrunk-the-ESG-Alpha.pdf).

ShareAction, 2020, "Point of No Returns: A Ranking of 75 of the World's Asset Manager Approaches to Investment", March 9 (available at https://shareaction.org/reports/point-of-no-returns-a-ranking-of-75-of-the-worlds-asset-managers-approaches-to-responsible-investment).

ShareAction, 2021, "USD 2.4 Trillion Investor Group Files Climate Resolution at HSBC", January 11 (available at https://shareaction.org/news/usd-2-4-trillion-investor-group-files-climate-resolution-at-hsbc).

Stevens, P., 2020, "Stock Performance Study Shows Companies should take Environmental and Social Factors Seriously", CNBC, February 7 (available at https://www.cnbc.com/2020/02/07/esg-high-controversy-events-can-cost-stocks.html).

Wilkes, T., 2022, "Four in Every 10 Euros of European Fund Assets now Sold as 'Sustainable' - Morningstar", Reuters, February 7 (available at https://www.reuters.com/business/finance/four-every-10-euros-european-fund-assets-now-sold-sustainable-morningstar-2022-02-07/).

2

Case Study 1: Applying ESG considerations to a pension fund's equity portfolios

Jens-Jakob Kratmann Nissen and Christian Kjær

ATP

As a public (pillar 1) pension scheme (see Figure 2.1) for almost the entire population of Denmark, acting as good and responsible stewards of our beneficiaries' asset is our most important task. A central aspect of responsible investing is to deal with ESG aspects of portfolio construction. This chapter will therefore discuss some of the ideas and principles underlying the choices ATP has made for the integration of ESG considerations across all types of investments.

To illustrate, we will use our global smart beta equity portfolio as an example. Our aim here is to summarise how we integrate

Figure 2.1 ATP's fundamental role in the Danish pension system

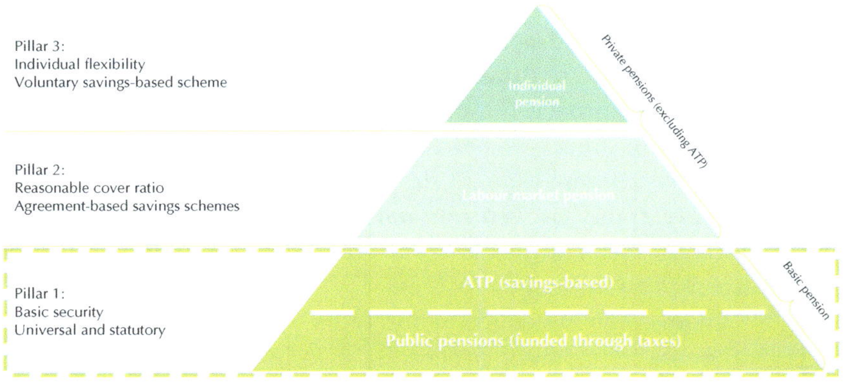

ESG considerations in the portfolio construction process and analyse their implications.

The chapter is organised as follows. First, we will outline the general guiding principles and investment beliefs underpinning our approach, and resolve the dilemmas that naturally arise in the actual implementation. Second, we will discuss the aspects highlighted above using the smart beta equity portfolio that we manage at ATP. The discussion is broken down into three parts: guiding principles/investment beliefs; integration and active ownership; and the ESG investment process at ATP. The objective is to provide a clear idea of how we use ESG in our investment process to fulfil our responsibilities to our members.

GUIDING PRINCIPLES AND INVESTMENT BELIEFS

The approach to ESG at ATP was initially formulated as an investment belief. We believe that we can, and should, make use of relevant aspects of the ESG universe to improve our understanding of risks and to identify potential investment opportunities. In other words, our ESG effort is primarily driven by a risk and return trade-off as opposed to a pure desire to appear green and/or good. There is no inherent contradiction between achieving a high level of financial return and assuming our social responsibility as our objective is not to generate the highest possible level of return at any cost. Instead, our aim is to maximise risk-adjusted returns in a responsible way, and we believe this can be partly achieved through a deep understanding of ESG aspects.

ESG is a broad concept and different areas are interesting to different people. Not every aspect of ESG is necessarily a relevant return driver across all investments. As with traditional financial data, the value of different datapoints varies across investments. The ESG approach therefore needs to be tailored to the various investment processes and cannot be a "one size fits all" approach. Like any other investment strategies, it also needs a well-described and preferably proven rationale. Integrating ESG should not be fundamentally different from integrating any other traditional aspect in an investment process.

To leverage ESG information to its fullest extent across a broad range of investment processes, it is important to have strong in-house expertise. We believe that financial markets are very efficient, and that there are no "free lunches". Without the right expertise, it is very hard to strike the right balance between risk and return.

As a data-driven investor, we are heavily reliant on the availability and quality of data. ESG data are still in the early stages of development, and there are significant gaps in terms of both coverage and quality. Therefore, working for transparency and disclosure of ESG data is also part of our active ownership efforts as we need sufficient and precise data to be able to make informed decisions. This is particularly important given that we are very precise about what ESG information we use.

We are also strong advocates for active ownership, and believe that we can influence companies to create long-term value. Indeed, as a responsible large investor, we have an obligation to ensure that the company acts in the best interests for shareholders so that value can be created over the long run. In addition to this, we also believe active ownership matters and that it adds long-term value to the portfolio.

Being explicit about ESG as an investment belief, it is only natural to integrate ESG issues in the active ownership responsibility as well. This can be achieved by supporting a given strategic direction or trying to change a company's strategic direction. Our bargaining power as an investor differs across our investments, as does our active ownership approach. We have a close and frequent dialogue with companies in Denmark, where we have a relatively large ownership share and easy access to management. Abroad, we typically have a relatively low ownership share and limited access to management, and therefore mainly push our agenda in writing and through our votes at general assemblies. All of this is carried out in-house as we do not want to outsource our opinions to third parties. Nevertheless, our ability to set an agenda and push through is naturally larger in Denmark.

Particularly abroad, we therefore tend to prefer companies that broadly align with us on pivotal issues. Active ownership complements ESG integration, and vice versa. We will stick with a company for as long as we believe in the long-term value creation proposition. Therefore, we divest on the back of an engagement process if we no longer believe in the long-term value creation proposition (expected return-driven divestment) or if the engagement reveals legal or moral issues that we cannot tolerate regardless of the expected return (with the company also being put on a restriction list).

Guiding principles regarding restrictions and integration

ESG restrictions represent a simple and crude way of dealing with ESG issues in a portfolio context. They represent the view that expected returns cannot compensate for everything. To the extent that ESG-grounded restrictions are binding, they cannot contribute positively to expected returns in the short term. At best they do not matter.

Note that divesting certain assets out of concerns of lower expected return and/or higher risks related to ESG does not constitute a restriction. These are portfolio decisions like any others in portfolio management. As will be clear later, restrictions can be a costly affair. Nevertheless, we do use restrictions to send a clear signal that a certain behaviour cannot be tolerated no matter the expected return. Although they can be warranted, restrictions are costly on the margin but only have a minor impact.

ESG integration represents a more nuanced approach to ESG. Whereas restrictions eliminate certain assets irrespective of expected risk and return, ESG integration is about integrating ESG issues in the traditional investment process considerations. We believe integrating ESG can lead to both better returns and less risk. On the return side, this has been materialised, for instance, in investing in a partly coal-powered utility company transitioning into a green utility company. On the risk side, it has materialised in divesting from coal-powered utility companies without ambitious transition plans.

However, on the margin we also value ESG in its own right. If differences in the risk and return properties in investment opportunities are indistinguishable, ESG considerations can be pivotal. It is important to note, nonetheless, that adopting ESG as an investment belief does not imply that all aspects of the ever-growing ESG spectrum are critical in the investment decision. On the contrary, ESG aspects are considered with the same rigour as any other input in the investment process. Just as a value manager is very precise in selecting value companies with strong return potential, you need to be very precise in judging the return potential within the ESG spectrum. It is key to have sufficient and precise data to be able to make informed decisions. In addition, we are very precise about which ESG data points are used as not all of them are relevant and sufficiently precise to be useful.

THE ESG INVESTMENT PROCESS AT ATP

Grounded in the principles detailed above, a wide range of ESG aspects have been implemented at ATP. As we do not believe in a "one size fits all" approach, the implementation has been tailored to the individual investment processes.

To make it as concrete and relevant as possible, the following will focus on the implementation in global equities. A full description of everything going on would be either too comprehensive or only allow us to scratch the surface of the different areas. The description is therefore divided into three areas (with some overlap):

- ESG restrictions;
- ESG integration; and
- measuring impact.

Before we get started, the next section provides a short description of the investment process for global equities at ATP. Without it, a concrete description of how we deal with ESG aspects is hardly possible. When our general portfolio construction is defined, we are in a position to quantify the effect of restrictions in our universe, which is covered in the following section. This is followed by a description of the actual integration of a quantitative ESG signal in our portfolio construction for global equities. Lastly, we will discuss the impact our different choices have resulted in. As will be explained, active ownership is important in each part of our investment process, whether looking at restrictions or integration.

Smart beta equity investment process

To concretely exemplify how the fundamental principles are implemented, we will use our global equity smart beta portfolio. It is a long-only quantitative equity strategy whose construction is based on more than a half century of academic research. Formally, the equity selection hinges on the idea that equity returns are driven by a limited set of underlying factors (originally formulated in the arbitrage pricing theory, APT). As such, equity returns are driven by the risk-free rate (*rf*), return of the underlying factors (f_k), the factor loadings ($\beta_{i,k}$) and idiosyncratic risk (ε_i):

$$r_{i,t} = rf_t + \sum_k \beta_{i,k} f_{k,t} + \varepsilon_{i,t}, i \in U_t$$

for all equities in our universe of investable equities at time t (U_t). Apart from the market factor, we operate with five factors: low risk; momentum; value; quality; and ESG. For each factor we rank all equities from best to worst. The ranks are subsequently transformed into factor scores such that the best gets the highest score and the worst gets the lowest score. The transformation from rank to score is non-linear but is designed so that the best equities get a higher score and the worst get a lower score. Therefore, worst-in-class ESG laggards are heavily penalised and unlikely to make it to the portfolio. The factor scores are in turn aggregated to get one final score for each stock. Now, with a single score per stock, we can rank all equities from best to worst and construct the final portfolio.

The effect of restricting your investment universe

It is not an easy task *ex ante* to quantify the cost of applying a given restriction in a strategy. However, *ex post* it is possible for us to quantify the price of restrictions, because of the systematic approach in our smart beta strategy.

Figure 2.2 shows an analysis based on return data of companies in our investment universe in the period 1995–2017. The analysis follows our portfolio construction in the smart beta process. We let U_t denote our universe at time t – that is, U_t represents the set of stocks available in the time period $[t,t+1]$, $t \in \{0,1,2,\ldots,T-1\}$. In each time step, we create $m \cdot l$ new universes where m is the number of simulations for each restriction in the set $res = \{res_i\}_{i=1}^{l}$ and l is the number of different restrictions tested. In our analysis, *res* = {2%, 4%, 6%, 8%, 10%, 12%, 14%, 16%}, and therefore $l = 8$.

We denote one of these simulated universes by $\tilde{U}_t^{i,j}$, where $i \in \{1,\ldots,l\}$ and $j \in \{1,\ldots,m\}$. Each of these simulated universes is created by randomly applying restrictions res_i, $i \in \{1,\ldots,l\}$ (ie, removing a specified number of companies) from the original universe.

Figure 2.2 Simulations of estimated annual costs based on the number of exclusions of companies from the ATP's investment universe (1995–2017)

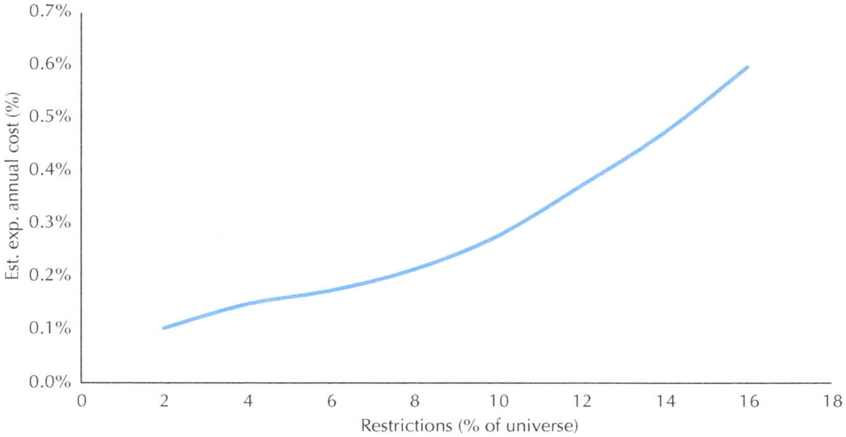

Having created the simulated universes, we proceeded to apply on them our smart beta strategy. This involves selecting the best available companies from the restricted universe based on the scoring mechanism below. It can be summarised mathematically as follows:

$$P_t^{i,j} = \{x \mid S(x) \geq S_{80\%}, x \in \tilde{U}_t^{i,j}\}$$

As we are dealing with historical data, we can calculate the portfolio return in each time step for each simulation. We sum the returns to get the backtested return for each simulation, ie:

$$r_{p^{i,j}} = \sum_{t=0}^{T-1} r_{p_t^{i,j}}$$

We calculate our expected cost for each restriction as the unrestricted return value minus the restricted return:

$$cost^i = r_p - \frac{1}{m}\sum_{j-1}^{m} r_{p^{i,j}}$$

In the analysis, we maintain that the ESG restrictions are not grounded in risk/return considerations and simply select companies for the restriction list randomly from our investment universe. This may seem an extreme (or even provocative) approach to deal with ESG restrictions, but it is a simple and effective way to represent restrictions not grounded in risk/return considerations. As discussed, divesting a company (or refraining from investing in the first place) based on risk or return expectations guided by ESG considerations should not be mistaken for restrictions.

The cost of restrictions is low in the beginning but increases more than linearly as the number of restrictions grow. The fact that restrictions are increasingly costly is related to how our investment process works. On average, the selection process can add value but restricting the investment universe often comes with an expected cost. Initially, there are plenty of good substitutes but as the share of restricted companies increases it gets more difficult to find good substitutes, and the cost starts to kick in. Therefore, although restrictions can be necessary and warranted, they do not constitute a free lunch and should be used with caution.

Restrictions can also be used as a signalling tool in the active ownership process. A case in point is how we dealt with utilities companies in our portfolio. We want to avoid stranded assets and at the same time send a clear signal on which direction we want our portfolio companies to focus. If the green transition is not on the agenda in a company, the direction is wrong in our view. Further, green transition and new coal plants do not go together – it is not a long-term profitable strategy and is at high risk of becoming a stranded asset. More broadly, the transition out of coal is imminent and if companies have more than 50% of their energy production coming from coal, they are too far behind the curve. Therefore, we have divested those companies out of an ESG-driven risk concern. To send a clear signal, we have also put the companies on our restriction list.

We further engage with and support companies with high greenhouse gas (GHG) intensities that pursue a realistic and profitable transition strategy. Based on the dialogue, we have rejected multiple companies because they did not have sufficiently ambitious plans for improvement. As a measure of the active owner impact, we are delighted when a company subsequently informs us of their plan to change direction, retire the coal capacity and replace it with renewables.

Figure 2.3 MSCI ESG scores and their underlying issues

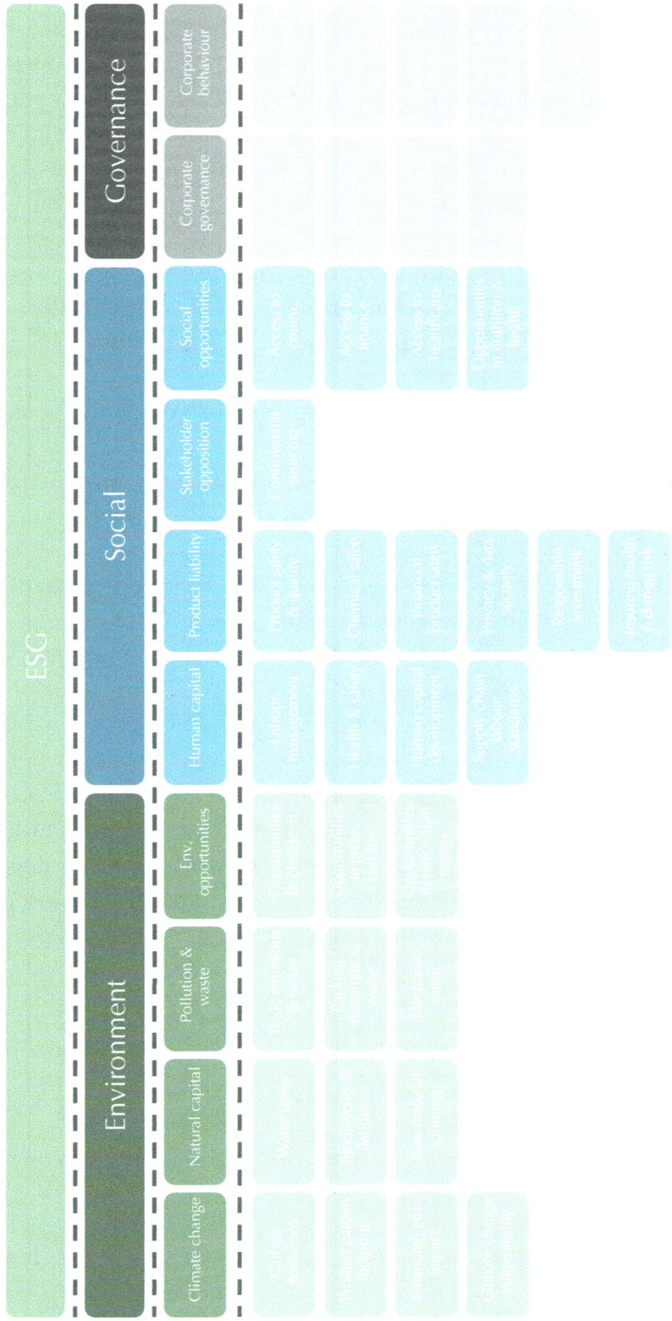

Source: MSCI Inc.

Integration

In the following, we will see how we use the MSCI's ESG dataset in our investment process. The MSCI ESG scores and their underlying issues are described in Figure 2.3. We will refer to the level below "environment", "social" and "governance" as the "issue level".

To illustrate the challenge with adopting a broad ESG metric, consider the following simple analysis.

- ❑ Rank all equities from best to worst based on their aggregate ESG score, and construct an approximately market-neutral portfolio that is long the top 20% and short the bottom 20% of rated companies.
- ❑ Do the same for the aggregate E-score, S-score and G-score.

Table 2.1 shows the annualised Sharpe ratio for the portfolios in North America and Europe, respectively.

- ❑ The European ESG portfolio delivers a positive Sharpe ratio, while the North American does not.
- ❑ The North American E-portfolio delivers a positive Sharpe ratio, but the European does not. And so on.
- ❑ There is no clear systematic link between ESG scores and returns.

Since there is no clear relationship between aggregated ESG-scores and portfolio returns, we have decided on an approach tailored to support our investment strategy as well as our ESG strategy. One of the areas where we have worked most intensively on integrating ESG issues in our global developed marked equity portfolio is in

Table 2.1 Comparing the annualised Sharpe ratio for the portfolios in North America and Europe

	Region	
Factor	**America**	**Europe**
ESG	–0.03	0.59
E	0.21	–0.14
S	0.07	–0.03
G	–0.17	0.45

GHG-intense sectors. As we progress in the green transition, the carbon intensity of production will come under increased scrutiny.

We believe that future carbon emissions and intensities will be a key metric in determining winners and losers in GHG-intense sectors. With this reasoning, we began to dig into the available ESG dataset to investigate whether this could help improve our equity selection process within these sectors. There is no reason to believe that an aggregated ESG score would be the most precise guide to single out companies that are most likely to excel in the carbon-intensity reduction race.

A high aggregated ESG score could be the result of certain governmental, or social aspects linked to a company, rather than the result of a company's E and S externalities themselves. Equally, the ESG score may be skewed because a company might score strongly in one ESG area but score weakly in another. That being said, we chose to focus on the environmental part of the ESG spectrum to look for a quantitative signal for the purpose of this analysis. The environment area is divided into four categories, where "climate change" and "environment opportunities" are obvious candidates when the focus is on carbon intensity. On an issue level, "carbon emissions" and "opportunities in renewable energy" are both linked to an "exposure metric score" and a "management metric score".

To understand whether a company is adequately managing an ESG risk, it is important to understand how exposed it is to the risk ("exposure") and which management strategy it has employed ("management").

- The management effort to develop renewable energy solutions is based on whether a company has declared ambitious goals to increase its production of green energy, whether it has effective structures to support this transition, whether it has planned new green capacity within the next five years, and other criteria.
- The carbon emission management score is based on efforts to reduce exposure through comprehensive carbon policies and implementation mechanisms. This includes carbon reduction targets, production process improvements, and installation of depollution or emissions capture equipment. This could also include a switch to cleaner energy sources.

It is worth highlighting here that our integrated ESG score is a combination of MSCI's "carbon emissions" and "opportunities in renewable energy" scores. The first score contributes to the final score in all sectors where carbon emission is a key issue, and the latter is used only when we score utility companies. We only use opportunities in renewable energy in utilities since this sector accounts for most of the GHG emissions in listed equity – more than 60% of the GHG emissions from our universe (scope 1) comes from utilities.[1] Again, our quantitative investment process allows us to backtest the implications of potential changes to the strategy. A data-driven strategy is heavily dependent on data. The availability of ESG data limits the strengths of quantitative studies.

In our MSCI ESG dataset, we have data on "management" efforts related to carbon efficiency dating back to 2008. The importance of GHG efficiency has undoubtedly been rising since then. Although the challenge of global warming and the link to GHG emissions has been known since the 1980s, it only became a mainstream issue for investors, company and public policy, and regulation since the mid-2010s. In the early part of the dataset in particular, it is not clear whether carbon efficiency is already captured in the pricing. Nonetheless, we do find a slightly positive link between carbon efficiency focus and portfolio returns. This will be explained and illustrated in the next section.

In our analysis, we rank companies on their ability to manage the carbon emission issue in industries where carbon emission intensity is an important issue. The factor score received from this ranking is a cross-sectional score that, as described above, is a non-linear score normally distributed with mean zero and volatility one.

All in all, this means that when included in our general integrated factor score, all else being equal, companies that are more proactive towards the transition to green energy, in high emitting industry groups, are favoured compared to those that are not proactive. When running a backtest from 2008 going forward, we do not see a statistically significant outperformance when carbon emission management is considered in our final company score. However, the inclusion does not lead to an underperformance. Returns are slightly higher, but not statistically significantly. As we will see in the next section, the impact of incorporating carbon emission management in our score also has a great environmental impact.

Impact

Impact investing is often confined to small niche private investments rather than sizable portfolio-wide efforts. In small private investments with a large ownership, share impact can be relatively tangible. For instance, if you build and operate a windmill farm you create tangible green energy that (presumably) would not have been there without you. However important investments like these are, they are always going to be small in scale and cannot be scaled up to any sizeable investment portfolios. The listed market and the transformation needed to take place there leaves a much greater potential for real impact. Unfortunately, targeting and measuring impact and its implications for returns is a lot less tangible here. Nonetheless, this is presumably where we can have most impact both on the environment and returns.

Again, as the main emitter of GHG, utilities is one of the key sectors that is going to take centre stage in the green transition. This will create both great threats and great opportunities, with the GHG intensity and the evolvement of GHG intensity in utility companies being very crucial parameters. By blending a novel and innovative approach to stock selection while having simple minimum requirements that are easy to communicate, we have devised a strategy we believe will enable us to pick the winners, avoid the losers and have the maximal impact on the green transition.

One way to avoid losers and foster more profitable strategies is by excluding laggards and companies moving in the wrong direction. Another more proactive approach with a higher success rate is to actively target companies already on the right track. Combining ESG, GHG emissions and traditional financial data, we have established that systematically picking utility companies going green is a possible and attractive strategy in terms of both returns and expected GHG impact. To invest in the most progressive utilities, you need to be able to identify companies that will most reduce GHG intensity in the future. To analyse this, we merged a large ESG dataset with present and historic ESG ratings of utility companies and a dataset with present and historically estimated GHG emissions.

The management of renewable power will be useful in determining which utilities are pursuing an effective transition strategy. To test this hypothesis, we analysed the relationship between the metric at a given point in time and the subsequent development in GHG intensity on a one-, two- and three-year horizon. The analysis shows that the companies scoring the highest on our ESG score, on average, reduce GHG intensity by almost 25% over the following three years, whereas the GHG intensity in the lowest scoring companies remains unchanged. The effect is smaller on a one- and two-year time horizon, but there is still a clear relation between score and subsequent development in GHG intensity. The results of the analysis are summarised in Figure 2.4.

The analysis thus supports the initial hypothesis and establishes that we can use elements of the ESG dataset as a leading indicator for future reductions in GHG intensity. The best scoring companies include low GHG-intensity utilities, but also utilities in the mid-range. This shows that among the utilities focusing the most on renewable energy, we can find both green utilities and "olive-green" utilities working towards a transition. Further, our analysis shows that the largest absolute GHG emission reduction is found in the mid-range utilities scoring best.

Figure 2.4 GHG-intensity reduction is closely related to score

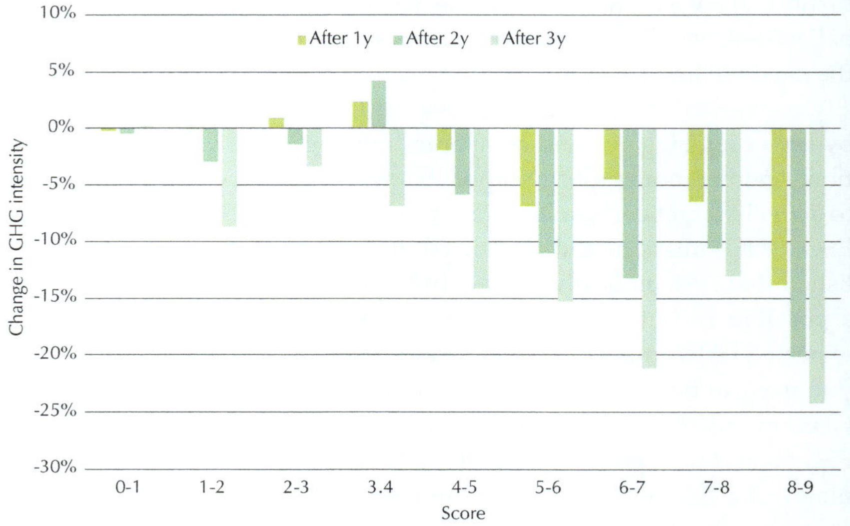

Table 2.2 Average GHG reduction on a three-year horizon

	[0–2]	[2–4]	[4–6]	[6–8]	[8–10]	Total
[0–200]	0%	1%	2%	8%	0%	11%
[200–400]	0%	–1%	3%	2%	3%	8%
[400–600]	2%	–1%	7%	23%	4%	35%
[600–800]	–1%	9%	13%	3%	2%	26%
[800–1000]	8%	9%	3%	0%	0%	20%
Total	9%	17%	27%	37%	10%	100%

A given percentage point reduction matters the most for the companies with medium/high intensities. Table 2.2 shows how the average GHG reduction on a three-year horizon is split into initial GHG intensity and the renewable energy score. For instance, it shows that 23% of the total GHG reduction has been done in utilities with an initial GHG intensity between 400 and 600 GwH/tCO_2 and a score between six and eight.

In terms of impact, you thus get maximal impact on the absolute emission level supporting companies in the mid-range (between 400 and 800) in terms of carbon intensity, but at the high end on the management score (between six and ten). If we solely invested in the very low intensity utilities, we would not support this low carbon transition and consequently have less impact on the environment. There is therefore a trade-off between looking good and doing good.

When looking at returns, they also show a clear pattern of where the winners are found. GHG-intensity reductions seem to be rewarded by the market. Our analysis shows that the companies scoring best on the ESG renewable energy measure outperformed the companies scoring the worst by a wide margin.

Again, we constructed long short portfolios to analyse the implication of different strategies. In one strategy we systematically buy the most GHG-intensity efficient utilities and sell the least intensity efficient utilities, irrespective of their focus on developing renewable energy – basically, maxing out on looking good. In the other strategy we systematically buy utilities with the most focus on renewable energy development and sell the ones with the least focus. Annualised returns from the different strategies are shown in Figure 2.5. While the utilities focusing on renewable energy

Figure 2.5 Annualised returns from the different strategies

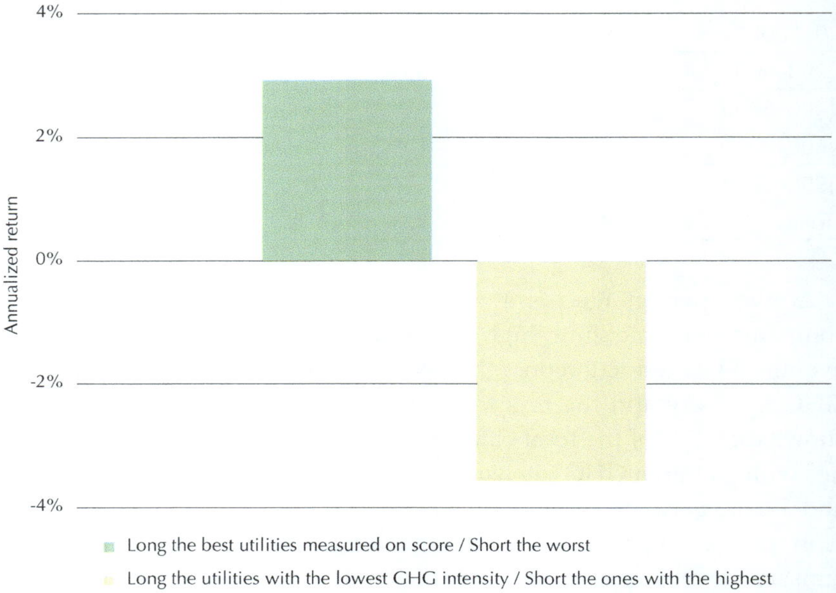

outperform the utilities with little focus, the already most efficient utilities underperform the least efficient. This is illustrated in Figure 2.5.

Thus, we see from our analysis above that pursuing maximal impact and maximal return are mutually compatible. Identifying the companies with the strongest future carbon intensity reduction projection is the same as identifying companies with positive portfolio performance potential. The reason could be that companies that have gone through a green transition have already been rewarded by the market, whereas companies with green potential still have a reward to collect.

Besides putting our investments to work where it matters the most, the strategy has also reduced our current carbon footprint significantly. Comparing the carbon intensity in our global equity portfolio in 2022 with the portfolio from 2018, it has been reduced by a staggering 54%. Notably, this has been achieved without altering the sector exposure in the portfolio. The changes helped put the portfolio on a stronger footing for the future as it managed to reduce its carbon emission intensity.

CONCLUSION

ESG is an integrated component of ATP's investment strategy. As the pension fund for all Danish citizens and the manager of one of Europe's largest pension funds, ATP holds great responsibility. To live up to that responsibility and maintain the public's trust, it is necessary to regularly make balanced, long-term decisions that result in a sustainable value creation.

We believe that incorporating ESG in our portfolio construction is fully compatible with pursuing high returns and sustainable value creation. Throughout our analysis we have seen no clear link between an overall ESG score and returns. Instead, we have found that future carbon emissions and intensities are key metrics both for the environment and for returns. This means that, while favouring companies on a path towards a greener environment, we can still create portfolios with great return potential.

Our analysis has shown us that if we use MSCI's ESG dataset as an indicator for future reductions in GHG, and choose to hold companies with the most reduction potential, we will indeed get companies with the greatest return potential because it seems that GHG reduction is rewarded by the market. Identifying companies with the strongest future carbon intensity reduction trajectory also means identifying companies with a positive portfolio performance potential.

1 We have used Trucost emission data for this estimate.

3

Case Study 2: Applying ESG concepts to wealth management portfolios

Edmund Shing

BNP Paribas Wealth Management

This chapter will assess the most effective approach to sustainable investing based on a client-centred focus, including: (i) identification of clients' ESG-related values and goals using our proprietary tool, myImpact; (ii) education on key sustainable themes; and (iii) long-term engagement with clients on these sustainability issues.

In constructing a comprehensive ESG-compliant product range, we offer a wide range of sustainable investment products (including individual securities, mutual and private market funds) in line with both BNP Paribas Group's sustainability objectives and Wealth Management's proprietary ESG criteria embedded within the BNP Paribas Wealth Management "clover rating" system. Product suitability for clients is based on the results of the myImpact tool and know your client data, incorporating risk tolerance, investment objectives and time horizon, together with sustainability values and objectives.

The UN's 17 Sustainable Development Goals (SDGs) are the starting point for BNP Paribas' sustainability objectives, with BNP Paribas' responsibility policy being structured around four pillars and 12 commitments, developed in line with the UN SDGs. By integrating ESG into the heart of investment strategy rather than as a "bolt-on" element to investment strategy, we embed ESG considerations and themes into our asset allocation and investment themes frameworks. The focus is therefore on the additional risk dimension from ESG criteria, including stranded asset risk, and the beneficial overlap between ESG/socially responsible investing (SRI) criteria and the quality factor.

Figure 3.1 The BNP Paribas wealth management positive impact approach

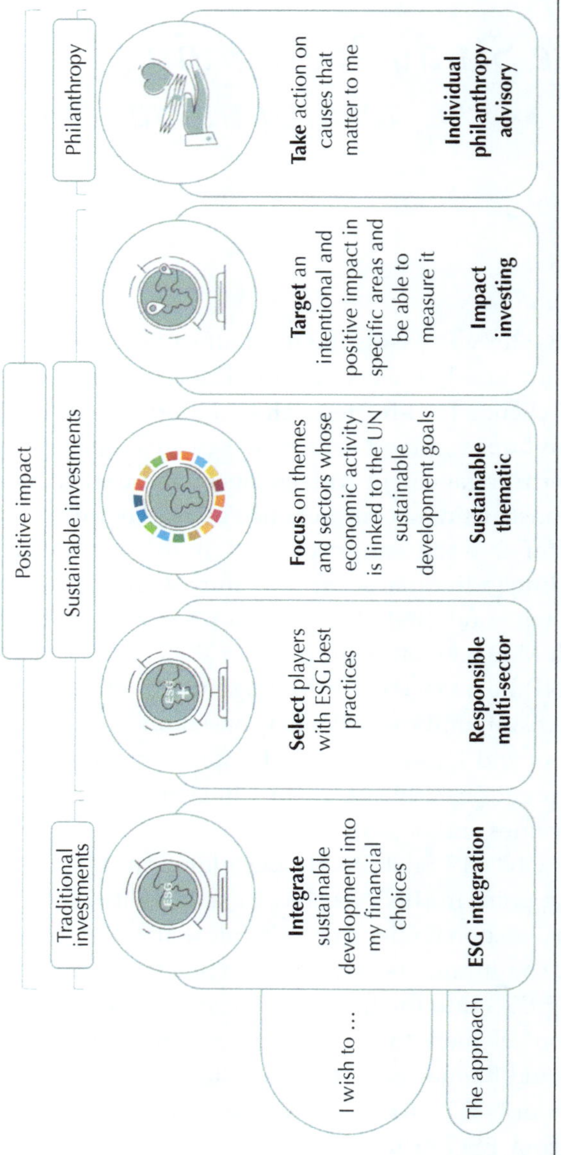

THE BNP PARIBAS GROUP'S OBJECTIVES: THE STARTING POINT

BNP Paribas, in its capacity as a bank, has sought to position itself as a leader in the sustainability and ESG space. To this end, we try to apply the principles of sustainability and ESG to the company purpose, which is "we serve our clients, and the world we live in". Concretely, how do we do this? We start by embedding major environmental and social challenges within the group strategy. The UN's 17 SDGs serve as a guiding force for BNP Paribas, leading the company to undergo a profound transformation in the way it does business (see Figure 3.1).

FOCUS ON SUSTAINABILITY IN WEALTH MANAGEMENT

At BNP Paribas Wealth Management, we adopt as a base the sustainability goals of the broader BNP Paribas Group. This is effectively achieving sustainable economic growth that increases people's wellbeing, and ensures a better future for the next generations, which requires:

- generating equitable economic growth;
- improving social inclusion; and
- protecting the environment so that natural resources remain sustainable.

Client-centred approach: Identifying clients' sustainability investment and philanthropic profile using the myImpact tool

In 2021, BNP Paribas Wealth Management launched a proprietary innovative tool to help clients get started on, or continue their impact journey. myImpact, an educational questionnaire, was originally designed for clients to provide them with information about their sustainability investor profile, working in tandem with their investment portfolio.

A quick and easy questionnaire, myImpact is enriched with comprehensive positive impact insights designed to investigate and clarify clients' views and personal objectives with respect to:

- sustainable development;
- responsible investment; and
- philanthropy.

These results then help to guide clients to make a positive impact on sustainable development through their wealth. We can use these personal insights to: (i) help identify; and then (ii) develop financial and wealth solutions that correspond to our clients' personal convictions.

Developing a broad and sustainable multi-asset product range to suit all forms of risk profile, both general ESG/SRI products and more specific thematic products

Once we have identified our clients' positive impact profile and objectives, we can then focus on making sure that we offer sustainability investment products that are appropriate both in positive impact and also investment terms.

We have to deal with a very wide range of client profiles, from the mass affluent to ultra-high net worth entrepreneurs and families, encompassing varying levels of financial market knowledge and experience, as well as very different investment objectives.

To provide our clients with innovative and appropriate investment products, we first select investment products on the basis of their suitability for our client base, their investment appeal and, crucially, their level of fit with our sustainability objectives. Such investments include:

- individual stocks and bonds;
- public mutual funds and exchange-traded funds (ETFs);
- alternative Undertakings for the Collective Investment in Transferable Securities (UCITS) (hedge) funds;
- private market real estate, infrastructure and private equity funds; or
- structured products.

(Re)educating our clients in sustainable topics

We have a large range of clients, ranging from the very sophisticated to those with little financial knowledge. For our clients at the bottom end of the spectrum in terms of financial expertise, education is a key plank in our client service strategy. We need to make sure that our clients understand financial language, including sustainability concepts, to allow them to make an informed decision on investing in a sustainable fashion.

One of the first steps in a client's sustainability journey is education – so we need to make sure the client is aware of sustainability and ESG issues. Then, we try to ensure that our clients understand the moral as well as financial reasons why this is a good way to invest. We find that clients in different countries move at different speeds when it comes to understanding sustainability issues and wanting to invest in a sustainable fashion. For instance, Belgium is a leader for BNP Paribas in this respect, with ESG criteria and benchmarks becoming a key factor underpinning our discretionary portfolio management offering. In contrast, Asian clients have been somewhat slower in embracing sustainability investing until more recently. However, through a consistent programme of education and marketing, we are now seeing these clients taking an ever-greater interest in such topics.

SUSTAINABILITY CRITERIA EMBEDDED IN BNP PARIBAS WEALTH MANAGEMENT'S CLOVER RATING

Since April 2020, most of our funds (whether sustainable or not) in addition to our recommended list of individual assets (eg, bonds and stocks), have been rated from zero to 10 clovers. They are evaluated on sustainability and are comparable across asset classes. The same has been true of ETFs since June 2020. As such, we can now offer our clients a view of how sustainable their overall portfolio is.

Example: Applying the Clover Rating to funds

The Clover Rating is an objective comparison of sustainability, allowing for a comparison of sustainability between funds of different asset classes and different asset management companies (not just single lines within their portfolios), within BNP Paribas Wealth Management's open architecture.

We assess the sustainability approach of each asset management company and the impact achieved via the financial instruments of each fund (see Figure 3.2). Under this rating system, 10 clovers thus represent the highest level of sustainability in a fund/asset, while zero clovers suggests no real effort to integrate ESG criteria or sustainability concerns into the fund's investment process. This clover rating is comprised of 130 criteria in the case of funds, grouped under six key sustainability categories (see Figure 3.3).

Figure 3.2 Level of sustainability of funds

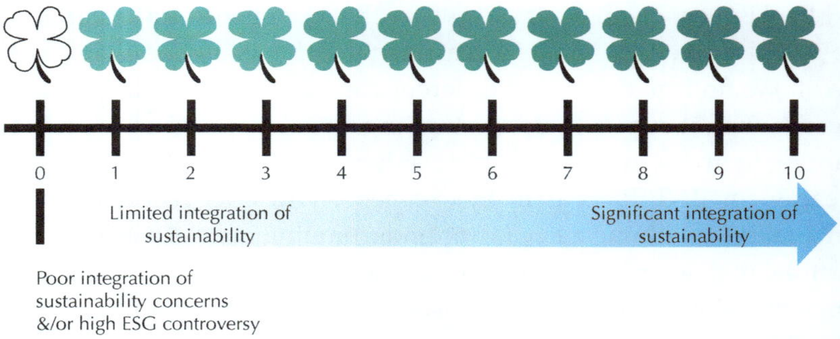

Figure 3.3 Clover rating: 130 criteria assessed under six categories

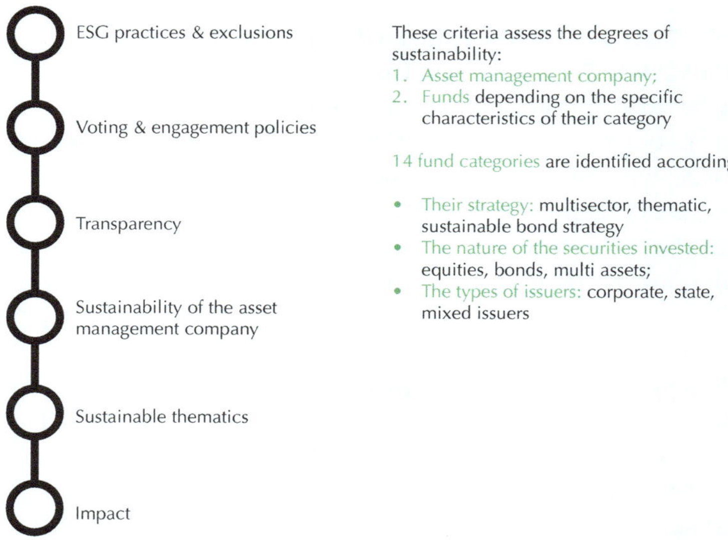

Why is the Clover Rating methodology key?

- It measures the sustainability level of all recommended funds, whether labelled "responsible" or not, in a unique and exclusive manner.
- It compares the sustainability of funds of all asset managers in an objective way.
- It follows the same logic and a common approach across all asset

classes to compare all financial instruments (funds, equities, bonds, etc) in a portfolio.

INTEGRATING SUSTAINABILITY INTO OUR INVESTMENT STRATEGY PROCESS

Thus far, we have dealt with building a client's sustainability profile using our myImpact questionnaire, and then selecting a broad and innovative range of investment products using our clover rating system. How do we then integrate these notions of ESG and sustainability into our everyday investment strategy that we communicate to our clients?

One obvious point to make is that sustainability in ESG is not a simple bolt-on to an existing investment strategy process. You cannot take your traditional asset allocation investment strategy – for instance, allocating between stocks, bonds and other asset classes – and then bolt on considerations of ESG criteria at the end. On the contrary, the whole investment strategy process needs to be rethought so that sustainability and ESG considerations are integral to the conception of the investment strategy, themes, and also strategic asset allocation over time.

Incorporating ESG into our thematic investing

One obvious avenue for incorporating sustainability into investment strategy thinking is via investment themes. The power of this narrative is clear when explaining the attractions of a potential investment theme and associated products to a client. Within sustainability, there are a huge number of potential narratives to allow us to tell effective stories to our clients. We use the UN's SDGs as inspiration for these ESG investment themes, focusing on goals such as zero hunger, quality education, affordable and clean energy, climate action and life below water.

Zero hunger

There are several ways in which this can be achieved. First, by investing in more sustainable farming techniques, such as better irrigation (which allows higher agricultural productivity); second, by investing in new techniques (such as vertical farming, which can allow greater productivity of agricultural produce); and third by developing new systems of diet, moving towards a vegetarian or vegan diet, for instance, given the difficulties of sustainably eating a protein-rich diet dominated by meat and fish.

In many developing countries there are still high rates of hunger and malnutrition. The focus is not just on growing crops, but equally on bringing crops to market and avoiding food waste. In Africa, fully 50% of the food grown perishes before it reaches the market. In other words, it is never eaten because it goes rotten and has to be disposed of.

Therefore, it is not just about improving water irrigation and increasing agricultural productivity, but also about ensuring that, once produced, this food then makes its way to market and the final consumer. Investing in logistics and infrastructure is thus a key target in tackling hunger. How do we transport the product in good time? Does it require refrigeration, for instance, or does it simply need better infrastructure in terms of lorries, roads, trains, and so on?

There is also the key issue of food waste, one of the biggest problems facing the Western world. We allow food to go off, and merely throw it away, which is incredibly wasteful. Efforts therefore have to be made in terms of recycling, but also (perhaps) how to improve the lifecycle. It is also a question of education to ensure that people eat the food that they have and do not throw it away. These are all goals that we attempt to invest in via our investment themes, which we propose four times per year and market to our clients. An important role for BNP Paribas Wealth Management with regards to implementing sustainability and ESG strategies is, indeed, to educate our clients, and this is the first port of call.

Quality education

This is perhaps less of an issue in the Western world and more important in the emerging markets. This goal focuses on offering equal opportunities to all, which starts with access to quality education, thus equipping people with the skills to do a wide range of jobs. Key to this is reading and writing, and then developing more advanced skills thereafter.

This is an area where certain countries (such as China) have made huge strides, but there are still many others where further progress must be made to bring longer-term potential prosperity to the majority of their population. To a large extent, the impact of quality education also depends on its delivery. This can be as simple as logistics, building schools, training teachers, and giving them the necessary teaching materials (books, blackboards, etc). This may involve digital infrastructure such as Internet access and installing simple computers (such as the ultra-low-cost Raspberry Pi). In many ways, the advent of the World Wide Web may be considered as one of the best educational tools ever invented! Of course, access to the Internet is very limited in many developing countries, and unfortunately this education pipe is not available to the majority of the population of these countries.

Affordable and clean energy

Even after the efforts to grow productive capacity of energy generated from solar, wind, hydroelectric and even biomass, the truth is that most countries (and particularly developed ones) still depend on fossil fuels, whether petrol or diesel heavy oil, natural gas, or even coal, for the majority of their energy consumption. There is still a long way to go to decarbonise the global economy and achieve the ambitious net zero carbon targets that have been set.

Linked to this goal are the issues around the storage of renewable energy. The sun does not always shine, the wind does not always blow. So, what do we do to supply electricity at these points in time if we increasingly rely on renewable forms of electricity generation? We need to store the electricity, although unfortunately industrial storage of electricity within national networks remains in its infancy.

Climate action

Decarbonising the global economy can be achieved, for instance, by using more and more renewable energy, but it is also linked to the issue of food production. How do we produce enough food to feed the planet while reducing carbon emissions? Remember that agriculture represents 26% of global carbon emissions, which is another reason to favour a vegetarian or vegan diet, and to eat less and less beef, for example, since beef (and dairy) production is heavily linked to carbon emissions by methane. Within climate action, we can also look at carbon offsetting and carbon capture strategies, which we try to encapsulate in investment funds and investment strategies as we believe there will be significant growth in these areas in the years to come.

Life below water

One form of carbon capture that will be very important is through the promotion and preservation of marine ecosystems. A huge amount of carbon is captured within our oceans globally, particularly marine life such as seaweeds and algae.

Another major challenge is to combat pollution. Marine pollution, particularly of plastics, is becoming a very pressing issue, with sea life being increasingly poisoned. This is a very good reason for us to abandon the use of single-use plastics and promote the growth and maintenance of marine ecosystems, particularly those close to land, because they can capture a lot of carbon in the atmosphere over time.

These are only five of the 17 UN SDGs that BNP Paribas Wealth Management embeds both in our long-term strategic allocation within our investment strategy but in particular also within the investment themes we propose to our clients.

IS THERE A TRADE-OFF BETWEEN SUSTAINABLE INVESTING AND PERFORMANCE?

It is clear that increasing amounts of investment capital are being devoted to ESG-friendly investment products across the world, led perhaps by Europe, but with other regions (such as the US) catching up very quickly. We can see this in the substantial inflows to ESG-rated investment funds and ETFs over the last few years, which have witnessed a veritable avalanche of inflows for these types of products with more traditional funds and ETFs, in contrast, suffering. It is clear that investors are "voting with their feet" and want to combine personal considerations of sustainability with their own investment portfolios. They would prefer their investment portfolios not only to maintain their value or increase in value over time, but also to do so while investing sustainably.

However, this needs to be balanced with investment performance. There has been a long debate about whether investing sustainably involves a cost to the investor – ie, by investing in a sustainable fashion using ESG-aware funds, do investors achieve lower long-term growth of their portfolios?

Interestingly, according to our analysis since the mid-2010s at least, the answer is no. If anything, investing sustainably via funds that have as an underlying benchmark the MSCI ESG leaders index, or even SRI benchmark indexes, have actually delivered positive alpha over and above the traditional non-ESG oriented benchmarks. This is true not only in Europe, which has been a leader in ESG investing, but also in the US, and is gaining momentum in Asia as well.

Exploiting the ESG/SRI and quality factor overlap

We encourage our investors, at least in the context of stock market exposure, to focus on the quality factor, as in quality stocks with higher-than-average profitability, better-than-average balance sheets, and lower-than-average debt. Over the long term, stock portfolios composed of companies demonstrating higher quality factor scores have delivered a higher Sharpe ratio (return per unit of risk) via a combination of better absolute performance and at lower maximum drawdowns in bear market phases.

This dovetails neatly with our focus on sustainability, as there tends to be a large overlap between stocks represented in quality factor portfolios and stocks represented in ESG- and SRI-heavy portfolios. This suits our investment objectives since our clients then benefit from a quality exposure when investing through a sustainability lens. When stock markets rise, the market beta of a typical quality factor portfolio tends to be around one. However, quality portfolios tend to suffer less during market corrections or bear markets, with a downside market beta historically around 0.8.

Of course, investors will still lose money in a bear market. Nevertheless, we argue that they would lose less by following a quality strategy than by simply investing in the underlying market benchmarks. Investing sustainably is achieving a similar result, since you are implicitly taking a positive bias towards the quality factor when you invest according to ESG or SRI criteria.

An ESG approach can reduce portfolio exposure to tail risks

If companies neglect issues related to ESG, they are exposed to higher risks, such as environmental accidents (E), reputational risk linked to labour conditions or gender inequality (S), and risks linked to corporate governance, such as fraud, compensation schemes and lack of risk control (G).

Lee and Faff (2009) find that "leading corporate social performance firms exhibit significantly lower idiosyncratic risk and that idiosyncratic risk might be priced by the broader equity market". Ilhan, Sautner and Vilkov (2021) also show that "the cost of option protection against downside risks is larger for firms with more carbon-intense business models". This suggests the perception of large tail risks (low probability events but often with huge consequences) for some firms. In addition, the 2019 IMF Global Financial Stability Report stresses that "Environmental risk exposures can lead to large losses for firms and climate change may entail losses for financial institutions, asset owners and firms" (IMF, 2019).

The integration of ESG factors into a firm's business model may help mitigate these risks. Beyond the environmental issues, reputational risks can lead to lasting negative effects on a company's valuation, and even default in extreme cases. Typical examples are negative news flow surrounding labour conditions, gender inequality, and governance issues such as compliance and risk control. Consequently, implementing improvement in ESG issues reduces tail risk for investors. This includes stranded asset risk in fossil fuels and corporate governance risks from fraud and lack of risk control, thus reducing idiosyncratic stock risks in a diversified portfolio.

CHOOSING A GENERAL ESG, SRI EXPOSURE OR FOCUSED THEMATIC EXPOSURE

The first question to ask yourself is this: "am I aiming to replace general equity portfolio exposure, or seeking specific thematic exposure for more aggressive growth?". The choice here is between a more generalised and thus diversified ESG/SRI exposure on the one hand, or a specific thematic exposure to one sub-theme within sustainability depending on one's investment objectives on the other.

Investors looking simply to replace overall equity portfolio exposure with a sustainable equity exposure should opt for diversified funds or ETFs tracking a broad ESG/SRI benchmark index. However, investors wishing to target a specific sustainability subtheme for a small part of their overall equity exposure to generate higher growth can look to specific thematic funds/ETFs in ESG themes, such as the future of food, water, the energy transition, or diversity and inclusion.

Clearly, there is greater risk in specific thematic funds. Given the larger concentration on a particular theme and fewer stocks, specific thematic funds (eg, clean energy) naturally tend to have higher risk metrics than more diversified ESG funds. There is high risk, but also decent rewards, in clean energy, carbon credit and electric vehicle/battery thematic funds as they are closely correlated with the technology sector, and the growth investment style more generally. This is evident in the elevated correlation between the Wilderhill Clean Energy index and the ARK innovation ETF since 2019.

In contrast, latterly there has been steady outperformance from future of food, water, and diversity and inclusion funds. These three thematic sustainability indexes have performed in a more consistent fashion since the mid-2020, all outperforming the diversified MSCI World ESG Leaders index by varying amounts but each remaining highly correlated to this broad equity index, exhibiting similar levels of volatility. This is indeed unsurprising since the composition of each of these thematic indexes includes a considerable weighting of stocks drawn from more defensive sectors, such as food and beverages, and utilities.

SUMMING UP THE BNPP WM ESG APPROACH

Our foundation is the BNP Paribas Group approach to sustainability, with a particular focus on the UN's 17 SDGs. Each client's sustainability views and objectives are analysed using our proprietary myImpact tool to propose suitable investment strategies and solutions. We put heavy emphasis on educating and informing our clients on a variety of sustainability topics so that they remain informed in today's fast-changing environment, including discussions of the EU's new taxonomy for sustainable activities and an ever-expanding range of ESG investment funds and products.

We assess the investment solutions that we offer our clients for their level of sustainability by applying our proprietary clover rating system, the aim being to offer clients funds and products with high clover ratings. Finally, we embed sustainability considerations into our formulation of investment strategy at source. We focus explicitly on a range of sustainability investment themes. We also look to align the investment portfolios of our clients with their ever-increasing awareness of the urgency to live in a more sustainable world, and to align their investment portfolios with their sustainability objectives.

HOW SUSTAINABLE INVESTING COULD EVOLVE IN WEALTH MANAGEMENT

The explosion in interest and investment flows in the sustainability fund space since the start of the 2020s has driven a huge proliferation of actively managed funds and passive index-based ETFs that purport to invest sustainably. However, many of the early ESG and SRI index benchmarks provided by the main index providers have implemented an exclusion methodology – ie, classifying stocks in binary terms as either "good" or "bad" in ESG or SRI terms, thus rendering them either eligible or ineligible for index inclusion.

However, if investing sustainably is ultimately to use investment capital to drive improvements on ESG criteria, then we need to engage with companies that are not necessarily the highest-ranking companies on ESG criteria. Rather, it is by investing in and engaging with those companies that may not start with the highest ESG scores today, but that are actively trying to improve their standing with respect to these criteria, that we can drive the biggest improvements in those companies. In short, as investors we should focus more on the transition towards more responsible corporate ESG strategies and policies, not simply on companies' static ESG ratings today.

After all, the greatest improvements can likely be made on the ESG/SRI front by companies that start from a low base – so-called "low-hanging fruit". An ultimately lower cost of equity and debt capital can be a powerful financial incentive for companies to implement more ESG-friendly policies, alongside the obvious moral imperative and the ongoing regulatory pressure from governments. In turn, this can then drive a valuation re-rating on the back of greater economic value creation. This is a powerful reason for investors to buy-in to drive the strategy shift that can ultimately trigger such a re-rating, from which they will benefit in portfolio performance terms.

Wealth management will increasingly have to implement

investment according to ESG and SRI principles as a key risk management tool. Investing sustainably should therefore enable wealth managers to reduce client portfolio exposures to a host of risks, including:

- stranded asset environmental risk (eg, to fossil fuel exposure);
- poor talent acquisition and retention social risks (eg, by not implementing diversity initiatives to cast the employment net as widely as possible); and
- reputational risk from poor governance (lack of independent board of directors, combined CEO/chairman roles) and even from fraud in the most extreme cases.

As stewards of our clients' capital, our approach is to use a sustainability strategy as part of our risk management toolbox in constructing and managing client portfolios, optimising portfolios returns per unit of risk taken in line with our clients' objectives.

REFERENCES

Ilhan, E., Z. Sautner and G. Vilkov, 2021, "Carbon Tail Risk", *The Review of Financial Studies*, 34(3), March, pp. 1,540–71.

IMF, 2019, "Global Financial Stability Report", October (available at https://www.imf.org/en/Publications/GFSR/Issues/2019/10/01/global-financial-stability-report-october-2019).

Lee, D. D. and R. W. Faff, 2009, "Corporate Sustainability Performance and Idiosyncratic Risk: A Global Perspective", *The Financial Review*, 44(2), May, pp. 213–37.

PART II

ENVIRONMENTAL AND CLIMATE RISKS

4

Managing environmental and climate transition risks and opportunities within portfolios

Karl Wilhelm Lange, Michael Leithead and Stefano Montobbio

EFG Asset Management

Climate change is one of the biggest issues we face today. It is ubiquitous, knowing no geographic, economic or social bounds, and has potentially devastating effects. Policymakers, corporations and investors have started to recognise and mitigate those effects, with pledges and commitments in favour of a more climate-friendly way of living, and producing goods and services. A climate transition is already under way. This transition to a low carbon economy cannot be ignored, as societal (and regulatory) pressures will continue to increase and force companies to act. While this creates marked risks for investors – with certain industries and geographies impacted more than others – it can also create opportunities. In some cases, return and risk objectives may conflict with climate objectives and require judgement on the appropriate strategy.

This chapter will discuss the key metrics that might be used to evaluate exposure to carbon risk, and highlight the approaches that could be adopted to align portfolios with decarbonisation and net zero[1] carbon ambitions. Finally, it will reflect on the advantages and disadvantages of these approaches with regards to returns, risk and philosophical alignment within portfolio construction.

We try to answer to some of the challenges investment managers face when looking to align investment and climate objectives, with a specific focus on how to measure climate exposure and emissions risk and incorporate these metrics within portfolios. In addition, we briefly explore how different portfolio and security selection approaches might be aligned with climate objectives. These will inevitably come with potential trade-offs in terms of return or risk.

In considering such challenges, it should be noted that investment and transition objectives could be looked at from two dimensions: downside protection and upside opportunities. This also aligns nicely with the two basic components of a capital structure, related to equity and fixed income.

- Equity-style investing: This stands to gain from the search for opportunities that can yield returns, leverage on earnings and which can theoretically multiply initial capital deployed.
- Credit-style investing: This in its simplest form has a binary outcome, survival or failure, where the payout is capped but the downside may far exceed the upside return. Inherently, credit investors will focus on negative risks to the credit profile rather than the potential opportunities for a company. Of course, when considering returns, investors may have to weigh up their ability to hold debt to maturity, and thus time horizons, restrictions and maturity may all play a part in the investment strategy.

CLIMATE RISK ANALYSIS: STATUS AND APPROACHES

From an investor perspective, climate change creates opportunities and risk, with the latter usually being divided between transition and physical. Transition risk is linked to the efforts that the society will put in place to move away from fossil fuels in the form of new policies, taxes, regulatory change, consumer preferences and market dynamics. The greater a company's exposure to CO_2 emissions, the higher its transition risks. Physical risks, on the other hand, are those that arise from damage to production or physical infrastructure as a result of a change in environmental conditions or following extreme events, such as floods or droughts. These risks will become increasingly relevant in the future, and their importance will be inversely correlated with society's transition efforts: a stringent regulatory framework able to reduce the worst effect of climate change could significantly reduce the future physical risk.

Figure 4.1 Illustration of scopes 1, 2 and 3 emissions with examples

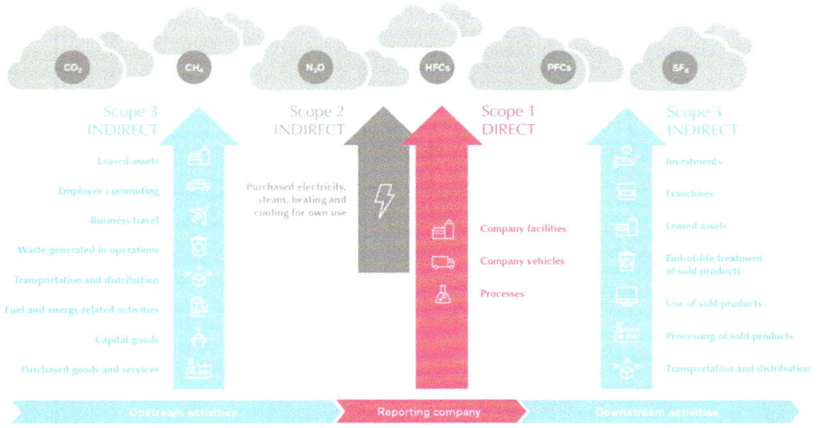

Source: CDP (2018)

This chapter will mainly focus on transition risks as they are the most relevant at this point in time, and because they will play the biggest role at the corporate level. First, however, it is key to appreciate the main classification systems for emissions, which are divided as follows (see Figure 4.1).

- Scope 1: Direct emissions from producing goods or services from owned or controlled sources.
- Scope 2: Indirect emissions such as those used to generate electricity, heating or cooling consumed.
- Scope 3: All other indirect emissions that occur in the value chain and which are a consequence of the use of the products or services.

The complexity of measuring emissions increases with respect to scope 3 emissions as:

- they are not completely controlled by companies;
- they are not 100% owned by one single company (eg, car emissions are at least attributable to two parties – the manufacturer and the oil company);

- their financial impact is dependent upon other parameters, such as the elasticity of the demand for the good; and
- they can be influenced by how a good is utilised (eg, how a car is driven).

As such, even if scope 3 emissions are estimated to be around three to four times larger than direct emissions, the lack of reliable data means many managers generally focus on scopes 1 and 2 only. However, it is worth highlighting that, as soon as the quality of data improves, scope 3 emissions should also be taken into account in the computation of total carbon emissions.

Carbon footprint

The measurement of the carbon footprint of a portfolio is typically done by summing total carbon emissions based on ownership (see Table 4.1). The carbon footprint of the sample portfolio in Table 4.1 is therefore the sum of the share of ownership, in this case equal to 4,250 tons of CO_2 emissions.

This approach is very simple and straightforward, but although it has the power to directly link a portfolio to its emissions, it has significant limitations.

- Larger portfolios will show a higher level of emissions irrespective of the climate risks of the holdings. While this issue can potentially be solved by indexing the amount of emission with the size of the portfolio, this is not a common practice.
- This approach is ill-suited for debt portfolios, although some advocate replacing the market value of a company with its enterprise value (EV). This substitution would, however, still have some major drawbacks since conceptually it is assumed that

Table 4.1 Absolute carbon footprint of a sample portfolio

	A: Emissions (CO_2 tons)	B: Market value (000s)	C: Value of investment	D: Ownership (C/B)	E: Attributable emissions (A*D)
Company 1	1,000,000	2,500,000	10,000,000	0.40%	4,000
Company 2	2,500,000	100,000,000	10,000,000	0.01%	250
			Total portfolio emissions		**4,250**

equity and bonds share equally in carbon intensity, whereas the legal responsibility, the payout and risks are not equally shared. This could present various issues when comparing levered versus unlevered companies, or with respect to companies that are private or with very high cash balances that could theoretically end up with negative attributable emissions.

Carbon intensity

To achieve climate objectives, the absolute level of emissions must be reduced, but companies with a growing market share, involved in mergers and acquisitions (M&A) or in a growing industry might not be able to cut their total GHGs. As such, using emissions intensity, which measures emissions per unit of sales, provides a better and easier metric than the absolute level of emissions. Additionally, the use of intensity enables comparison between peers across regions and market caps. This second approach focuses less on absolute weights and more on the weights of the portfolio, and thus solves some of the methodological issues embedded in the carbon footprint metric.

The approach described in Table 4.2 is no longer linked to the absolute size of the portfolio, and since emissions intensity is an intrinsic characteristic of any company it is better suited than the previous one, particularly for fixed income portfolios.

The carbon intensity of the sample portfolio in Table 4.2 would be equal to 0.15, meaning that it creates 0.15 tons of emissions per unit of sales.

While we believe this approach is a step forward, it is not perfect.

Table 4.2 Carbon intensity of the sample portfolio

	A: Emissions (CO_2 tons)	**B: Revenues (000)**	**C: CO_2 intensity (A/B)**	**D: Value of investment**	**E: Portfolio weight (Dn/Σ_D)**	**F: Portfolio CO_2 intensity (C*E)**
Company 1	1,000,000	2,500,000	0.40	10,000,000	33.3%	0.13
Company 2	2,500,000	100,000,000	0.03	20,000,000	66.7%	0.02
				Total portfolio carbon intensity		**0.15**

- In multi-asset portfolios it will evenly attribute carbon intensity to equity and fixed income holdings, which might not be ideal as previously described.
- Additionally, the approach has limitations as it may not reflect risks to profitability or work where companies have alternative accounting methodologies, or even revenues at all.

While these two approaches are both static, it is possible to use them to align a portfolio with climate transition or net zero goals dynamically. Year-on-year emissions of the portfolio should be measured and constantly reduced to reach net zero.[2] The portfolio must therefore be regularly monitored and optimised to respect such goals. However, although this approach allows aligning with the climate needs, it says nothing about how well or badly a company is managing its emissions, or what the future opportunities or challenges are likely to be.

Carbon pathways and temperature of portfolio assessments

According to the Intergovernmental Panel on Climate Change (IPCC), humanity needs to reach net zero carbon emissions by 2050 to stay within a 1.5°C temperature increase compared to pre-industrial levels. This is a significant reduction in a short period of time, but it also means that transitioning away from fossil fuels is a dynamic process.

The climate risk of a company or portfolio does not only lie in current emissions, but more in the future path of reduction. A company with high emissions today, but with a significant and credible cutting programme, might offer more in terms of positive climate impact and risk reduction than a company with lower numbers but no planned improvements. Reducing emissions in line with what is required by the scientific community may also protect against negative surprises that could arise from almost any carbon tax scenario.

However, being able to measure future trajectories requires some preliminary steps. First, emissions pathways aligned with different temperature scenarios are required. The work of science and the IPCC *in primis* is paramount as it demonstrates a clear relationship between cumulated emissions and warming potential. Figure 4.2 shows this link: the slower the emissions reduction (slope), the

Figure 4.2 Two carbon pathways for decarbonisation (for illustrative purposes only)

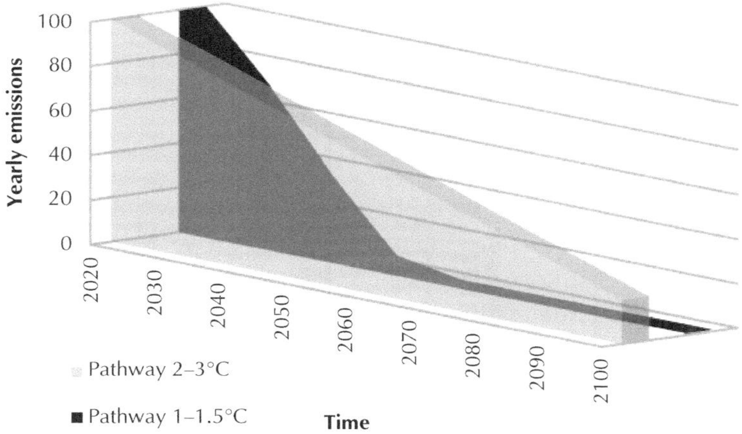

greater the cumulated emissions and consequent temperature increase. A company whose emissions are aligned with pathway 1 is therefore consistent with a lower implied temperature, such as 1.5°C in the example. The one aligned with pathway 2 is consistent with a higher temperature (3°C in the example).

Second, the pathways need to be corrected on the basis of the industry, as the technological feasibility for reducing emissions differs from sector to sector (SBTi, 2015). Third, and finally, the specific company carbon reduction pathway must be verified. Many companies have announced their intention to be aligned with 1.5°C – ie, to reach net zero emissions by 2050 or earlier – but not all the claims are equal nor followed by consistent actions. It is therefore crucial for investors to assess the credibility of those plans. It is beyond the scope of this chapter to enter into the details, but we can highlight a few checks worth applying to understand the strength of the commitments: such as verifying the perimeter of the reduction; the expected timeframe; any external assessments from rating agencies or associations such as CDP; application of Task Force on Climate-Related Disclosures (TCFD) guidance and other measures. Actions speak louder than words, and the most robust approach is arguably to assess both the commitments and the slope of a company's GHG reduction to monitor the consistency between declarations and facts.

Table 4.3 Implied temperature from the sample portfolio

	A: Temperature pathway alignment	B: Value of investment	C: Portfolio weight (Bn/ (Bn+Bn+1))	D: "Warming contribution" (A*C)
Company 1	1.5°C	10,000,000	33.3%	0.5°C
Company 2	3°C	20,000,000	66.7%	2°C
		Total portfolio temperature		**2.5°**

Transforming the temperature of multiple companies into the temperature of a portfolio is something that can be done in multiple ways. Utilising portfolio weights is perhaps the simplest, but using more elaborate methodologies that take into account the company market capitalisation, enterprise value or others are also possible.[3] Considering the high degree of assumption in this exercise, we think that a simple portfolio weighted average of different temperature pathways, as illustrated in Table 4.3, would suffice. It also does not create the problems that can be encountered when using market cap, EV or some of the other alternatives.

While we believe this approach is probably the best among the three highlighted, it is not without problems. The number of companies with consistent and reliable historical emission data is still limited, which limits the accurate modelling of future emissions pathways. Clearly, given that the model aims to identify future emissions, it is also exposed to estimation errors or risk of companies not delivering on their promises.

An additional complexity with forward looking metrics, such as implied temperatures, is that the focus lies on future potential rather then current absolute emissions. A portfolio aligned with 1.5°C might therefore have emission intensity higher than the market but should move below the market at a faster pace as we approach 2050. Although this is not a problem *per se* and potentially addresses the decarbonisation needs, it might create some uneasiness or confusion among investors.

Building scenarios

The approaches described above are useful to monitor and build portfolios that are aligned with the climate needs, but don't allow investors to measure the risk to the financial bottom line. Even if there is a high degree of uncertainty around future regulatory

Table 4.4 Three scenarios over three time periods for company A

Company A	Scenario 1			Scenario 2			Scenario 3		
	Impact on revenues (%)	**Impact on operating income (%)**	**CO_2 price**	**Impact on revenues (%)**	**Impact on operating income (%)**	**CO_2 price**	**Impact on revenues (%)**	**Impact on operating income (%)**	**CO_2 price**
Year 2025	1.8	13.0	US$95	0.4	2.6	US$31	1.4	9.9	US$53
Year 2030	3.5	24.8	US$127	1.5	10.9	US$62	5.9	41.5	US$108
Year 2035	7.0	49.4	US$169	1.8	24.7	US$96	12.8	90.2	US$167

developments, investors can evaluate risks by building scenarios that combine a set of data, such as company emissions, transition pathways, carbon price assumptions (for example, IPPC or Network for Greening the Financial System, NGFS),[4] physical climate change impacts, and economic and financial indicators. Scenarios may also consider scope 3 emissions, and integrate different estimates about demand elasticity or additional strategies that companies might put in place to protect their margins. While not perfect, scenarios represent an informative tool to illustrate future risk and quantify future impact on company financials (as illustrated in Table 4.4). By transforming financials, some assumption on the valuation of a bond or equity could also be assumed – eg, adjusting a discounted cashflow (DCF) valuation.

Frameworks

If data is needed to measure the climate risk of portfolios, a framework to govern and give order to actions is also needed. Among a few existing, we highlight two: the TCFD, which can be used by all companies and sectors, and the Net Zero Investment Framework (IIGCC, 2021), which focuses on asset owners and managers.

Figure 4.3 Overview of the "four core elements"

Core Elements of Recommended Climate-Related Financial Disclosures

Governance
The organisation's governance around climate-related risks and opportunities

Strategy
The actual and potential impacts of climate-related risks and opportunities on the organisation's business, strategy, and financial planning

Risk Management
The processes used by the organisation to identify, assess, and manage climate-related risks

Metrics and Targets
The metrics and targets used to assess and manage relevant climate-related risks and opportunities

Source: TCFD (2017)

TCFD

The TCFD framework recommends acting on four "core elements" to better meet the challenges: governance; strategy; risk management; and metrics and targets (see Figure 4.3). For all four areas, the TCFD recommends a set of disclosures and information that help investors understand how the reporting organisation is assessing and managing climate-related risk and opportunities. For some sectors, financials included, the TCFD has also developed supplemental guidance to highlight some additional relevant matters. One of the TCFD's key recommended disclosures focuses on climate-related scenarios. It acknowledges that scenario analysis is still nascent and will improve over time, but recommends that organisations build scenarios as they can help provide a better understanding of climate-related issues and their potential financial implications.

Net Zero Investment Framework

This framework has been designed to support asset owners and asset managers wanting to commit some or the totality of their assets to be invested in alignment with net zero objectives. It consists of the following strategic areas.

- ❑ Governance and strategy: The first intervention consists in defining the beliefs and stating the goals. Reporting should be performed in line with the TCFD recommendation highlighting the action plan, the metrics, targets and responsibilities.
- ❑ Data, targets and objectives: These are needed to inform the Strategic Asset Allocation (SAA).
- ❑ The SAA: Needs to consider the climate information and the desired goals. Optimisation should happen with emissions and solution constraints, and should eventually be aligned with the stated objectives.
- ❑ Asset class alignment: This should be consistent with the SAA and ideally expanded to increase the percentage of asset entering the scope. Portfolio construction tools, engagement and divestment should also be coherent and support the stated goals.
- ❑ Policy advocacy and market engagement: These should finally target main stakeholder with the aim to reinforce the process and the rules.

STRATEGY COMPARISON: EXCLUSION, BEST IN CLASS, DELTA OR THEMATIC

Broadly speaking, we apply four key approaches for ESG investing. Each approach has its advantages and disadvantages from both an investment performance and climate-alignment perspective. Equally, some combination could be used to align stakeholder interests.

- ❑ Exclusion: Removing companies or sectors based on specific climate criteria or exposure.
- ❑ Best in class: Looking to include the "best" performers in any sector.
- ❑ Integration and delta: Looking to maximise the carbon reduction profile.
- ❑ Thematic: Picking securities based on their gearing to climate change and transition.

In each case, varying degrees of quantitative and fundamental research may be applied. For example, exclusion could be based on specific metrics (such as coal exposure) or analysis could be applied with a view to estimating financial costs.

Exclusion

The fundamental arguments for this strategy can be based around avoiding the negative-associated financial risks of potential business decline through substitution, risk associated with new regulation, and elevated capital expenditure to reduce emissions. It also has the advantage of having clear boundaries to explain to end-investors.

For equity investors, removing low performing sectors or companies already provides a relative gain. With proper risk engines, the exclusion approach, unless applied to a significant portion of the benchmark, does not significantly increase tracking error, as demonstrated by many socially responsible investing (SRI) indexes that can achieve TE <1% relative to their benchmarks. However, it is clear that this strategy might change the factor exposure to the investment strategy, leading to higher/lower performance than the initial benchmark (as discussed later in the chapter).

For fixed income, ESG exclusion may enable credit investors to avoid extreme negative returns and generate positive excess returns versus a parent benchmark. However, as noted previously, large discounts on shorter duration assets are unlikely to be impacted by climate risk in the near term, and might provide investors with superior returns, particularly if balance sheets are robust and the probability of financial default is lower than implied by spreads.

A drawback of exclusion approaches is that they avoid addressing the need to transition and decarbonisation. While this strategy may align well with carbon intensity and carbon footprint metrics, it is debatable how well aligned it is with carbon pathways, as it may deny capital to companies having the greatest impact on decarbonisation.

Best in class

Selecting companies or issuers based on their best in class profile provides investors with the lowest possible carbon footprint/intensity while maintaining exposure to all sectors of the global economy. In theory, selecting those with the best emissions profile should result in a natural bias away from transition risk, but this does assume direct comparability of businesses. This approach may also allocate capital to the companies with the lowest climate footprints – ie, the most carbon efficient.

Determining the "best" company on the basis of quantitative carbon emissions metrics alone may not fully account for the risk to credit or earnings that a company may incur. A company with greater leverage and more narrow profit margins may be more negatively impacted than a company that has a more resilient financial profile, despite higher CO_2 to revenue or absolute CO_2 metrics. For example, if the transmission mechanism of transition risk is through revenue (eg, oil price declines), then higher margin businesses may well survive and outperform lower emitters.

Equally, as investors select companies with better carbon profiles, "greeniums" (green premium, ie, the premium the market assigns to green investments) over time may reduce potential investment upside. Additionally, while the definition of best in class might not be completely aligned across investors, there is a risk that this approach can lead to partial loss of diversification and concentration in a smaller number of investments.

Integration and delta

Exclusion and best in class approaches are important tools for security selection and high-level screening, but for investors willing to keep a closer tie with their benchmark and who are less value-based oriented, an integration approach can also be a suitable strategy.

This approach implies that companies with weak climate credentials might provide a good investment opportunity if, for example, the sustainability risks are already more than discounted by the markets, if the firm is on an improving and yet unappreciated path, or if the duration of the investment is sufficiently short. The approach requires a complex balancing of different aspects related to ESG, climate risk/opportunities and financial valuation that are inherently difficult to balance, and might be negatively perceived by some investors due to their different judgements or sensibility. Additionally, it means that climate characteristics are reduced to only one piece of the investment puzzle. One example of a particular form of integration is what we would call "delta", where we identify companies able to make rapid adjustments to their carbon profile.

A forward-looking perspective such as investing in companies that are making the most rapid adjustment to CO_2 emissions can result in a positive climate alignment of the portfolio. As a weaker emission profile today may also be accompanied by a higher credit risk or equity risk, this approach could provide some additional alpha by capturing the trend early (Kazdin *et al*, 2021).

A 10% reduction from a high base (eg, 200 tons of CO_2) could be a better result for the environment than the same reduction from 100 tons of CO_2. As climate risks are mitigated fast and from a higher base, this might also represent the greatest delta in terms of credit and equity risk, and consequently be positive for valuations. For example, discounting future opportunities, reducing liabilities and increasing cashflows might result in greater expected profitability and higher multiples, generating better investment outcomes.

An individual or collaborative engagement strategy is also closely aligned with this approach, and indeed may be complementary. Identifying those companies with the highest potential to improve, and engaging with management to change or maintain the positive reduction path, may yield positive results. There is some evidence that this approach might offer higher financial and climate returns (Dimson, Karakaş and Li, 2015). In the fixed income space, sustainability-linked bonds or loans could be complementary, incentivising management to align to the interest of the bondholder.

Having said that, the strategy does not come without potential flaws. Clearly companies with high carbon reduction potential may score poorly on current screens and be at a more elevated risk of sudden shifts in regulation or carbon pricing. As previously highlighted, the risk of pathway miscalculation or execution risk may be higher, creating greater investment risk. This approach arguably demands linkage with fundamental equity and credit analysis to assess the investment payout.

Thematic

Thematic climate approaches are typically focused on the upside – ie, on companies whose business strategy is particularly geared to addressing climate challenges. Thematic approaches are most likely to centre around exploiting business adaptation to climate change often for specific megatrends or areas of key climate risk – eg, transportation, renewables or agriculture. They arguably demand deeper bottom-up analysis to assess the investment opportunity. In comparison to other strategies, they are perhaps easier for end-investors to understand conceptually, and can still be linked with carbon pathways or carbon intensity.

There are a few issues with this approach, particularly with respect to pure play businesses. Foremost, while there may be some breadth in sector exposure, investors may be exposed to similar factor risks – ie, exposure to a limited number of megatrends yielding a similar factor exposure. Companies with new technologies may deliver scope 3 savings (eg, electric cars) that may not be captured in carbon metrics. Finally, the asymmetric payout of new technologies or products is better suited for an equity portfolio than for fixed income investors, especially equity investment, and especially where execution risk exists, as credit investors' participation in the upside is limited. It is perhaps in sectors most impacted by climate risk that the more interesting thematic opportunities appear.

SECTOR-BASED APPROACHES

Understanding risk adaptation becomes critical to aligning investment returns and climate objectives. The strategies used above can help to screen and evaluate companies and provide a base framework, but the return on climate adaptation ultimately depends on how successfully companies evolve. Companies essentially have the following three options to adapt to climate risk.

- Efficiency: It is possible to make changes within the current business model that will produce less emissions – eg, through innovation or disruptive technology. For example, changes to the manufacturing process and operations, from energy efficiency and waste reduction to the use of best available technologies (BATs). The extreme version is revolutionary disruption, where new technology and business models replace older versions altogether, creating a meaningful opportunity.
- Exit: Companies can divest from emissions-intensive business lines and move to low emissions areas. They can also provide products or services that help other companies reduce emissions.
- Offset: It may be difficult for certain companies, particularly within very carbon-intensive industries, to greatly reduce their carbon intensity through efficiency or exit. Instead, they can mitigate high carbon budgets by offsetting. This means balancing their own carbon production by taking carbon out of the atmosphere (ie, Carbon Capture and Storage, CCS), or from planting trees or other net-negative carbon projects.

Putting these options into context of some of the most exposed sectors helps to illustrate how opportunities may arise and the consideration investors may make.

Food

Agrifood is directly or indirectly responsible for 25–30% of global GHG emissions, and a reduction of approximately 13GT of GHG emissions is required by 2050 (Xu, 2021). Livestock uses nearly 80% of agricultural land but produces less than 20% of the world's calorie supply, and is responsible for most GHGs. To address nutrition needs and meet rising population growth, the land surface for crops and animal agriculture will need to be increased, but without destroying forests or exacerbating already deteriorating soil conditions. Carbon efficiency can be achieved through reducing transportation and packaging footprint, or increasing yield, or reducing wastage on crops and food. This creates growth opportunities in precision agriculture, sustainable fertilisers, improved animal health and, of course, protein substitution.

Energy and utilities

Power generation is one of the greatest sources of CO2 emissions globally. To achieve net zero by 2050, the sector will need to decarbonise a decade earlier than other sectors. There is marked regulation in this sector that need to be adapted, which could lead to delays. Despite long-term structural concerns, renewable systems may not yet provide a universal solution, and fossil fuels will continue to play a part in the transition. While the exit from fossil fuels is clear, there are also opportunities in terms of efficiency in existing fossil fuel production, through carbon capture, utilisation and storage (CCUS) technologies for example. Indeed, with a large amount of capital chasing fewer projects and lowering returns on capital, investors may also consider these as a source of climate change delta and attractive returns.

Materials

Globally, materials production from extraction to industrial production, transportation and consumption contribute to nearly half of GHG emissions globally.[5] Growth opportunities to decarbonise come in the form of both efficiency and substitution. Circular economy principles and remanufacturing can also be applied to the materials industries – for example, by maximising the use of end-of-life steel or recycling and reusing cement clinker (Bataille, 2019). Negative emissions technology (NET) could be used to actively pull carbon dioxide out of the air and create carbon sinks, including CO_2 capture and storage, using carbon-scrubbing technologies (Brownell, 2017), and material substitution, switching from carbon-intensive polymers to those that are more environmentally friendly, such as biopolymers and biodegradable polymers (Jaber, 2020).

Transport
Transport accounts for nearly a quarter of the EU's GHG emissions, and has not seen the same level of emissions reductions as other sectors (European Commission, n.d.). Indeed, transport is expected to be the fastest-growing source of global emissions (Wang and Ge, 2019), so any pathway towards net zero will necessarily include decarbonisation of the sector. Investment in electric vehicle (EV) technologies will be a key feature in reducing the carbon intensity of the transport sector. Opportunities exist in various points in the lifecycle, from enhancing the efficiency of batteries and vehicles to infrastructure, and indeed end-of-life management of components such as batteries.

Chemicals
Chemical products play an important role in processing and manufacturing, and will even play a vital role in the transition to net zero (Brudermüller, 2020). The sector is the biggest industrial consumer of oil and gas,[6] both as a source of energy and as feedstock, and therefore efficiency changes will be necessary to reduce the industry's GHG emissions. Companies can switch to renewables as direct energy sources and using artificial intelligence could improve energy efficiency. Approximately half of the chemical sector's energy consumption derives from hydrocarbons used as a feedstock, so more sustainable energy inputs will be needed (Levi and Fernandez Pales, 2018). CCUS has the potential to reduce emissions and then reuse the captured CO_2 in chemical production.

New technologies based on renewable feedstock, biomass and recycled materials could result in more seismic shifts – for example, Dow Chemical using pyrolysis oil feedstock, made from recycled plastic waste, in the production of new polymers. Increasing circularity in plastics and alternative sustainable packaging solutions also present opportunities for growth.

RELATIONSHIP BETWEEN THEMES AND ESG
This section will examine four thematic product concepts that may adopt positive and negative screening: water; climate (Paris-aligned);[7] clean energy; and general ESG. These represent two styles, namely narrow thematics such as water and clean energy, and broad thematics such as "climate" and general ESG. As with

Figure 4.4 Weighted regional exposure of four sample portfolios

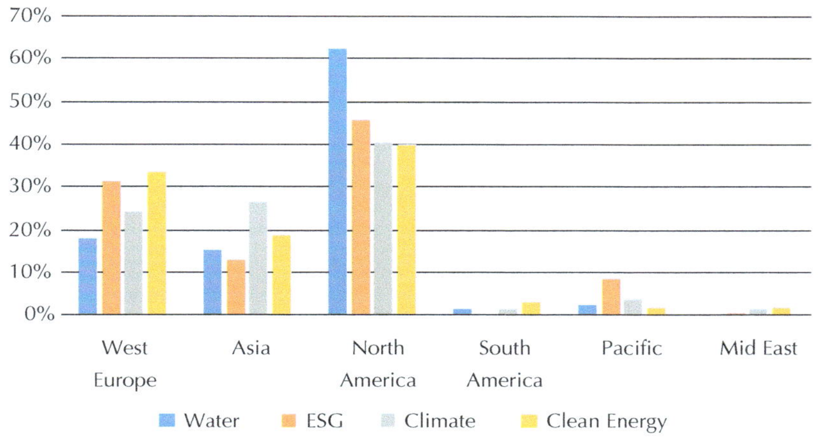

many investors, in some instances these groups will be compared to a benchmark, in this case a proxy for the global market. We have constructed thematic indexes by weighting a number of products in each theme to capture the thematic effect rather than the style of one individual product. There are both financial and ESG characteristic trade-offs to be considered. We also highlight some of the best practices in terms of exclusion, fund management and portfolio construction.

Diversification in climate portfolios

Notably, the four thematic groups have a similar regional exposure where regionally US weights remain high, as shown in Figure 4.4. This is to be expected given the relative weight of the US market in the global financial system. From a risk point of view, this indicates good risk diversification: the products are spreading the risk across regions at least as well as the benchmark while still maintaining an overweight to the largest financial region, North America.

From a climate point of view, this could also add some benefits – for example, limiting the exposure to physical climate risk by investing in several countries and regions. The probability of extreme climate events such as hurricanes, droughts or monsoons occurring globally at the same time is very low, which is why diversification can be important in that aspect as well. However, this

Figure 4.5 Weighted regional over or under exposure compared to a proxy for the global markets

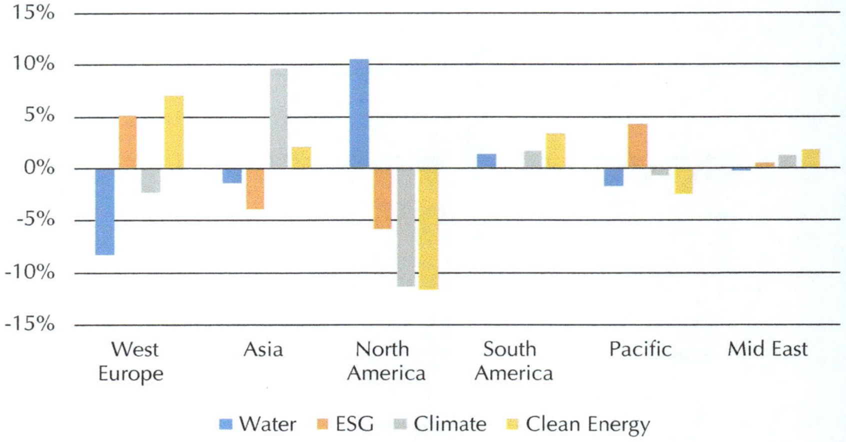

does depend on bottom-up analysis of individual company exposure as it might hinge on the exposure of underlying holdings.

When comparing the regional exposure to our proxy for the global market, we observe some interesting results in Figure 4.5. The composite clean energy thematic is relatively overweight in Europe and Asia and underweight in North America and the Pacific region, which is aligned with the general development of clean energy. North America and the Pacific is more heavily reliant on fossil fuels compared to Europe, which has transitioned towards more sustainable energy sources.

However, this highlights the importance of having appropriate benchmarks for thematic products such as these. If the world market were to be used to measure portfolio risk, the results would likely be skewed by differences in regional exposure. The water thematic is the only product group that shows a relative overweight to North America against the world market proxy.

Diversification can be double-edged. On the one hand, it helps to reduce the risk in the portfolio by splitting the risk between different regions and sectors. On the other hand, from a climate and ESG perspective, some sectors are so polluting that investing can be difficult – and some regions are still struggling with trustworthiness of ESG data to the point where having data could provide a false sense of security. The point of sustainability data is to drive better decisions and reduce risk, but false data reduces the intended effect and could expose the portfolio to more risk than intended.

Portfolio managers often have to balance trade-offs between financial and ESG/climate risk. On the one hand, diversifying regional exposure can lower the financial sensitivity of a portfolio; on the other hand, however, this can expose the portfolio to negative sustainability surprises, especially if the sustainability assessment was based on faulty data. The probability of ESG black swan events are higher outside developed markets due to the lack of transparency, on average. The greater gap risk associated with data, the greater risk that data does not comply with ESG policies, forcing portfolio managers to sell at an inappropriate level. There are no right or wrongs here, but awareness of the complete spectrum of risk is advisable, as is balancing the different sources of risk to reach the objective of the portfolio.

One could assume water-themed portfolios should exclusively invest in water-related securities, and likely have concentration in the utility sector. However, this is demonstrably not the case, as can be seen in Figure 4.6. Second-order thinking enables portfolio managers to capture the theme from different angles and in different stages of the supply chain. This approach not only focuses the immediate effects of an investment, but also considers the consequences of that investment.

Figure 4.6 Weighted sector distribution of four sample portfolios

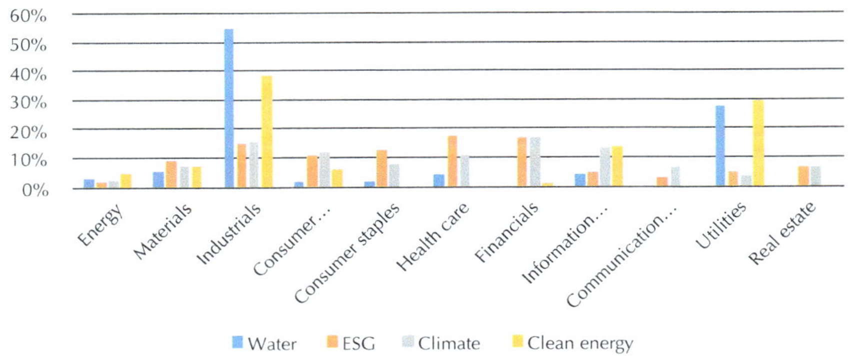

Figure 4.7 Financial performance over three years for the sample portfolios; portfolio, benchmark and delta are plotted

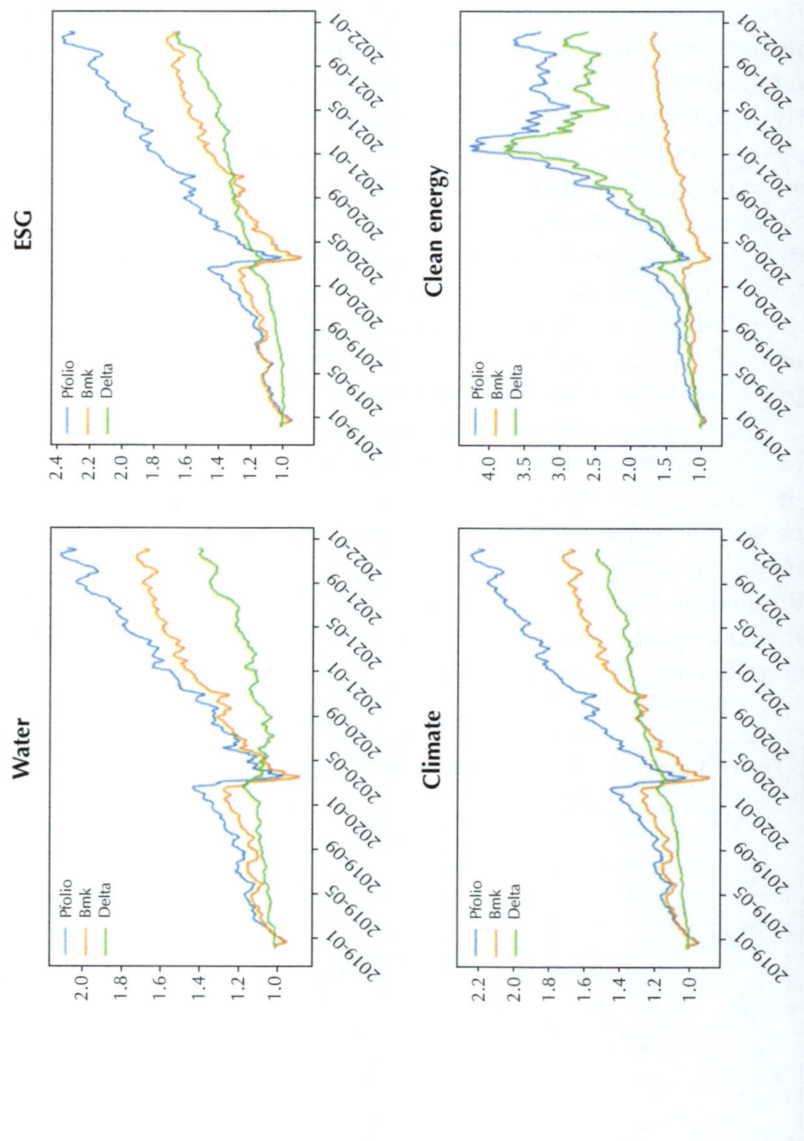

While this is a great way to diversify the portfolio, limiting risk and capturing opportunities, it does come at a price – namely the risk of double-counting emissions. It can, however, help the portfolio manager see the larger picture, and identify new trends and more efficient ways of solving problems that can have a positive climate impact.

A thematic product is generally concentrated in specific sectors, but we see that climate and ESG are more balanced than the other sample portfolios. Likewise, they are also more regionally diversified. This shows that it is possible to construct a climate product while still avoiding too many biases in the portfolio. This may be expected since the lower constraints from a more general ESG product can allow for a wider mandate and universe. In both cases, one needs to balance the trade-off between regional/sector exposure with data availability and quality.

Quantitative considerations

Looking at the financial performance of thematic and sustainable products, we have calculated the past performance of our four product groups compared to the world market proxy in Figure 4.7. The blue line is the portfolio and the orange is the proxy we use for the world market.

Drawdowns as a result of Covid-19 are obvious, but there is notable outperformance from all products. While recent performance has been skewed by extraordinary events and regime change, we have limited history to examine. Clean energy has had spectacular performance, which can be partly explained by the

Table 4.5 Risk metrics for the sample portfolios

Metric	Water	ESG	Climate	Clean energy
Portfolio risk%	21.19	20.49	19.53	33.46
Benchmark risk%	19.04	19.04	19.04	19.03
Portfolio Tracking Error %	8.29	4.84	3.56	22.72
VaR 99% 1d	–2.56	–2.50	–2.32	–2.72
Expected Shortfall 99% 1d	–3.20	–3.11	–2.92	–4.48
Portfolio beta	1.02	1.05	1.01	1.33
Portfolio alpha%	6.62	10.05	8.86	16.74
Portfolio R^2	0.85	0.95	0.97	0.57
Diversification	14.78	6.54	12.38	10.06

heavy sector exposure to industrials and utilities. However, it could also be a case of having a poorly fitting benchmark. As we can see from Table 4.5, the R^2 of the regression is very low and does not hold much explanatory power, so the high alpha of the strategy is highly artificial.

Since clean energy is a niche product it should also have an appropriate benchmark. However, ESG and climate both provide good results in terms of benchmark fit and performance, as seen in the portfolio alpha and R^2 row in Table 4.5. This illustrates the importance of having well-fitting benchmarks, especially for thematic products that otherwise would indicate results that only partly explain the behaviour of the portfolio.

Generally, niche thematics will struggle against core portfolios in terms of diversification and risk profile given the higher degree of concentration risk. Climate may not be as affected as it potentially can invest in a broad universe while still respecting the theme. Finally, we note that the diversification score of the different products differ as well, with water and climate being the best diversified and ESG the lowest. Additionally, we should note that the water product had a significantly higher number of securities compared to the other sample portfolios, which did result in a higher diversification. For reference, the diversification score of the world proxy is around 17, although not shown in Table 4.5.

It is worthwhile highlighting that the lower diversification compared to the global market is probably a consequence of the negative/ethical screening applied by the sample products. This is mostly noticeable in the ESG product as that will probably have the strictest exclusion rules. This could potentially expose the ESG portfolio to larger financial risks, which is important to balance particularly if ESG products are positioned to reduce the overall risk of the investment. As always, a portfolio manager needs to balance sustainability and financials. To add diversification, the least correlated stock should be selected, but that stock may often also be "unsustainable".

ESG considerations

Moving from the financial assessment to climate and ESG, we observe some notable results for our four product groups, as illustrated in Table 4.6. The world proxy provides a base of reference to

Table 4.6 Sustainability and climate data for the four sample portfolios[8]

Source	Metric	World	Water	ESG	Climate	Clean energy
Provider A	ESG score	100	96	103.3	101.1	94.1
Provider B	ESG score	100	111.5	107.7	103.8	98.1
Provider A	Weighted CO_2 emissions (scope 1+2) ('00)	5,747,408	2,167,270	1,319,309	1,091,434	1,157,498
Provider A	Weighted CO_2 emissions (scope 1+2+3) (00s)	42,902,128	3,482,174	12,793,822	5,157,182	4,177,568
Provider B	Weighted CO_2 emissions (scope 1+2) (00s)	4,285,022	1,995,234	1,279,038	1,389,108	995,126
Provider B	Weighted CO_2 emissions (scope 1+2+3) (00s)	31,730,439	3,343,557	11,509,626	7,505,101	4,623,624

compare the ESG scores for all product groups. The ESG and CO_2 metrics are derived from two different providers to highlight the differences and similarities a portfolio manager could face when working with different ESG data providers. The two providers are aligned in most cases, except for water.

There could be several reasons for this. First, no one provider would cover everything. Indeed, when looking into the data, we noted that provider B does not cover the two companies deemed worst by provider A in the water product group. This would naturally give the product an artificially high score. However, the effect is limited since the ESG score is weighted and the total weight in the companies can compensate or amplify the effect depending on portfolio construction.

Second, each provider has their own methodology, which translates into different scores for the same companies (Dimson, Marsh and Staunton, 2020). ESG scores can usually be treated as a relative ranking system within the same provider, but do not necessarily translate between different providers.

The first thing to note in Table 4.6 is that only clean energy has a worse ESG score than the global market proxy when comparing both providers. However, the difference is small, and the result is by no means a bad score. The different product groups have different objectives, and ESG stands out as a heavy emitter in relative terms while still performing well below the global market portfolio.

We can also see that clean energy is among the higher polluters. This may be counterintuitive given the name, but the clean energy spectrum is full of industrial and utilities, and light on media, insurance and financials, which are low emitting industries. Additionally, many clean energy companies are still engaged in polluting activities and the proportion of the "clean business" may be expanding. These companies are probably much cleaner than other energy companies but, as energy production is one of the most polluting activities, emissions remain elevated.

It is worth highlighting that as soon as scope 3 emissions are considered, the emissions in the world portfolio greatly exceeds the other portfolios from previously being more in line. This is mainly due to the heavier allocation in oil and gas, material and the automotive sectors, which are assigned lower weight in the other

Figure 4.8 Estimated price per tonne of carbon emissions according to the SSP1–19 scenario

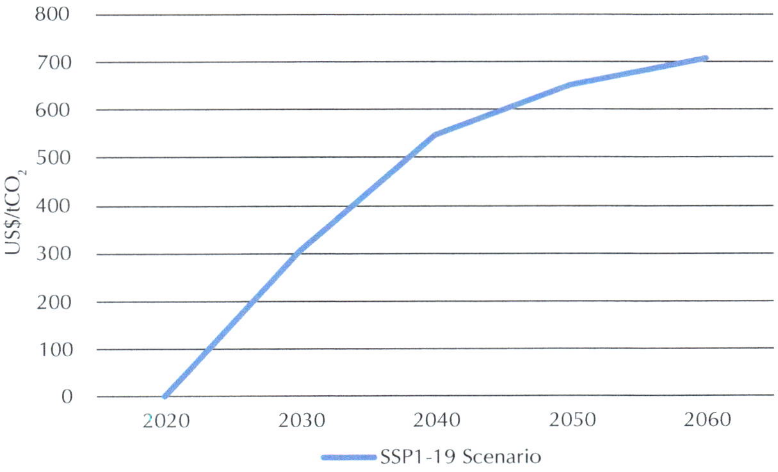

sample portfolios due to the specific characteristics of the thematic portfolios.

The risk of carbon exposure

A portfolio with high emissions could have a negative effect not only on sustainability metrics but also on financial risk since companies will probably have to internalise the cost of the emissions in the not too distant future. For some sustainable energy companies, this could partly be compensated by the carbon credit systems, but clearly polluting companies will have to adjust to a new environment. We need to take emissions into consideration and control the carbon risk of all portfolios, as illustrated in Figure 4.8.

In IPCC (2021), the price of carbon was discussed. There are many scenarios and pricing regimes associated with the cost of carbon, but one of the most commonly used is the SPP1–19, which respects the sub-two degrees global warming concept. As shown in Figure 4.8, the price of carbon has been zero but will quickly rise and become more expensive over time. This could provide insight into the carbon risk that highly polluting companies are exposed to. The gradually higher price translates into increasing risk exposure that needs to be mitigated either through carbon credits or change of production, both of which are expensive. As suggested, this could be aligned with the climate pathways and scenarios described earlier in this chapter.

Final remarks on portfolio construction

To conclude this section, we would briefly highlight challenges faced today by portfolio managers wishing to align their portfolios. What is notable from this chapter is that thematic approaches can skew portfolios according to underlying biases. While broader thematic (eg, climate) strategies can improve relative ESG characteristics and proxy benchmarks, they can also come at the expense of unforeseen impacts – eg, higher scope 3 emissions. Narrow thematics such as clean energy illustrate how regional impacts could affect usage, and weaker headline ESG scores may also represent a headwind for some investors and portfolio managers trying to align with broader selection and portfolio construction considerations.

Many sustainable products have rules on exclusion of certain activities, companies or regions that are deemed non-investable. Although there are some benefits to negative screening, it can be a very blunt tool. This can be described as the ESG integration paradox (Cappucci, 2018), where only partly integrating ESG criteria to a portfolio such as only having hard exclusions could lead to worse performance, while completely integrating both positive and negative screening show good results in providing alpha. We wonder why so many still only rely on the prior, missing the opportunity to construct better portfolios, both financially and for the environment.

CONCLUSION

The IPCC report of August 2021 concludes that climate change is without doubt a direct result of human behaviour. Most scientists also agree that the negative effects of not acting on climate change will have catastrophic impacts. The financial sector is increasingly aware of the issues, but much more must be done.

Meanwhile, multiple challenges persist.

- Data availability is arguably the biggest challenge, particularly for emerging markets, small caps and private companies.

- The quality of data is also questionable due to different reporting systems and lack of reporting obligations. Very often ESG data are also unaudited.
- Improved conceptual frameworks are also needed to better attribute and measure scope 3 emissions as they are fundamental to correctly measure the impact of products and companies. Existing models such as the PACTA webtool, ESG Book initiative or benchmarks that provide a guide to emission reductions trajectories are useful guidance and support, but the climate revolution comes with costs: for many small and medium firms, the need for improved climate (and ESG) data represents an additional burden that will put additional pressure on margins.

It is clear that the integration of ESG and climate data opens a new era for portfolio management. While the risk premium for smaller or emerging companies might increase due to their limited transparency, it is too early to judge to what extent the efficient market hypothesis will be challenged. Clearly, it enters into a new phase and investors will have to seriously consider how much of the information in their hands is already discounted by markets. Investment managers will be confronted with new problems at the border between ethics and financial materiality that will be difficult to assess.

We believe in this new complex scenario it is difficult to define the "best" approach as it is also a consequence of portfolio objectives that are different among investors. Exclusion or best in class strategies reduce the investable universe or increase exposure to specific market factors that can worsen the risk/return profile of the portfolio, but can potentially remove the most critical companies. From an investment perspective, integration appears to be the winning strategy as it counterbalances the integration of climate consideration with the assessment of the risk premium, but we recognise this might be more difficult to explain and demonstrate. All emission reductions and adaptations efforts come at a cost, which needs to be factored into any investment decision. Being too green or too early could in fact be a risk in itself if regulation and market practices do not move in the anticipated direction.

We are, however, strong believers that more information is better than less, and that a more-informed investor will construct better portfolios. Errors and underperformance risks always exist, but considering what is at stake it is more advisable to take a more proactive approach than a more passive one. Notwithstanding, this all highlights the importance of clear, coherent and globally aligned regulatory clarity for climate risk mitigation and adaptation frameworks, data and metrics. The Apollo mission may have managed to reach the moon with less computational power than we have in our smartphones, but they had something much more powerful: a unified objective.

We would like to express our deepest thanks to the following colleagues that helped us better understand the challenges and opportunities of companies belonging to different sectors, and for improving the readability of the content: Sam Glover, Jeff Li, Jonathan Rawicz and Gabrielle Steele.

1 Net zero refers to a state in which the greenhouse gases (GHGs) going into the atmosphere are balanced by removal out of the atmosphere. The term net zero is important because – for CO_2 at least – this is the state at which global warming stops getting worse. The Paris Agreement underlined the need for net zero, requiring states to "achieve a balance between anthropogenic emissions by sources and removals by sinks of GHGs in the second half of this century".

2 EU Regulation 2019/2089 on Paris-aligned and climate transition benchmarks defines the characteristics that benchmarks require in order to be classified as Paris-aligned or climate transition. In addition to an initial delta of 30% or 50% (respectively for climate transition and Paris-aligned benchmarks), the climate benchmarks have to reduce GHG intensity or absolute emissions by 7% per annum.

3 For alternative measures, see CDP and WWF (2020).

4 See, as examples, Nakicenovic and Swart (2000) and the Network for Greening the Financial System (NGFS) Scenarios Portal (https://www.ngfs.net/ngfs-scenarios-portal/).

5 See the Raw Materials Information System (RMIS) at the EU Science Hub (https://rmis.jrc.ec.europa.eu/?page=climate-low-carbon-cda228) and Hertwich (2021).

6 See https://www.iea.org/fuels-and-technologies/chemicals.

7 Within Paris-aligned, we focus on products that aim to align the emissions of the portfolio to the target of the Paris agreement – ie, emission reduction consistent with a temperature increase of well below 2°C by 2050.

8 The difference between the CO_2 emissions of the two providers is mainly a consequence of two factors: different coverage and different results for estimated data. The delta becomes even wider when scope 3 emissions are considered. As explained previously, estimating scope 3 emissions for companies in the oil, materials and automotive sectors is challenging, and results are different between providers. Indexes with significant allocation to those sectors amplify the difference.

REFERENCES

Bataille, C., 2019, "Low and Zero Emissions in the Steel and Cement Industries: Barriers, Technologies and Policies", Issue Paper, OECD GGSD Forum, November 26/27, Paris (available at https://www.oecd.org/greengrowth/GGSD2019_IssuePaper_CementSteel.pdf).

Brownell, B., 2017, "The Materials Industry is Pitching in to Reduce Greenhouse Gas Emissions", *Architect*, December 14 (available at https://www.architectmagazine.com/practice/the-materials-industry-is-pitching-in-to-reduce-greenhouse-gas-emissions_o).

Brudermüller, M., 2020, "How to Build a More Climate-friendly Chemical Industry", WEF, January 21 (available at https://www.weforum.org/agenda/2020/01/how-to-build-a-more-climate-friendly-chemical-industry/).

Cappucci, M., 2018, "The ESG Integration Paradox", *Journal of Applied Corporate Finance*, 30(2), pp. 22–28 (available at https://ssrn.com/abstract=3233222).

CDP, 2018, "Closing the Gap: Scaling up Sustainable Supply Chain Practices", Global Supply Chain Report 2017/18 (available at https://cdn.cdp.net/cdp-production/cms/reports/documents/000/003/014/original/CDP_Supply_Chain_Report_2018.pdf?1518084325).

CDP and WWF, 2020, "Temperature Rating Methodology: A Temperature Rating Method for Targets, Corporates, and Portfolios", October 1 (available at https://cdn.cdp.net/cdp-production/comfy/cms/files/files/000/003/741/original/Temperature_scoring_-_beta_methodology.pdf).

Dimson, E., O. Karakaş and X. Li, 2015, "Active Ownership", *The Review of Financial Studies*, 28(12), August 12, pp 3,225–68 (available at https://academic.oup.com/rfs/article/28/12/3225/1573572).

Dimson, E., P. Marsh and M. Staunton, 2020, "Divergent ESG Ratings", *The Journal of Portfolio Management*, 47(1), pp. 75–87 (available at https://jpm.pm-research.com/content/47/1/75).

European Commission, n.d., "A European Strategy for Low-emission Mobility", EU Climate Action – Transport Emissions (available at https://ec.europa.eu/clima/policies/transport_en).

Hertwich, E. G., 2021, "Increased Carbon Footprint of Materials Production Driven by Rise in Investments", *Nature Geoscience*, 14, March, pp. 151–55 (available at https://www.nature.com/articles/s41561-021-00690-8.pdf).

IIGCC, 2021, "Net Zero Investment Framework: Implementation Guide", March (available at https://www.iigcc.org/download/net-zero-investment-framework-implementation-guide/?wpdmdl=4425&refresh=6271179c71e671651578780).

IPCC, 2021, "Climate Change 2021: The Physical Science Basis", contribution of Working Group I to the Sixth Assessment Report (available at https://www.ipcc.ch/report/sixth-assessment-report-working-group-i/).

Jaber, S., 2020, "Five Ways Manufacturers can Reduce Carbon Emissions", Matmatch, blog, March 11 (available at https://matmatch.com/blog/five-ways-manufacturers-can-reduce-carbon-emissions/).

Kazdin, J., K. Schwaiger, V.-S. Wendt and A. Ang, 2021, "Climate Alpha with Predictors also Improving Firm Efficiency", *The Journal of Impact and ESG Investing*, 2(2), November, pp. 35–56 (available at https://papers.ssrn.com/sol3/papers.cfm?abstract_id=3889640).

Levi, P. and A. Fernandez Pales, 2018, "From Energy to Chemicals", IEA, July 2 (available at https://www.iea.org/commentaries/from-energy-to-chemicals).

Nakicenovic, N. and R. Swart (Eds), 2000, "Emissions Scenarios", IPCC (available at https://www.ipcc.ch/report/emissions-scenarios/).

SBTi, 2015, "Sectoral Decarbonization Approach (SDA): A Method for Setting Corporate Emission Reduction Targets in Line with Climate Science", May (available at https://sciencebasedtargets.org/resources/files/Sectoral-Decarbonization-Approach-Report.pdf).

TCFD, 2017, "Recommendations of the Task Force on Climate-related Financial Disclosures", Final Report, June (available at https://assets.bbhub.io/company/sites/60/2020/10/FINAL-2017-TCFD-Report-11052018.pdf).

Wang, S. and M. Ge, 2019, "Everything You Need to Know about the Fastest-growing Source of Global Emissions: Transport", WRI, October 16 (available at https://www.wri.org/insights/everything-you-need-know-about-fastest-growing-source-global-emissions-transport).

Xu, X., P. Sharma, S. Shu, T.-S. Lin, P. Ciais, F. N. Tubiello, P. Smith, N. Campbell and A. K. Jain, 2021, "Global Greenhouse Gas Emissions from Animal-based Foods are Twice those of Plant-based Food", *Nature Food*, 2, pp. 724–32 (available at https://www.nature.com/articles/s43016-021-00358-x).

5

Considering physical climate risks and resilience in real asset investment

Lucy Carmody and Carlos Sánchez

For the Coalition for Climate Resilient Investment

"BUILDING IN" RESILIENCE TO CLIMATE CHANGE

Climate change makes a fundamentally unknowable future even more uncertain for investors, scientists and policymakers alike. It poses a systemic risk to society, the economy and financial markets and, regardless of global national and corporate commitments to reduce greenhouse gas (GHG) emissions, we are all certain to experience some degree of climate change over the coming decades that could be slow and challenging to reverse. The Intergovernmental Panel on Climate Change (IPCC), the body of the United Nations responsible for advancing knowledge on human-induced climate change, concluded in their Sixth Assessment Report that "many changes due to past and future greenhouse gas emissions are irreversible for centuries to millennia, especially changes in the ocean, ice sheets and global sea level" (IPCC, 2021).

In parallel, investors and bankers globally have become increasingly aware of the financial materiality associated with climate risks that threaten real assets, supply chains and systemic stability. The impacts of these risks can derive from both physical impacts – the chronic and acute effects of climate change – and from imbalances caused by the transition to low carbon industrial futures.

Transition risks may entail policy, legal, technological and market changes that may pose varying levels of economic, financial and reputational risk. These are slowly being addressed by realigning incentives and taxes, and by mitigation and adaptation innovations on a sectoral basis, along with the use of carbon credits to offset the remaining emissions. Even if we are successful on all mitigation fronts and achieve our net zero targets, our physical world will continue to be affected by the consequences of two centuries of GHG emissions and associated global warming and changing climate. In other words, even if we get to net zero, we need to build in resilience now. Adaptation and mitigation need to be achieved in tandem as they are mutually reinforcing.

To efficiently integrate the immediate and longer-term physical climate risks (PCRs) now forecast by climate data scientists along the whole investment decision-making value chain, we need to swiftly develop and pilot end-to-end solutions, practical tools and financial instruments.

CLIMATE DATA USE IN INFRASTRUCTURE INVESTMENT DECISION-MAKING

Our growing understanding of climate scenarios and the likely range of hazards and necessary adjustments across all geographies, points to the looming climate crisis delivering a disproportionately painful shock to infrastructure as an asset class. However, real asset developers and investors are in general not currently considering resilience to physical risks in the asset design, structuring and funding of their projects, despite sophisticated natural catastrophe and climate scenario modelling being available from specialist providers. Rather, decisions are primarily influenced by the long-term functionality and durability of the asset alongside the desire to minimise capital expenditure (Capex) and operating expenditure (Opex) and time to completion, while delivering infrastructure that does not pose a risk to the lives and well-being of the people using, servicing and living near the asset.

When climate factors are considered, they are often based on an understanding of historic climate and extreme events rather than a consideration of future climate likely to be experienced over the lifetime of the asset. If future climate is considered, there tends to be a blanket approach – for example, applying an uplift in flows to account for changes in rainfall in drainage design – but this generally does not result in a level of resilience that will protect either the investor's asset or the local environment and affected communities. These "factors of safety in design" – the engineer's version of discount rates in finance – are often used to account for any future variability in climate scenarios, but do not necessarily equate to the severity, frequency and type of the expected climate risks under various scenarios.

At this stage along our collective journey towards net zero, investors performing fiduciary duties should not only be decarbonising portfolios and investing in transition innovation, but also be considering specific exposure and vulnerability of an asset to the various specific risks related to climate change. These can be modelled by climate data providers such as Verisk, One Concern, Lobelia, Trucost, Jupiter and XDI. Unless investors are aware of these risks there is the potential for over-specification, which often conflicts with mitigation objectives related to embodied carbon.

Latterly, several tools have been developed to evaluate certain elements of climate risk. These include:

- guidelines from the Institutional Investors Group on Climate Change (IIGCC, 2020);
- the United Nations Environment Programme Finance Initiative Real Estate Impact Analysis Tool;[1]
- the Canadian Institute of Chartered Accountants Climate Risk Asset Valuation Methodology (CPA Canada, 2021);
- the Inter-American Development Bank's "Climate Resilient Public Private Partnerships: A Toolkit for Decision Makers" (IDB, 2020);
- the International Institute for Sustainable Development's Sustainable Asset Valuation (SAVi) tool;[2] and
- Acclimatise Aware for Projects;
- the Investor Leadership Network's Physical Climate Risk Toolkit (Investor Leadership Network, 2021); and
- the European Investment Bank's Climate Change Risk Country Scoring Model (Ferrazzi, Kalantzis and Swart, 2021).

It is our belief, however, that the perils associated with climate change remain insufficiently incorporated into investment decisions in real assets, especially those having to do with infrastructure in developing nations.

RESILIENCE AND VULNERABILITY

Vulnerability is the degree to which a system, region or asset is susceptible to, or unable to cope with, adverse effects of climate change, including climate variability and extremes. It is a function of the character, magnitude and rate of climate variation to which the area is exposed, its sensitivity, and its structural attributes. In this regard, resilience is described as the capacity of an asset at a given point in time to withstand, recover and evolve from climate shocks. As exposure to physical climate risks increases and is not matched by structural improvements (resilience building), all nations and regions are beginning to experience growing levels of vulnerability at a societal level.

Attention to resilience building has, to date, mostly been focused on the poorer regions of the world, which have been disproportionately affected due to their multiple fragilities. We have seen the devastating effects of acute hazards on the Philippines, India, Pakistan, Sri Lanka and Myanmar. Small Island Developing States (SIDS) such as Madagascar, Fiji, Puerto Rico and Haiti have been particularly hard hit, with the Bahamas seeing climate-related losses amounting to almost 32% of annual GDP in 2019 (Eckstein, Künzel and Schäfer, 2021). According to research by Swiss Re, Indonesia is now the most vulnerable overall to the physical risks of climate change (Swiss Re Institute, 2021) once sea level rise is included. The Climate Vulnerable Forum (CVF) was established in 2009 as an "international partnership of countries highly vulnerable to a warming planet" and the Vulnerable 20 (V20) coalition was launched in 2015. By 2018, there were 55 member countries in the CVF representing over 1.4 billion people.

The "global adaptation gap" is widening, with these vulnerable and developing countries potentially requiring as much as US$300 billion per year by 2030 (UNEP, 2021), yet less than 6% of climate finance flows annually towards adaptation. Climate change, and particularly its associated tropical cyclones and hurricanes, threatens vital strategic infrastructure assets in these locations, which in turn will present challenges to the smooth functioning of society with risks to livelihoods, lifestyles and, in extreme cases, life itself.

During COP26 in November 2021, an entire day was dedicated to "adaptation, loss and damage", with 12 donor governments pledging US$413 million in new funding for a Least Developed Countries Fund (LDCF),[3] hosted by the Global Environment Facility. The LDCF is the only dedicated source of climate resilience funds currently available to the 46 least developed countries that have contributed the least to carbon emissions and face some of the highest risks from the effects of climate change. The debate on loss and damage will continue through the COP process with the Paris Agreement having reaffirmed the Warsaw International Mechanism for Loss and Damage[4] as the main vehicle to avert, minimise and address loss and damage associated with climate change impacts, including extreme weather events and slow onset events. Support for the most vulnerable regions and populations must continue to ensure investment allocated to resilience is allowed to begin immediately, and in ways most appropriate to their conditions, vulnerabilities and geographies. Dedicated efforts should also be made without delay to avoid capital flight from climate vulnerable regions as insurance for climate risks becomes less affordable.

Resilience building is, however, no longer simply a non-OECD, "vulnerable nation" discussion. Climate extremes are also causing damage beyond developed nation worst-case scenarios, as we have seen with flooding and wildfire events across Europe, Canada, the US and Australia. In 2021, in the US alone there were over 20 separate US$1 billion+ weather and climate disasters, ranging from the Western wildfires to hailstorms in Texas, Hurricanes Ida and Nicholas, as well as deadly tornadoes and droughts.

The increasing understanding of PCR impacts is causing tensions and internal political rifts as governments manage the budget requirements of their own pandemic relief programmes and domestic infrastructure resilience alongside the expectations of commitments to V20 "loss and damage". We need to incentivise the private sector to fund projects that build resilience, such as natural disaster defences that prevent loss of operational efficiency during extreme events. We also need to regulate the industry to "bake resilience in" using standardised tools and reporting.

A COALITION FOR CLIMATE RESILIENT INVESTMENT

To this end, the Coalition for Climate Resilient Investment (CCRI) was launched in 2019 to mobilise private finance, in partnership with key public institutions, to develop and implement practical solutions for the effective integration of PCRs and the acceleration of investments flows in climate resilience – with an initial focus on infrastructure. The 123 CCRI members (asset managers and owners, data providers, lenders, consultants, rating agencies, standard setters, public institutions and insurers) are developing and testing practical and effective tools and frameworks to integrate physical climate impacts, financial modelling, asset management resilience and adaptation measures in a systematic, objective, auditable and repeatable fashion.

The solutions under development are split into three workstreams: systemic; asset design and structuring; and financial innovation. All solutions will require investors to resource and implement additional steps, and we therefore expect additional time and collaboration will be required for their refinement, validation and systemic – and systematic – adoption. Rapid delivery of the solutions, when developed, should enable investors to ensure that every dollar invested will maximise the protection of economic, social and ecosystem value from PCRs, while also enhancing risk-adjusted returns.

By integrating PCRs into traditional and accepted economic markers of value, such as GDP and net present value (NPV), we hope to allow for an effective bridging of the gap between private and public approaches for resilience. This will bring targeted redeployment of risk sharing, risk transfer and policy incentive instruments to attract a greater share of private capital towards resilience building. It will also contribute to redefining the incentive structures of the future and, accordingly, to prepare actors across public and private spaces for a repricing of economic and social activity worldwide once climate risks are properly accounted for and integrated into decision-making.

MACROECONOMIC IMPLICATIONS OF IGNORING PHYSICAL CLIMATE RISKS

In 2015, Mark Carney, the governor of the Bank of England and chairman of the Financial Stability Board (FSB) at the time, stated that climate change was a systemic risk to financial markets, and that the speed at which the associated repricing of physical, transition and liability risks occurs "could be decisive for financial stability". Subsequently, there has been an unparalleled rapid mobilisation of investment capital to find solutions that will mitigate climate change. More than 100 countries have proposed, or are considering, a net zero target (ECIU, 2021), with mitigation solutions a priority, yet current national and regional investment into resilience is comparatively low. Around 20% of the largest corporates across the globe had pledged to become net zero by early 2021 (with only a fifth of those targets aligning with the scientific consensus and recommendations of the International Energy Agency and IPCC; Bindman, 2022), yet very few have begun to consider the resilience of even their own asset base to the effects of chronic and acute PCRs.

We believe this is due to a lack of analytical tools to quantify the exposure of a "real asset" to PCRs, the difficulty in determining and comparing resilience options, and the fact that investors do not currently adjust their expected returns or cost of capital to account for such risks. This situation corresponds to a market failure, the main consequence of which is that incorporating long-term resilience to PCRs is not explicitly rewarded by the equity, credit or insurance markets. Existing investment appraisal frameworks do not consider these risks and are not properly structured to assess the range of exposure of a real asset to PCRs, let alone identify ways to reduce such exposure. Institutional investors such as pension funds and insurance companies are now, understandably, keen to comprehend the potential repricing of investments due to resilience, and to see how the long-term risk and return profiles of financial portfolios might improve through the incorporation of these risks into the investment process.

Climate change threatens to damage economic systems and destroy vital infrastructure assets, posing perils that reveal the vulnerabilities of both our built and natural assets. The financial system must address PCRs to real assets by both making infrastructure more resilient, so it better withstands chronic changes and climatic extremes, and by "mutualising" those risks and offsetting them in the financial and insurance markets. Both approaches are vital components of a more resilient future that complement each other.

It is important, however, that practitioners and investors understand that, due to the scale of the issue and the limitations of the insurance industry to absorb losses from ever more extreme climate events, our priority needs to shift away from offsetting risk to "baking in" adaptation and resilience. Mutualisation should still be considered but only when resilience options have been explored and incorporated, in the same way carbon offsets are appropriate only when all available mitigation actions have been explored and implemented.

ADDRESSING THE "RESILIENCE" MARKET FAILURE

There is incontrovertible evidence of a looming global climate crisis that will lead to higher sea levels, droughts, violent storms and flooding. These severe climatological phenomena pose considerable risks to physical infrastructure. Yet, investors have changed very little about how they plan, design and finance large-scale infrastructure when it comes to climate resilience. If the tools of finance are as forward-looking and sophisticated as they appear, we should have seen by now significant changes in how infrastructure investment decisions are made. Market actors, however, do not always rationally process the evidence of the impending perils associated with PCRs as we would expect them to.

Markets fail for a variety of reasons. They work well when there are reasonable fees, benign oversight of legal and regulatory frameworks to govern market activity and raw information, analytical tools and readily available platforms for market players to interact with each other. In the case of climate change, the most common form of market failure arises because of so-called "negative externalities": adverse consequences from economic activity (the CO_2 that enters the atmosphere from the burning of fossil fuel) whose environmental and social costs are not sufficiently borne by private actors. Aligning private and social interests may require a combination of taxes, regulations and financial incentives.

Framing the mispricing of PCRs as market failure highlights that the private sector alone cannot solve the resilience issue, and that it is vital to create well-designed regulation, taxation and other forms of intervention that can help markets operate properly. However, if we are to achieve the ambitions set out in the Paris Agreement, to "hold the increase in the global average temperature to 'well below' 2°C above pre-industrial levels", we need to also immediately address the lack of integration of PCRs in global investment decision-making. For this to happen, we need to deliver open source solutions that can be used across national and regional infrastructure investment programmes and all relevant industries in the private sector. Private finance must be mobilised, in partnership with key public institutions, to develop and implement practical solutions for the effective integration of PCRs that will increase investments flows to climate resilience.

Markets will need to mobilise hundreds of billions of dollars of climate-resilient investment over the 2020s and beyond, and we must therefore collectively work towards an agreed consistent method of incorporating acute and chronic PCRs. There is currently insufficient, and sometimes poor quality, data available to support the rational pricing of risk, as well as a lack of analytical tools for investors to convert raw data into information that is relevant to investment decisions. It is imperative that we swiftly identify the tools needed to harness information about climate to inform investment decisions, and to analyse how financial instruments and market mechanisms could help market players, including governments and regulatory authorities, interact more productively.

ACHIEVING RESILIENCE THROUGH COLLABORATION AND ADAPTATION

Financial markets are crucial to overcoming the market failures we observe, but market participants need clear guidance and support. Within the next few years, we envisage a series of principles, guidelines, models and frameworks, developed by the CCRI working groups, which investors in real assets will be able to incorporate into their decision-making process to address the different PCR levels within the global economy.

These frameworks will be structured from both the top down, firstly looking at systemic risk and resilience for local and national governments, to the bottom up, looking at how investors should integrate PCR considerations in the asset design and structuring of specific investments. Others will focus on the financial innovations required to ensure that all investments consider and integrate PCRs as a matter of course.

Each output will flow into the others, so there will be an exchange of learning both within and between the groups of members developing them and then on into the markets. To demonstrate the practicality of these models and frameworks, investors, asset operators, climate data providers and other practitioners will continue to develop specific case studies of national programmes and individual projects or assets. The more robust case studies that can be presented, across different geographies and sectors, the more applicable the theoretical models will become. Finally, it is important for investors and other market participants to build alliances with other leading initiatives in this area, as outlined below.

ROADBLOCKS TO RESILIENCE

Infrastructure projects have historically faced, and continue to face, serious challenges in design, delivery and operations. Cost overruns, delivery delays, procurement failures and issues in securing private financing are common. Many of these problems arise due to the lack of a structured, forward-looking approach to risk management across all stages of the value chain and throughout the project lifecycle. Effective risk management goes some way to improving project processes and procedures, as do improving linkages to planning and budgetary cycles, good reporting and performance management, risk assessment frameworks, risk registers and audit programmes.

Poor risk assessment and risk allocation during the early phases of design and procurement can lead to higher materialised risks later. During these early stages, there is also a tendency to focus on risk prevention from an insurance lens, which tends to be restricted to loss and damage. Thus, impacts of other (non-loss related) risks are not always considered despite being material to the asset. This is especially true for PCRs. Decisions made regarding asset delivery and management, especially in the design and procurement phases, are often not informed by climate projections and a robust understanding of future PCRs under various scenarios in the relevant geographies. Historic climate data is often used in the design of climate-specific thresholds – temperature, humidity level, wind speed, etc – for infrastructure assets and individual components.

Infrastructure asset delivery and management decisions are driven by the need to optimise for a handful of key parameters. First, there is the desire to minimise Capex, Opex and the time to completion, while delivering infrastructure assets that do not pose a risk to the lives and well-being of users, employees, local communities and other stakeholders who are expected to benefit from the use of these assets. Second, any decisions or suggested changes ought not to compromise the serviceability of infrastructure assets (ie, asset functionality and durability). Finally, as infrastructure assets tend to exist in a regulated environment, decisions need to respond to and comply with regulatory frameworks and design codes. Regulators, such as the UK's Office of Gas and Electricity Markets (Ofgem), present stringent requirements in industry codes and standards to ensure fair treatment of end-users and compliance with legislation. In addition, design codes such as British Standards or Eurocodes, and asset management standards such as ISO 55000, provide guidance and often dictate how infrastructure assets are to be designed, procured and managed.

The infrastructure industry, when launching a new project, currently focuses on minimising cost and schedules for clients, preventing loss of life, serviceability, and existing regulation and code compliance. In general, a lack of appreciation of PCRs, combined with a corresponding lack of regulatory incentives to guide them to resilience-appropriate decisions, mean that future climate projections and associated climate risks are often not prioritised. This is true for both public and private sector project design and delivery. As a result, future negative externalities and potential remediation costs are simply being transferred outwards to the public sector. Integrating climate risk assessment from the outset to adapt infrastructure assets could, in fact, lead to significant reductions in the cost of climate adaptation measures later on. In essence, investing in resilience needs to be seen as offering multi-stakeholder benefits, instead of simply increasing Capex and Opex and lengthening the schedule to completion.

TOOLS, METHODOLOGIES AND GUIDELINES FOR RESILIENCE

For resilience to begin to be built into infrastructure projects, large and small, private and public, we need specific tools, case studies, methodologies and guidelines. These need to be both technical for asset managers to incorporate PCRs into their projects and for national governments to prioritise resilience options. We also need a set of climate-resilient investment principles to help asset owners insist that their asset managers incorporate the new tools. These tools are now under development with separate and active "resilience" working groups created to address the three separate issues of systemic resilience, asset design and structuring, and financial innovation.

The Systemic Resilience Forum (SRF) aims to mobilise public finance at scale for resilient investments by governments – national, regional and local – and multilateral development agencies. It was formed with the goal of supporting sovereign institutions to better assess and manage national exposure to PCRs, bringing together perspectives, practice and research from these various partners to help policy and investment decision-makers to better assess the exposure of notional value at risk from PCRs, and manage that risk through improved metrics and prioritisation of investments. The group includes international organisations, financial institutions and technical experts, and supports investment and policy decision-makers in making more effective decisions and managing their exposure to the social, economic and biodiversity impacts that come alongside PCRs.

The tools under development within the SRF aim to facilitate increased and consistent capital flows into climate-resilient infrastructure. These will be essential to progressing local, national and global efforts to implement national economic development plans, nationally determined contributions and long-term strategies (LTSs). The SRF will gradually build a solid economic and business case for investing in resilience and facilitating the development of project pipelines. The outcomes of these working groups will then play a critical role in pricing these PCRs into investment and financing decision-making.

The Asset Design and Structuring group is developing an important tool for investors, the Physical Climate Risk Assessment Methodology (PCRAM), shown in Figure 5.1. This tool has been developed under the auspices of the CCRI and guided by Mott MacDonald, the global engineering, management and development consultancy. The PCRAM is a "bottom-up" framework where component-based risk assessments (at individual asset or system level) are assessed using climate projections, engineering and financial modelling data. It aims to incorporate highly complex components from across a range of critical professional disciplines into infrastructure project decision-making in both the public and private space. The method starts by quantifying the impacts of climate change (on performance, lifecycle and maintenance) based

Figure 5.1 The Physical Climate Risk Assessment Methodology

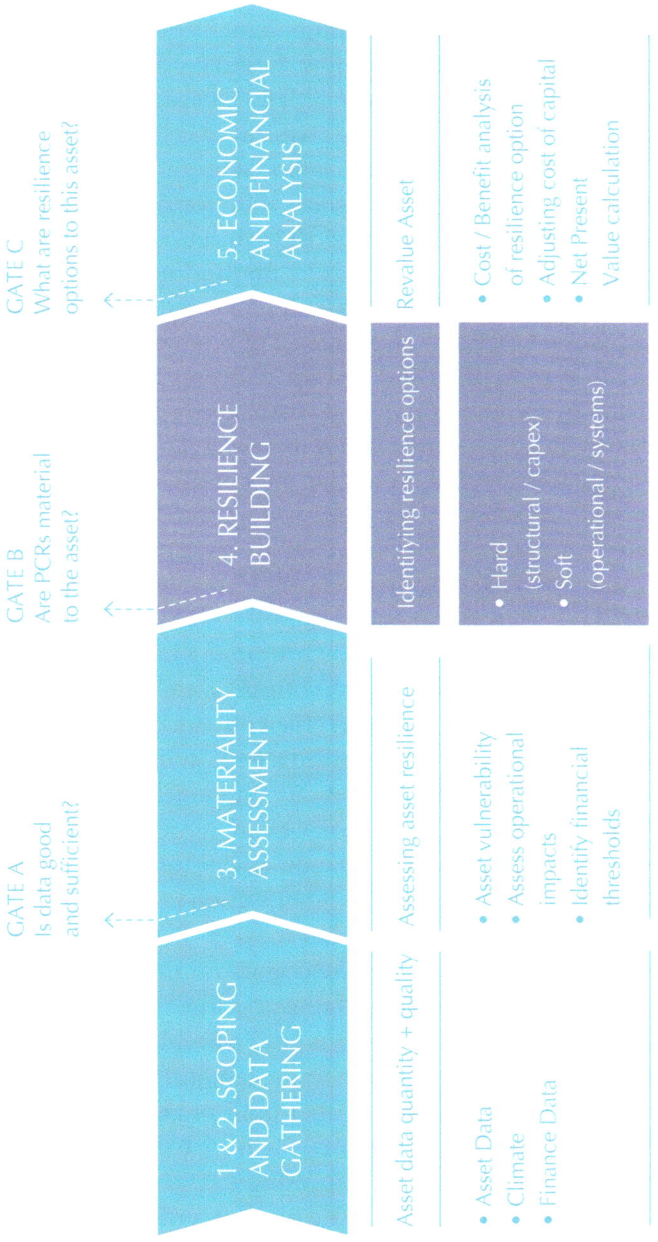

Source: CCRI, guided by Mott MacDonald

on climate scenario projections, followed by identifying resilience options and then conducting a cost–benefit analysis on them. The first important resilience-building element of the PCRAM is the process of adjusting the cashflow forecasts of all infrastructure assets to integrate known (chronic) PCRs based on certain climate scenarios, and ensuring that the physical characteristics of an asset are adjusted to them as needed. Other stages include a data audit, materiality assessment, and ongoing monitoring and prioritisation of resilience impacts for future consideration.

The development of this "live" methodology is an iterative process: the tool will be refined and enhanced as case studies are developed. The PCRAM is the result of open collaboration across many critical industries and sectors, and will continue to be open source and non-commercial. Asset managers will be able to use the accompanying developing guidelines, which instruct how each step is implemented and highlights the pitfalls along the way. Asset owners and investors will be able to adopt the Principles of Climate Resilient Investment to ensure that all their managers adopt the PCRAM as a way of building resilience into infrastructure investment.

Understandably, there will be a time lag before the proposed guidelines see widespread global uptake among finance practitioners such that all investments efficiently incorporate PCRs. This implies that the "resilience funding gap" will continue to grow unless practical financial solutions are implemented to reward such practices.

It is with this in mind that the Financial Innovation group has been structured to allow capital mobilisation to resilience at a huge scale. Through this group, capital market instruments are being developed with the support of regional and multilateral development agencies to incentivise and reward infrastructure projects that can prove they have effectively modelled and integrated climate resilience considerations into their design and structuring phases. They will also seek to support operating projects that implement incremental resilient investments. Such instruments are likely to combine insurance and credit products. Ultimately, these resilience-incentive instruments can be used to certify that a project has incorporated and priced in PCRs, and reinforce a key attribute of infrastructure as an investment asset class: a predictable, secure and long-term source of cashflows. Massive-scale pilot transactions are underway that both fund resilience investments in infrastructure assets and incentivise the efficient pricing of PCRs. Parametric insurance solutions are being woven in to address bankability issues linked to asset PCR exposure.

Preliminary work on potential adjustments to the traditional methodology for real asset valuation, the capital asset pricing model (CAPM), now over 60 years old, is scheduled to continue over the next few years. CAPM projects lifetime cashflows and discounts them back to a present value so that those further out, which are more uncertain and therefore riskier, are valued less than those realised sooner. In the model, the expected rate of return is the "risk-free" rate plus an "equity risk premium" (the market risk premium multiplied by beta for that specific asset type). The downside of this approach is that it does not allow users to "weight" the risks against time factors, as it assumes that risk and time effects are interchangeable. Essentially, in CAPM, risks are a function of time and independent of source, which is problematic when we begin to consider acute PCRs.

The various workstreams highlighted here will complement the many other initiatives (outlined below), regulatory frameworks and existing analytical frameworks in development. They are all intended to support key regulatory and analytical initiatives by providing "proof of concept" of efficient pricing of PCRs. All major organisations working on global resilience initiatives are in constant communication with the executive office of the UN Secretary General as the network of partnerships and collaborations grows, to avoid duplication and redundancy. The work underway in each of these groups will create practical outputs available for investors in the coming years.

GLOBAL RESILIENCE INITIATIVES: COMPLEMENTARY AND COLLABORATIVE

In April 2015, the G20 finance ministers and central bank governors asked the FSB to convene a review of how the financial sector should take account of climate-related issues. As part of its review, the FSB identified the need for information to assess and price climate-related risks, and subsequently established an industry-led task force: the Task Force on Climate-Related Financial Disclosures

(TCFD). The TCFD disclosure recommendations have, by early 2022, been endorsed by over 3,000 supporting organisations with market capitalisation of over US$25 trillion and representing assets of around US$200 trillion.

The recommendations put in place have already been incorporated into many frameworks and regulations that aim to identify and report on climate-related financial risks in a standardised way. Investors seeking to build resilience into their real asset base are advised to follow the eight TCFD-recommended activities below, as well as becoming collaboratively involved through industry associations in the development of specific methodologies for their particular asset class:

- climate change scenario analysis;
- engagement with companies along their value chain;
- analysis of evolving legislation on climate change;
- risk mapping, materiality assessments and balanced scorecards;
- enhanced due diligence applied to projects and transactions;
- use of an internal carbon price;
- integrating climate risk management plans into enterprise risk management; and
- adaptation of business models so resilience to PCRs is part of long-term business strategy.

The resilience tools, methodologies, guidance and principles under development by the CCRI's three working groups (Systemic Resilience, Asset Design and Structuring, and Financial Innovation) complement these TCFD recommendations by providing a valuation framework that incorporates PCRs in the appraisal of infrastructure assets. The process under development not only puts a value on downside risks, but also captures the benefits of climate-resilient infrastructure assets. Investors are expected to incorporate climate-related risks and opportunities into governance structures as well as strategy and risk management processes, using additional climate-related scenario analysis and stress tests. TCFD is an incredibly powerful initiative and a true driving force in mobilising interest in resilience across regions and industries. CCRI will continue to provide actionable recommendations on how to achieve this.

Since the TCFD was launched, other notable organisations have sprung up to support markets to build in future resilience and urgently close the trillion dollar sustainable infrastructure investment gap. The Global Infrastructure Outlook estimated in 2018 that there would be a "global infrastructure investment gap" of about US$15 trillion, equal to a 16% infrastructure investment deficit, by 2040. Closing the gap will require annual infrastructure investment to increase from the current level of 3.0% of global GDP to 3.5%. We highlight some of these initiatives below, including the Coalition for Disaster Resilient Infrastructure (CDRI), Finance to Accelerate the Sustainable Transition-Infrastructure initiative (FAST-Infra), the Global Center on Adaptation (GCA), the Blue Dot Network, the Resilience Shift and the Race to Resilience (R2R).

CDRI is a partnership of national governments, UN agencies and programmes, multilateral development banks and financing mechanisms and thinktanks that together promote the resilience of infrastructure systems to climate and disaster risks with a view to supporting sustainable development. They focus on technical support, capacity building, research, thought leadership, advocacy and building strong partnerships with a focus on public and international decision-making related to resilience investments.

FAST-Infra aims to transform sustainable infrastructure into a mainstream, liquid asset class. It was launched in 2020 by the Climate Policy Initiative, HSBC, the International Finance Corporation, OECD and the Global Infrastructure Facility. FAST-Infra is creating a global labelling system for sustainable infrastructure assets that includes a category on resilience.

GCA, hosted by the Netherlands, has been brokering solutions to accelerate action and support for adaptation since its launch in 2018. It focuses on high-level policy, research and technical assistance to governments and the private sector in food security, infrastructure and nature-based solutions, climate finance, and water in urban areas, and has special programmes on accelerating adaptation in Africa and on engaging youth to promote activities at a local level.

The Blue Dot Network aims to promote open, inclusive, transparent and economically viable infrastructure investment of the highest quality. Their ambitions are for this infrastructure to be Paris-aligned, environmentally and socially sustainable, and compliant with international standards, laws and regulations. The standards build on detail already laid out in the G20 Principles for Quality Infrastructure Investment, the G7 Charlevoix Commitment on Innovative Financing for Development, the Equator Principles, and guidelines such as the OECD Guidelines for Multinational Enterprises. The voluntary network, launched by the US, Japan and Australia, is developing robust criteria and standards to certify infrastructure projects against climate change. It will regularly review developments in standards to ensure inclusion of the leading international standards at any time. The aim is long-term sustainable growth and a resilient economic recovery post-pandemic.

The Resilience Shift aims to catalyse resilient solutions for acute shocks and chronic stresses. It is a resilience accelerator, incubator and champion of platforms that supports systemic change by convening and hosting organisations which help ensure the safety and continuity of the critical infrastructure and services, focusing on innovation and creativity.

Lastly, R2R is a campaign to achieve global climate resilience, where people and nature thrive despite climate shocks and stresses. It focuses particularly on strengthening the resilience of the four billion people living in climate-vulnerable communities by 2030, helping communities build resilience and adapt to impacts of climate change, such as extreme heat, drought, flooding and sea-level rise in urban, rural and coastal areas. R2R stresses that pledged finance for climate adaptation and resilience falls catastrophically behind that for climate mitigation and decarbonisation, and is often left off the agenda completely, with less than 6% of all climate finance tracked globally being attributed to adaptation. The United Nations Environment Programme (UNEP) estimates that up to US$300 billion will be required annually for adaptation in developing countries alone by 2030.

BUILDING MULTI-STAKEHOLDER RESILIENCE

A multitude of stakeholders are affected by, and involved in, creating more resilient infrastructure assets globally. They are all interconnected and should be supported as they address the resilience issue practically and collectively, eventually setting industry standards and implementing policies and guidance.

Table 5.1 Stakeholder resilience

Investors: Equity and debt	**Ecosystem: Platforms, data intermediaries, technology**	**National frameworks**	**Supranational frameworks**
❑ Pension funds ❑ Insurance companies ❑ Municipalities ❑ Governments ❑ Development banks ❑ Retail investors ❑ Corporates	❑ Insurance industry and actuaries ❑ Academic institutions and research ❑ Investment banks (bond and equity issuance) ❑ Asset managers ❑ Sovereign wealth funds ❑ Ratings agencies ❑ Risk assessors ❑ Consultancies ❑ Stock exchanges ❑ Data and technology (risk, artificial intelligence, AI, geospatial) ❑ Architects, planners, engineers and designers	❑ Central banks and financial regulators ❑ Regional authorities ❑ Cities ❑ Planning ❑ Flood management agencies ❑ Sectoral regulatory and advisory bodies ❑ Government ministries: ❍ power ❍ housing ❍ transport ❍ environment ❍ food and agriculture	❑ United Nations ❑ Conference of the parties ❑ G7/20 ❑ Non-governmental organisations (NGOs) ❑ Thinktanks ❑ Multilateral development agencies ❑ Global sectoral coalitions

These stakeholders can be considered to sit in the "market segments" shown in Table 5.1, all of which have their own taxonomies and approaches.

FUTURE CHALLENGES TO BUILDING IN RESILIENCE

In an ideal world we would already have developed a supercomputer that uses AI, machine learning and geospatial analysis to compare the cashflows of individual infrastructure projects against the likely climate hazards produced within the different IPCC Representative Concentration Pathway (RCP) climate models and Shared Socioeconomic Pathways (SSPs). In this world, we would not only be able to assess the resilience options that should be built in from the outset, but also the point at which additional resilience options are less attractive as de-risking through insurance and derivatives becomes more valid. Due to the enthusiasm and energies of people working in the resilience space, this world is not far away. Even if, in the lull following COP26, the mobilisation of climate finance to accelerate resilience and to help the most vulnerable populations seems crushingly slow, solutions are underway. Many challenges remain, however, on the rocky road to resilience.

First, very long-term cashflow and internal rate of return (IRR) forecasts are extremely sensitive to the time value of money and inflation. Investors and lenders looking at distant costs and revenues are understandably cautious over the additional uncertainty that loans for infrastructure, especially in climate vulnerable developing nations, will not be repaid due to the impacts of both chronic and anticipated PCRs, but also the acute hazards and unknown unknowns due to the potential for tipping points and thresholds to be crossed. As a result, at the very time that vulnerable nations need to be building resilience in, the high premiums required on loans to fund these projects often makes them unattainable. This is where resilience finance must come in, and where the Financial Innovation group is working to smooth the path by piloting multiple investment funds for resilience, possibly with concessional finance, as proof of concept.

Second, there is a theoretical hurdle to cross. The cost of capital of a project that benefits from an investment in resilience should theoretically be lower, reflecting its lower exposure to future disruption of earnings and higher remedial costs. When we introduce systematic risk, however, things get a little complicated. Hazards occur simultaneously and compound each other as asset-specific risks correlate with climate shock-induced macro risks. To illustrate the complexity, imagine a renewable energy project connected to a national electricity network, and therefore the wider economy. Would building in overall resilience against an acute event deliver enhanced long-term cashflows? The same hazard event that causes disruption may result in an overall reduction in total generation capacity, and therefore increase the value of the assets production capacity as the "shadow" electricity price rises. Could flooding in the coastal area it is located in also impact transmission and distribution, meaning that the benefit of building in resilience is not fully captured?

We could also write a whole separate chapter here on the highly debated topic of the appropriate discount rate for financial modelling that includes climate risk and building in resilience through adaptation. Discounted cashflow models tend to break down in the face of extreme risks (fat tails) in the long term, and it is unclear how we should adjust discount rates for very varied long-term risks across varied assets and geographies. Taking averages of multiple climate scenarios and then performing sensitivity analysis causes us to ignore extremes and tail risk, and investors must avoid losing precision when smoothing for risks. There is also the question of which scenario we should be using. Is it time for standardisation and for all practitioners to use the RCP 8.5 "very high baseline emission scenario" as a standard climate scenario, essentially admitting we are still in a "business as normal" fossil fuel world for the foreseeable future? Perhaps we should all be using stochastic scenario modelling as standard? How should we account for the growing realisation that tipping points and thresholds take us to unknown unknown futures that are utterly unpredictable.

Due to the lack of clarity on these issues, many feel that current best practice for assessing projects is to use IRRs instead of NPVs (even with sensitivity tests using multiple discount rates). Long-term risks are unlikely to affect NPVs in a material way, and discount rate assumptions are continuing to stimulate debate. For this reason, we are setting up a global academic council to further these discussions. This group of leading climate finance academics will address the challenges ahead for integrating PCRs into decision-making from a theoretical perspective. Cost is always a major issue, and the cost of sophisticated climate modelling analysis is beyond the developer of a small single infrastructure asset. Standard generalised frameworks need to therefore be developed and applied. We also need to take into consideration climate risk adjustment long-term costs that were not anticipated in earlier agreements. Should they be built into periodic climate risk adjustment charge "breaks" over the life of the asset? If so, what is an appropriate period for this? Perhaps these restatements could be tied into the IPCC assessment cycle?

As we have seen, there is an urgent need for public policymakers to support, and investors to develop, long-term sustainable infrastructure at reasonable cost. Nevertheless, the bulk of firms that must carry out this work are seemingly unaware of the immediacy of physical climate risks. At the firm level, analysts are not being incentivised to integrate the predictable (chronic) and unpredictable (acute hazards) impacts of climate change into their models. Often, within the colossal companies of today with employees in the 100,000s, there can be many different silos of practitioners all working on their own version of risk and adaptation, without the ability to plan collectively and integrate this developing knowledge area in a standardised way. Ultimately, until firms and investors see resilience building as an opportunity, we will not be able to move swiftly enough to protect vulnerable assets and populations.

At the individual project level there are several roadblocks. First up is persuading planners to move away from using records of historic climate data and to include climate data providers at an early stage in discussions about potential climate variables. For this to happen, there needs to be renewed focus on retraining and adding additional modules to university and professional engineering courses. Practitioners must identify the technical, commercial and financial needs of the project with respect to climate risks, crucially including an understanding of what data and metrics are available for site or specific asset location. With long, linear assets such as roads and railways it can be preferable to get gridded projections for the entirety of the route, rather than just a series of latitudinal and longitudinal points. Flood hazards, for example, can be highly localised but could affect the larger impact zone surrounding an asset. Assessment and expected outcomes tend to evolve as the project progresses, and scope and schedules can change materially during the design, structuring and construction phases. Lastly, resilience options for a particular type of asset are often untested, and it can be difficult to determine the quantum and timing of potential changes to cashflow forecasts as a result of including the option. In some instances, it can be helpful to use Monte Carlo simulation or other statistical techniques to predict the probability of different outcomes when random variables are introduced, but this comes with its own set of issues.

On the cost side, market pricing of hedging or insuring against physical climate risk is currently very opaque. It relies on expensive research and development (R&D) into creating the relevant actuarial data that increasingly uses sophisticated satellite imagery and catastrophe modelling. There is often a lack of data available for the developing markets, where resilience to increasingly extreme climate change-related weather events is so crucial. An additional technical issue is that infrastructure projects are normally structured as special purpose vehicles (SPVs), and often do not satisfy the collateral requirements for derivatives providers. It is also hard to test the developing methodologies, especially when there is no market pricing of climate-related risks for large, complex assets of national security, or in emerging market contexts. As a result, in most private and public infrastructure deals to date, acute climate risk events are almost always transferred away from the private sector and borne by the taxpayer or government.

There are additional hurdles regarding the data required on PCRs and impacts of resilience options. The data tends to be sensitive and could affect business confidence, other investments in the area, property prices or even cause misunderstanding or panic among local populations if it was in the public domain. Due to concern over confidentiality, data encryption has become very important, and in the future blockchain could also prove critical. Different data providers use different metrics and proxy indicators for climate hazards, present their data in different ways, and charges vary wildly. Finally, the availability of detailed climate projections beyond 2100 is poor, even when most assets being built today would anticipate a design life beyond this.

There is little reliable open source data available at a scale that would be useful to individual project developers. Due to the high R&D costs embedded in data – from satellites, AI, machine learning, light detection and ranging (LiDAR) and drone technology – competing service providers are keen to protect their intellectual property (IP), even though the data has an extremely high "public good" value. This is somewhat similar to a successful new pharmaceutical drug or vaccine that has been developed in the private space but is required for urgent and life-saving use as a public good. We are optimistic that this issue can be scaled, primarily as we have seen how, in the case of the Covid-19 crisis, over 10 billion vaccine doses and the research that made them possible were funded by the public sector to the tune of around US$100 billion, just 0.1% of the global GDP for 2022.

Despite this multitude of challenges, we believe that by properly pricing climate risk in infrastructure decision-making, investors will be encouraged to build infrastructure that is more resilient and capable of withstanding the present and future impacts of climate change, as we head towards net zero 2050 and potentially ward off the most ravaging impacts of global warming.

CONCLUSION – A BRAVE AND RESILIENT NEW WORLD

As the world edges tentatively towards this mid-century net zero, we must ensure measures are in place so that every financial decision not only takes chronic climate change into account but also incorporates resilience to acute climate risks. As shown in 2021 in Glasgow, we cannot solely rely on the COP process to deliver the far-reaching commitments needed to reach the Paris goals, and must recognise that avoidance and mitigation are only half the story. Much of the damage to be caused by acute climate risks has already been "baked in", and the surface and marine temperature increases caused by global warming cannot be swiftly reversed.

We must therefore focus on the immediate practical implementation of tools and guidelines for infrastructure and other asset classes to build in resilience to protect assets and populations. We need measures in place now so that every financial decision incorporates resilience to physical climate risks. We need central banks and regulators to begin to build climate change resilience into financial systems, and banks, insurers and investors to commit to align to net zero. Disclosure should be aligned with the new frameworks for resilience – the TCFD and the Taskforce on Nature-related Financial Disclosures (TNFD) – so that real assets, humanity and biodiversity are protected from physical climate risks going forward.

Successful resilience building will also require enhanced corporate disclosure, increased rigour of project due diligence, and the development and adoption of new technologies and solutions to assess risks and more easily incorporate available scientific data. We also need institutional and sovereign asset owners to engage with, and endorse, the Principles for Climate Resilient Investment, and for infrastructure asset managers to adopt the new Guidelines for Resilient Investment, scheduled for release in 2022.

Resilience building may appear costly upfront but should enhance long-term risk-adjusted returns on assets and, as with the entire green energy transition, present new business opportunities, intellectual capital and job creation. If most climate scenarios in use are to be believed, it will also reduce vulnerabilities, especially in developing countries.

Over the course of the next few years, and as climate data becomes more trusted and hazards more predictable, there will be a need for additional actions and advances in investment structuring, financial modelling and the theory of asset valuation. Infrastructure practitioners will also have to focus collaboratively on climate risk-related regulatory initiatives around the world, and work towards the delivery of open source climate risk databases as a public good on shared platforms. This is where large, climate-focused donors and multilateral agencies must step up as it is difficult for the private sector, with their competing stakeholder interests, to give away climate risk IP. We need climate risk experts to continue to innovate, and for the pace of development of technical tools and methods of analysis not to be stifled.

If all this were to happen, and across all asset classes not just infrastructure, then the global financial industry and the system in which it operates will see: key incentive structures aligned with future climate resilience; regulation that efficiently promotes the adequate integration of physical climate risks in investment decision-making; and the long-term cost of capital reduced. These are the steps that must be in place for our brave and resilient new world to reveal itself.

This chapter was assisted by contributing members of the Coalition for Climate Resilient Investment

1 See https://www.unepfi.org/positive-impact/unep-fi-impact-analysis-tools/real-estate-impact-analysis-tool/.
2 See https://www.iisd.org/savi/#:~:text=Sustainable%20Asset%20Valuation%20%28SAVi%29%20An%20assessment%20methodology%20that,investors%20make%20informed%20decisions%20on%20financing%20sustainable%20infrastructure.
3 See https://www.thegef.org/what-we-do/topics/least-developed-countries-fund-ldcf.
4 See https://unfccc.int/wim-excom.

REFERENCES

Bindman, P., 2022, "Exclusive: The Companies with the Most Ambitious Net-zero Targets", Capital Monitor, October 27 (available at https://capitalmonitor.ai/factor/environmental/which-sectors-are-the-most-ambitious-on-net-zero/).

CPA Canada, 2021, "A4S Essential Guide to Valuations and Climate Change: A Framework to Assess the Impact of Climate Change on Business Valuations", CFO Leadership Network, February 25 (available at https://www.cpacanada.ca/en/business-and-accounting-resources/other-general-business-topics/sustainability/publications/a4s-cfo-leadership-network-canadian-chapter/a4s-guide-valuations-climate-change).

Eckstein, D., V. Künzel and L. Schäfer, 2021, "Global Climate Risk Index 2021: Who Suffers Most from Extreme Weather Events? Weather-related Loss Events in 2019 and 2000–2019", Briefing Paper, Germanwatch (available at https://germanwatch.org/sites/default/files/Global%20Climate%20Risk%20Index%202021_1.pdf).

Ferrazzi, M., F. Kalantzis and S. Swart, 2021, "Assessing Climate Change Risks at the Country Level: The EIB Scoring Method", EIB Working Paper 2021/03, May (available at https://op.europa.eu/en/publication-detail/-/publication/1a42783a-c283-11eb-a925-01aa75ed71a1/language-en).

IDB, 2020, "Climate Resilient Public Private Partnerships: A Toolkit for Decision Makers", (available at https://publications.iadb.org/publications/english/document/Climate-Resilient-Public-Private-Partnerships-A-Toolkit-for-Decision-Makers.pdf).

IIGCC, 2020, "Understanding Physical Climate Risks and Opportunities", May 27 (available at https://www.iigcc.org/download/understanding-physical-climate-risks-and-opportunities-a-guide-for-investors/?wpdmdl=3388&refresh=62f241f0590e51660043760).

Investor Leadership Network, 2021, "Climate Change Physical Risk Toolkit", November (available at https://investorleadershipnetwork.org/en/resource/physical-climate-risk-toolkit/).

IPCC, 2021, "Sixth Assessment Report", August 9 (available at https://www.ipcc.ch/assessment-report/ar6/).

Swiss Re Institute, 2021, "The Economics of Climate Change", April 22 (available at https://www.swissre.com/institute/research/topics-and-risk-dialogues/climate-and-natural-catastrophe-risk/expertise-publication-economics-of-climate-change.html).

UNEP, 2021, "Adaptation Gap Report 2021", November 1 (available at https://www.unep.org/resources/adaptation-gap-report-2021).

6

Case Study 3: Practical issues and considerations for implementing a Net Zero emissions strategy for asset owners

Marc Olivier Dines

The Velux Foundations

This chapter aims to provide practical guidance on how to align an investment portfolio towards a trajectory that achieves net zero greenhouse gas (GHG) emissions by 2050 in accordance with the EU's Green Deal (2019/20) and the expectations set out in the Paris Agreement (2015/16). The focus will be on an asset owner-centric approach. It begins with the rationale for using a net zero framework and an overview of different selected frameworks, before a roadmap is presented that illustrates the practical steps and considerations that can be used to create a net zero-aligned portfolio. Then different carbon metrics and alignment evaluation tools are analysed to outline sensible tracking of a given investment portfolio's GHG stance. This is followed by a discussion of common issues related to the collection of relevant data, dealing with gaps in, the lack of, or even incorrect, data, with results being mapped to visualise the GHG emissions profile of an investment portfolio. Finally, guidance is given on practical steps and considerations for achieving portfolio alignment with a net zero emissions targets and pathways by 2050.

WHY USE A NET ZERO FRAMEWORK?

Organisations representing asset owners have a fiduciary duty to manage risks prudently and achieve satisfactory returns. This duty necessitates the integration of ESG issues into financial decision-making. In fact, the final UNEP FI and PRI (2019) report "Fiduciary Duty in the 21st Century" cites three reasons why such integration is required: ESG incorporation is the investment norm; ESG issues are financially material; and policy and regulatory frameworks are changing to require ESG incorporation. The latest updated version of the UK Stewardship Code from 2020 also includes the integration of ESG factors as part of a responsible investor's conduct.[1]

As part of this incorporation of relevant and material ESG issues, a growing number of institutional investors and financial intermediaries are recognising the need to ensure that their activities are not financially vulnerable from, nor contribute to, increasing environmental risks. One of the biggest environmental and existential risks – defined as the first planetary boundary by the Stockholm Resilience Centre – is climate change due to rising atmospheric carbon dioxide concentration.[2]

With the Paris Agreement, a legally binding international treaty on climate change adopted by almost all countries, the global task of addressing this environmental challenge has been manifested into the goal of limiting "global warming to well below 2, preferably 1.5 degrees Celsius, compared to pre-industrial levels". This in turn, has been translated into a growing consensus among countries and organisations on achieving the more practical (and dividable) target of net zero GHG emissions by 2050.

It is against this backdrop that more and more non-exclusive net zero frameworks have emerged among different types of financial companies. Table 6.1 lists the sub-sectoral net zero initiatives that have the broadest coverage, all of which are UN-convened and in the UN's Race to Zero campaign united through the Glasgow Financial Alliance for Net Zero (GFANZ), representing about 300 financial firms responsible for roughly US$90 trillion.[3]

According to GFANZ, all sub-sector alliance members are required to "use science-based guidelines to reach net zero, cover all emission scopes, include 2030 interim targets and commit to transparent reporting and accounting". The bulk of these financial entities' emissions come not from their direct operations (scope 1) or purchased energy consumption (scope 2), but instead indirectly from their investment exposure by financing and owning GHG-emitting companies and assets (scope 3). All of the alliances

Table 6.1 Net zero frameworks

Framework (member types) representation	**Major source of emissions**	**Selected items from commitment statements**
Net Zero Banking Alliance (NZBA) Banks 38% of global banking assets or about US$58 trillion	Loans (financed emissions) to and portfolio investments in companies.	Banks commit to align lending and investment portfolios to align with net zero by at least 2050. Set initial 2030 targets (or sooner) and intermediary five-year targets from 2030 onwards. Banks' first 2030 targets to focus on GHG-intensive (priority*) sectors with further sector targets set within 36 months. Take a robust approach to the role of offsets in transition plans (restricted to certified carbon removals where limited viable alternatives to eliminate emissions).
Net Zero Asset Managers Initiative (NZAM) Asset managers US$43 trillion in AUM	Debt and equity investments in operating companies and real assets	Asset managers commit to work in partnership with asset owner clients to reach net zero emission by at least 2050 or sooner across all assets under management (AUM) Set interim targets at least every five years for the proportion of assets to be managed in line with a net zero emissions by 2050 goal, with an intention of eventually covering 100% of AUM. Set interim targets for 2030. Prioritise achieving real economy emission reductions. If using offsets, then invest in long-term carbon removal where no viable alternatives exist to eliminate emissions. Create investment products aligned with net zero by 2050 and encourage increased investment in climate solutions. Implement stewardship policies and engagement strategies with clear escalation and voting policies consistent with net zero by at least 2050. Engage with key actors to the investment system, such as rating agencies, auditors, exchanges, consultants, and data and service providers, to facilitate the development of investor products and services that are consistent with a goal of net zero by at least 2050.

Framework (member types) representation	Major source of emissions	Selected items from commitment statements
Paris Aligned Investment Initiative (PAII) Asset managers and asset owners (pension funds) US$34 trillion in assets	Debt and equity investments in operating companies and real assets	Asset managers and asset owners transitioning investments to achieve net zero portfolio GHG emissions by at least 2050. Set interim targets for 2030 or sooner. If using offsets, then invest in long-term carbon removal where no viable alternatives exist to eliminate emissions. Ensure any policy advocacy supports policy and regulation consistent with reaching net zero by at least 2050. Implement a stewardship and engagement strategy consistent with an objective for all portfolio assets to reach net zero by at least 2050. Engage with key actors in the investment system, such as rating agencies, auditors, exchanges, consultants, and data and service providers, to facilitate the development of investor products and services that are consistent with a net zero by at least 2050 goal. Emphasise GHG emission reduction outcomes in the real economy. Set a target to reduce operational (scope 1 and 2) emissions consistent with reaching global net zero emissions by at least 2050.
Net Zero Asset Owner Alliance (NZAOA) Asset owners (pension funds and insurance companies) US$9.3 trillion in assets	Debt and equity investments in operating companies and real assets	Asset owners commit to transition investment portfolios to net zero GHG emissions by at least 2050. Set intermediate targets every five years. Embed net zero by at least 2050 commitment in a holistic approach to managing sustainability considerations by considering, but not limited to, climate change. Emphasise GHG emission reduction outcomes in the real economy.

Framework (member types) representation	Major source of emissions	Selected items from commitment statements
Net Zero Insurance Alliance (NZIA) Insurers and reinsurers Founded by eight of the world's leading insurers and reinsurers (AXA, Allianz, Aviva, Generali, Munich Re, SCOR, Swiss Re, and Zurich)	Insurance and re-insurance underwriting portfolios	Transitioning all operational and attributable GHG emissions from insurance and reinsurance underwriting portfolios to net zero emissions by 2050. Set, to the extent permissible by applicable laws and regulations, intermediate science-based targets every five years. Set intermediary targets within six months of joining alliance. Consider emerging frameworks such as the Taskforce on Nature-related Financial Disclosures (TNFD). Support global policy frameworks relevant to a net zero transition and the insurance industry, such as the UN Sustainable Development Goals (SDGs) and the Post-2020 Global Biodiversity Framework, including nature-based solutions to climate change that absorb GHG emissions and build climate resilience. Sign the UN Principles for Sustainable Insurance at the latest one year after joining alliance. Develop and offer insurance and reinsurance products, solutions and arrangements for low-emission and zero-emission technologies and nature-based solutions that are key to the net zero transition. Aim to transition investment portfolios to net zero GHG emissions by 2050 and consider joining relevant initiatives (eg, NZAOA) to achieve a consistent approach to net zero. Advocate for, and engage in, governmental policies for a science-based and socially just transition of economic sectors to net zero. Integrate independently determined, company-specific net zero and decarbonisation-related risk criteria into risk management frameworks (eg, ESG/sustainability risk management frameworks) applicable to underwriting portfolios and promoting human rights, including the right to free, prior and informed consent (FPIC).

Framework (member types) representation	Major source of emissions	Selected items from commitment statements
		Work together with insurance associations, insurance and financial regulators and supervisors, governments, trade bodies, policymakers, the UN and other intergovernmental organisations to promote the goals of the NZIA, and to seek consistency of regulatory, supervisory and governmental policy frameworks with the net zero transition. Engage with non-member insurance industry, financial sector peers and trade bodies; leading scientific methodological and data-related organisations; academia; non-governmental organisations; and other key stakeholders on the goals of the NZIA.
Net Zero Financial Service Providers Alliance (NZFSPA) Auditors, consulting firms, rating agencies, index providers, investment advisors, financial exchanges, and other financial data and service providers BDO, Bloomberg, Deloitte, Ernst & Young, Grant Thornton, KPMG, London Stock Exchange Group (LSEG), Moody's, Morningstar, MSCI, PWC, SGX, Solactive, S&P Global, and others	No significant emission sources but provide services to members in all of the above alliances	Align all relevant services and products to achieve net zero GHG emissions by at least 2050, scaling and mainstreaming Paris Agreement-alignment into the core of the business. Build internal capability to understand the risks and opportunities of the net zero transition using best-practice net zero methodologies where they exist and, where methodologies or data are missing, proactively and collaboratively work to address those gaps. Set interim targets for 2030 or sooner consistent with a fair share of a 50% global reduction in carbon emissions. Review and update such targets at least every five years with a view to increasing the proportion of services and products to achieve full alignment. Set interim science-based reduction targets within 12 months of joining for no later than 2030 across all operational emissions. Consistently raise with key stakeholders the importance and implications of setting net zero targets and strategies across scopes 1, 2 and 3 emissions, and understanding the impact businesses can have to help reduce GHG emissions.

Framework (member types) representation	Major source of emissions	Selected items from commitment statements
		Advance efforts by proactively engaging with stakeholders and policymakers on corporate and industry action, as well as public policies, that support a net zero transition of economic sectors in line with science and with regard to social impacts. Contribute to GFANZ efforts within the NZFSPA, which will aim to bring together existing tools and alliances.
Net Zero Investment Consultants Initiative (NZICI) Investment consultants (more than 4,400 signatories across investment managers, asset owners and service providers)	No significant emission sources but provide services to members in all of the above alliances	Integrate advice on net zero alignment into all investment consulting services as soon as practically possible and within two years of making net zero commitment. Work with institutional asset owner clients to identify the investment risks from climate change, highlight the importance of net zero alignment and, where applicable, support clients in developing policies that align their portfolios to a net zero pathway. Support efforts to decarbonise the global economy by helping clients prioritise real economy emissions reductions, reflecting the target of 50% global emissions reduction by 2030 or sooner using existing decarbonisation methodologies. Align with the NZAM as soon as practically possible and within two years of making this commitment. Where suitable net zero methodologies do not exist, work collaboratively for the benefit of clients to address these challenges, seeking harmonised methodologies.

*Priority sectors include oil and gas, utilities, aviation, shipping and heavy and light duty road transport
Source: GFANZ and each member site for the alliances

require at least accounting for scope 1 and 2 emissions of these underlying investment exposures. Accounting for scope 3 emissions is, for now, not required due to the recognition that reliable, if any, data may be difficult to obtain. It is, however, expected to be included to the extent possible and as soon as possible by all initiatives in GFANZ.

This chapter will take the perspective of an asset owner following the NZAOA guidelines based on the "Net Zero Asset Owner Alliance 2025 Target Setting Protocol" (UNEP FI and PRI, 2021): An asset owner's own scope 3 emissions are "portfolio emissions". Each portfolio holding may be an ownership stake or financing exposure towards governments, companies, projects or other types of investments that emit greenhouse gases. It is in the measurement of each of these underlying holdings' emissions where the asset management industry sees assessment challenges. Most companies only report scope 1 and 2 emissions, and scope 3 emissions will likely comprise the vast majority of total, direct emissions (Funk, 2020). Emissions contributions, whether directly or indirectly, are particularly significant for the so-called "priority sectors" identified in the NZAOA 2025 Target Setting Protocol, which include oil and gas, utilities, aviation, shipping, and heavy and light duty road transport (see Figure 6.1).

Data on scope 3 emissions of companies is particularly difficult to obtain, however, and far from being reported by all companies. A *Financial Times* article (Murray, 2021) identified poor quality or even lack of relevant data and analytics to be the biggest obstacle to

Figure 6.1 Structure of asset owner's emissions

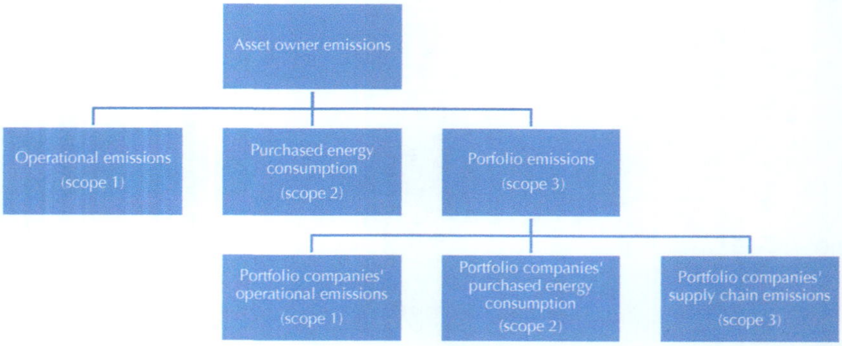

ESG investing in general. There is therefore no way around relying on the use of estimated data.

Poor data coverage is an often-heard argument against including scope 3 emissions on underlying company holdings, even though these emissions on average account for the majority of total corporate emissions.[4] Overlooking these emissions, however, could give a distorted, if not misleading, picture of a given portfolio's carbon profile. Therefore, while acknowledging that the uncertainty surrounding scope 3 estimates is significant, it would be better to strive to be roughly right using estimates than completely wrong from ignoring scope 3 emissions from underlying companies in setting portfolio targets.

A known critique of including scope 3 emissions is that it may cause double, or even triple, counting if multiple companies within the same supply chain are owned. For instance, if an oil producer sells fuel to a transportation company both companies will include the burning of the same fuel in their emissions (scope 3 for the oil producer and scope 1 for the transportation company). However, it is unlikely for a portfolio to include, say, an oil producer's entire supply chain as the before-mentioned transportation company is likely to consume fuel from many different suppliers. Again, by overlooking scope 3 emissions an asset owner would definitely underestimate (in addition to distorting the emissions distribution across sectors) the true emissions of one's portfolio as many downstream scope 3 emissions are caused by governments, private households and companies outside the investment universe. By including scope 3 emissions there is a potential multiple counting of emissions of negligible size, which becomes more and more unlikely with increasingly concentrated portfolios, where supply chain overlap is even rarer. Including scope 3 emissions also shows the real-world impact of a given portfolio company's emissions and therefore better reveals its transitional risks. While double counting may affect the level of portfolio emission, it would equally occur from the emission reduction changes that are the result of portfolio companies decarbonising. As will be argued, investors should not only track current emissions. Even more importantly, they should focus on aligning the forward-looking trajectory of portfolio emissions with a net zero target (Odier, 2021).

Returning to the poor availability of scope 3 emissions data, it should also be noted that companies themselves, as well as third-party data providers, are producing increasingly better estimates over time. This is because guidance is emerging from relevant sources such as the Greenhouse Gas Protocol, the Partnership for Carbon Accounting Financials (PCAF) and the Climate Disclosure Project (CDP) on how to measure and account for carbon emissions.

In particular, the CDP (2021) asserts that supply chain emissions (scope 3), which are likely to include small and medium-sized enterprises (SMEs), may be over 10 times higher than operational emissions (scope 1). According to the Organisation for Economic Co-operation and Development (OECD), SMEs represent over 90% of businesses and over half of worldwide employment. They also account for over half of GDP in OECD economies and about a third of GDP in emerging economies (Cusmano, 2017). Recognising that SMEs lack the same resources and means for reporting emissions as larger corporations, the CDP in collaboration with the SME Climate Hub launched a climate disclosure framework "to empower SMEs to make strategic and impactful climate commitments, track and report progress against those commitments, and demonstrate climate leadership" (CDP, 2021).

The NZAOA recommends setting sub-sector emissions targets covering scope 1, 2 and 3 on the mentioned "priority sectors" as soon as possible, but do not expect to set scope 3 targets at the portfolio level before the data has been deemed to be sufficiently reliable by the alliance (UNEP FI and PRI, 2021).

THE ASSET OWNER ROADMAP FOR NET ZERO

A roadmap to constructing a Paris-aligned net zero portfolio should include the steps and considerations shown in Figure 6.2.

In the TCFD's "Proposed Guidance on Climate-related Metrics, Targets, and Transition Plans" from June 2021 (TCFD, 2021b), an

Figure 6.2 A roadmap to constructing a Paris-aligned portfolio

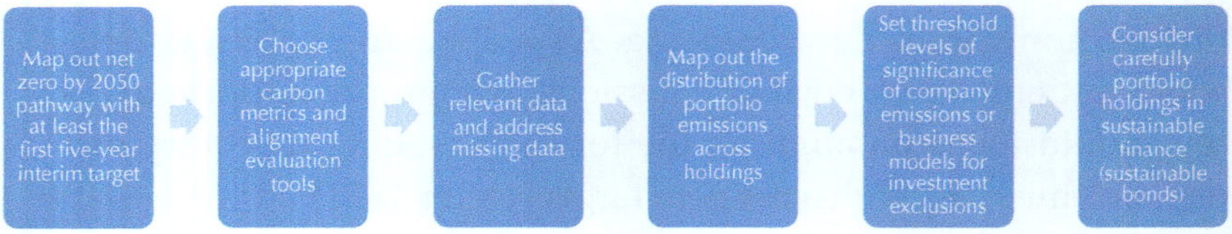

example illustration of a net zero by 2050 trajectory with five-year interim targets including at least a 50% emissions reduction by 2030 is given (see Figure 6.3).[5] It is built on the TCFD's general principles that climate-related targets should be:

- based on recognised metrics;
- quantified and granular;
- designed with consideration of an organisation's strategy and forecasting, and informed notably by scenario analysis and climate science;
- clearly specified over time, and in particular include:
  - a baseline period;
  - a time horizon; and
  - interim targets.
- reviewed and updated, when appropriate; and
- reported annually.

Figure 6.3 An example of a path towards net zero portfolio emissions from the TCFD

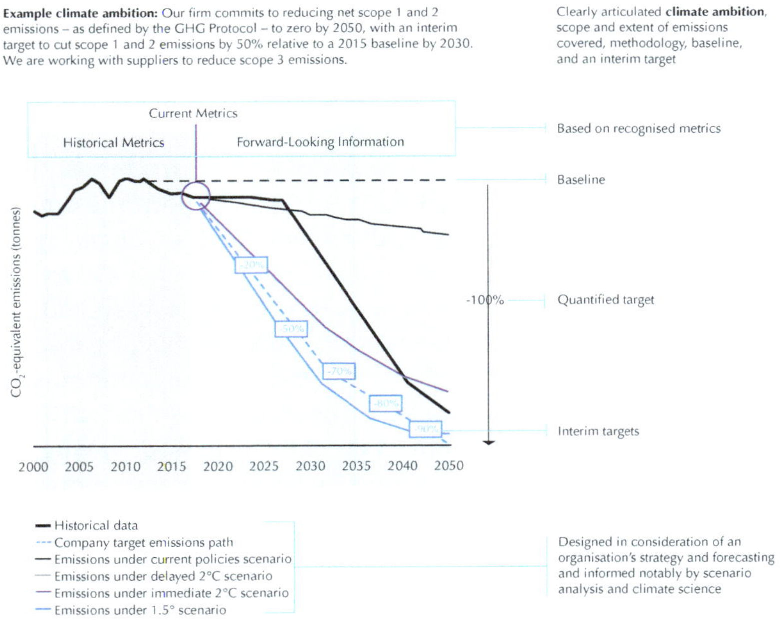

Source: TCFD (2021b)

The NZAOA's stated five-year emissions target is a reduction of –16 to –29% by 2025.[6] This range is aligned with the mitigation pathways compatible with limiting global warming to 1.5°C in the context of sustainable development mentioned in the Intergovernmental Panel on Climate Change's (IPCC) special report "Global Warming of 1.5°C". In that report, the IPCC defines these mitigation pathways, or more specifically climate-resilient development pathways (CRDPs), as: "Trajectories that strengthen sustainable development at multiple scales and efforts to eradicate poverty through equitable societal and systems transitions and transformations while reducing the threat of climate change through ambitious mitigation, adaptation and climate resilience".[7]

By following intermediary targets that are only specified for five years at a time, investors have certain leeway in considering which strategy to use on this pathway towards net zero. It gives room to adopt a more gradual and sensible change of direction rather than trying to find a complete solution to portfolio emissions in an investment environment that is rapidly changing, and with new sustainable business models and investment opportunities that have yet to emerge.[8] It is also important to acknowledge that guidance on what constitutes sustainable investing from an environmental standpoint is quickly evolving. In addition, there are many unresolved issues around measurement that remain to be settled.

As a creditor or minority owner of an asset or company, investors have limited ability to directly control portfolio emissions. Rather than simply selling holdings with high emissions – ie, divest the assets (which does not reduce emissions for the world but merely transfers them to other owners) – investors should seek to finance or hold stakes in assets or companies that, by themselves and perhaps even with the engagement of the investor, actively pursue a strategy to decarbonise over time and thus achieve real-world emission reductions. As will be discussed, having a clear approach on whether to divest or exercise active ownership through engagement is key to a net zero portfolio strategy.

An asset owner's portfolio objective should focus on a Paris-aligned decarbonisation trajectory towards net zero emissions, by at least 2050, while maximising expected risk-adjusted returns. This requires being more selective when investing within sectors, especially when it comes to the so-called "priority sectors". This selectiveness can be improved by doing an ESG analysis of companies, which includes the metrics and tools discussed in next section, to further identify investment risks and opportunities.

CHOOSING APPROPRIATE CARBON METRICS AND ALIGNMENT EVALUATION TOOLS

There are many ways to assess emissions data and evaluate both historical developments, as well as the degree of portfolio alignment towards net zero emission trajectories. Table 6.2 lists some of the most common metrics and alignment evaluation methods that can be applied to investments in listed equities and corporate debt.[9]

It should be noted that the TCFD originally proposed the market capitalisation of a company as a denominator for weighting an investment ownership or financing share. Based on recommendations from PCAF, Finance Denmark and others, it seems more appropriate to use enterprise value including cash (EVIC) as a better measure for a company's value. In fact, the TCFD references new carbon footprinting and exposure metrics based on PCAF methodologies across many different asset classes, which all are based on EVIC rather than market capitalisation even though the TCFD's own definitions are still based on market capitalisation in their latest public consultation on metrics, targets and transition plans from 2021.[10]

The advantage of using EVIC is that equity and debt investments can be measured on an equal footing, whereby a given investment should have the same carbon emissions exposure regardless of whether it is in the form of a stock or a bond. From the company's perspective, the capital structure should also be irrelevant for carbon metrics.

A weakness of using EVIC-based measures is that fluctuations in market capitalisation or the market value of debt may also cause EVIC to fluctuate without any significant changes in emissions. Thus, a stock market bubble or crash may cause the carbon footprint of a company to fall or increase dramatically without any significant change in that particular company's business practices or emissions.

A weakness of using company revenue-based metrics such as carbon intensity (CI) and weighted average carbon intensity

(WACI) is that fluctuations in revenues from cyclical businesses or, for instance, large energy price movements may cause intensity measures to change without reflecting significant real-world changes in company emissions.

The recommended measure to use, besides aiming for net zero absolute carbon emissions (CE), is the carbon footprint (CF) because of the greater stability in using EVIC compared to revenues as a denominator for a relative carbon measure. CF as a relative measure makes it comparable across different sized portfolios, and thereby makes it easier to use as a tool for setting interim targets for different types of portfolios. By having an (expectedly) more stable denominator (EVIC), it is also easier to interpret changes in this measure over time as arising primarily from changes in carbon emissions.

All the above measures have one common weakness insofar as they are backward-looking – that is, they only paint a picture of the recent carbon emissions profile of a given portfolio. If an asset owner would achieve net zero by 2050 emissions in substance, it is clearly not satisfying to steer one's portfolio by only looking in the rear-view mirror. A forward-looking measure to ensure that such a portfolio is aligned in its trajectory towards net zero emissions is clearly needed. Using a forward-looking measure would also reduce the pressure to simply "greenwash" one's portfolio by selling high emission companies and buying low emission companies.

Two such measures that can be recommended and are easy interpretable, although uncertain, are implied temperature rise (ITR) and climate value-at-risk (VaR).[11] They are both model- and scenario-based. This implies a dependency on the reliability and availability of such data from third-party providers, and leaves asset owners with the complication of dealing with missing data (as will be discussed later in the chapter). However, if a satisfactory data coverage can be achieved, they are also powerful tools for assessing portfolio alignment with a net zero trajectory, and therefore highly recommendable for both portfolio evaluation as well as identification of investment risks and opportunities on an individual company level. It is a huge advantage that these measures can be aggregated at the portfolio level as this allow for better

Table 6.2 Recommended carbon metrics and forward-looking tools for alignment evaluation for listed equities and corporate debt

Metric/tool	Unit	Formula/description	Pros	Cons
Carbon emissions (CE)	tCO_2e (tonne of carbon dioxide equivalent)	$\sum_i \frac{\text{Current value of investment}_i}{\text{Investee company's EVIC}_i} \times \text{Investee company carbon emissions}_i$	Additive. Easy to understand. Comparable across portfolio holdings.	Affected by portfolio size and in/outflows.
Carbon footprint (CF)	tCO_2e/US$ million invested	$\frac{\sum_i \frac{\text{Current value of investment}_i}{\text{Investee company's EVIC}_i} \times \text{Investee company carbon emissions}_i}{\text{Current value of all investments}}$	Relative and more stable metric. Easy to understand and interpret. Comparable across portfolio holdings. Good metric for setting intermediary targets.	Large market value fluctuations may cause huge shifts in CF from changes in EVIC without reflecting significant changes in emissions. Differences in the size of companies (ie, carbon efficiency of company) not taken into account.
Carbon intensity (CI)	tCO_2e/US$ million revenue	$\frac{\sum_n^i \left(\frac{\text{current value of investment}_i}{\text{Investee company's EVIC}_i} \times \text{issuer's GHG emissions} \right)}{\sum_n^i \left(\frac{\text{current value of investment}_i}{\text{Investee company's EVIC}_i} \times \text{issuer's \$M revenue}_i \right)}$	Relative and more stable metric. Comparable across portfolio holdings. Illustrative of company "business model"-impact on carbon.	Large energy prices swings or cyclical revenues may cause carbon intensity to fluctuate without significant changes in emissions. More complex calculation that is difficult to communicate.

Metric/tool	Unit	Formula/description	Pros	Cons
Weighted Average Carbon Intensity (WACI)	tCO_2e/US$ million revenue	$\sum_{n}^{i}\left(\frac{current\ value\ of\ investment_i}{current\ portfolio\ value}\times\frac{issuer's\ GHG\ emissions_i}{issuer's\ \$M\ revenue_i}\right)$	Recommended by the TCFD. Same as for carbon intensity. Fairly simple calculation and easy to communicate.	Same as for carbon intensity. Metric is sensitive to outliers.
Implied temperature rise (ITR)	Degrees celsius	Converts current and all future projected GHG emissions – taking into consideration each company's emission reduction plans – into an estimated rise in global temperature by 2050. ITR is calculated by comparing projected emissions with a company's fair share of a global carbon budget that remains if the world is to remain within a 2°C temperature rise by the end of the century. Follows TCFD recommendations based on IPCC data.	Forward-looking. Portfolio alignment tool. Recommended by the TCFD. Science-based. Simple interpretation.	High estimate uncertainty and dependency on model assumptions Dependency on third party data providers Difficulty of addressing missing data.
CDP temperature rating (TR)	Degrees celsius	Similar to ITR. Temperature pathways derived from the IPCC 1.5°C and the Integrated Assessment Modelling Consortium (IAMC) compiled database of climate scenarios.	Forward-looking. Portfolio alignment tool. Science-based.	Same as ITR.
Climate VaR	US$ million or percentage of portfolio value	A forward-looking and return based evaluation metric to identify climate related risks and opportunities based on scenario analysis taking into account company specific data, sector outlook data, macroeconomic impacts, climate data and climate policy outlooks.	Forward-looking. Risk measure. Identification of long-term climate-related physical and transition risks and opportunities.	High estimate uncertainty and dependency on model assumptions. Dependency on third-party data providers. Difficulty of addressing missing data.

Metric/tool	Unit	Formula/description	Pros	Cons
Transition Pathway Initiative (TPI)	Multiple measures	The TPI is a global initiative led by asset owners and supported by asset managers. Aimed at investors and free to use, it assesses companies' preparedness for the transition to a low carbon economy, supporting efforts to address climate change.	Forward-looking. Multiple assessment tools.	High estimate uncertainty and dependency on model assumptions. Dependency on third-party data providers. Difficulty of addressing missing data.
2DII (PACTA)	Multiple measures	2DII has introduced the Paris Agreement Capital Transition Assessment (PACTA) tool. The PACTA tool provides multiple types of reports based on forward-looking data to assess the overall alignment of investor portfolios with various climate scenarios and the Paris Agreement.	Forward-looking. Multiple assessment tools.	High estimate uncertainty and dependency on model assumptions. Dependency on third-party data providers. Difficulty of addressing missing data.

Sources: TCFD (2021a; 2021b); Finance Denmark (2020); MSCI, CDP, 2DII and TPI. Formulas are author's own updated versions based on TCFD and Finance Denmark guidance

comparability of different portfolios: "What can be measured, can be better managed".[12]

In addition, there are also comprehensive solutions from the Transition Pathway Initiative (TPI) and the 2 Degrees Investing Initiative (2DII), which both provide more detailed alignment evaluation reports and assessments of climate risks and opportunities for companies that may inform and support portfolio construction. Finally, the Science Based Targets initiative (SBTi) evaluates individual companies' own net zero targets, and provides certification when these targets are found to be ambitious and credible enough to be aligned with the Paris Agreement objectives.

GATHERING RELEVANT DATA AND ADDRESSING MISSING DATA

With poor data, or even lack thereof, being the biggest obstacle towards constructing ESG relevant portfolios, investors are forced to adopt a pragmatic and iterative approach towards collecting and assessing emissions data. Some of the more widely used data providers for comprehensive and continually updated ESG data are MSCI, Morningstar, Sustainalytics, S&P Sustainable 1, Moody's ESG Solutions and Bloomberg, to mention but a few. Their data generally cover a wide set of environmental (including emissions data), social and governance metrics. In addition, corporate controversies are being monitored. Coverage is very high and increasing for listed instruments such as stocks and bonds, especially within the developed world.[13] Consider which data provider(s) cover your investment universe best.[14]

For investments in the developing world and non-listed investments, emissions data are much more limited. In addition, many listed (mostly fixed income) securities are constantly being created out of newly formed subsidiaries or affiliate companies that are yet to be "mapped" to their relevant operating company by the data providers. Other changes to corporate structures such as mergers and acquisitions (M&A), joint ventures and spin-offs may also not be recognised and "mapped" by the data providers until after they have become part of an investor portfolio.

It is hence almost impossible to get 100% emissions data coverage even if an investor portfolio is based on listed securities from companies that all report emissions data. So, what is an investor to do when getting only a partial picture of one's portfolio emissions from the biggest data providers?

Here are the options that asset owners should consider for portfolio positions that do not have any emissions data:

- identify whether the position simply needs to be "mapped" correctly (ie, linked to the relevant portfolio company or project);
- use reliable third-party data provider estimates for the company;
- use reliable third-party data provider averages for the sector;
- create your own estimates;
- "normalise" your emissions data using sampling techniques; and
- make a list of your top emitting positions ordered by descending total estimated carbon emissions, and investigate directly with the company or project whether there may be actual carbon emissions data available or more reliable estimates can be obtained.

It is obviously essential to track the exact source of your emissions data, whether reported or estimated. For estimates, it is also important to keep track of what method has been applied. Using a data priority waterfall is a good idea (see Figure 6.4). When reported and perhaps even audited data from the underlying company or investment project is not available, there should be an independent assessment of what kind of estimates to use and how to prioritise them. This would, of course, depend on your own continued

Figure 6.4 An example of a data priority waterfall structure for listed equities or corporate bond (with example data coverage indicated in parentheses)

Table 6.3 An illustrative example of emissions data source coverage for an asset owner

Data category	Bonds	Stock	Total
Reported	**63.03%**	**89.03%**	**85.92%**
MSCI reported	59.87%	88.48%	85.06%
Bloomberg reported	3.16%	0.55%	0.86%
Estimated	**36.97%**	**10.97%**	**14.08%**
MSCI E.Segmt-Moderate	5.79%	4.35%	4.52%
MSCI E.CSI	8.26%	3.85%	4.37%
Internal Model	15.18%	0.33%	2.10%
MSCI E.Segm-Moderately High	2.09%	1.02%	1.15%
MSCI E.Segmt-Moderately Low	1.66%	0.85%	0.94%
MSCI E.Segmt-Low	3.47%	0.57%	0.92%
MSCI E.Segmt-High	0.50%	0.00%	0.07%
Bloomberg estimated	0.02%	0.00%	0.01%
Total	**100.00%**	**100.00%**	**100.00%**

evaluation of the reliability of different sources of estimates. Any given prioritisation could also differ, say between asset classes or even between regional or sector estimates. The important thing is to formalise this priority list for any given type of position to ensure consistency of the data.

Normalising your data means, in effect, that you treat your investment position with unknown emissions as if it had the same emissions profile as your similar investments with known emissions. This may function as a last resort for estimating unknown carbon emissions if none of the higher priority sources seem reliable or viable. Normalising could also best be justified if the position is very small and not a source of expected heavy emissions. As with any statistical sampling method, one should balance relevant "population" group size with having close characteristics with the sample investment in question. Therefore, controlling for sector, geography and company size would be a good starting point.

Finally, an investor who wants to continually improve on their data quality for estimated emissions data should investigate, say, the top 15 heaviest estimated emitters more deeply on a recurring basis. While the gathering of data in all the steps in Figure 6.4 can be automated, it makes sense to verify the quality of the estimated most impactful emitters in a more hands on way.

In reality, a third-party data provider could (temporarily) miss reported – and even audited – data from the underlying company or investment project in question. An investor may sometimes successfully obtain carbon emissions data from a company when reaching out to their investor relations department, even if they have not been registered by third-party data providers. When such numbers are not provided by companies, a direct investor request for such disclosure may in any case influence or accelerate the companies' decisions to disclose. A growing number of companies are committing to report ESG, and especially climate-related data.

For estimated emissions data, it can also happen on occasion that a comparison between multiple third-party estimates reveals huge disparities in emissions numbers. Asset owners should therefore continually seek to improve on the reliability of estimated emissions data, particularly for heavy emitters.

MAPPING THE DISTRIBUTION OF A PORTFOLIO'S EMISSIONS ACROSS HOLDINGS

With emissions data in place, it is possible to profile how one's portfolio holdings are contributing to the chosen key performance indicator (KPIs). It turns out that most diversified portfolios follow a "power law", whereby a select few positions account for a disproportionally large share of total carbon emissions and thus a portfolio's CF and WACI as well.

To illustrate this, consider an article from the Bank for International Settlements (BIS) where a reported study rated around 16,000 firms on a carbon intensity scale, ranging from the "greenest" GGGGG to the "most polluting" PPPPP companies (Ehlers, Mojon and Packer, 2020). Table 6.4 illustrates the uneven rating category sizes along a percentile scale for carbon intensity, and Figure 6.5 illustrates the distribution of total emission by rating.

To quote the results from the study: "Even though our PPPPP rating bucket contains only the 1% of firms with the highest carbon intensities, these are responsible for close to 40% of total Scopes 1–3 emissions in 2018". It is very likely that a diversified investor

Table 6.4 Carbon intensity (tCO2e/US$m of revenue) distribution

Green rating – carbon intensity cutoff points										
Financial year 2018										Table 1
	Rating label									
	GGGGG	**GGGG**	**GGG**	**GG**	**G**	**P**	**PP**	**PPP**	**PPPP**	**PPPPP**
Percentile of carbon intensity distribution	5th	25th	50th	75th	85th	90th	95th	97.5th	99th	>99th
Threshold Scopes 1–3 carbon intensity*	50	133	401	985	1,847	3,112	6,293	9,128	16,812	>16,812
Rounded threshold Scopes 1–3 carbon intensity*	50	130	400	1,000	1,800	3,100	6,300	9,100	17,000	>17,000

* In tonnes of CO_2 per US$ million of revenue. Includes both upstream and downstream Scope 3 data.
Source: Ehlers, Mojon and Packer (2020)

Figure 6.5 Share of total emissions by carbon intensity rating

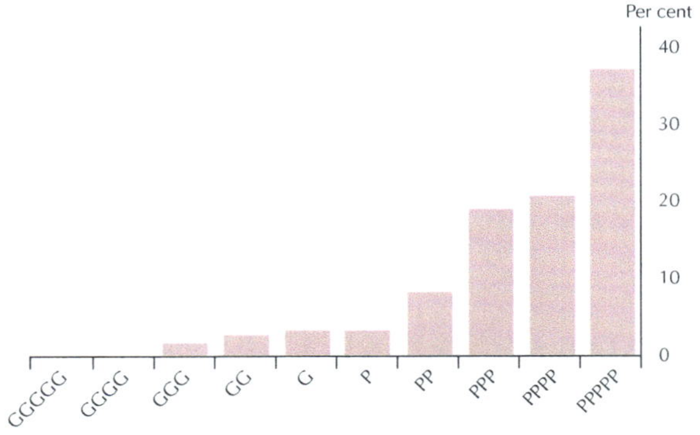

Source: Ehlers, Mojon and Packer (2020)

portfolio will have a profile that is qualitatively similar to the distribution found in this study, with heavy emitters mainly located in the "priority sectors".

ASSESSING PORTFOLIO IMPLICATIONS

Therefore, what are the portfolio implications of having gathered a clearer picture of the carbon emissions stance of one's portfolio in terms of achieving net zero? The first obvious consideration for investors who intend to fulfil on their net zero ambitions is of course to take a closer look at one's likely concentrated set of existing high emission holdings, as well as taking a more selective look at potential investments that are carbon intensive today by integrating climate-related data into the investment analysis.

Broadly, there seems to be two types of strategies for achieving net zero (Edward and Davies, 2021).

- Reduction techniques: Investors here aim to reduce portfolio emissions as much as possible and as soon as possible. This, in effect, means that investors sell high emitting assets or reduce emissions in other ways. These may include short-selling, buying green-labelled securities and buying carbon offsets.
- Alignment strategies: Investors main focus here is on long-term decarbonisation. This means that even positions with high emissions today are considered for portfolio inclusion if the

companies or assets in question are deemed to have credible and meaningful decarbonisation strategies or determined to be susceptible to an effective engagement strategy that can encourage a company's increased effort to reduce GHG emissions. With this strategy, investors may even aim to create a portfolio that is aligned with a credible transition pathway towards net zero emissions by at least 2050 – and by doing so contribute towards achieving real-world reductions in carbon emissions.

While reduction strategies reduce reported portfolio emissions, alignment strategies are obviously the right choice for investors who intend to fulfil on their net zero ambitions while contributing to real-world emission reductions. Therefore, rather than changing the sector composition of an investor portfolio – a likely by-product of a reduction strategy – an alignment strategy would seek to focus on being more selective towards company exposures within sectors.

Are there opportunities to replace top emitters in the so-called "priority sectors" with other investments in the same sectors with similar (or better) return/risk characteristics, but a much healthier transition pathway for carbon emissions? By focusing on top percentile emitters, an investor may reduce carbon exposure or at least improve the portfolio emissions trajectory without a significant worsening of the overall return/risk profile.[15] Further, there should be a distinction made between heavy emitters who are actively and ambitiously moving to decarbonise from those who are not.

Investors should also question whether the potentially substantial transition risks faced by some of the most polluting companies in terms of emissions are fully reflected in today's market valuations. Fines or new stricter regulations from governments or organisations with oversight of these companies may be very difficult to predict but could still have a fundamental impact on those companies' business models. As an example, take the ruling in 2021 where Royal Dutch Shell was ordered by the district court in The Hague to ensure its net carbon emissions were 45% lower in 2030 than in 2019 (Raval, 2021). Other transition risks may occur in the form of litigation risk, risks of increasing financing costs to portfolio companies from changing investor preferences, and the imposition of carbon taxes or emissions quotas.

The advantage of using a more nuanced investment approach with a more careful company selection that better accounts for both physical and transition risks is not only the avoidance of large potential investment losses. Companies that actively work to decarbonise and focus on adjusting business models towards more sustainable practices may become "sector champions" and obtain premium valuations. By owning or financing such companies, even if they are heavy emitters today, investors may hold positions with exposure to priority sectors that have falling carbon footprints over time and potentially earn above average risk-adjusted returns.

It may be helpful to categorise top portfolio emitters into laggards, learners and leaders in portfolio construction to continually assess whether exclusion, an active ownership strategy or simple inclusion is warranted (see Table 6.5).

As a general observation, an investor must also be mindful of their portfolio composition across asset classes and the trends in portfolio emissions over time. In general, equities have in terms of market share been shifting from high emission, capital-intensive companies towards more asset-light business sectors, such as technology, healthcare services and pharmaceuticals, with far lower emissions. If this mega-trend continues or does not reverse, one could reasonably expect carbon footprints or carbon intensities to fall over time on a diversified equity portfolio – even with unchanged allocations.[16]

Fixed income corporate debt seems to be weighted more towards capital-intensive sectors that tend to have higher emission

Table 6.5 Categorisation of top portfolio emitters that already meet required risk/return objectives

Emissions category	Implications for portfolio holding
Laggard	Consider active ownership Substitution of investment within sector to other company or asset with similar (or better) return/risk characteristics and a better expected decarbonisation pathway, possibly due to an active ownership approach
Learner	Consider active ownership
Leader	Keep position

intensities. According to Bloomberg, the utilities, materials, industrials and energy sectors comprise 24% of global debt. In comparison, these sectors comprise 16% of, for instance, the S&P 500. Furthermore, the capital and emissions light technology sector comprises 3% of global debt, compared to 28% for the S&P 500.[17]

However, with the introduction of sustainable finance instruments, as defined by the International Capital Markets Association (ICMA), there may be complimentary ways for debt investors to align their portfolios towards net zero emissions (at least in substance) in addition to using the earlier discussed metrics and alignment evaluation tools. More on that later.

SETTING THRESHOLD LEVELS FOR INVESTMENT EXCLUSIONS

An investor may also, for more ethical reasons or to adjust according to evolving stakeholder values, choose to restrict investments in certain business practices that are deemed to be particularly controversial, polluting and/or unsustainable. Examples of those relevant to an investor with a net zero portfolio emissions ambition in mind are:

- unconventional oil and gas production, including shale gas and tar sands;
- coal production and processing, including energy production from thermal coal and production of liquid fuels and petrochemicals from coal; and
- Arctic drilling.

It should be noted that decisions to restrict the investor universe limits an investor's flexibility in constructing portfolios and should therefore, all else being equal, be expected to deteriorate portfolio return/risk characteristics.[18]

By adopting a zero-tolerance policy towards certain business practices and operating with exclusion lists on companies that have any links to controversial business practices, an investor runs the risk of excluding potential future "sector champions" that are committing to transition towards more sustainable business practices. When excluding, for instance, companies associated with energy production from thermal coal, an investor will also exclude a very large portion of existing energy companies.[19] That includes large integrated energy companies where thermal coal is a minor, and perhaps even decreasing, part of their income source. This holds especially true for emerging market investments where the current reliance on thermal coal is much higher for energy production than in the developed world.

It may in fact be more sensible to avoid simply excluding most large energy companies, and to recognise and include potential or established "sector champions" in the investment opportunity set. As a practical matter, investors should instead consider setting thresholds for how big a share of revenues controversial business practices may account for in underlying companies to be considered "material" or even warrant exclusion.

There are advantages to adopting a threshold rather than a pure zero-tolerance approach. One is that investments are not exposed to forced selling from event risks such as M&A activity or the news indication that a given portfolio company has exposure to controversial business practices, such as oil sands production or energy generated from thermal coal. Thresholds create room for nuances and issues that committed net zero investors should think about in terms of balancing the day one "KPI costs" of having exposures to currently heavy emitters with participating in investments that do credibly follow the right path towards net carbon neutrality and potentially earn above average risk-adjusted returns.

Is it sensible to divest from an integrated energy company that has 2% of revenues generated from oil sands production? Or, say, 30% of revenues attributed to the use of thermal coal for energy production? What if the company purchases or creates "carbon offsets" corresponding to the emissions coming from thermal coal? Should companies based in emerging economies be evaluated by the same thresholds as those based in developed economies?

No simple answer exists to these types of questions, but they should be considered nonetheless to establish acceptable levels for thresholds on company emissions or business practices. It is a balancing act between adhering to ethical or moral-based values and keeping investment room for "transitional" investment opportunities. Emerging market countries and companies should be able to undergo a "just transition" from extractive economies to regenerative and sustainable economies even when their starting point for doing so is much lower than for the developed countries and companies. Obviously, there should be exclusion policies made in cases where certain business practices or company behaviours are deemed to be egregious and cross certain "red lines", such as violating basic human rights or other moral values held by an asset owner.

As mentioned, simply divesting does not in itself solve the world's emissions problems. It only results in a transfer of emission "ownership". By leaving room for investments into (potentially emerging) "sector champions", an investor may also contribute to lowering emissions in substance without sacrificing returns or distorting sector allocations. It could be argued that an energy company based on burning fossil fuels that cuts emissions in half (through its conversion towards renewables) does more for the environment (in terms of absolute emission reduction) than, say, a software company with an already very low emissions baseline would by going to net zero (and thus reducing net emission by 100%). Of course, both outcomes should be welcomed.

When allowing exposures into high emitting companies, an investor should investigate whether any given company is moving in a more sustainable direction and with adequate speed to be on the right path towards becoming a net- zero emissions company by 2050. Just as "portfolio emissions" may be easily reduced by simply divesting from portfolio holdings, underlying companies themselves may also reduce their thermal coal exposures by simply selling their coal-related assets (which does nothing to reduce global emissions) rather than winding them down (which does). Asset owners should be mindful of such practices as well and, if worthwhile, engage with companies to consider the latter option.

There may also be win–win situations in owning stakes in "sector laggards" if an investor can reasonably expect to impact and affect a company's strategy towards more environmentally sustainable practices via active engagement, while at the same time earning a risk-adjusted return premium for doing so.[20] When pursuing this road, the UN endorsed Climate Action 100+, which consists of the world's leading asset owner and asset managers, providing a good investor forum for implementing a coordinated and science-informed engagement strategy.[21]

On the fixed income side, many traditional energy companies and utilities that have historically had operations based on coal production are beginning to issue green or sustainability bonds to finance investments into renewables. These are investments that are directly financing the transition towards clean energy. In fact, more and more energy companies and utilities are phasing out coal and committing to become net carbon neutral by 2050 or earlier.[22] Therefore, even with unchanged investment allocations, portfolio emissions (at least measured in terms of intensity) should be expected to fall over time for exposure to such companies, reducing one's need to make drastic changes to portfolio composition.

There are useful third parties that may help inform investors on whether a company's stated emissions targets are ambitious and realistic. One such party is the SBTi, which evaluates and opines on how aligned such company targets are to a 1.5° degree temperature rise scenario.[23] An example for a second party opinion (SPO) provider that evaluates companies who fund themselves through sustainability-linked bonds (SLB) is CICERO. The firm opines on the ambitiousness of the carbon emissions targets used in SLBs.[24] SLBs often contain targets for GHG emissions reductions, especially for companies in the energy sector and utilities. There are also practical ways to implement thresholds on revenue sources within portfolio companies. Some third-party ESG data providers such as MSCI provide data on figures, including share of revenue derived from thermal coal or oil sands.

CONSIDERING PORTFOLIO HOLDINGS IN SUSTAINABLE FINANCE (SUSTAINABLE BONDS)

Sustainable bonds, as described by the ICMA, are comprised of green bonds, social bonds, sustainability bonds and SLBs.[25] The first three types of these are (in their purest form) forward-looking due to their use of the proceeds principle whereby any issued bond is financing specific (ideally new) investment into sustainable business practices.[26] While there are uncertainties regarding how to properly account for such instruments in the backward-looking emission measures (CE, CF, CI and WACI), it is clear that the emissions profile of assets financed by green and sustainable bonds may very likely differ from the overall emissions profile of a given portfolio company.

Consider, for instance, green bonds issued by the German utility RWE whose operations are segmented into wind and solar energy, then hydro, biomass and gas, and finally coal and nuclear.[27] While the bonds are exclusively used to finance investments in renewables (RWE, 2020), current emissions accounting would (as of November 2021) still be based on the entire company's emissions reported in the annual report.[28] Reported emissions in this case would clearly be overstated.

It seems possible that a distinction between measuring emissions for conventional and sustainable finance instruments would be made in future guidance, perhaps from the TCFD. In fact, PCAF has proposed a framework for carbon accounting for green bonds that will require a disclosure and distinction of carbon emissions from activities financed by them. This proposed framework is being developed through public consultation.[29] In the meantime, asset owners should make this distinction clear in their emissions reporting by, for instance, also showing emission KPIs, excluding green and sustainable bonds and/or the share of green and sustainable bonds within fixed income portfolios, and perhaps even within "priority sectors".

A simpler measure would be to exclude emissions on green and sustainable bonds in emissions numbers but to include them in portfolio value numbers. Thus, CF or WACI would be "ex emissions attributed to green and sustainable bonds". The effect of owning green and sustainable bonds within utilities, transportation and the energy sector is obviously material for what real portfolio emissions would be as opposed to reported emissions.

As the stylised Figure 6.6 shows, a fixed income investor may experience increased reported CO_2e emissions due to the purchase of, or rebalancing into, green or sustainable bonds, even though emissions attributed to the investor's holdings of conventional bonds are declining. True total emissions should be somewhere in between emissions from conventional bonds alone and total reported emissions since emissions from green or sustainable bonds are very low, but not necessarily zero. Investors who wish to truly align their portfolios towards a net zero trajectory should report and illustrate these issues until a proper accounting for emissions standard has been established for such instruments.

When using the more practical carbon footprint measured in tonCO_2e/US\$m invested, investors should at least use a measure that excludes "green or sustainable emissions" in the numerator

Figure 6.6 Stylised example of the effect of additional investments into green bonds

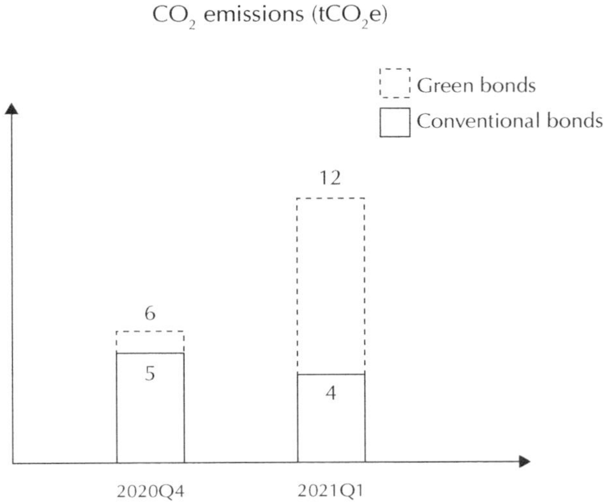

but includes investment value in the denominator. Reporting such a measure illustrates the range within which true carbon emission are likely to be by providing a bottom. In addition, an "ex green or sustainable carbon emissions" measure does not penalise asset owners for investing in assets that contribute to the transition towards net zero emissions even if the issuing companies are in high emission sectors (se Figure 6.7).

By illustrating these issues, fixed income investors should therefore not simply divest from "priority sectors" and as a result increase portfolio tracking error, but rather think carefully about using sustainable finance instruments to uphold sector diversification. This issue is, however, a major stumbling block for achieving the NZAOA's milestone CO_2e reduction target of 16 to –29% by 2025.

The price for switching from conventional bonds into green or sustainability bonds still seems relatively small (and perhaps with less risks associated in doing so). A meta study that reviewed all estimates on the so-called "greenium" (green premium) found that, on average, it ranged from –1 to –9 basis points (MacAskill *et al*, 2021).

Figure 6.7 An illustrative example of the carbon emissions profile of a sustainable fixed income portfolio with and without green emissions excluded

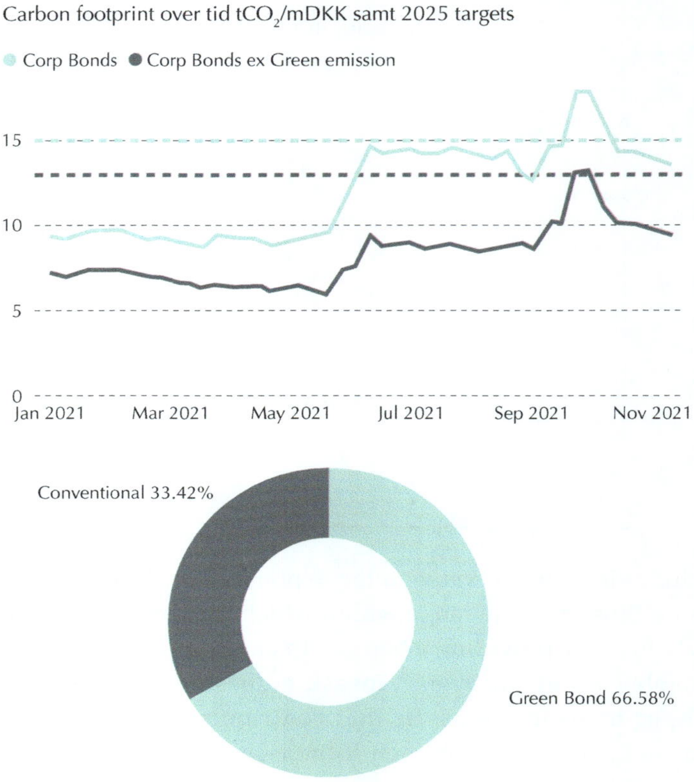

Note: Portfolio is a sustainable fixed income portfolio, 66% invested in green bonds mainly in priority sectors with a focus on long-term sustainability

CONCLUSION: TYING IT ALL TOGETHER BY CONSTRUCTING A 2050 NET ZERO EMISSIONS ALIGNED PORTFOLIO

The challenge for asset owners aiming to align their investment portfolios towards a trajectory that reaches net zero emissions by 2050 is a very practical matter in terms of implementing a measurement framework for portfolio emissions. Here, the first step would be to set up credible intermediary emission reductions targets, such as those five-year milestones suggested by the UN-convened NZAOA.

In addition to identifying total carbon emissions as a KPI,

investors would be well served by utilising relative measures such as CF and WACI, which are independent of portfolio size and therefore useful for comparison across portfolios. With the right KPIs in place, investors can then identify focus areas. By mapping out emissions distributions across sectors, asset classes or other dimensions, asset owners with a diversified portfolio are likely to find that emissions follow a power law with very few positions accounting for an outsized share of emissions.

In terms of portfolio construction, the challenge for investors who aim to reduce emissions now lies in balancing a few different trade-offs. Obviously, implementing exclusionary policies could quickly reduce portfolio emissions with a few divestments from high emissions companies. However, such policies, if implemented too broadly, have a few downsides.

- By divesting, an investor is merely transferring "ownership" of emissions to a new owner, and thus only reducing emission accounted for rather than reducing real-world emissions.
- There is some evidence to suggest that the potential worsening of the return/risk profile from an increase in tracking error of a diversified portfolio is very low initially. For larger increases in tracking error, the potential price in terms of lower returns/ higher risks are increasing exponentially.
- Investors run the risk of excluding companies in "priority sectors" that are moving in the right direction and who may be part of the solution towards reaching net zero emissions. Such "sector champions" may in some cases already have committed themselves towards reaching net carbon neutrality by 2050 (or even earlier), and provide massive capital expenditures into research and development (R&D) and building renewable energy or other low-emitting energy generation capacity.

A practical way to take advantage of such nuances would therefore be to consider using thresholds (in terms of share of revenues or other relevant comparable metrics) on certain high emission or controversial business practices. This would have the benefit of limiting sector concentration build-up in the remaining non-priority sectors. It should also be recognised that simply buying "best in class" investments may not at all times be the optimal investment strategy for achieving the best risk-adjusted returns, as these business traits may have already been "priced in". On the other hand, owning business that do in fact transition significantly towards sustainable business practices from a poorer initial standpoint may sometimes yield better investment returns and contribute to greater total carbon emissions reductions over time than already efficient and well-run companies.[30]

To guide investment decisions in high emission companies, it may be helpful to classify these within the proposed categories of laggards, learners and leaders. Here, opportunities to engage in active ownership towards improving companies' environmental impact (as well as other ESG factors) may justify investments in laggards or learners by increasing their expected risk-adjusted returns while keeping an investment portfolio aligned to a net zero trajectory.

When adopting a forward-looking framework, there are helpful measures and Paris-alignment evaluation tools available for identifying sustainable companies. Those are the measures implied temperature rating and climate VaR. In addition, tools are provided by TPI, SBTi and 2DII's PACTA. In fact, a portfolio-level implied temperature rating below 2 degrees, and preferably no more than 1.5 degrees, may serve as a good target if a high enough data coverage allows it.

Finally, by keeping room for allocations into "priority sectors" and identifying companies with credible transition plans towards sustainable business practices, fixed income investors may consider substituting their traditional bonds with sustainable finance instruments such as green bonds or sustainability bonds (and, in the future, by the EU Green Bond Standard). One may even argue that thresholds should be "waivered" or set much higher for "use of proceeds" based green bonds or sustainability bonds when such proceeds bypass high emission business practices covered by those given thresholds.

Still, there remains many unanswered questions.

- There does not yet seem to be a consensus on the proper emissions accounting for green bonds or sustainability bonds.
- It is still being debated whether non-renewables such as nuclear power may qualify for inclusion into a future version of the EU

Green Taxonomy due to improvements in technology that may deal with both hazardous waste issues and the risk and consequences of meltdowns (World Nuclear News, 2021).[31]

- The use of carbon offset or carbon sinks that remove carbon from the atmosphere are likely to become a bigger and more recognised part of companies' business practices. Although there are some serious issues in terms of lack of oversight and varying credibility in many of today's use cases of carbon offsets, they are a critical piece in the broader quest to build a carbon neutral world (Finucane, 2021; Hodgson and Nauman, 2021).

Recognising and being mindful of issues that in substance contribute to a reduction in portfolio emissions may be a sensible way for forward-looking investors to position themselves for future improvements in generally used methods to account for portfolio emission and sustainable investments.

APPENDIX 6.1 SECTOR DISTRIBUTIONS

Table 6.6 Global debt (US$m)

	Outstanding amt	Num. issuers	% of all	% of all ex govt
All	116,673,081	34,540	100%	
Communications	1,779,787	806	2%	5%
Consumer discretionary	2,837,512	3,551	2%	7%
Consumer staples	1,276,167	1,170	1%	3%
Energy	2,058,842	1,490	2%	5%
Financials	21,280,448	13,160	18%	55%
Healthcare	1,407,911	1,093	1%	4%
Industrials	3,283,973	4,942	3%	8%
Materials	1,288,718	1,654	1%	3%
Technology	1,109,638	1,072	1%	3%
Utilities	2,522,174	2,251	2%	6%
Government	77,827,910	3,351	67%	

Source: MAPD function in Bloomberg: "Global Debt Map", November 2021

Figure 6.8 S&P 500 sector breakdown

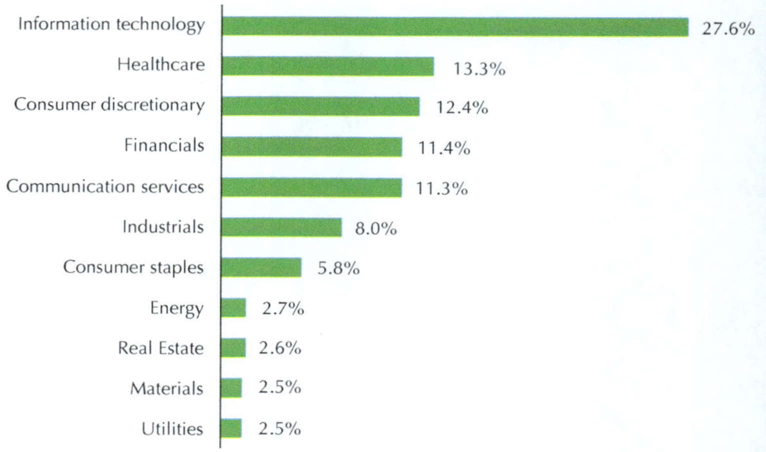

The author would like to thank his former colleagues in the investment department at PensionDanmark for helpful comments and valuable inputs. Particular thanks go to Erik Bennike, Head of Credits, and Jan Kæraa Rasmussen for sharing your insights. This chapter represents my own opinions and impressions, and is not necessarily reflective of my former or current employers' views. All data shown are for illustrative purposes only and do not reflect the particulars of my former or current employer.

1 The latest 2020 UK Stewardship Code from the Financial Reporting Council (FRC) lists its Principle 7 for asset owners and asset managers as: "Signatories systematically integrate stewardship and investment, including material environmental, social and governance issues, and climate change, to fulfil their responsibilities". Principles 9–12 cover engagement and voting activities (see https://www.frc.org.uk/getattachment/5aae591d-d9d3-4cf4-814a-d14e156a1d87/Stewardship-Code_Final2.pdf).

2 See https://www.stockholmresilience.org/research/planetary-boundaries.html.

3 Financial organisations may be members in more than one alliance. Therefore, the sum of assets represented by each alliance may supersede the total represented amount of assets by GFANZ.

4 See the Greenhouse Gas Protocol website (https://ghgprotocol.org/standards/scope-3-standard) or Funk (2020).

5 The often-cited intermediary target of a 50% emissions reduction by 2030 comes from the Intergovernmental Panel on Climate Change (IPCC), although it is from a baseline of 2019 levels.

6 See UNEP FI and PRI (2021). It should be noted that one reason for the NZAOA's intermediary targets being stated as intervals is that some investor groups have already implemented active restrictions on investments into energy companies that engage in controversial and high emission business practices by burning or extracting thermal coal and oil sands. It is clearly easier for investors that still have exposures to these companies to reduce their portfolio emissions by a wider margin than for those that do not have any exposure.

7 See IPCC (2018) on the impacts of global warming of 1.5°C above pre-industrial levels and related global GHG emission pathways in the context of strengthening the global response to the threat of climate change, sustainable development and efforts to eradicate poverty.

8 Consider the International Energy Agency (IEA) and their own roadmap to net carbon neutrality for the energy sector by 2050. On their website, they state that: "Most of the reductions in CO2 emissions through 2030 come from technologies already on the market today. But in 2050, almost half the reductions come from technologies that are currently at the demonstration or prototype phase. Major innovation efforts must take place this decade in order to bring these new technologies to market in time." (IEA, 2021).

9 See TCFD (2021) and the table for carbon footprint metrics for financed emissions (p. 72), and the original carbon footprint metric based on market capitalisation (Table 3C, p. 73). For the rationale on using EVIC, see PCAF (2020).

10 See TCFD (2021); PCAF (2020), including Box 5: "Rationale for EVIC as denominator in the attribution factor".

11 CDP provides a metric called the CDP temperature rating, which has a similar interpretation to ITR and is also measured in degrees celsius.

12 Derived from a quote usually attributed to Peter Drucker: "What gets measured, gets managed", although the exact meaning in this case is different.

13 For instance, MSCI states that their climate data coverage spans "more than 9,600 companies including large, mid and small cap developed and emerging market equities, as well as investment grade, high-yield and emerging market fixed income issuers; 198 countries for select/relevant metrics" (https://www.msci.com/our-solutions/esg-investing/climate-solutions/climate-data-metrics).

14 There are many different ESG data providers, including but not limited to Bloomberg,

Sustainalytics, MSCI, ISS, RepRisk, Truvalue Labs, FTSE Russell, Thomson Reuters, Vigeo Eiris, Inrate, Carbon Disclosure Project (CDP) and S&P (including Trucost).

15 Blitz and Swinkels (2021) estimates the effect of the first 1% point increase in the tracking error of a diversified equity portfolio to result in an expected return loss of one basis point. A tracking error of 3% points results in a 10 basis point lowering of expected returns. Of course, this only holds if divestments from exclusions are redirected to poorer substitute investments with worse return/risk profiles.

16 For a good visualisation of this, see Desjardins (2019). The data source is Global Financial Data.

17 From Bloomberg (Global Debt Map, November 2021) and SIFMA (2021); see also Appendix 6.1.

18 One study on developed market high-yield bonds by AQR illustrates how *ex ante* return capture falls from an initial 100% level by only a few percentage points when the carbons emissions profile in the portfolio is up to almost 60% lower than the benchmark emissions with minimal portfolio distortion. For higher relative reductions, return capture falls much quicker. This effect is obviously a consequence of the power law distribution for emissions mentioned earlier (see Diep, Pomorski and Richardson, 2021).

19 According to IEA (2018), coal's share of the global electricity generation was 38% in 2018.

20 An example of an ongoing engagement strategy against a major energy company is that of the hedge fund Engine no. 1 vs Exxon Mobil. Engine no. 1 managed to get three of their own four board member nominees elected in a proxy fight pushing for the company to commit to a net zero emissions plan by 2050 (Matthews and Glazer, 2021).

21 See https://www.climateaction100.org.

22 For instance, Enel Group is phasing out coal by 2030: "Enel boosts its 2030 greenhouse gas emission reduction target to 80% from 70%, SBTi-certified" (Enel Group, 2020), and RWE is aiming for carbon neutrality by 2040 (RWE, 2019).

23 The SBTi is a partnership between CDP, the United Nations Global Compact, World Resources Institute (WRI) and the World Wide Fund (WWF), see https://sciencebasedtargets.org/about-us.

24 CICERO Shades of Green provides second opinions on SLBs (see https://cicero.green/slbs), sustainable finance instruments as described by ICMA.

25 See https://www.icmagroup.org/sustainable-finance/. It should be noted that a EU Green Bond Standard (EUGBS) is also under development after a proposal by the European Commission (see https://ec.europa.eu/info/business-economy-euro/banking-and-finance/sustainable-finance/european-green-bond-standard_en).

26 Companies may simply relabel existing assets as "green" and use the proceeds from refinancing activities towards the servicing of these assets. A relabelling of existing assets does not in itself change company emissions. In their purest form, green bonds finance new capital expenditures into new climate-friendly projects and thereby reduce a company's carbon footprint or emission intensity on the margin. The difficulty of sub-dividing emissions between a company's assets is probably a reason why it can be a challenge to distinguish between "emission ownership" of green bonds and conventional bonds.

27 See https://www.rwe.com/en/investor-relations/reasons-to-invest/key-data.

28 At least there does not yet seem to be a consensus on how emissions should be calculated for sustainable finance instruments. Ehlers, Mojon and Packer (2020) discuss some of the drawbacks from not properly accounting for carbon emissions from green bonds on an instrument level. Rather, emissions from green bonds are not distinguished from those from traditional bonds even though green bond funds are earmarked for sustainable and therefore (most likely) low emission business practices. According to Alliance Bernstein (Lamdour and Wong, 2021), no distinction is made between green and conventional bonds in terms of measuring emissions: "existing carbon intensity reporting tools do not differentiate between carbon footprints from conventional bonds and those from green bonds or other ESG bond structures".

29 PCAF launched a public consultation on three new draft methods and a discussion paper on capital market instruments (see https://carbonaccountingfinancials.com/newsitem/public-consultation-three-draft-methods-capital-market-instruments#newsitemtext).

30 Brøgger and Kronies (2021) document for equity investors how predicting ESG ratings or score upgrades may yield better returns than remaining invested in top quartile ESG companies.

31 European Union lawmakers have since voted to allow natural gas and nuclear energy to be labeled as green investments https://www.bloomberg.com/news/articles/2022-07-06/eu-lawmakers-remove-last-hurdle-for-gas-nuclear-as-green

REFERENCES

Blitz, D. and L. Swinkels, 2021, "Does Excluding Sin Stocks Cost Performance?", *Journal of Sustainable Finance & Investment,* September (available at https://www.tandfonline.com/doi/full/10.1080/20430795.2021.1972789).

Brøgger, A. and A. Kronies, 2021, "Skills and Sentiment in Sustainable Investing", Copenhagen Business School, August 27 (available at https://papers.ssrn.com/sol3/papers.cfm?abstract_id=3531312).

CDP, 2021, "SMEs Equipped to Join Race to Net-zero with Dedicated Climate Disclosure Framework", November 25 (available at https://www.cdp.net/en/articles/companies/smes-equipped-to-join-race-to-net-zero-with-dedicated-climate-disclosure-framework).

Cusmano, L., 2017, "Small, Medium, Strong. Trends in SME Performance and Business Conditions", OECD (available at https://read.oecd-ilibrary.org/industry-and-services/small-medium-strong-trends-in-sme-performance-and-business-conditions_9789264275683-en#page3).

Desjardins, J., 2019, "Visualizing 200 Years of U.S. Stock Market Sectors", Visual Capitalist, January 25 (available at https://www.visualcapitalist.com/200-years-u-s-stock-market-sectors/).

Diep, P., L. Pomorski and S. A. Richardson, 2021, "Sustainable Systematic Credit", September 7, AQR (available at https://www.aqr.com/Insights/Research/Working-Paper/Sustainable-Systematic-Credit).

Edward, C. and Z. Davies, 2021, "Net Zero Investing: The Other 'Tragedy of the Horizon'", Barclays Research/ESG Research.

Ehlers, T., B. Mojon and F. Packer, 2020, "Green Bonds and Carbon Emissions: Exploring the Case for a Rating System at the Firm Level", *BIS Quarterly Review,* September 14 (available at https://www.bis.org/publ/qtrpdf/r_qt2009c.htm).

Enel Group, 2020, "Enel Boosts its 2030 Greenhouse Gas Emission Reduction Target to 80% from 70%, SBTi-certified", October 30 (available at https://www.enel.com/media/explore/search-press-releases/press/2020/10/enel-boosts-its-2030-greenhouse-gas-emission-reduction-target-to-80-from-70-sbti-certified).

Finance Denmark, 2020, "Framework for Financed Emissions Accounting: Principles and Methods", November (available at https://finansdanmark.dk/media/47145/finance-denmark-co2-model.pdf).

Finucane, A., 2021, "Carbon Offsets Can Help in the Transition to Net Zero", *Financial Times,* June 8 (available at https://www.ft.com/content/62da50a8-2d89-4bae-8369-5fec1be66b05).

Funk, C. M., 2020, "Carbon Footprinting: An Investor Toolkit", State Street Global Advisers, September (available at https://www.ssga.com/library-content/pdfs/insights/carbon-footprinting-an-anvestor-toolkit.pdf).

Hodgson, C. and B. Nauman, 2021, "Carbon Offsets: A Licence to Pollute or a Path to Net Zero Emissions?", *Financial Times,* August 31 (available at https://www.ft.com/content/cfaa16bf-ce5d-4543-ac9c-9d9234e10e9d?shareType=nongift).

IEA, 2018, "Coal 2018: Analysis and Forecast to 2023", December (available at https://www.iea.org/reports/coal-2018).

IEA, 2021, "Net Zero by 2050: A Roadmap for the Global Energy Sector", Flagship Report, May (available at https://www.iea.org/reports/net-zero-by-2050).

IPCC, 2018, "Summary for Policymakers", in "Global Warming of 1.5°C", Special Report (available at https://www.ipcc.ch/site/assets/uploads/sites/2/2019/05/SR15_SPM_version_report_LR.pdf).

Lamdour, S. and T. Wong, 2021, "Understanding Your Bond Portfolio's Carbon Footprint", Alliance Bernstein, April 28 (available at https://www.alliancebernstein.com/corporate/en/insights/investment-insights/understanding-your-portfolios-carbon-footprint.html).

MacAskill, S. E. Roca, B. Liu, R. A. Stewart and O. Sahin, 2021, "Is There a Green Premium in the Green Bond Market? Systematic Literature Review Revealing Premium Determinants", *Journal of Cleaner Production,* **280**(2), January (available at https://www.sciencedirect.com/science/article/abs/pii/S0959652620345352?via%3Dihub).

Matthews, C. M. and E. Glazer, 2021, "Exxon Considers Pledging 'Net Zero' Carbon by 2050", *Wall Street Journal,* August 5 (available at https://www.wsj.com/articles/exxon-considers-pledging-net-zero-carbon-by-2050-11628161201).

Murray, S., 2021, "Measuring What Matters: The Scramble to Set Standards for the Sustainable Business", *Financial Times,* May 14 (available at https://www.ft.com/content/92915630-c110-4364-86ee-0f6f018cba90?shareType=nongift).

Odier, L., 2021, "Calculating a Company's Carbon Footprint: Debunking 7 Misconceptions on Scope 3 Emissions", August 4 (available at https://www.lombardodier.com/contents/corporate-news/responsible-capital/2021/august/calculating-a-companys-carbon-fo.html).

PCAF, 2020, "The Global GHG Accounting & Reporting Standard for the Financial Industry Standard", November (available at https://carbonaccountingfinancials.com/files/downloads/PCAF-Global-GHG-Standard.pdf).

Raval, A., 2021, "Dutch Court Orders Shell to Accelerate Emissions Cuts", *Financial Times,* May 26 (available at https://www.ft.com/content/340501e2-e0cd-4ea5-b388-9af0d9a74ce2).

Rockström, J., *et al,* 2009, "Planetary Boundaries: Exploring the Safe Operating Space for Humanity", *Ecology and Society,* 14(2), art. 32 (available at https://www.ecologyandsociety.org/vol14/iss2/art32/).

RWE, 2019, "The New RWE: Carbon Neutral by 2040 and One of the World's Leading Renewable Energy Companies", press release, September 30 (available at https://www.rwe.com/en/press/rwe-ag/2019-09-30-the-new-rwe).

RWE, 2020, "RWE Green Bond Framework", April (available at https://www.rwe.com/-/media/RWE/documents/05-investor-relations/anleihen-und-rating/2020-05-04-RWE-Green-Bond-Framework.pdf).

SIFMA, 2021, "SIFMA Research Quarterly - 3Q21", October (available at https://www.sifma.org/wp-content/uploads/2021/07/US-Research-Quarterly-Equity-2021-10-19-SIFMA.pdf).

TCFD, 2021(a), "Measuring Portfolio Alignment: Technical Considerations" (available at https://www.tcfdhub.org/wp-content/uploads/2021/10/PAT_Measuring_Portfolio_Alignment_Technical_Considerations.pdf).

TCFD, 2021(b), "Proposed Guidance on Climate-related Metrics, Targets, and Transition Plans", June (available at https://assets.bbhub.io/company/sites/60/2021/05/2021-TCFD-Metrics_Targets_Guidance.pdf).

UNEP FI and PRI, 2019, "Fiduciary Duty in the 21st Century", Final Report (available at https://www.unepfi.org/wordpress/wp-content/uploads/2019/10/Fiduciary-duty-21st-century-final-report.pdf).

UNEP FI and PRI, 2021, "Inaugural 2025 Target Setting Protocol" (available at https://www.unepfi.org/wordpress/wp-content/uploads/2021/01/Alliance-Target-Setting-Protocol-2021.pdf).

World Nuclear News, 2021, "Unions Repeat Call for Nuclear' s Inclusion in EU Taxonomy", July 27 (available at https://www.world-nuclear-news.org/Articles/Unions-repeat-call-for-nuclear-s-inclusion-in-EU-t).

PART III

SOCIAL RISKS AND IMPACT INVESTING

7

Evaluating social criteria in fundamental and thematic investment portfolios

Lydia Harvey

The "S" pillar has trailed the "E" and "G" pillars in terms of integration within modern ESG approaches; it could even be described as suffering from "middle child syndrome". Compared to governance topics that are closer in spirit to traditional financial analysis, and environmental topics that are underpinned by scientific consensus, investors to date have struggled to incorporate social topics into financial analysis.

However, social issues can present very real risks to companies and the consequences of failing to properly manage material social issues can involve significant financial costs and reputational damages. Examples of social failures include exploiting workers in a supply chain, mismanaging customer data or failing to meet product safety standards. While these impacts are not immediately captured within a company's financial statements, there are several ways in which they may cause material financial costs, including regulatory implications (fines, taxes, etc), operational disruptions and reputational damages.

Managing social issues well not only reduces the level of risk a company faces but may also contribute positively to improved reputation and even performance. Research from Boston Consulting Group (Lorenzo *et al*, 2017) found that companies that establish favourable work conditions for employees have higher earnings before interest and taxes (EBIT) margins (17%) than those that do not (13%). In addition, research from McKinsey (Dixon-Fyle *et al*, 2020) found that companies in the top quartile for gender diversity on executive teams were 25% more likely to have above-average profitability than companies in the fourth quartile. Organisations in the top quartile for ethnic/cultural diversity among executives were 36% more likely to achieve above-average profitability than those in the fourth quartile.

This chapter aims to provide an overview of social ("S") investing, beginning with its origins before outlining the wide variety of topics included within the social pillar. Reporting frameworks and metrics used by companies and investors to disclose performance on material social issues are introduced. Key developments both in terms of market and policy momentum for social investing are also outlined, and the commonalities and differences within social investing strategies in the market are evaluated. Finally, there is a summary of the many challenges faced by investors looking to integrate social factors into their investment process, as well as some potential solutions.

THE CONTEXT OF SOCIAL INVESTING

Origins of "S"

ESG investing has its roots in the socially responsible investing (SRI) movement, believed to date back more than 200 years to the money management principles of the Methodists (Schueth, 2003). These principles involved avoiding investments that profited at the expense of others, as well as investments in so-called "sin stocks" such as tobacco, weapons and gambling. However, it wasn't until the 1960s that SRI gathered momentum more broadly, driven by protests against the Vietnam War. Students and young people began boycotting companies that provided weapons to the war effort. These exclusionary principles continued to gather momentum during the 1970s as concern over environmental pollution, racial inequalities and wars continued to influence the development of SRI.

In the 1980s, the apartheid system in South Africa became a notable focus of the SRI movement, with investors pulling money from companies with operations in the country. At this time, investors began to cater to clients' preferences by offering screening based on both positive and negative selections. Filters were based on the Methodist church principles and began with weapons, alcohol, tobacco and gambling. This quickly grew to include other issues such as nuclear energy, labour rights and environmental pollution.

The world's first SRI index, the Domini Social Index, was launched in 1990. It was comprised of 400 primarily large-cap US corporations, and provided a benchmark to measure the performance of screened investments versus their unscreened counterparts. These historic SRI roots continue to underpin modern ESG efforts, with the "S" pillar firmly focused on human rights and community relations.

The expanding scope of "S"

The scope of the social pillar has expanded considerably over recent decades, reflecting the increased scope of social risks that businesses face. The growing digitalisation of economies requires businesses to increasingly invest in cybersecurity measures to keep both company and client data safe.

Globalisation has increased the complexity of international supply chains, making it more challenging for businesses to monitor social issues such as labour rights and community relations. With rapid advancements in technology and electronics, rare earth minerals are being mined in areas where the labour force is unregulated and at risk of including child labour.

In addition, the ethical standards by which companies are held to account have broadened and evolved. Practices that were common in the past, such as company boards being all male, are now viewed as unacceptable. In some cases, practices have been outlawed, such as unsafe working conditions. As such, companies face an increasing challenge to maintain full oversight of material social issues.

Market momentum for "S" strategies

The social pillar has traditionally played a smaller role compared to "E" and "G" within financial analysis. However, market momentum for "S" strategies is growing, and several pivotal events have thrust the social pillar firmly into the spotlight and spurred investor action. This section illustrates two such events: the global Covid-19 pandemic and the Black Lives Matter (BLM) movement in the US.

Covid-19

Covid-19 sparked a global health crisis at a speed and scale not seen in recent history and caused the largest global recession since the great depression of the 1930s. As governments tried to navigate arguably the period of greatest economic uncertainty since the Second World War, the toll on individuals, businesses and communities accumulated.

Social issues quickly became a high priority. Companies with large workforces faced operational disruptions and health and safety issues as workers contracted the virus. Unemployment rose sharply as businesses were forced to lay off workers, with the International Labour Organisation estimating that, globally, 114 million jobs were lost in 2020 relative to 2019. Companies faced reputational and even litigation risks associated with their protection of employees from the spread of Covid-19 at work. One such example is the retail giant Amazon which, in 2021, faced a lawsuit filed by the New York State Attorney General for failing to protect workers and unlawfully firing workers who complained.

Black Lives Matter

Since its inception in 2013, the BLM movement has protested against incidents of police brutality and all racially motivated violence against black communities. On May 25, 2020, George Floyd was murdered by a Minneapolis police officer in an act of extreme police brutality, an incident that spurred a national uprising, with civil unrest and protests supporting the BLM movement both within the US and internationally. It is estimated that between 15 million and 26 million people participated in the demonstrations, making it the largest civil unrest movement in US history (Burch *et al*, 2020).

As of August 2021, America's 50 biggest public companies had committed US$49.5 billion in the form of lending and grants since George Floyd's murder to tackle racial inequality (Jan, McGregor and Hoyer, 2021). While quantifying the impact of these pledges at scale is difficult, the scrutiny and pressure for US corporations to show accountability and transparency regarding their racial equality performance has tangibly increased.

Trends: Labelled bonds

Investors focused on the social impact of their investments are increasingly turning to social bonds: use of proceeds bonds that raise funds for new and existing projects with positive social outcomes. Launched in 2006, the social bond market has remained relatively modest compared to the green bond market (US$1 trillion as of December 2020). However, social bonds became the fastest growing category of labelled bonds in 2020, with a 10-fold increase in issuance year-on-year (US$249 billion), bringing the total market to US$315.6 billion (Harrison and Muething, 2021). This dramatic growth can be attributed to the global Covid-19 pandemic, and a sharp increase in bond issuers aimed at addressing health and social issues in a more strategic way. So-called "pandemic bonds" comprised 34% of 2020 social bond issuance, with China's domestic bond market introducing the 'covid-19 prevention and control' bond label in February 2020.

In response to the unprecedented growth in the social bond market, the International Capital Market Association (ICMA) updated its Social Bond Principles (SBP) in June 2020 to include an expanded list of social project categories and target populations. The SBP are a set of voluntary guidelines that recommend transparency and disclosure, and foster integrity in the development of the social bond market.

Impact investing

A growing investment approach that targets social impacts is impact investing. Integral to impact investing is the measurement and management of impact. The Global Impact Investor Network (GIIN) defines impact investments as "investments made with the intention to generate positive, measurable social and environmental impact alongside a financial return". The GIIN Annual Impact Investment Survey of 2020 collected responses from 294 impact investors with a combined assets under management (AUM) of US$404 billion. Of these, approximately 60% are exclusively impact investors, with the remainder additionally allocating a portion of their AUM to impact-agnostic investments (Hand *et al*, 2020). The survey found that 60% of respondents targeted both social and environmental impacts, while 34% targeted social impacts exclusively and the remaining 6% targeted environmental.

The survey also found that 15% of respondents were more likely to commit more capital to impact investments because of Covid-19.

The "Impact Fund" flag on Morningstar's ESG screening tool captures funds that "seek to make a measurable impact alongside financial return on specific issue areas through their investments. Impact funds are often focused on specific themes or use the 17 United Nation Sustainable Development Goals (UN SDGs) as a framework for evaluating the overall impact of the portfolio". As of December 2021, there were 494 parent and sub-funds with the Impact Fund flag on the ESG screening tool.

Policy context

A lack of clear definitions, disclosures and agreed metrics hinders the development of social investments. Increasing regulation on ESG disclosures globally is improving the transparency and disclosure of social metrics. ESG regulation is most developed within Europe, with the region acting as a "blueprint" for regulators globally. The European Commission's Action Plan on Sustainable Finance has developed a mandate to create a social taxonomy, or classification system, similar to the existing environmental taxonomy. The overarching aim is to direct capital to entities and activities that operate with respect for human rights and to support capital flows to investments that improve living conditions, especially for the disadvantaged.

One particular social topic that is increasingly being incorporated into regulation globally is diversity and inclusion (D&I). For instance, New York regulators asked the financial institutions they supervise to disclose data on the diversity of their boards and senior leadership from June 2020. In August 2020, the US Securities and Exchange Commission (SEC) adopted additional disclosure requirements on the human capital of public companies. The rule requires companies to identify the number of persons employed, and any human capital measures or objectives such as gender and ethnic diversity and inclusion goals. Stock exchanges are also implementing D&I listing rules – in August 2021, the NASDAQ implemented the Board Diversity Rule, approved by the SEC, as a disclosure standard designed to encourage a minimum board diversity objective for listed companies.

DEFINE "S" IN INVESTING

Frameworks for "S"

There are a growing number of voluntary reporting frameworks and standards that capture social issues and measurements. A 2020 review of 12 of the most referenced frameworks classified them into three broad categories: company-focused; investor-focused; and human rights-focused (O'Connor and Labowitz, 2017). However, key ESG frameworks are commonly referenced and used by companies and investors alike.

There are two frameworks that dominate this space: the Global Reporting Initiative (GRI); and the Sustainability Accounting Standards Board (SASB), now a part of the Value Reporting Foundation (VRF) industry standards.

GRI

The GRI standards[1] are designed to enable organisations to report on their impacts on the economy, environment and people in a comparable way, thereby improving transparency. The GRI standard follows the dual or double materiality concept, and hence acknowledges that risks and opportunities can be material from both a financial and non-financial perspective. The standards apply to all organisations, and incorporate reporting on human rights and environmental due diligence in line with intergovernmental expectations. Individual sector standards enable consistent reporting on sector-specific impacts. As of December 2021, the first of a planned 40 sector standards had been published, for the oil and gas sector. This standard identifies the likely material ESG topics for organisations in the sector, as well as a list of disclosures to report in relation to each material topic. In addition, the standard maps each material ESG topic to the relevant UN SDGs to assist disclosure and reporting using this framework.

SASB

SASB is linked to the financial materiality concept, and is hence a primary resource for both companies and investors to guide the identification, disclosure and evaluation of ESG factors that are financially relevant. SASB standards identify the subset of environmental, social and governance issues most relevant to financial performance in each of 77 industries. The SASB Materiality Map,[2] conceived in 2010, provides this breakdown of material ESG factors across industries and sectors.

Other frameworks often referenced by companies and investors include, for example, the UN SDGs, the UN Global Compact (UNGC), the World Benchmarking Alliance's (WBA) thematic and sector benchmarks, the Carbon Disclosure Project's (CDP) climate and environmental risk reporting frameworks, the Carbon Disclosure Standards Board (CDSB) reporting framework, the Impact Reporting and Investment Standards (IRIS), the Global Steering Group for Impact Investment (GSG), and the UN Guiding Principles Reporting Framework (UNGPFR) for human rights in business. The UN SDGs in particular is a key framework that has gained strong momentum for ESG and impact reporting and investing.

UN SDGs

The "2030 Agenda for Sustainable Development", adopted by UN member states in 2015, is a framework for peace and prosperity for people and the planet. The framework is centred around the 17 UN SDGs, which are an urgent call for action by all countries. The goals recognise that ending poverty and other deprivations must go hand in hand with strategies that improve health and education, reduce inequality and spur economic growth – all while tackling climate change and working to preserve oceans and forests. The UN estimates that US$5–7 trillion of annual investment is required globally between 2015 and 2030 to achieve the UN SDGs (Lavigne-Delville, n.d.), which have emerged as a common framework for investors to align impact themes. The 2020 GIIN survey found that, on average, investors target eight different UN SDG-aligned impact themes across their portfolio. SDG 8 (decent work and economic growth) was the most common, targeted by 75% of impact investors, followed by SDG 1 (no poverty) at 62% and SDG 3 (good health and well-being) at 59%.

In November 2020, the International Financial Reporting Standards (IFRS) Foundation announced the creation of a new International Sustainability Standards Board (ISSB), and a consolidation with the CDSB and VRF/SASB, and the publication of new prototype disclosure requirements (IFRS, 2021). At the same time, the EU's European Financial Reporting Advisory Group (EFRAG)

Project Task Force on Non-Financial Reporting Standards (PTF-NFRS) is working on establishing a new sustainability reporting framework in alignment with the EU's Corporate Sustainability Reporting Directive (CSRD, formerly the Non-Financial Reporting Directive, NFRD). EFRAG follows the dual materiality concept, and has announced a close collaboration with GRI in 2021 (EFRAG and GRI, 2021).

To summarise, the GRI, SASB, IFRS/ISSB, WBA and EFRAG can be classified as rules-based sustainability reporting and accounting standards, with the UN SDGs, and the UNGC being key examples for principles-based frameworks that highlight industry practices.

Data points and metrics

The social component of ESG focuses primarily on organisational policies and practices relating to human rights, business ethics, supply chain management, diversity and inclusion, and the social impacts resulting from corporate operations. Put simply, this pillar encompasses how a company manages its relationships with its staff, customers and the broader community. In fact, the continued acceptance of a company's standard business practices and operating procedures by these groups is known as the "social licence to operate". Companies build their social licence to operate over time by consistently operating with integrity and transparency, and by following ethical business practices. However, as with brand value and reputation, the social licence to operate can be damaged instantly by corporate controversies.

Social data points are inherently more qualitative in nature than governance and environmental factors, which are grounded in financial analysis and science, respectively. By contrast, social metrics are underpinned by ethical principles and standards, often formalised in international agreements, such as the UNGC. The UNGC is a set of 10 normative principles that apply to businesses regardless of location or sector, and covers four themes: human rights; labour rights; environment; and anti-corruption. The two that focus on social issues are human rights and labour rights. These principles in particular are derived from the Universal Declaration of Human Rights and the International Labour Organisations Declaration on Fundamental Principles and Rights at Work.

Social metrics take several forms: they may be binary (the presence or not of a health and safety policy); quantitative (the number of fatalities or lost time injury days); or qualitative (an evaluation of labour standards). The bulk of social data that investors rely on comes from voluntary corporate disclosures, accessed either directly through company reporting or more commonly via third-party ESG vendors (such as MSCI, Sustainalytics and RepRisk).

ESG rating agencies

ESG ratings provided by third-party data vendors are relied upon by investors to evaluate and measure company ESG performance over time and compared to peers. Ratings are often informed by a mixture of corporate ESG disclosure, news and controversy analysis, and expert analyst views. While ESG ratings cover comparable high-level topics within each of the "E", "S" and "G" pillars, they are characterised by considerable measurement divergence where the choice of indicators used to measure the same issue differs between vendors. Taking labour practices as an example, one vendor may consider a company's workforce turnover, while another may consider the number of workplace grievances. Neither approach is incorrect, but the way a company performs against peers will differ accordingly. As a result, there is a considerable level of inconsistency in final ESG ratings within the market. This lack of consistency is a common bugbear of investors, something that is discussed later in the chapter.

Despite the challenges associated with third-party ESG ratings, they are a central tenet of the ESG investing landscape. The burden falls on investors to identify the ESG rating that most aligns to their view on "S". Increasingly, investors are utilising a combination of ESG ratings, or alternatively using the underlying metrics to create custom in-house ESG scores. Both approaches require an understanding of the core components of "S" in the ESG ratings. Analysis of the leading third-party ESG rating agencies by the Harvard Law School Forum (Neilan, Reilly and Fitzpatrick, 2020) has identified the following five core "S" themes in common.

- Workforce, engagement and training: This encompasses metrics related to internal stakeholders and employees, covering their working conditions, equality diversity and inclusion, and ability to have a voice, whether individually, collectively or through a union.

- Customers: This includes topics relating to the businesses' consumer base, and includes topics such as consumer safety, product quality and safety, customer welfare, access and affordability, and customer privacy.
- Human rights: Traditionally an area of focus for investors, all companies regardless of activity or location are expected to have clear human rights policies and the means to comply with them, regardless of the complexity of their business operations.
- Community and society: This captures the interaction of a company with external stakeholders and the broader community, and may include controversies, stakeholder opposition and community relations.
- Data and IT security: An increasingly important theme, this covers topics relating to cybersecurity such as the number and severity of data breaches, volume of customer data handled and exposure to privacy regulation.

"S" categories in the market

According to fund tracker Morningstar (Bioy, 2021), global sustainable fund assets reached US$3.9 trillion at the end of September 2021, driven mainly by ESG disclosure regulation. While the number of ESG investing products, including funds and exchange-traded funds (ETFs), has grown considerably, those that focus specifically on the "S" pillar are still relatively rare.

A search of the mutual funds (this analysis excludes ETFs) on Morningstar UK as of December 2021 for the key social terms of "social", "gender", "women", "diversity", "inclusion" and "human" found 33 parent funds with these labels. The majority are listed equity funds, with only six fixed income funds and one direct property fund. The most common benchmark used by these funds is the MSCI ACWI, with 10 funds referring to this index as their benchmark. The majority of the funds are also actively managed, with only three passive funds, tracking the MSCI World SRI Index, the FTSE4Good US Select Index and the MSCI KLD 400 Social Index.

Figure 7.1 displays these funds by inception date and social label. The most common label is "social", with 23 funds

Figure 7.1 Mutual funds with a social label inception date

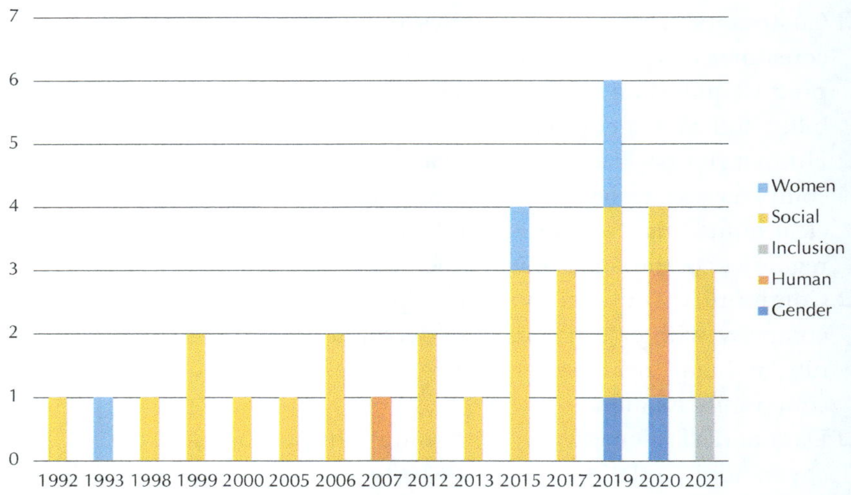

incorporating the term within their name, followed by diversity and inclusion funds, of which there are seven. There are also 23 funds with a track record of over 10 years, and only six funds with a track record of over 20 years. The three funds with the longest track record are the 1919 Socially Responsive Balanced Fund (1992), the Pax Ellevate Global Women's Leadership Fund (1993) and the Payden California Municipal Social Impact Fund (1998).

The funds with a social label can be divided into two distinct categories: those with an investment objective that focuses on a specific social theme or topic, such as gender diversity; and those that apply a broader SRI approach. The majority of the funds with a social label follow the SRI approach.

The SRI funds are in effect ESG funds, considering a full range of ESG factors in the investment process. These funds apply ESG factors in a range of ways, including full ESG integration, positive screening and negative screening. It is a common approach, at a minimum, to apply exclusionary screens on certain sectors not deemed to be socially responsible, such as tobacco and controversial weapons. This is in keeping with the origins of SRI investing.

A smaller number of funds with the social label are those tailored to focus on specific social topics. An example here is the Nordea

Global Social Empowerment Fund, which allocates capital in three central thematic areas: vital needs (eg, nutrition and sanitation); inclusion (eg, learning and education); and empowerment (eg, health and wellness). A second example is the AXA Framlington Social Progress Fund, which invests in companies that support those UN SDGs with a social theme. A third is the Pacific Longevity and Social Change Fund, which invests in companies that are linked to the ageing of the population and the improvement of life expectancy.

The second most common label used by funds in the sample analysed is diversity and inclusion, with seven funds having the labels of "gender", "diversity" or "women". The clear focus is on gender diversity, with six funds looking specifically at the issue of women's empowerment, with only one fund, the M&G Diversity and Inclusion Fund, looking more broadly at both gender and ethnic diversity. For the funds focused on gender diversity, the investment process applied varies – however, broadly speaking, a set of criteria and thresholds are applied using company-specific metrics. For example, the Glenmede Women in Leadership Fund outlines four characteristics that define "women in leadership": the board chair is a woman; the board of directors is over 30% women; the chief executive officer (CEO) is a woman; and women comprise over 30% of senior management. For a company to be considered for the fund, they must include at least one of these criteria.

The final three funds have a "human" label. Both the Multi Manager Access II Future of Humans Fund and the Pictet Human Fund are focused on key demographic shifts such as a growing global population, urbanisation and an ageing population. The third fund, the AXA World Funds ACT Framlington Human Capital Fund, applies a broad SRI approach, with a particular focus on the human capital practices of companies.

Hurdles and limitations

Translating concepts into meaningful metrics

The social pillar of ESG has traditionally been the most challenging for investors to consider. A 2019 global ESG study from BNP Paribas (2021) found that 51% of investors surveyed found the "S" the most difficult to analyse and embed in investment strategies, partly due to a lack of the right data. Compared to the environmental pillar where the concepts and metrics are well defined and underpinned by scientific concepts, the social pillar is characterised by a lack of consensus on how social topics should be defined and measured (IRSG and KPMG, 2021). For environmental topics, the decision-useful metrics required by investors to evaluate performance tend to be the data points disclosed, such as greenhouse gas (GHG) emissions. By contrast, social disclosures are often comprised of discrete, disconnected metrics and policy statements, rather than focused on the material social risks or impacts of the company.

Several studies have found that social reporting almost exclusively focuses on efforts rather than effects (O'Connor and Labowitz, 2017; Shift Project, 2019). A 2020 review of more than 1,700 "S" indicators found that 92% measured company efforts and activities, such as the presence of policies and procedures, training of staff and membership of particular bodies. In addition, over half of the indicators were focused on internal procedures over those that involved external stakeholders. This focus on internal, efforts-based "S" reporting means that companies will ultimately be evaluated predominantly by the internal exercises they are completing. A more meaningful evaluation, however, would be based on the effects of their operations. A company may have the correct policies and procedures in place, but if they are not implemented they cannot be effective. A 2017 study by NYU Stern Centre for Business & Human Rights (O'Connor and Labowitz, 2017) found that the measurement of "S" usually focuses on what is most convenient and available, rather than what is most meaningful.

Regional differences

An additional challenge that the social pillar faces is the fact that social issues are often domestic in nature and therefore subject to regional differences. This makes the imposition of global social standards particularly challenging. Climate change, by contrast, is a global phenomenon with clear, time-bound and science-based consequences of inaction. As a result, global consensus to tackle the problem has been built, as evidenced by the 2015 Paris Agreement signed by 196 countries.

Lack of standardisation in reporting frameworks

Despite the numerous frameworks available to investors to measure "S", there is little convergence between them. While all aim to improve the quality and usefulness of corporate disclosures, they have been developed with different ambitions and end-users in mind. The GRI is designed to meet the needs of a broad range of stakeholders, and focuses on disclosures around material social impacts. In contrast, SASB's standards focus more on the needs of investors and the disclosures required to support capital allocation decisions.

Voluntary frameworks also differ in the definitions used for social topics. Where some are principles-based and employ more overarching definitions of human and social capital, others begin with indicators and topics and build definitions around them. This inconsistency of framework hinders the ability of investors to compare companies, and contributes to a lack of comparability between ESG ratings.

Third-party ESG ratings

A common complaint by investors and companies alike is the lack of standardisation of third-party ESG ratings. A 2020 study of six core ESG ratings providers found the correlations between the ratings are on average 0.54, and range from 0.38 to 0.71, with some of the widest of all categories being social, in particular human rights and product safety (Berg, Kölbel and Rigobon, 2020). When it comes to evaluating a company's GHG emissions or executive remuneration, the market has established metrics and tools for investors. However, as social data points are frequently qualitative in nature it is arguably less likely that ESG rating providers will provide a consistent view.

O'Connor and Labowitz (2017) compared the social pillar of 12 ESG rating agencies, and concluded that there are four fundamental gaps:

- social measurement evaluates what is most convenient, not what is most meaningful;
- current approaches to disclosure are not likely to yield the information needed to identify social leaders;

- the lack of consistent standards underpinning social measurement increases costs and creates confusing "noisiness" across the ESG industry; and
- existing measurement does not equip investors to respond to rising demand for SRI strategies and products.

INVESTMENT STRATEGIES

Diversity of strategies

There is a significant amount of variety within the funds analysed on Morningstar with a social label in terms of asset class, regional focus, social issue(s) targeted and the method of integration into the investment process. The lack of common frameworks and approaches does make the comparison of funds more difficult. Investors would benefit from a standardisation of social labelling terms more broadly. However, despite the wide variety of approaches, there are a number of notable trends and common characteristics.

First, every fund with a social label relies to some extent on third-party ESG data and ratings. There are two main datasets utilised as the building blocks for social investing strategies: the "S" pillar of ESG ratings; and data on sector involvement screens (such as tobacco, gambling and thermal coal). Some approaches rely on negative involvement screens, whilst others target specific social issues such as gender diversity, utilising the underlying 'S' metrics of ESG ratings. In some cases, third-party data is supplemented with proprietary in-house analyst research to further define the investment universe.

Second, it is common for all funds with a social label to include some consideration of ESG factors either through ESG integration or negative screens. Although most funds did this by including negative sector screens on industries such as tobacco, weapons and fossil fuels, some do integrate ESG through third-party ESG ratings. In practice, this means that a fund with a social label will also likely apply negative screens and/or integration of environmental and governance factors. For example, the RobecoSAM Global Gender Equality Impact Fund looks to invest in companies that consciously recognise and promote gender equality, while in addition excluding companies that exhibit an inferior overall ESG assessment. The fund also applies an exclusion list based on controversial

Figure 7.2 Exclusionary screens applied by funds with a social label

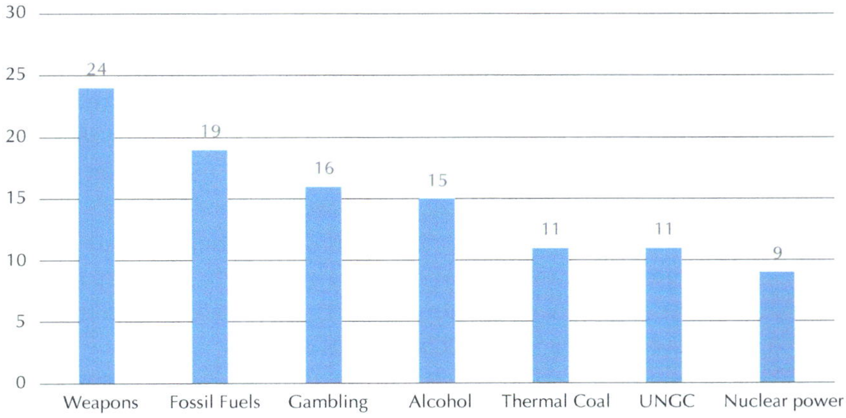

behaviour, products (including controversial weapons, tobacco, palm oil and fossil fuel) while avoiding investments in thermal coal, weapons, military contracting and companies that severely violate labour conditions.

Figure 7.2 highlights some of the ethical exclusionary screens applied by the funds on Morningstar with a social label. For this analysis, broad sector definitions have been applied that cover multiple controversial activities. For example, fossil fuel as a category covers exclusions of individual fossil fuels, such as coal, through to full exclusions of all fossil fuel activities. Thermal coal is, however, often as a specific exclusion on its own, and hence it has been considered separately. Similarly, weapons as an exclusion category includes all weapons-related exclusions such as small arms, military contracting, nuclear weapons, controversial weapons and other weapons-related exclusions. For all exclusion categories, funds will apply various revenue thresholds for exclusion, with a 0% revenue tolerance representing the most conservative approach. As shown in Figure 7.2, the most common exclusion is weapons, with 24 funds excluding companies involved in some way with weapons. The second most common exclusion is fossil fuels, followed by gambling and alcohol.

Finally, for recently launched ESG funds, there is a clear preference to aim for the highest classification of EU sustainability regulation. Articles 6, 8 and 9 are three classifications of investment strategy that apply to investment products under the European Union's Sustainable Finance Disclosure Regulation (SFDR). The regulation came into force in March 2021, and requires asset managers with funds promoted as ESG to categorise their funds according to the level of sustainability integration to improve transparency and prevent greenwashing. Article 6 funds do not integrate sustainability into the investment process; article 8 funds promote environmental or social characteristics; and article 9 funds are those that have an environmental or social goal as their objective. Of the 33 funds analysed, eight have SFDR classifications, with three classified as article 8 and five classified as article 9.

Case studies

This section looks at three funds with a social label in more detail: Nordea Global Social Empowerment Fund; AXA World Funds Framlington Social Progress; and RobecoSam Global Gender Equality Impact. These are all article 9 funds that target specific social outcomes and objectives.

The Nordea Global Social Empowerment Fund and the AXA World Funds ACT Framlington Social Progress have been chosen as case studies as they both aim to contribute to the UN SDGs with a focus on the social themes. Beyond this shared objective, however, the key investment themes and UN SDGs targeted by each fund differ substantially, a result of the broad focus of the UN SDGs. This highlights the difficulties that investors face in comparing and contrasting funds with a social label even when they have a common objective. Table 7.1 lists the UN SDGs targeted by the investments of each fund.

The RobecoSAM Gender Equality Impact Fund has been included to showcase how a fund with a narrower investment objective is structured. In this case, RobecoSAM have developed proprietary gender scores based on a combination of third-party data and internal research. In addition, while this fund is not based on a UN SDG framework, the literature notes the fund contributes to SDG 5 – gender equality, and SDG 8 – decent work and economic growth.

Table 7.1 UN SDGs targeted by the Nordea Global Social Empowerment Fund and the AXA World Funds Framlington Social Progress

UN SDG goals	Nordea Global Social Empowerment Fund	AXA World Funds Framlington Social Progress
1 – No poverty	X	
2 – Zero hunger	X	X
3 – Good health and well-being	X	X
4 – Quality education		X
5 – Gender equality	X	X
6 – Clean water and sanitation	X	
8 – Decent work and economic growth	X	X
9 – Industry, innovation and infrastructure	X	X
10 – Reduced inequalities	X	
11 – Sustainable cities and communities	X	X
13 – Climate action	X	
14 – Life below water	X	
15 – Life on land	X	
16 – Peace, justice and strong institutions	X	X
17 – Partnerships for the goals	X	

PANEL 7.1 CASE STUDY 1

Fund **Nordea Global Social Empowerment Fund**

Benchmark MSCI ACWI Net Return US$

Inception 2020

SFDR Article 9

Objective To create positive social impact by investing in companies that contribute to the UN SDGs that relate to social issues. Nordea identify the large opportunity for growth in the social segment, noting that there is an investment gap of US$2–4 trillion per year on Global Social Empowerment (Nordea Asset Management, 2021).

Strategy The fund invests in companies taken from a proprietary investment universe of almost 1,000 companies identified as social solutions providers. Company-specific metrics are linked to the underlying indicators of the

	relevant UN SDG targets. These companies are broken into three main themes and nine sub-strategies, mapped to the relevant UN SDG goals: ❑ Vital needs: Companies that provide minimum foundational resources required for long-term well-being, including water and sanitation, food and nutrition, and affordable housing (SDGs 2, 6, 13, 14 and 15). ❑ Inclusion: Companies that empower human capital, improve digital connectivity and build infrastructure to support economic, technological and social inclusion (SDGs 9, 10 and 11). ❑ Empowerment: Companies that target health and wellness solutions, innovators that help reduce operational costs while driving productivity and income generation possibilities of small and medium-sized enterprises (SMEs) (productive innovation), and providers that democratise the access to financial products (financial engagement) (SDGs 1, 3, 5, 8, 16 and 17). To implement this strategy, Nordea use a range of external data providers of ESG data, as well as internal research and proprietary ESG scores. Country ESG analysis data sources include Maplecroft, Freedom House, Transparency International, Eurasia and MSCI sanction lists. Corporate ESG analysis data sources include internal research, ISS ESG and SDG, Transition Pathway Initiative, Carbon Disclosure Project, Bloomberg, RepRisk, TrueValue Labs, MSCI ESG and Clarity AI.
Exclusions	❑ Companies and countries involved in UN Global Compact violations: ❑ 5% of revenue from weapons ❑ 0% revenue from controversial weapons ❑ 5% revenue from tobacco ❑ 5% revenue from coal extraction ❑ 0% revenue from unconventional oil and gas extraction ❑ 5% revenue from conventional oil and gas extraction ❑ Exclusion of electricity generation companies with carbon intensity of over 393g CO2/kWh ❑ Tolerance for improving oil and gas and electricity companies – maximum of 5% share of the portfolio.
Performance	There is insufficient data to provide a useful indication of past performance (as at November 2021)

PANEL 7.2 CASE STUDY 2

Fund	**AXA World Funds – ACT Framlington Social Progress**
Benchmark	MSCI ACWI Total Return Net
Inception	2017
SFDR	Article 9
Objective	The fund aims to support on the long run the UN SDGs established by the UN with a focus on the social themes. Formerly the AXA World Funds Framlington Women Empowerment Fund, which focused on companies that promoted gender diversity, this fund was rebranded in 2021 to expand its investable universe. However, promoting gender diversity remains a continued focus of the fund.
Strategy	❑ The new social mandate follows all UN SDGs with a social focus, in particular: ❑ Access to affordable housing, essential infrastructure, and financial and digital inclusion (SDGs 8, 9 and 11) ❑ Protection through healthcare solutions and safety (SDGs 2, 3, 11 and 16) ❑ Progress by investing in companies that foster education, and entrepreneurship and well-being (SDGs 4, 5, 8 and 9). First, the fund applies both sectorial exclusions and a "best-in-class" approach to selecting the best issuers in the investable universe based on their contribution to the socially focused UN SDGs. Second, the investment manager uses a combination of macroeconomic, sector and company-specific analysis, with a focus on the medium to long-term benefits from companies that demonstrate a strong commitment to promoting social progress. The ESG data used are based on methodologies relying in part on third-party data and in some cases are internally developed.
Exclusions	❑ 30% revenue from thermal coal ❑ Mining companies that extract >20 million tonnes of coal per year ❑ Utilities with >30% coal share of power production ❑ Companies with coal power expansion plans of over 300MW ❑ Mining companies developing new coal mining and coal industry partners with significant new coal assets ❑ Utilities with more than 10GW of installed coal-based power production

- ❑ Mining companies with >20% revenue from tar sands and pipeline companies with >20% revenue from tar sands transportation
- ❑ Companies that produce, use, store, trade, maintain, transport, finance or provide support, research or technology dedicated to controversial weapons and their components
- ❑ Companies that breach the Treaty on the Non-Proliferation of Nuclear Weapons
- ❑ Companies that own over 50% of an excluded weapons company
- ❑ 5% revenues from palm oil production, or own over 30,000 hectares of palm oil plantations
- ❑ Companies with controversial land use and biodiversity practices, environmental supply chain incidents, operational incidents or environmental product incidents (significant, high and severe controversies)
- ❑ Companies classified as "critical" for their impact on forests (according to the Carbon Disclosure Project).

Performance Performance is calculated in euros and expressed as a percentage change of the fund's net asset value at each year end

	2018	**2019**	**2020**
Fund	0.1	26.1	9.5
Benchmark	–4.8	28.9	6.7

PANEL 7.3 CASE STUDY 3

Fund **RobecoSam Global Gender Equality Impact**
Benchmark MSCI World Index TRN
Inception 2020
SFDR Article 9
Objective To invest globally in companies that are leaders in promoting gender diversity and equality
Strategy RobecoSAM Gender Equality Equities invest in companies that are leading with regard to the promotion of gender equality. It employs systematic, bottom-up stock selection that combines proprietary ESG data and research throughout the investment process. ESG criteria for exclusions and fund-specific suitability are applied during universe construction. An in-house sustainability investing (SI) research team integrates financially

material sector and company-specific sustainability analysis into investment cases.

RobecoSam has developed proprietary Gender Scores comprised of the following criteria:

- ❑ Diversity among executives, management and the total workforce
- ❑ The consideration of diversity in the board nomination process
- ❑ Retention of female talent
- ❑ Equality of remuneration
- ❑ Approach to employee health, safety, well-being and satisfaction.

Companies that exhibit an inferior overall ESG assessment are also excluded. While this fund is not based on a UN SDG framework, the literature notes the fund contributes to SDG 5, gender equality, and SDG 8, decent work and economic growth.

Exclusions

- ❑ Companies involved in UNGC principles and Organisation for Economic Co-operation and Development (OECD) guideline violations
- ❑ >0% revenue from controversial weapons
- ❑ >0% revenue from tobacco production, over 5% tobacco key parts
- ❑ >20% revenue from non-Roundtable on Sustainable Palm Oil (RSPO) certified palm oil
- ❑ >10% revenue from thermal coal
- ❑ >10% revenue from oil sands
- ❑ >5% revenue from arctic drilling
- ❑ >5% revenue from military contracting
- ❑ >0% revenue from firearms production
- ❑ >30% revenue from nuclear power
- ❑ >5% revenue from alcohol production, over 10% alcohol retail
- ❑ >5% revenue from gambling
- ❑ >5% revenue from adult entertainment.

Performance Performance prior to the launch date has been simulated on the basis of the past performance of the absorbed fund that had similar investment policy and applied higher or comparable charges. The ongoing charges are included in the calculation of past performance, excluded are the entry and exit charges.

	2016	2017	2018	2019	2020
Fund	9.0%	9.6%	–0.8%	28.6%	3.3%
Benchmark	10.7%	7.5%	–4.1%	30.0%	6.3%

RobecoSAM evaluated whether their proprietary gender scores are a useful predictor of investment performance using a portfolio approach. All companies in the investment universe were ranked according to the gender score, adjusted for transparency biases stemming from region, sector and size. Two portfolios were created: the high gender score portfolio comprised of the top 33% of companies; and the low gender score portfolio comprised of the bottom 67%. Both portfolio components are equal weighted. The resulting analysis found that the high gender score portfolio outperformed the low gender score portfolio by 0.5% annualised per year, over the period June 2004 to June 2019, and with slightly lower volatility (Hafner-Cai, 2020).

Hurdles and limitations

The rise of "social washing"

Greenwashing refers to the practice of deliberately disseminating information to present an environmentally responsible public image. Investors and companies must be cautious of "social washing", and avoid overstating or misrepresenting their social credentials to improve their reputation. As the "S" pillar becomes a firmer focus of investors, the incentive for companies to undertake social washing also increases. Unlike environmental impacts, which are typically quantifiable, social issues are often evaluated quantitatively, increasing the risks associated with social washing to investors.

Interdependencies within ESG

Although ESG data and frameworks are structured with three pillars, in practice environmental and social topics rarely sit within one pillar. There are often synergies and trade-offs between environmental and social issues. The United Nations SDGs are a case in point, characterised by many potential conflicts that make achieving them more difficult. For example, looking specifically at SDG 7 ("ensure access to affordable, reliable, sustainable and modern energy for all") and SDG 13 ("take urgent action to combat climate change and its impacts"), investing in new fossil fuel projects to target more affordable and accessible energy would be achieving SDG 7, while being in direct conflict with SDG 13. Similarly, initiatives targeted at achieving SDG 2 (zero hunger) may focus on intensifying agriculture to boost productivity and yields, conflicting with SDG 15 ("sustainably manage forests, combat desertification, halt and reverse land degradation and halt biodiversity loss").

CONCLUSION

While described in isolation for the purposes of this chapter, "S" underpins all business decisions in practice. Fundamentally capturing the concept of acting responsibly, "S" represents the minimum ethical standards to abide by, in order to maintain a social licence to operate. Conversely, mismanagement of "S" can present a material risk to companies and may result in significant costs and reputational damages.

Despite ESG investing developing from deep SRI roots, social topics remain arguably the most challenging for investors to address, characterised by a lack of consensus on how they should be defined and measured. Social data points are often qualitative in nature, and corporate disclosure is focused on what can be easily measured rather than what presents a material risk or opportunity for the business. In addition, the scope of the "S" pillar is constantly evolving and expanding, driven by changing social norms and an increasingly interconnected global economy.

Market and policy momentum together have increased the scrutiny of company performance on material "S" issues, as well as the credibility of investor "S" strategies. In particular, the Covid-19 pandemic has forced social topics to the top of the agenda for governments, investors and businesses globally. As a result, the market is increasingly incentivised to overcome the many hurdles facing the "S" pillar of ESG.

Investors wield significant power to influence how companies manage and report on "S" through the allocation of capital, engagement with management and exercising voting rights. However, improving corporate disclosures around social topics will require more than just investor demand. Increased sustainability regulation is fundamental to driving greater disclosure and transparency on ESG performance. While the market would benefit from standardisation of the many voluntary ESG frameworks in the market, of more immediate importance is a concerted regulatory push for transparency and accountability to combat the risks of "social washing".

Bridging the gaps will require collaboration between companies and investors, not only to reward the companies performing best in social issues but also to support those that need to improve. "S" disclosures must move away from efforts-based towards effects-based metrics, in order to allow the meaningful integration of social factors into investment approaches. A shift towards quantitative metrics will further support the transition of "S" reporting away from what is easily measured towards what is most meaningful. Finally, a fundamental shift is required by all market participants towards becoming more proactive and less reactive, and investing the necessary resources to measure and manage the "S".

1 See https://www.globalreporting.org/standards/.
2 See https://navigator.sasb.org.

REFERENCES

Berg, F. J. Kölbel and R. Rigobon, 2020, "Aggregate Confusion: The Divergence of ESG Ratings", MIT Sloan School of Management, May 17.

Bioy, H., 2021, "Global Sustainable Fund Flows: Q3 2021 in Review", Morningstar Manager Research, November (available at https://www.morningstar.com/content/dam/marketing/shared/pdfs/Research/Global-ESG-Q3–2021-Flows.pdf?utm_source=eloqua&utm_medium=email&utm_campaign=none&utm_content=27223).

BNP Paribas, 2021, "The ESG Global Survey 2021", September 13 (available at https://securities.cib.bnpparibas/esg-global-survey-2021/).

Burch, A. D. S., W. Cai, G. Gianordoli, M. McCarthy and J. K. Patel, 2020, "How Black Lives Matter Reached Every Corner of America", *The New York Times*, June 13 (available at https://www.nytimes.com/interactive/2020/06/13/us/george-floyd-protests-cities-photos.html).

Dixon-Fyle, S., K. Dolan, V. Hunt and S. Prince, 2020, "Diversity Wins: How Inclusion Matters", McKinsey & Company, May 19 (available at https://www.mckinsey.com/featured-insights/diversity-and-inclusion/diversity-wins-how-inclusion-matters).

EFRAG and GRI, 2021, "Landmark Statement of Cooperation", July 8 (available at https://www.efrag.org/Assets/Download?assetUrl=%2Fsites%2Fwebpublishing%2FSiteAssets%2FEFRAG%252 0GRI%2520COOPERATION%2520PR.pdf&AspxAutoDetectCookieSupport=1).

Hafner-Cai, J., 2020, "Gender Equality and Corporate Performance: Seeking Gender Balance Inside and Outside of the Boardroom", RobecoSAM, White Paper, March (available at https://advisers.fpinternational.com/fund-centre/responsible-investing/downloads/robecosam-gender-equality-paper-0320.pdf).

Hand, D., H. Dithrich, S. Sunderji and N. Nova, 2020, "2020 Annual Impact Investor Survey", Global Impact Investing Network, June (available at https://thegiin.org/assets/GIIN%20Annual%20Impact%20Investor%20Survey%202020.pdf).

Harrison, C. and L. Muething, 2021, "Sustainable Debt: Global State of the Market 2020", Climate Bonds Initiative (available at https://www.climatebonds.net/files/reports/cbi_sd_sotm_2020_04d.pdf).

IFRS, 2021, "IFRS Foundation Announces International Sustainability Standards Board, Consolidation with CDSB and VRF, and Publication of Prototype Disclosure Requirements", November 3 (available at https://www.ifrs.org/news-and-events/news/2021/11/ifrs-foundation-announces-issb-consolidation-with-cdsb-vrf-publication-of-prototypes/).

IRSG and KPMG, 2021, "Accelerating the S in ESG – A Roadmap for Global Progress on Social Standards", June (available at https://assets.kpmg/content/dam/kpmg/uk/pdf/2021/06/irsg-kpmg-accelerating-the-s-in-esg-report.pdf).

Jan, T., J. McGregor and M. Hoyer, 2021, "Corporate America's $50 Billion Promise", *The Washington Post,* August 24 (available at https://www.washingtonpost.com/business/interactive/2021/george-floyd-corporate-america-racial-justice/).

Lavigne-Delville, J., n.d., "UN Alliance for SDG Finance", United Nations Global Compact (available at https://www.unglobalcompact.org/take-action/action/globalallianceforsdgfinance).

Lorenzo, R., N. Voigt, K. Schetelig, A. Zawadzki, I. Welpe and P. Brosi, 2017, "The Mix That Matters: Innovation Through Diversity", Boston Consulting Group, April 26 (available at https://www.bcg.com/publications/2017/people-organization-leadership-talent-innovation-through-diversity-mix-that-matters).

Neilan, J., P. Reilly and G. Fitzpatrick, 2020, "Time to Rethink the S in ESG", Harvard Law School Forum on Corporate Governance, June 28 (available at https://corpgov.law.harvard.edu/2020/06/28/time-to-rethink-the-s-in-esg/).

Nordea Asset Management, 2021, "The Importance of Socially Responsible Investing (and Why it Makes Economic Sense): Nordea's Global Social Empowerment Strategy", January (available at https://www.nordea.lu/en/professional/documents/in-focus/IF_GSEMF_eng_INT.pdf/).

O'Connor, C. and S. Labowitz, 2017, "Putting the 'S' in ESG: Measuring Human Rights Performance for Investors", NYU Stern Center for Business and Human Rights, March (available at https://static1.squarespace.com/static/547df270e4b0ba184dfc490e/t/58cad912e58c6274180b58b6/1489688854754/Metrics-Report-final-1.pdf).

Schueth, S., 2003, "Socially Responsible Investing in the United States", *Journal of Business Ethics*, 43(3), pp. 189–94.

Shift Project, 2019, "The Problem with How we Measure Business Respect for Human Rights", September (available at https://shiftproject.org/wp-content/uploads/2019/09/ValuingRespect_TwoPager_Sept2019.pdf).

8

Case Study 4: Defining impact investing for today's ethical investor – evaluating the efforts of Evangelisches Johannesstift

Jens Güldner

Johannesstift Diakonie

This chapter outlines the fundamentals of a leading ethical asset owner in Germany, Evangelisches Johannesstift's (EJS) integrated, ethical and sustainable investment philosophy. It highlights the interconnectedness between its ethical, impact and mission-led investment approaches, and describes how it identifies and measures socially oriented, targeted outcomes using some of the United Nations' Sustainable Development Goals (UN SGDs) and underlying targets.

Evangelisches Johannesstift, a charitable foundation, makes investments with the intention of achieving measurable, positive social and/or ecological impacts, in addition to achieving a traditional financial return. The foundation thus strives to achieve a "double dividend" and aims to address solving social, economic and ecological problems.

With the launch of an endowment fund, the EJS Endowment Fund in February 2010, the social impact investment approach has ultimately been applied to all parts of EJS's investment strategy with the aim of reducing possible "negative" effects and bringing the investment into line with EJS's articles of association and mission statements.

DEFINING ETHICAL, MISSION-LED AND SOCIAL IMPACT INVESTING

Ethical, mission-led and social impact investing are key building blocks of EJS's investment philosophy and investment strategy. This investment philosophy considers the foundation's mission to integrate ethical criteria into the investment process, and to achieve a social impact without losing sight of due diligence, substance and performance.

The foundation's vision and mission are focused on climate and environmental protection, on improving resource efficiencies, and on providing better social outcomes for future generations in terms of their lives and places of work.

The investment strategy aims to support EJS's investment philosophy of establishing a more sustainable, long-term oriented economy, and to contribute to societal and social values, outcomes and impacts. It thereby focuses on three key areas:

- assessing financial criteria such as security, liquidity and profitability – ie, the "magic tetrahedron";
- evaluating an investment opportunity, decisions based on economic, sustainable and ethical criteria – ie, the "integrated future model"; and
- aligning a broad spectrum of fundamental, and thematic ESG and impact investment approaches used across asset classes, where activities are benchmarked against the UN SDGs.

Figure 8.1 Magic tetrahedron

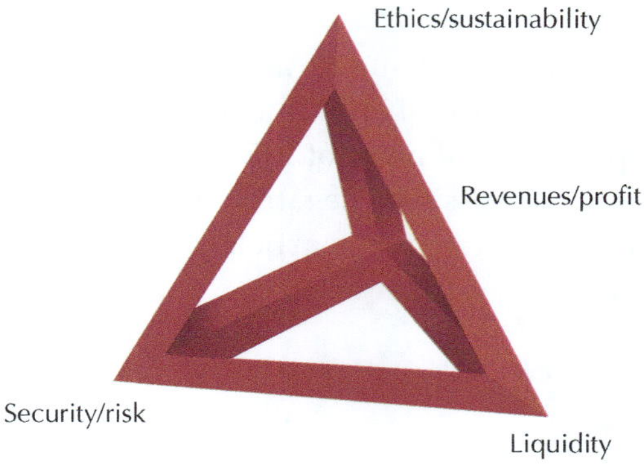

Figure 8.2 Integrated future model

We have classified this approach as a "magic tetrahedron" for investment decision-making that encompasses financial and extra-financial dimensions, and which is supported by a rigorous due diligence approach adhering to tax and compliance regulation in Germany (see Figure 8.1).

Our "integrated future model" and their interdependencies are also considered in the implementation of our investment policy and approach, across asset classes (see Figure 8.2).

LEVERAGING A BEST-IN-CLASS INVESTMENT APPROACH

The focus here is on selecting best in class companies in the context of our ethical and mission-led investment approach. For equity portfolios, we select companies and/or industries that best meet our faith-based and foundation-specific requirements in relation to ecological and social safeguards and standards, as well as minimum requirements in relation to good corporate governance. We follow a systematic approach for active asset allocation that is both fundamental (qualitative) and quantitative.

MANAGING EXTRA-FINANCIAL RISKS

Evangelisches Johannesstift always considers associated environmental, social and governance (ESG) risks in its investment strategy, including managed and pooled funds. The aim as a faith-based asset owner is to become a role model and "multiplier" for

Figure 8.3 Avoiding extra-financial risks

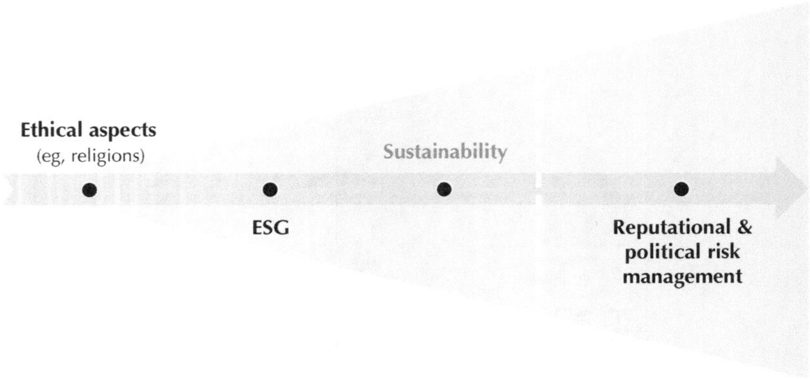

the integration of ESG factors into ethical and mission-led investment strategies. ESG factors are, by definition, so-called "extra-financial" risk factors that can influence portfolio performance on the one hand, and the reputation of the foundation on the other. If not treated appropriately, ESG issues and controversies can escalate and become significant risks to the foundation and its well-established work in and among faith-based communities.

Examples of ESG risks include human rights violations, illegal logging activities or serious allegations of corruption. Together with its partners (AGI, ISS ESG, Commerzbank, LBBW and DPG), the foundation's asset management team takes care of the management of a wide range of ESG risks and controversies to ensure that they do not become "business" risks for the foundation (see Figure 8.3).

IDENTIFYING ESG OPPORTUNITIES THROUGH THEMATIC INVESTING AND ACTIVE OWNERSHIP

The foundation also aims to identify positive investment opportunities such as investments in renewables or alternative energy, in future technologies and/or in socially responsible financing solutions for emerging markets.

It has established a dedicated corporate dialogue and engagement strategy to support positive change trajectories among investee companies. In addition, as discussed below, EJS links these efforts to its social impact investment efforts.

ASSESSING SOCIAL OUTCOMES AND IMPACTS

Every investment, whether "traditional" or "ethical/sustainable", has to also deliver a positive social impact. Measuring social impact remains a challenge and requires a dedicated impact thesis and approach *ex ante* (see Table 8.1).

The foundation's social impact investment aims to focus on the following.

- ❑ Intentionality: An investor sets out to exert a positive impact.
- ❑ Return: It should generate a positive return on the investment.
- ❑ Measurability: The benefits should be measurable and transparent.

To achieve these goals, we have created a dedicated and demonstrable impact criteria catalogue that looks at impact objectives, and a dedicated policy that is followed through by a long-term

Table 8.1 Assessing social impact

Impact thesis	Impact approach	Engagement policy
Financial and impact objectives to be set at the same level	Alignment of the impact investment philosophy and process	Long-term engagement focus proportional to the impact objectives to:
Ex ante definition of impact objectives:	Mapping of positive and negative externalities for each potential investment	❑ maximise the impact
❑ quantification/qualification of the impact (key performance indicators, KPIs)	Proactive selection based on the expected impact	❑ reduce negative externalities
❑ linked to UN SDGs (two/three max)	Dedicated impact investment governance structure (committee, policies, processes)	❑ achieve long-term positive change trajectories
❑ time horizon		Continuous monitoring and measuring of effects of the engagement for targeted outcomes
Investment policy aligned with the impact objectives (documentation)		
Compensation of the investment team aligned with the impact achieved		

Figure 8.4 UN SDGs

impact philosophy and process. In addition, this social impact investment effort is complemented by a dedicated long-term active ownership and engagement approach.

We map our ambitions against specific UN SDGs to meet our environmental and societal goals for ethical, mission-led and impact investing: SDG 3, SDG 4, SDG 7, SDG 8, SDG 10, SDG 12 and SDG 13 (see Figure 8.4).

ESTABLISHING IMPACT LOANS FOR PRIVATE INVESTORS: EJS STIFTSDARLEHENS

Among other things, the Evangelical Johannesstift offers private individuals the opportunity to gain access to other impact vehicles, such as through a dedicated loans programme (EJS Stiftsdarlehen).[1]

Lenders to Evangelisches Johannesstift receive comprehensive information on these types of regulated debt instruments, and Evangelisches Johannesstift pays the lenders interest at the end of each year. The lenders can decide whether they will use the proceeds of the loan for commercial purposes or if they would like to donate the interests gained through their lending activities to the community projects run by the EJS. Most of the proceeds are donated to one of the foundation's community projects, and hence contribute once again to an "outcome with a social impact".[2]

CONCLUSION

Non-profit foundations such as the Evangelisches Johannesstift can achieve a long-term positive social impact. The foundation's investment arm represents an important building block to ensure intergenerational equity is being maintained and preserved for generations.

Social impact investing in accordance with the faith-based "statutes" and a dedicated mission statement forms the basis for the implementation of an ethical and mission-led investment philosophy. The EJS thus aims to achieve a "double dividend" from both a financial and extra-financial perspective. The assets invested by EJS are also intended to make a visible contribution to addressing social, economic and ecological problems.

However, investments are just one financial instrument to implement a holistic, mission-led philosophy. Through dedicated impact loans, the EJS also offers private individuals the opportunity to gain access to targeted social impact debt instruments in line with their, and the EJS's, beliefs and values.

1 Subordinated loan, coordinated with BaFin, term <=five years.

2 These include donor loans, donations, investments in one of the foundation's three thematic funds, and "testamentary dispositions".

PART IV

GOVERNANCE AND ACTIVE OWNERSHIP

9

Developing governance and active ownership frameworks for investment analysis

Carol Nolan Drake, J.D. and DR. Christine Chow

International Corporate Governance Network

For more than a quarter of a century, the International Corporate Governance Network (ICGN) has advanced high standards of corporate governance and investor stewardship for its growing membership, while its principles and guidance has also helped inform global regulatory bodies and international organisations. Led by investors responsible for assets under management in excess of US$70 trillion, ICGN is a leading authority on global standards of governance and stewardship at a time when issuers and investors have been challenged to navigate a continually changing world. Its membership is based in more than 45 countries, and includes companies, investors, advisors and other stakeholders. ICGN's mission is to promote high standards of professionalism in governance for investors and companies alike in their mutual pursuit of long-term value creation contributing to sustainable economies worldwide. ICGN offers an important investor perspective on corporate governance and sustainability to help inform public policy development and to encourage good practices by capital market participants.

ICGN has provided a tiered approach to its policy outreach in its publication of principles, guidance and viewpoints for the membership and broader investment community.

- Principles: The Global Governance Principles (GGP) are ICGN's primary standard for well-governed companies. The ICGN Global Stewardship Principles (GSP) set out ICGN's view of best practices in relation to investor stewardship obligations, policies and processes (ICGN, 2020a; ICGN, 2021a).
- Guidance: The Guidance, which are adopted by the membership on a range of governance themes, are issued periodically to elaborate on key concepts and practices. Guidance pieces are often used by ICGN members as benchmarks in assessing investee company governance practices, and serve as an international source of best practice that influences corporate governance regulatory developments and standard setting around the world. The Guidance that serves to inform this chapter includes ICGN, Guidance on Investor Fiduciary Duties, 2018.
- Viewpoints: Viewpoints are "short and topical reports produced by ICGN Policy Committees on key governance themes. They are meant to enhance member awareness and understanding of emerging governance issues, along the range of themes covered by the ICGN Policy Committees." Two Viewpoints are particularly relevant to this chapter: ICGN, Shareholder Proposals – An Essential Instrument for Ensuring Corporate Accountability, 2021 and ICGN, Investor Framework for Addressing Systemic Risks, 2019.

While the Global Governance Principles and Global Stewardship Principles are principle-based and carry no hard law or soft law mandate, they have been revised in such a way as to recognise the movement from voluntary to mandatory reporting in many jurisdictions, and newer regulatory requirements under the European Union (EU) Shareholder Rights Directive requirements, among others. The final section of the Global Stewardship Principles outlines the "ecosystem of stewardship and the pre-conditions for effective adoption within the context of a 'comply or explain' system of corporate governance oversight".

THE CALL FOR CLARITY: STEWARDSHIP PRINCIPLES

ICGN published its GSP in 2016 (and revised in 2020); however, ICGN's commitment and policy work on stewardship dates back to its 2003 Statement on Institutional Shareholder Responsibilities, the predecessor to the current Principles. The GSP are a natural addition to the GGP, which were first published in 2001 and revised in 2021. In the GSP preamble, ICGN provided a global definition of the word "stewardship" to provide context for its meaning and as a straightforward interpretation for action by investor fiduciaries (ICGN, Global Stewardship Principles, 2020):

> The term "stewardship" does not always translate readily into some languages, so it is important to clarify what is meant by stewardship and how this is relevant to institutional investors. In general terms stewardship can be defined as the responsible management of something entrusted to one's care. This suggests a fiduciary duty of care on the part of those agents entrusted with management responsibility to act on behalf of the end-beneficiaries. In the investment context, institutional investors are the agents acting on behalf of beneficiaries, who are often long-term savers or members of pension funds. At an individual company level, investor stewardship helps to promote high standards of corporate governance, which contributes to sustainable value creation, thereby increasing the long-term risk-adjusted rate of return to investors and their beneficiaries or clients. At an investor level, stewardship is about preserving and enhancing long-term value as part of a responsible investment approach. This includes the consideration of wider ethical, environmental and social factors, and the consideration of relevant systemic risks as core components of fiduciary duty. In a broader context, stewardship enhances overall financial market stability and economic growth, and, by focusing on long-term value creation, stewardship is directly linked to sustainable benefits for the economy, environment, and society.

While the Global Governance and Stewardship Principles are ICGN's foremost guidance on governance and stewardship, ICGN has published additional reference materials, including Guidance and Viewpoints to provide greater detail on governance and stewardship practices. As Kerrie Waring, chief executive officer (CEO) of ICGN, wrote in the Foreword of Dallas and Lubrano (2021):

> The important role investors play in holding companies to account for sustained value creation is the bedrock of ICGN's work and underpins the rationale for our own Global Stewardship Principles. Now more than ever, society is questioning the role of corporations in society and their licence to operate this extends to the effectiveness of investors in holding them to account.

Active stewardship: Investment and engagement approaches

As highlighted in the ICGN GSP, at an investor level, "stewardship is about preserving and enhancing long-term value as part of a responsible investment approach" (ICGN, 2020a). Stewardship activities have a spectrum of approaches, from voting shares, to thematic stewardship, also known as "beta stewardship", which focuses on market risk (or "beta"), to taking a more active role in public policy advocacy and engagement with companies.

Opportunities for taking an active role in stewardship occur across the investment spectrum, prompted by asset allocation to diversify and spread out risk among a variety of investment strategies, including fixed income, credit and bond instruments, global equities, private equity/hedge funds, positive and negative screening for certain investments, and by passive and/or active management. Stewardship may include engagement with the investor or as part of a collaborative engagement with like-minded investors, regulators and policy setters, underwriters, financiers and others who bankroll capital, initial public offerings (IPOs), and mergers and acquisitions (M&A). The bottom line is that any area in which an investor has assets invested, stewardship practices lead to opportunities to enhance long-term value creation.

All of these activities culminate in action by investors with the adoption of stewardship practices to effectively discharge their fiduciary duties over longer-term horizons. As stated in the ICGN, Guidance on Investor Fiduciary Duties, 2018:

> Investors are stewards of an ever-growing percentage of global investible assets. The rapid institutionalisation of savings has increased with corresponding systemic effects. As markets have become more complex and investors' asset allocations have become increasingly global and diversified, the investment service provider sector has also grown.

ICGN has issued policy on stewardship responsibilities within allocation strategies. Table 9.1 provides examples of asset allocations, cross-referenced with the applicable ICGN policy. The GGP and GSP are incorporated by reference.

COLLABORATIVE ENGAGEMENT STRATEGIES

As noted in the ICGN Global Stewardship Principles (ICGN, 2020a), engagement with investee companies is an important area of stewardship, enhanced, where appropriate, by collaboration with other like-minded investors:

Table 9.1 ICGN policy/guidance/viewpoints by asset allocation

Asset allocation	ICGN Policy/Guidance/Viewpoints
Fixed income, credit and bond instruments	ICGN, Global Stewardship Principles, 2020, Part 3, considers the role of the creditor in the context of the "ecosystem" of stewardship. Investors may serve as creditors with other investors. This can provide a framework for fixed income investors to factor governance-related issues into investment analysis and stewardship activities. According to the ICGN, Investor Framework for Addressing Systemic Risks, 2019 Viewpoint, investors should build sensitivity towards reconciling the different, but legitimate, perspectives of corporate creditors and shareholders, and seek to identify common areas of alignment as an aspect of stewardship and engagement. Taking a long-term view, a constructive tension between protecting creditors' interests, while generating fair returns for shareholders, can hopefully steer companies from the extremes of unwarranted financial risk or conservatism to enable them to achieve their overall mission, including satisfying the requirements of all its financial stakeholders. As a matter of stewardship and engagement, creditors and shareholders should aspire to find common ground to engage with companies to adopt business models, corporate strategies and financial policies that are positioned to stand the test of time. Bond holders in particular provide long-term risk capital to companies, and share with equity holders an interest in promoting responsible and sustainable corporate governance and investor stewardship practices. Creditor engagement can be particularly relevant in the due diligence process leading to new bond issues (or the refinancing of outstanding debt), and can influence company governance by establishing covenants in indenture agreements to protect creditor rights. A key focus of stewardship from a creditor's perspective will be on a company's risk management oversight and on maintaining financial policies that appropriately balance the interests of shareholders and creditors. The stewardship principles of monitoring and engagement are both relevant to creditors in this context.
Global equities–proxy voting, engagement, shareholder proposals	According to the ICGN, Investor Framework for Addressing Systemic Risks, 2019 Viewpoint Viewpoint, investors can use their voice to encourage both policymakers and investee companies to address the commonly shared long-term ethical and systemic risks that impact companies, investors, individuals, markets and societies. Through engaging with company management and boards, investors gain insights as to how effectively investee companies are addressing relevant ethical issues and systemic risks. ICGN encourages its members to make effective use of all available shareholder rights to hold corporations and their boards to account. This includes utilising voting rights and addressing risks in a company's ESG policies and practices, through dialogue and engagement.

Asset allocation	ICGN Policy/Guidance/Viewpoints
	According to the ICGN, The Inclusion of Non-voting or Limited Voting Shares in Stock Market Indices, 2017 Viewpoint, its long-standing policy position is that the optimal share structure for companies wishing to benefit from access of public capital should be one vote for each share within the same class. ICGN's general view is that the mismatch of ownership and control through differential ownership rights can create significant governance risks for minority shareholders such as management entrenchment and a lack of accountability (see also ICGN, Guidance on Securities Lending, 2016).
Alternatives, private equity/hedge funds	According to the ICGN, Investment Exclusions: Some Technical Considerations, 2018 Viewpoint, private equity poses issues both of control (the general partner of the private equity firm, not the institutional investor, which is generally a limited partner, selects the investments) and timeframe (such partnerships tend to be for multi-year periods, usually 10 years, with some potential annual extensions). Investors should discuss their exclusion policies with general partners before making an investment, and should seek a side letter stating their policy, although general partners may not agree. Also, investors may want to ask for a position on the partnership's limited partner advisory committee, where it can engage with the general partner and use its power of persuasion to try and affect portfolio choices.
Positive and negative screening practices	According to the ICGN, Investment Exclusions: Some Technical Considerations, 2018 Viewpoint, it is relatively easy for investors seeking to operate an exclusion policy to remove relevant companies from an actively managed equity portfolio. Complications arise, however, with companies that are involved indirectly in the activity that is being excluded. One solution to this is for the fund to set a threshold on the basis of turnover. More complicated is investment in pooled funds, including index products. Here, it may not be possible to exclude specific companies because the investor making the exclusion decision does not directly control the investments in the pool. Some investors with exclusion policies may be able to find pooled products that align with those policies. However, in the event such a solution is not possible, a typical response for investors might be to set a limit that gives some leeway for investment in pooled funds and other asset classes.

> Principle 4: Investors should engage with investee companies with the aim of preserving or enhancing value on behalf of beneficiaries or clients, and should be prepared to collaborate with other investors to enhance engagement outcomes.

Investors recognise that successful engagement may take time to see results. Therefore, ICGN has offered Global Stewardship Principle 4.3 to provide tools for escalation, if necessary ICGN, Global Stewardship Principles, 2020:

> 4.3 Engagement escalation: Investors should clarify how engagement might be escalated when company dialogue is failing, including: a) expressing concerns to corporate representatives or non-executive directors, directly, in writing or in a shareholders' meeting; b) expressing their concern collectively with other investors; c) making a public statement; d) submitting shareholder resolutions; e) speaking at general meetings; f) submitting one or more nominations for election to the board as appropriate and convening a shareholders' meeting; g) seeking governance improvements and/or damages through legal remedies or arbitration; and h) formally adding the company to an exclusion list or otherwise exiting or threatening to exit from the investment.

Active stewardship through equity ownership and proxy voting considerations

One of the primary ways that investors hold boards to account is through the effective use of proxy voting in response to matters presented on company ballots. ICGN recognises proxy voting is a key stewardship obligation, as an underpinning of fiduciary duty. Investors are encouraged to establish and disclose their voting policies, and disclose how the voting decisions are made. Included in the Global Stewardship Principles is "Principle 5. Exercising and protecting voting rights":

> Principle 5.1 Voting policies. Investors should publicly disclose clear voting policies, which should be reviewed periodically. The voting policy should outline the principles guiding voting decisions, highlight scope for derogation in specific cases and make clear any differences in approach between domestic and international holdings. Where an investor chooses not to vote in specific circumstances, for example where holdings are below a certain threshold, this should be disclosed.
>
> Principle 5.2 Voting process. Investors should disclose the process by which voting decisions are reached, including how potential conflicts of interest are addressed and how due diligence is undertaken. Disclosure should clarify who is responsible for the vote decision, including if this differs depending on the nature of the resolution, geography or scale of holdings.

Stewardship coordination

Due to the nature of portfolio construction, asset owners, institutional investors and investment professionals will have complex portfolios that allocate holdings in a variety of asset classes, thereby attempting to limit risk and actualise returns on these investments.

In the global investment space, some investors (particularly those with passive index-based strategies) may have ownership in thousands of companies. While the number of shares held may be a small fraction of the overall company shares, those shares give investors the right and fiduciary responsibility to vote effectively on corporate issues. The global allocations by investors, which shifted dramatically after the global financial crisis in 2008, provided investors with the opportunity to vote on thousands of public companies ballots each year.

Into this environment, investors, who may have portfolio managers, active ownership and stewardship teams, will need to make voting decisions, or delegate voting decisions, regarding director elections, executive pay and compensation packages, remuneration reports and advisory votes on executive pay, and/or proposals filed by management and shareholders. These engagements are important: portfolio managers may deal more directly with the CEOs and senior management of companies on quarterly reporting, dividends, and short- and long-term financial performance. The teams focus on active ownership and stewardship with a broader range of subject experts, including the board of directors on board-related issues, such as diversity, long-term strategies, CEO succession, remuneration policies and audit independence. More importantly, they will be looking to guide companies on emerging trends and the dynamic materiality of the risk landscape. Taken together, the valuable perspectives of these individuals should offer more complete assessment of companies. This dialogue can also be quite useful to inform an investor's proxy voting and stewardship responsibilities.

Proxy voting guidelines help investors determine whether to support, withhold or vote against the directors, and how to cast votes for the remaining ballot items. The key provisions will generally include the vote for the directors, ratification of the auditor (in some jurisdictions), "say on pay" (executive pay and compensation), and any management or shareholder proposals that have been included for shareholders to consider. More recently, proxy voting guidelines for investment managers have been developed to include guidance on social (such as board and company diversity, health and safety) and environmental (such as climate reporting and climate risk response, decarbonisation strategy) resolutions.

Figure 9.1 The objective of stewardship

There are three primary ways in which effective stewardship can enhance investment outcomes:

1. Driving growth

At its essence, stewardship is acting in the best interests of asset owners. This means holding boards accountable for execution oversight. It also supports spotting early sustainability themes and visionary companies behind new opportunities. As part of stewardship, engagement activities guide strategic growth plans by addressing stakeholder-related challenges.

2. Managing dynamic materiality of risks

Stewardship activities put constructive pressure on companies to evaluate how they will navigate an emerging landscape of risks.

3. Improving transparency and disclosure

Better disclosure means less uncertainty for investors, typically leading to lower costs of capital and the ability to finance positive change. Additionally, through the disclosure process companies can gain added insights into their business, leading to changes that enhance growth and risk management.

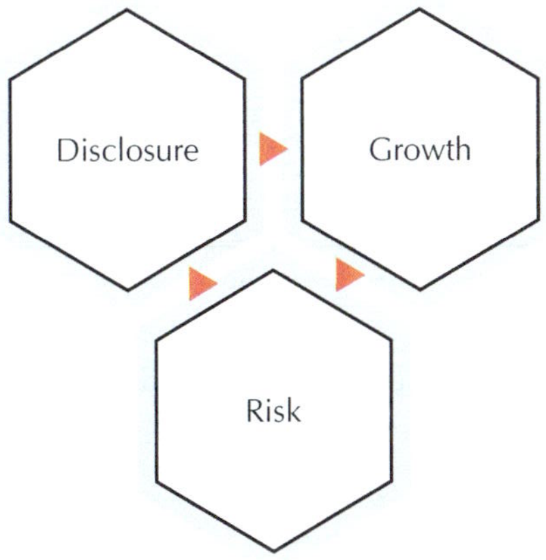

Source: HSBC Asset Management

Voting guidelines may contain detailed language to guide voting decisions that contain factors an investor has determined are essential for good governance practices at companies. While ICGN encourages a robust set of voting guidelines, a "check the box" system is discouraged. Thoughtful consideration and attention to voting are stewardship principles. Many votes may be relatively uncomplicated to cast based upon the investor's proxy voting guidelines. Other votes may be more difficult in determining the appropriate instructions since they may fall into a "grey area", requiring analysis and/or engagement prior to voting. This analyses can be time-consuming, and require reviews of voting results and proposals from past proxy seasons, while engagement also requires resources. Proposals presented by management and those requested by shareholders to be placed on the ballot are two categories of voting that may need extra time and attention before informed votes can be cast. Figure 9.1 presents an illustrative diagram on the objective of stewardship as it can help drive returns, support the consideration of risks and guide disclosure that could lead to a lower cost of capital

Stewardship matters

If there is any doubt about the value of stewardship at work, one needs to look no further than key proxy votes that occurred in 2021 (see also Panel 9.1).

- One example is the annual general meeting (AGM) at ExxonMobil on May 28, 2021, in which investment manager Engine No. 1 was able to align support with "Exxon's biggest institutional investors. BlackRock, Vanguard and State Street", which "voted against Exxon's leadership and gave Engine No. 1 powerful support". Three of four directors were elected in the activist proxy contest campaign (Phillips, 2021).
- The commitments of the "big 3" of BlackRock, Vanguard and State Street announced increasing levels of support for ESG-related proposals. According to Lazard (2021), in H1–2021, Vanguard supported 50% of diversity, equity and inclusion-related and 37% of environmental-related proposals. From July 1, 2020, until June 30, 2021, BlackRock supported 64% of environmental proposals and 47% of environmental and social (E&S)

PANEL 9.1 SEC PROPOSAL REQUIREMENTS FOR 2022 PROXY SEASON

The final amendments to the Securities and Exchange Commission's (SEC) Rule 14a-8(e) apply to proposals submitted for an annual or special meeting held on or after January 1, 2022. There is a transition period for the new ownership thresholds that allows shareholders who meet the US$2,000/one-year ownership threshold as of the effective date of the amendments to submit proposals for an annual or special meeting to be held prior to January 1, 2023, provided they continuously hold at least US$2,000 of a company's securities from the effective date through the date of submission.

The resubmission thresholds were changed to 5%, 15% and 25%, respectively.[1]

proposals overall. In H1–2021, State Street supported 46% of climate-related proposals and voted against board members at 43 S&P 500 companies for lack of board diversity data disclosure.

SHAREHOLDER PROPOSALS FROM THE STEWARDSHIP LENS

The ICGN, Shareholder Proposals – An Essential Instrument for Ensuring Corporate Accountability, 2021 stated:

> Over the last several years, there has been a proliferation of stewardship codes adopted around the world. These codes underscore the importance for institutional investors, fund managers, and retail investors to effectively utilise their shareholder rights and fiduciary responsibilities to hold investee companies to account. The filing of shareholder proposals (or resolutions) is one of the instruments in the shareholder toolkit to influence a company's policies, practices, and boards of directors/management related to environmental, social and governance (ESG) issues.

The analytics provided in this Viewpoint established that filings of shareholder proposals are on the rise in many countries in parallel with the adoption of stewardship codes. There are several factors that may have an impact on the success of a shareholder proposal passing, including specific language to the company, as well as being feasible, practical, timely and proportional to the remedy sought (ICGN, 2021b, p. 10).

The Viewpoint noted that there are still relatively low passage rates for many shareholder proposals. Support rates, however, are trending upward. According to Gibson Dunn (2021):

> Average support for all shareholder proposals voted on was 36.2% in 2021, up from the 31.3% average in 2020 and 32.8% average in 2019. In 2021, environmental proposals overtook governance proposals to receive the highest average support at 42.3%, up from 29.2% in 2020. Support for social (non-environmental) proposals also increased significantly to 30.6%, up from 21.5% in 2020 – driven primarily by a greater number of diversity-related proposals voted on with increased average levels of support. Governance proposals received 40.2% support in 2021, up from 35.3% in 2020. This year also saw a double-digit increase in the number of shareholder proposals that received majority support (74 in total, up from 50 in 2020), with an increasing number of such proposals focused on issues other than traditional governance topics.

As the Viewpoint mentioned, the filing of shareholder proposals triggers cost to the filer as well as the company, particularly if the proposal will be opposed. Management may counter with its own proposal or offer to add the shareholder proposal on the proxy if agreement is reached. Duelling proposals may ultimately land on the same proxy ballot, generating a review to determine which proposal should be supported by investors.

Given the "costs"[2] associated with proposals to both investors and companies, compared to the shareholder rights that may accrue with their passage, are there ways for other investors to evaluate proposals that may fall into these grey areas? Do shareholder proposals detract from management's ability to run the day-to-day activities of the company? Or do these proposals serve as a bellwether for issues on the minds of investors, who may have grown impatient with the slow adoption by the board and management or their outright refusal to consider what an investor is proposing? Under either scenario, what tools or analysis could be useful as these proposals are considered during proxy season?

In an interesting development, on November 3, 2021, the SEC's Division of Corporation Finance issued a Staff Legal Bulletin that addressed the exclusion of shareholder proposals under the "ordinary business exception". The exception "confines the resolution of ordinary business problems to management and the board of directors, since it is impracticable for shareholders to decide how to solve such problems at an annual shareholders meeting".

The Division will now use a modified approach to excluding shareholder proposals covering "issues with a broader societal impact", according to the Staff Bulletin. It said, "For example, proposals squarely raising human capital management issues with a broad societal impact would not be subject to exclusion solely because the proponent did not demonstrate that the human capital management issue was significant to the company". This means that the more restrictive amendments passed by the SEC for the current proxy season could pave the way for social-type proposals to have an easier path for inclusion on the proxy.[3]

The SEC has a long-established process in which companies may request that it provides an interpretation whether it will take "no action" on enforcement if the company does not add a shareholder proposal to the ballot. The Division of Corporation Finance will receive "requests from companies to state its informal, non-binding views on whether it concurs that there is a legal basis to exclude shareholder proposals from their proxy statements under Exchange Act Rule 14a-8 (Rule 14a-8)". On December 13, 2021, the Division issued a notice that "staff will once again respond to each shareholder proposal no-action request with a written letter, similar to those issued in prior years. Our response letters will be posted publicly on the Division's website in a timely manner."[4]

PANEL 9.2 THE ICGN MODEL MANDATE INITIATIVE

This initiative was launched in 2012 to provide model contract terms between asset owners and their fund managers in asset management agreements (ICGN, 2012). In 2022, ICGN partnered with the United Nations' supported Global Investors for Sustainable Development (GISD) Alliance to update the model mandate document and contract clauses (ICGN-GISD, Model Mandate, 2022).

BOARD ACTION ON WRITTEN CONSENT

According to D.F. King, the most frequent shareholder proposal filed in 2021 in Russell 3000 companies was "action by written consent" (written consent). Along with proposals in the US filed on climate change, diversity, racial equity audits, proxy access, special meetings or majority vote standards, action by written consent attracted a strong level of support. Written consent serves as a way to validate a course of action by shareholders without the requirement that a shareholder meeting actually take place; however, the board must take action if it needs to amend the articles of incorporation, even if shareholders support a proposal. In the first half of 2021, 77 proposals on this subject were filed in the US. The average level of support, among proposals voted on, was 41.1% (D.F. King, 2021b).

As a comparison, in 2019 there were only 34 proposals relating to written consent. In 2020, that number grew to 55. In 2019, the proposals faired rather well, with support at 39.4%, while there was a decrease in 2020 to 34.36% and then a high of 41.18% in 2021 (D.F. King, 2021a).

According to Minerva Analytics, during the 2020 AGM season a total of 735 shareholder proposals were filed in markets globally. Out of the overall total, only 12 proposals related to corporate actions, but 211 proposals related to shareholder rights. (). Specific proposals addressing the right to act by Written Consent were not as prevalent on a global basis. Other "shareholder rights" proposals made up almost 29% of the proposals filed, which demonstrated a heightened level of advocacy by shareholders, seeking governance changes.[5]

What caused the increase in shareholder proposals for written consent?

The increase in the filing of shareholder proposals may be partially attributed to the concerns raised by investors beginning in early 2020 when the pandemic caused companies to quickly pivot to virtual annual meetings. Some shareholders reported they had difficulty presenting proposals, asking questions and exercising basic shareholder rights. In its review of the 2020 proxy season, ICGN issued a Viewpoint that considered virtual and hybrid meetings, and recommended best practices for companies to provide optimal annual meeting formats to ensure shareholder rights (ICGN, Shareholder Meetings and Investor Dialogue: The New Normal, 2020).

Shareholders also reacted to the high threshold levels to set a record date for written consent that many companies included in their articles of incorporation. As one shareholder noted in their proposal, the high threshold will never be achievable for shareholders to meet, and therefore it is a meaningless shareholder right. The proposals requested that the boards approve a lower threshold to allow for written consent.

Finally, the ability to act by written consent was considered more viable than pursuing the right to call a special meeting. Given the pandemic's obliteration of in-person meetings, it did not seem advisable to ask for the right to call a special meeting that would become another virtual event, controlled by management. Allowing shareholders to act by written consent was a safer and effective alternative.

Management proposals for written consent

One of the byproducts of the increase in investor stewardship and advocacy is the effort by companies to offer their own management proposals for shareholders to consider. These proposals can serve as a counterbalance to investor demands that a company believes are not in the best interests of shareholders. If a company believes that more of its investors would support a management proposal rather than a shareholder proposal, duelling proposals may land on the same ballot.

There were US companies that included management proposals with governance overtones on their ballots in 2021 and in previous proxy seasons. Examples include the declassification of company boards, the right to call a special meeting, and action by written consent (Westcott, 2021). For example, some companies provided shareholders with the opportunity to vote to add action by written consent to the their articles of incorporation. Why would a company add another mechanism for shareholders to ratify certain actions? Companies had begun to recognise that the continual challenges of operating in a global pandemic could impact their own ability to bring necessary actions to shareholders for ratification. Waiting one year for the next annual meeting is a long time in the world of corporate actions.

CONSIDERATIONS

Why would shareholders need to look carefully at proposals on a topic as mundane as action by written consent? It is because AGMs were so disrupted by the impact of Covid-19 that companies have been forced to move to virtual shareholder environments. With respect to the management and shareholder proposals that competed in the same ballot, investors needed to analyse any duelling proposals and decide how to cast their ballots.

There are several considerations with respect to management or shareholder proposals, including written consent, which may help inform the proxy voting analysis. Proposed thresholds have ranged from a high of 25–35% (usually proposed by management) to a low of 10% (usually proposed by investors) to set a record date that would trigger written consent. The newly crafted proposals in recent proxy seasons, asking for written consent, are worded differently than past seasons, to contain provisions for notice to other shareholders, intended to limit any misuse by some investors. Acting by written consent in lieu of a meeting is one provision that shareholders would be able to utilise to raise important matters outside of the routine AGM cycle.

For global investors who have assets in US companies, the rationale of why companies may need to offer shareholders the right for action by written consent is important to consider. The state of Delaware Courts have opined that a provision implementing written consent for shareholders must be included in a company's articles of incorporation. If not, a shareholder cannot solely file a precatory (non-binding) shareholder proposal to acquire that right. Therefore, if a company wants to adopt a provision authorising written consent for shareholders under its own terms, the company has to seek the change in the articles of incorporation or other controlling documents from both the board and shareholders. If the company does not want to adopt a provision that triggers written consent, the shareholders may file a precatory proposal to gain shareholder support as a way to pressure the board to act.[6]

ICGN provides for consideration of proposals such as action by written consent and other "shareholder rights" provisions. According to ICGN, Global Governance Principles, 2021:

> 10.7 Shareholder proposals. Companies should ensure that shareholders have the right to place proposals on the agenda of AGMs, subject to reasonable limitations. All shareholder proposals should be voted upon and contingency provisions should be made to ensure that proponents are able to present their proposal should they have difficulties in attending an AGM, particularly in a hybrid or virtual AGM.
>
> 10.8 Thresholds. Any threshold associated with shareholder proposals or other such participation should balance the need to ensure the matter under consideration is likely to be of importance to

> all shareholders. The threshold should take into consideration the degree of ownership concentration to ensure minority shareholders are not prevented from putting items on the agenda.

Meredith Foster has written a seminal piece on written consent, where she noted that, in 2019, most US public companies' articles of incorporation still included provisions that barred shareholders from acting by written consent. She also observed that activist investors and hostile bidders for companies have used written consent solicitations in the past, particularly in the 1980s and early 1990s, to pressure companies for changes that may or may not be a benefit for other shareholders (Foster, 2019).

Two proxy advisory firms, Glass Lewis and Institutional Shareholder Services (ISS), provide their own guidelines for voting proposals related to shareholder rights and action by written consent. Glass Lewis (2021) recommended a vote against the chair of nominating/governance and/or the entire committee if the board adopted certain provisions that impacted shareholder rights. It noted:

> In addition, we may recommend that shareholders vote against the chair of the governance committee, or the entire committee, where the board has amended the company's governing documents to reduce or remove important shareholder rights, or to otherwise impede the ability of shareholders to exercise such right, and has done so without seeking shareholder approval. Examples of board actions that may cause such a recommendation include: the elimination of the ability of shareholders to call a special meeting or to act by written consent; an increase to the ownership threshold required for shareholders to call a special meeting; an increase to vote requirements for charter or by-law amendments.

Glass Lewis codified its global approach on shareholder proposals related to written consent for the proxy season commencing in 2022, requesting that companies lower the threshold required to initiate written consent under certain conditions:

> When evaluating these proposals, we will generally recommend in favour of lowering the ownership threshold when the company has no special meeting provision, or only allows shareholders owning more than 15% of its shares the ability to call a special meeting. We will generally oppose lowering the ownership threshold necessary to initiate written consent if the company in question has a 15% or lower special meeting threshold.

ISS (2021) also noted that, under shareholder ability to act by written consent, ISS will:

- generally vote against management and shareholder proposals to restrict or prohibit shareholders' ability to act by written consent;
- generally vote for management and shareholder proposals that provide shareholders with the ability to act by written consent, taking into account:
  - shareholders' current right to act by written consent;
  - consent threshold;
  - inclusion of exclusionary or prohibitive language;
  - investor ownership structure; and
  - shareholder support of and management's response to previous shareholder proposals.
- ISS will vote case by case if, in addition to the above, the company has these governance and anti-takeover provisions:
  - unfettered right for shareholders to call a special meeting at the 10% threshold;
  - a majority vote standard in uncontested director elections;
  - no non-shareholder approved pill; and
  - an annually elected board.

A CASE STUDY: COMPANY "A"

Background

In 2020 and 2021, company A, a US listed public company, included management or shareholder proposals on the ballots for annual meetings that provided approval for written consent and other related proposals that impacted company operations and/or shareholder rights. The company has less than 70 holders of record of its common stock. The number of beneficial owners is substantially greater because a large portion of common stock is held of record in broker "street names".

Board proposal in 2020

In 2020, the board proposed an amendment to its articles of incorporation that contained procedural safeguards to ensure that shareholder action by written consent would not occur without adequate notice, transparency, information or time. The threshold was set at 25%. The company noted that without these procedural safeguards, the right to action by written consent could create the potential for uninformed action, confusion and potentially disable the company from pursuing alternatives if an unsolicited takeover effort occurred. The management proposal was supported by 96% of shareholders.

Shareholder proposal in 2021

Notwithstanding the high level of shareholder support in 2020, a shareholder filed a proposal in 2021 to improve the company's procedure for triggering shareholder action by written consent, by seeking to lower the threshold to 10%. The shareholder provided the following arguments in support of the proposal.

- The threshold would be set at 10% of shares to request a record date to initiate written consent. Currently, it takes the formal approval of 25% of all shares that normally cast ballots at the annual meeting to ask for a record date for written consent. The 25% threshold effectively means that shareholders will not be able to request a record date.
- The company has a supermajority vote requirement for changes to the articles of incorporation, meaning that any action taken by written consent would still need to reach the 65% supermajority approval from the shares that normally cast ballots at the annual meeting. The supermajority vote requirement gives overwhelming protection to management that will remain unchanged.
- Taking action by written consent is a right that shareholders can use to raise important matters outside the normal annual meeting cycle, such as the election of a new director because a current director received a significant number of negative votes.
- Virtual shareholder meetings have limited engagement with other shareholders, management and directors. Written consent provides an alternative for corporate business.

Board response to the shareholder proposal

The board recommended a vote "against" the proposal for the following reasons.

- The company currently provides shareholders with the right to act by written consent, which was approved at the 2020 annual meeting, for a threshold of 25% of the company's common stock. This ownership threshold represents the right balance between providing shareholders with the right to take action by written consent and preventing possible abuse or misuse by investors with minority or misaligned interests, as well as avoiding significant costs and distractions to the board and management associated with the solicitation process.
- The proposal to adopt the right to act by written consent received the support of the holders of approximately 96% of shares present and voted on the matter in 2020.
- Most of the large institutional shareholders with whom the company engaged expressed the view that the right to act by written consent was unnecessary in light of existing shareholder rights, including the right to call special meetings. Nevertheless, they encouraged us to be responsive to the majority-supported shareholder proposal by adopting a written consent right with reasonable safeguards to prevent possible abuse.
- The board believes that lowering the ownership threshold for the shareholders' right to act by written consent is unnecessary because of the company's strong corporate governance practices, including:
  - annual election of directors and a majority-voting standard for the election of directors in uncontested elections;
  - the holders of at least a majority of the company's outstanding common stock can remove a director, with or without cause;
  - holders of 25% of the outstanding common stock have the right to call a special meeting of shareholders; and
  - the company's by-laws allow eligible shareholders to include their own nominees for directors in the company's proxy materials along with the board-nominated candidates.

The results

The 2021 shareholder proposal did not pass, although the vote was close: approximately 51.4% of shareholders voted against it, with 48.2% voting in favour. Broker non-votes played a part in the final vote totals.

SHAREHOLDER ANALYSIS: ACTIVELY USING STEWARDSHIP DURING VOTING

Due to the pattern in the case study on company A, investors may wish to consider how they would have voted on the 2020 and 2021 proposals. Action by written consent is just one type of proposal that may require a more detailed analysis by investors, whether it is filed by management or a shareholder. As noted in the case study, investors may need to look at previous company ballots to inform their votes.

To determine whether a management or shareholder proposal's threshold level is appropriate to implement written consent, investors may need to do the following.

- ❑ Analyse whether the company already provides for written consent in its articles of incorporation or other controlling documents. If not, a precatory shareholder proposal, even if approved by the level set for passage (either a simple majority or the supermajority standard the company has set) will not be enough to accomplish action by written consent without board action.
- ❑ Review the ownership concentration to determine whether shareholders will be able to utilise written consent. If a company has a dual or multi-class share structure or is a controlled company, minority shareholders may not be able to pursue action.
- ❑ Consider whether investors, including institutional investors and asset managers, will likely support a shareholder proposal for written consent given a company's current governance practices, the relationships with the board of directors and senior management.
- ❑ Analyse other shareholder "rights" in place – for example, the right to call a special meeting, a declassified board, a simple majority voting standard, a lead independent director (LID) if the chair/CEO positions are combined, one share/one vote standard without dual class or multi-class share structures, diversity among the board, board refreshment policies are in place, and no "overboarded" board members.
- ❑ Review the proposal, whether it is offered by management or a shareholder, to determine if safeguards are in place to provide adequate notice to all shareholders, given the threshold level

proposed to set a record date, and how it would be implemented, if supported.

ENGAGEMENT ISSUES TO INFORM STEWARDSHIP

ICGN has identified several questions to consider when evaluating the potentially conflicting areas of engagement or proxy voting in view of good governance practices, or a lack thereof within the board and a company (see Table 9.2). While this is not an exclusive list, these questions may inform voting, stewardship, and engagement with companies (ICGN, Global Governance Principles, 2021).

CONCLUSION

As more outreach and dialogue occurs between companies and investors, investors will be faced with the question of whether to escalate engagement by filing shareholder proposals to request that boards of directors take action on specific issues. While one shareholder may file a proposal, the rest of the investors will need to consider whether they will support the proposal or side with management.

As the global pandemic has shown us, the annual general meeting schedule of in-person meetings has been changed, perhaps permanently. In our interconnected global markets with increased M&A activity, changes in board and executive leadership, and geopolitical risks that impact entire sectors, shareholders may need additional opportunities to engage with directors and discuss the company's strategic direction.

This active stewardship role for investors will be increasingly important as they engage companies to address global risks, from climate change to widespread supply chain disruptions. Investors, too, can amplify their approach with a full review of factors, with a stewardship "lens", as they engage with companies on a broad approach to ESG issues and analyse proposals on company ballots.

ICGN would like to thank and acknowledge the following individuals and organisations for their review and contributions to this chapter: Marie Lehmann, Martina Macpherson and Daniel Ung for inclusion of the chapter in this book; Dr Christine Chow, ICGN Board of Governors, Head of Stewardship, HSBC Global Asset Management, for recommending that ICGN participate; and Robert Lewenson, ICGN Board of Governors, Head of Responsible Investment, Old Mutual Investment Group; ICGN Global

Table 9.2 Governance questions

Questions on governance	ICGN principles or guidance
Does the company have a classified or unclassified board of directors?	GGP 3.7 Director election process: Directors should be elected to the board preferably on an annual basis, or stand for election once every three years, and be accountable to shareholders by approval of a majority of shares voted in favour on each resolution.
What is the makeup of the board? Are the members diverse and do they represent diverse perspectives? What is the tenure of the members? Does the board have the requisite skillset? Are any board members overboarded?	GGP 3 Composition and appointment: The board should comprise a sufficient mix of directors with relevant knowledge, independence, competence, industry experience and diversity of perspectives to generate effective challenge, discussion and objective decision-making in alignment with the company's purpose, long-term strategy and relevant stakeholders. GGP 1.6 Directorships: The number, and nature, of board appointments an individual director holds should be carefully considered and reviewed on a regular basis, and the degree to which each individual director has the capacity to undertake multiple directorships should be clearly disclosed. This consideration should reflect the nature of existing board commitments, as well as any commitments relating to foundations or charities. Normally, an individual director should not hold more than three directorships of any sort, and this should be substantially less for executive directors, as well as for the board chair and committee chairs.[7]
Is there an independent board chair or LID? Does the board separate the role of the chairperson from the role of the CEO?	GGP 2 Leadership and independence: Board leadership requires clarity and balance in board and executive roles, and an integrity of independent process to protect the interests of shareholders and relevant stakeholders in promoting the long-term success of the company. GGP 2.1 Independent leadership: There should be a clear division of responsibilities between the role of the chair of the board and the CEO to avoid unfettered powers of decision-making in any one individual. This is particularly relevant in controlled companies when either the chair or CEO are significant shareholders. The board should be chaired by an independent director who should be independent on the date of appointment. Should the role of the chair and CEO be combined, the board should explain the reasons why this is in the best interests of the company in the annual report and keep the structure under review. The responsibilities of the chair, CEO, LID and committee chairs should be clearly described and publicly disclosed.

Questions on governance	ICGN principles or guidance
Does the company have internal and external audit reporting and records that are rigorous and independent? What is the reported performance against peers over time – longer term as well as quarterly reporting?	GGP 8 Internal and external audit: The board should establish rigorous, independent and effective internal and external audit procedures to ensure the quality and integrity of corporate reporting.
Has the company adopted supermajority voting requirements? Who are the majority shareholders – ie, who owns the company?	ICGN believes in one share/one vote. Thresholds may be harder to meet – ie, 35% threshold for action by written consent.
Has the company adopted a dual class share structure? If so, is there a sunset provision of no more than seven years, for example?	GGP 9.1 Share classes: Ordinary or common shares should feature one vote for each share. Divergence from a one share/one vote standard that gives certain shareholders power or control disproportionate to their economic interests should be avoided or, in the event of the existence of such classes, they should be disclosed and explained and sunset mechanisms put in place. Dual class share structures should be discouraged, and where they are in place kept under review and be accompanied by commensurate extra protections for minority shareholders, particularly in the event of a takeover bid. The board should disclose sufficient information about the material attributes of all of the company's classes and series of shares on a timely basis.
Has the company provided shareholders with recognised rights in its by-laws or corporate documents (for example, proxy access, right to call a special meeting, action by written consent)?	GGP 9 Shareholder rights: Rights of all shareholders should be equal and must be protected. Fundamental to this protection is ensuring that a shareholder's voting rights are directly linked to its economic stake, and that minority shareholders have voting rights on key decisions or transactions that affect their interest in the company. GGP 3.8 Shareholder nominated directors: The board should ensure that shareholders are able to nominate candidates for board appointment, subject to an appropriate threshold of share ownership. Such candidacies should be proposed to the nomination committee and, subject to an appropriate threshold, be nominated directly on the company's proxy. GGP 9.2 Major decisions: The board should ensure that shareholders have the right to vote on major decisions that may change the nature of the company in which they have invested.

Questions on governance	ICGN principles or guidance
Does the board have risk oversight as part of its duties, including anti-corruption, climate change, cyber risk policies and exposure? How often does management report these risks to the board? Have they publicly identified their material sustainability (E&S) risks and dedicated board oversight of those risks?	GGP 6 Risk oversight: The board should proactively oversee the assessment and disclosure of the company's key risks, and approve the approach to risk management and internal controls regularly or with any significant business change, and satisfy itself that the approach is functioning effectively (ICGN, 2019a).
Have the board of directors and the remuneration committee aligned executive compensation and remuneration to ESG key performance indicators (KPIs), tied to performance, sustainability reporting and relevant metrics? How are awards made, short-term and long-term payouts? Does the board have a clawback policy for rewards that should be returned by key executives for illegal or inappropriate behaviour? Vesting over three years for long-term investment plans (LTIPs)? Holdings requirements?	GGP 5 Remuneration: Remuneration should be designed to equitably and effectively align the interests of the CEO, executive officers and workforce with a company's strategy and purpose to help ensure long-term sustainable value preservation and creation. Aggregate remuneration should be appropriately balanced with the payment of dividends to shareholders and retention of capital for future investment, and the level of quantum should be defendable relative to social considerations in terms of inequality.
How do the board and management report on the company's financial position, human capital management, ie, diversity, equity and inclusion, Equal Employment Opportunity (EEO)-1 data? Does the company have a track record as a business model that is sustainable over time?	GGP 7 Corporate reporting: Boards should oversee timely and reliable company disclosures for shareholders and relevant stakeholders relating to the company's financial position, approach to sustainability, performance, business model, strategy and long-term prospects.

Questions on governance	**ICGN principles or guidance**
What is the history of regulatory fines, penalties, whistleblowers and/or lawsuits against the company, management and/or board?	GGP 1 Board role and responsibilities: The board should promote the long-term best interests of the company by acting on an informed basis with good faith, care and loyalty, for the benefit of shareholders, while having regard to relevant stakeholders.
What appears to be the "culture" of the organisation? Does the company report transparently on employee training, turnover or recruitment/retention challenges? Has the company made any statements related to purpose – is the company part of the global effort to address climate change, for instance? Has it adopted sustainability disclosures and materiality standards?	GGP 4 Corporate culture: The board should instil and demonstrate a culture of high standards of business ethics and integrity aligned with the company's purpose and values at board level and throughout the workforce. GGP 7.7 Materiality and sustainability: Sustainability disclosures should focus on materially relevant factors, with many environmental and social factors being sector-specific, linked to the company's management of its natural and human capital. Where possible, sustainability-related reporting should also seek to address "double materiality", for reporting on the company's external impacts on society and the environment, as well as internal impacts on the company's own financial performance. Moreover, boards should build an awareness of "dynamic materiality", recognising that materiality evolves over time alongside factors such as emerging technology, product innovation and regulatory developments.
Do board members on relevant committees engage with shareholders? Are they accessible to investors? Does the company have an investor relations division that coordinates outreach by the board?	GGP 1.1 Responsibilities: The board is accountable to shareholders and relevant stakeholders for preserving and enhancing sustainable value over the long term in alignment with a company's purpose and long-term strategy. In fulfilling their role effectively, board members are responsible for engaging constructively with shareholders on governance, sustainability and performance aligned with the company's purpose and strategy. GGP 1.4 Dialogue: The board, particularly the chair, lead (or senior) independent director and committee chairs, should constructively engage with shareholders and relevant stakeholders (particularly the workforce) for meaningful dialogue.

Stewardship Committee, Catherine McCall, Chair, Executive Director, Canadian Coalition for Good Governance and Peter Dervan, Director, ESG Research & Integration, Manulife Investment Management. Thank you also to Kerrie Waring, ICGN Chief Executive Officer; George Dallas, Policy Director and Francesca Phillips, Policy Coordinator, for their support and encouragement.

1 For more details, see https://www.sec.gov/rules/final/2020/34-89964.pdf.

2 With regard to management costs for shareholder proposals, in a letter to the SEC, Darla Stuckey, CEO of the Society for Corporate Governance, explained that while the highest costs could be more than US$200,000, a 2019 study by the Center for Capital Markets Competitiveness found that costs average about US$87,000 per proposal (Stuckley, 2019).

3 See https://www.sec.gov/corpfin/staff-legal-bulletin-14l-shareholder-proposals.

4 See https://www.sec.gov/corpfin/announcement/announcement-14a-8-no-action-requests-20211213.

5 For information on the requirements and deadlines for filing shareholder proposals in Australia, Canada, France, Germany, Italy, Japan, The Netherlands, South Africa, Spain, Sweden, Switzerland, UK and the US, see ICGN (2021b), p. 10.

6 See Del Code Ann, title 8, Section 242 (2018) at https://delcode.delaware.gov/title8/c001/sc08/index.html.

7 See also ICGN (2016a).

REFERENCES

D.F. King, 2021a, "Proxy Season Review and Fall Engagement Guide", August (available at https://lp.astfinancial.com/2021-debrief-guide.html).

D.F. King, 2021b, "Shareholder Proposal Review", December.

Dallas, G. and M. Lubrano, 2021, "Governance, Stewardship and Sustainability: Theory, Practice and Evidence", ICGN, June (available at https://www.icgn.org/education/e-book-governance-stewardship-and-sustainability).

Foster, M., 2019, "Special Meetings and Consent Solicitations: How the Written-consent Right Uniquely Empowers Shareholders", *The Yale Law Journal*, 128(6), April, pp. 1,478–791 (available at https://www.yalelawjournal.org/note/special-meetings-and-consent-solicitations-how-the-written-consent-right-uniquely-empowers-shareholders).

Gibson Dunn, 2021, "Shareholder Proposal Developments During the 2021 Proxy Season", August 19 (available at https://www.gibsondunn.com/wp-content/uploads/2021/08/shareholder-proposal-developments-during-the-2021-proxy-season.pdf).

ICGN, 2012, "ICGN Model Mandate", London: International Corporate Governance Network.

Glass Lewis, 2021, "Guidelines: An Overview of the Glass Lewis Approach to Proxy Advice – United States", Proxy Paper (available at https://www.glasslewis.com/wp-content/uploads/2020/11/US-Voting-Guidelines-GL.pdf).

ICGN, 2016, "Guidance on Diversity on Boards" (available at https://www.icgn.org/sites/default/files/2021–06/ICGN%20Guidance%20on%20Diversity%20on%20Boards%20-%20Final.pdf).

ICGN, 2016, "Guidance on Securities Lending" (available at https://www.icgn.org/sites/default/files/2021-06/ICGN%20Guidance%20on%20Diversity%20on%20Boards%20-%20Final.pdf).

ICGN, 2017, "The Inclusion of Non-voting or Limited Voting Shares in Stock Market Indices", November (available at https://www.icgn.org/sites/default/files/2021–05/5.%20ICGN%20Viewpoint%20Indices%20and%20non%20voting%20shares.pdf).

ICGN, 2018, "Guidance on Investor Fiduciary Duties" (available at https://www.icgn.org/sites/default/files/2021–06/ICGN%20Guidance%20on%20Investor%20Fiduciary%20Duties.pdf).

ICGN, 2018, "Investment Exclusions: Some Technical Considerations", ICGN Viewpoint, February (available at https://www.icgn.org/sites/default/files/2021-05/1.%20Viewpoint%20Investment%20exclusions%20some%20technical%20considerations.pdf).

ICGN, 2019, "Investor Framework for Addressing Systemic Risks", ICGN Viewpoint, June (available at https://www.icgn.org/sites/default/files/2021-05/1.ICGN%20Viewpoint%20on%20Systemic%20Risk.pdf).

ICGN, 2019, "What is the Role of the Creditor in Corporate Governance and Investor Stewardship?", ICGN Viewpoint, September (available at https://www.icgn.org/sites/default/files/2021-05/4.Creditors%20Governance%20and%20Stewardship.pdf).

ICGN, 2020, "Global Stewardship Principles" (available at https://www.icgn.org/sites/default/files/2021-06/ICGN%20Global%20Stewardship%20Principles%202020_1.pdf).

ICGN, 2020, "Shareholder Meetings and Investor Dialogue: The New Normal", ICGN Viewpoint, September (available at https://www.icgn.org/sites/default/files/2021-06/ICGN%20Viewpoint%20future%20AGMs.pdf).

ICGN, 2021, "Global Governance Principles" (available at https://www.icgn.org/sites/default/files/2022-04/ICGN%20Global%20Governance%20Principles%202021.pdf).

ICGN, 2021, "Shareholder Proposals – An Essential Instrument for Ensuring Corporate Accountability", December (available at https://www.icgn.org/sites/default/files/2021-12/ICGN%20Shareholder%20Proposal%20Viewpoint%20review%20021221%20Final.pdf).

ICGN-GISD, 2022, "ICGN-GISD Model Mandate", June (available at https://www.icgn.org/sites/default/files/2022-06/ICGN%20GISD%20Model%20Mandate%202022.pdf).

ISS, 2021, "Proxy Voting Guidelines: Benchmark Policy Recommendations – United States", December 13 (available at https://www.issgovernance.com/file/policy/active/americas/US-Voting-Guidelines.pdf).

Lazard, 2021, "Lazard's Annual Review of Shareholder Activism – 2021", January 19 (available at https://www.lazard.com/perspective/lazards-annual-review-of-shareholder-activism-2021/).

Minerva Analytics, 2020, "Shareholder Meetings (AGM/EGM)".

Phillips, M., 2021, "Exxon's Board Defeat Signals the Rise of Social-good Activists", *New York Times*, June 9 (available at https://www.nytimes.com/2021/06/09/business/exxon-mobil-engine-no1-activist.html).

Stuckley, D., 2019, "Society of Corporate Governance Letter, February 3, 2020, to the SEC, re: Procedural Requirements and Resubmission Thresholds under Exchange Act 14a-8".

Westcott, S., 2021, "2021 Proxy Season Review", Harvard Law School Forum on Corporate Governance, August 5 (available at https://corpgov.law.harvard.edu/2021/08/05/2021-proxy-season-review/).

10

Case Study 5: Applying active ownership and stewardship to a pension fund portfolio

Caroline Escott

Railpen

This chapter builds on the theory of active ownership by demonstrating how the in-house manager for one of the UK's largest pension schemes considers and undertakes engagement, voting and public policy activity on behalf of scheme members. It explores the Railpen approach to, and governance of, active ownership, as well as how it has evolved and what it looks like in practice.

ABOUT RAILPEN

The Railways Pension Trustee Company Ltd (the Trustee) is responsible for managing four railways pension schemes. The Railways Pension Scheme (RPS) is the largest of the four, created in 1994 after the privatisation of the UK railways industry and reorganisation of the British Rail Pension Scheme.

Railpen is the trading name of Railway Pension Investments Ltd, authorised and regulated by the Financial Conduct Authority (FCA), and acts as the in-house investment manager for the railways pension schemes. Railpen is responsible for the management of around £37 billion of assets on behalf of 350,000 members. The Trustee is Railpen's only client, which ensures that all Railpen's activities align with the interests of the schemes' members.

"Sustainable ownership" is the term given to Railpen's approach to incorporating a broad spectrum of sustainability considerations into the investments it manages on behalf of members.

RAILPEN'S MANDATE FOR ACTIVE OWNERSHIP

The railways pension schemes include many open defined benefit sections, and the Trustee invests based on the expectation that it will be paying the pension of an 18-year-old who is in their first job today out to 2100 and beyond. This means that Railpen's time horizons are very long, and therefore that long-term risks and opportunities are fundamental to managing the investment portfolio. This management includes Railpen's long-standing work on both incorporation of environmental, social and governance (ESG) factors into investment analysis and decision-making (which Railpen terms "ESG integration"). It also includes significant activity on engagement, proxy voting and public policy (collectively known as "active ownership", the main topic explored in this chapter).

The Trustee's investment beliefs guide Railpen's investment management activities. These include the following.

1. Incorporating and acting upon climate risk and other ESG factors is a significant driver of investment outcome and part of our fiduciary duty.
2. Environmental, social and governance (ESG) factors affect corporate financial performance, asset values and asset-liability risk. Well-informed and financially material ESG analysis, as part of a holistic investment process, supports the identification and ultimately the pricing of ESG risk and opportunity. Constructive engagement combined with thoughtful voting can protect and enhance investment value.
3. A long investment horizon exposes a pension scheme to societal and systemic risks, such as climate change. These risks are growing and need to be managed. Capital allocation by investors and corporates makes a difference in how these risks play out. Railpen has a responsibility to make a scheme's assets resilient to systemic threats and to position portfolios for long-term opportunities.

The Trustee is also clear in its Statement of Investment Principles (SIP)[1] that companies with good corporate governance practices and engaged shareholders are more likely to achieve the superior long-term financial performance that members need. This derives from a growing body of evidence to demonstrate the positive impact active ownership has on long-term value creation, including the following impacts on individual portfolio companies:

- a reduction in share price volatility and downside risk (Dimson *et al*, 2015; Hoepner *et al*, 2018);
- an increase in return on assets and sales per employee or sales growth in the wake of successful engagements (Dimson *et al*, 2015; Dimson *et al*, 2018); and
- an increase in ESG rates of target companies in the wake of shareholder proposals (Dimson, Karakas and Li, 2015, 2018; Hoepner *et al*, 2018; Barko, Cremers and Renneboog, 2017; Dyck *et al*, 2019).

If the pursuit of these positive impacts is targeted at those companies and sectors most material to the portfolio, and is successful in driving change or enhancing understanding of a company, then *ceteris paribus* we can assume that active ownership is beneficial to long-term value creation at the portfolio level. Railpen's active ownership activity on behalf of the Trustee, proactively engaging with portfolio companies, policymakers and exercising available voting rights, therefore enables Railpen to enhance long-term investment returns for members.

RAILPEN'S INTEGRATED APPROACH TO ACTIVE OWNERSHIP

Railpen's active ownership workstream is implemented by individuals in Railpen's sustainable ownership team, alongside ESG integration and analysis and work on climate change. The sustainable ownership team sits within the fiduciary business, which brings together those teams responsible for supporting the Trustee and other pension sub-committees in oversight and top-down investment responsibilities. Placing active ownership within the fiduciary business explicitly links the Trustee's – and in turn members' – needs and expectations to the sustainable investment decisions made on members' behalf.

Railpen's sustainable ownership and investment management teams work closely and collaboratively across all parts of the lifecycle of an investment (see Figure 10.1). Although the starting point

Figure 10.1 Sustainable ownership and investment management teams collaborative across all parts of the lifecycle of an investment

for good engagement is a robust analysis of the ESG profile of a company, it is the active ownership activity that forms the key focus of this section.

- Before a decision to invest: Individuals in the sustainable ownership team co-engage in partnership with the investment management team to probe any areas of interest or concern, and then recommend possible mitigating activities.
- After a decision to invest: The sustainable ownership and investment management teams co-engage with key portfolio companies on stock-specific issues, and discuss Railpen's overall thematic sustainability and governance priorities.
- Voting recommendations: Recommendations are, where relevant, made and implemented by the sustainable ownership team. In key portfolios, decisions to abstain or vote against, are referred to the relevant Railpen portfolio manager for approval. If the two teams cannot reach a consensus, there is a process for escalation to the chief investment officer (CIO).
- Class actions: The CIO provides final sign-off on the decision as to whether to participate in opt-in class action suits against a company. The sustainable ownership and legal teams feed in views, including whether there is a likelihood of influencing and improving corporate governance because of the class action or whether participating in the lawsuit risks undermining an engagement with the company.

Having a clear line of sight from the Trustee's investment beliefs and philosophy regarding the importance of active ownership to investment outcomes to the governance, oversight and processes that support and underpin Railpen's engagement, voting and public policy work is important for effective active ownership. However, the Trustee and Railpen's approach to active ownership does not operate in a vacuum. The next section will explore how Railpen's approach to active ownership reflects the specifics of its investment allocation and approach, and how this has evolved over time and in response to market and regulatory developments.

EVOLUTION OF THE RAILPEN APPROACH OVER TIME

Railpen has a long history as a leader in the UK pensions industry on sustainable ownership. It was an early pioneer in creating its own in-house corporate governance framework, explicitly recognising the materiality of good governance to long-term corporate success and the important role of an independent board that is truly accountable to shareholders. This framework was extended to include sustainable ownership principles, and Railpen was an early adopter of the Carbon Disclosure Project (2000) and the UN-backed Principles of Responsible Investment (2010). Railpen has also published its "Global Voting Policy" annually since 1992 (one of the first schemes to do so), and aims to vote its entire listed equity portfolio.

While Railpen has often been at the vanguard of developments in this space, both Railpen's and the Trustee's approach has changed over time and in a way that reflects both market and regulatory trends. Each development or shift in emphasis remains true to Railpen's corporate governance heritage, and the centrality of an effective and independent board to strategy and risk management.

The implications of internally managed portfolios

Railpen has the authority to delegate investment management to external managers. It has always sought to extend its influence over its external asset managers' activity on sustainable ownership issues, including voting practices. However, in 2013, Railpen undertook its "Investment Transformation Programme" and began to shift management of its assets to an in-house investment management team. This was to provide more cost- and resource-efficient, and effective oversight and implementation, of its long-term investment strategy on members' behalf.

This momentum towards internalisation has continued ever since, with a significant proportion of Railpen's assets invested in-house. This approach has clear benefits for Railpen's active ownership work as it allows more direct control of engagement and voting. While the sustainable ownership team still works to scrutinise and challenge its external managers where necessary, more internal resource has therefore been dedicated to engaging directly with the companies themselves.

Railpen focuses engagement (both direct/individual and collaborative) and voting resources on those most material holdings to the portfolio – ie, where there is the most potential value at risk and where engagement can have the greatest impact. This means that two of Railpen's four priority engagement lists in the listed equities portfolio are focused entirely on internally and actively managed portfolios (1 and 2 in the list below).

1. Fundamental equities: Companies that are held in the fundamental growth strategy. Railpen seeks to engage regularly with all these companies (there were approximately 70 as of Spring 2021).
2. Quantitative equities: Companies that are held in the quantitative strategy. Railpen seeks to engage with the largest holdings annually, covering a significant proportion of assets under management (AUM) in the portfolio.
3. Governance and conduct laggards: Problematic companies at risk of exclusion.
4. Thematic: Railpen engages directly with key holdings on thematic issues but often undertakes thematic engagement in collaboration with others. Resources are prioritised across those coalitions considered most impactful.

Portfolio allocation across asset classes and geographies

Where the nature of Railpen's exposure and portfolio changes over time, so do the jurisdictions and asset classes to which the team dedicates active ownership resource. This includes both the tangible engagement and voting activity, as well as the time spent on learning and understanding the particularities of a specific asset class, or a jurisdiction's regulatory framework and investor ecosystem.

Figure 10.2 AUM by region (December 31, 2021)

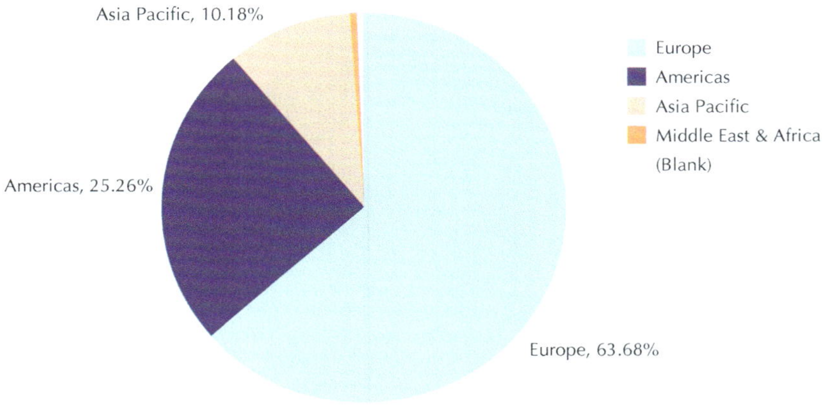

The Railpen portfolio is mainly concentrated in developed markets and, in particular, the UK and US (see Figure 10.2). In part, this reflects the nature of some of Railpen's private markets and real assets holdings, where the team believes greater oversight and capacity for a positive influence over holdings can be exerted in domestic markets. Furthermore, as a UK pension scheme, Railpen and the Trustee continue to be particularly keen to exercise voting rights and influence on UK holdings. This has led to the negotiation of direct voting rights on the UK holdings in some of Railpen's pooled, externally managed portfolios.

Similarly, as Railpen's allocation to the US has grown over time, with several sizable holdings in the fundamental and quantitative portfolios, it has sought to become more actively involved with the relevant US membership organisations – or those organisations that include a significant proportion of US investors. These include the Council of Institutional Investors (CII) and the Global Investment Governance Network (GIGN). Building and maintaining relationships with advocacy groups in core jurisdictions is important as it offers us additional insights into a given country's active ownership policies and practice, and helps build networks with other investors on topics of interest.

The length of Railpen's time horizons means there is a substantial allocation to growth assets such as listed equity, which is why a significant proportion of its in-house resource is dedicated to the

Figure 10.3 AUM by asset class (December 31, 2021)

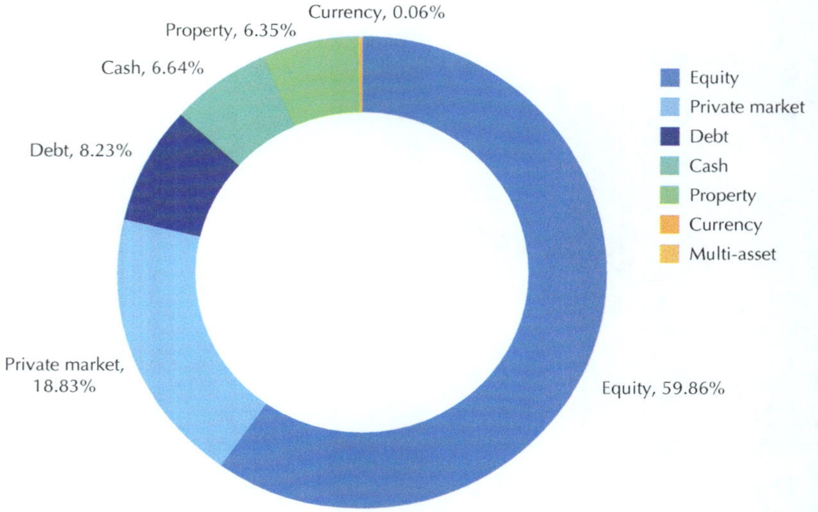

thoughtful exercise of substantial voting rights alongside constructive engagement of listed equity assets (see Figure 10.3).

As Railpen's allocation to private markets has grown, alongside an expansion of its internal investment management and sustainable ownership teams' capacity, so has its ability to engage and exercise voting rights beyond listed equities. This includes working closely with the private markets team to consider stockholder votes.

A shift in focus to thematic risk (and engagement)

As Railpen has continued to diversify its portfolio and the AUM have grown, it considers itself to increasingly be a "universal owner" of assets – ie, it has portfolios that can be considered sufficiently representative of broader capital markets. This position means that it effectively owns a "slice" of the overall market. The primary implication of this approach is that investment returns are dependent on the effective functioning of the wider market/overall economy and, in turn, on an investor's successful management of whole-of-economy risks faced by its portfolio, including systemic ESG issues.

Since 2020, Railpen has been dedicating a greater proportion of active ownership resources to managing these system-wide risks through its thematic engagement work. This activity includes some direct engagement, collaborative work and a small but increasing volume of public policy activity, recognising that effective management of system-level risks requires system-level, often regulatory or legislative, solutions.

Railpen uses a proprietary materiality matrix to ascertain which thematic issues it should prioritise in its engagement work. Criteria explicitly incorporated into this model include: materiality to the portfolio (likely impact and risk); the Trustee and member perspective; the expertise of the Railpen team; and the likely effectiveness of Railpen's intervention. These issues are further discussed to better understand current and future mechanisms for achieving change before a priority list is drawn up.

For 2021–25, Railpen's thematic priorities are:

- the climate transition:
  - biodiversity; and
  - net zero.
- responsible technology:
  - cybersecurity; and
  - ethical artificial intelligence (AI).
- sustainable financial markets:
  - audit and accounting; and
  - minority shareholder rights.
- worth of the workforce:
  - workforce disclosure;
  - diversity and inclusion;
  - fair pay; and
  - workers on boards.

Thematic issues are highlighted in Railpen's individual engagements with companies – both those in the fundamental equities portfolios and key holdings in the quantitative equities strategy – but collaborative engagement also has a key role to play in achieving the market-wide changes required.

Understanding the member perspective

A key input in Railpen's thinking around active ownership – particularly on thematic engagement priorities – is understanding member views. Railpen has several different mechanisms for doing so, including the following.

- The Trustee: All 16 members of the Trustee board are nominated by the members of employers of the scheme and bring a valuable understanding of member views to their trusteeship.
- The pensions and management committees (pension committees): These have been implemented by around a quarter of sponsoring employers, covering around 85% of the membership. They provide additional governance oversight and are important forums for understanding the member perspective.
- The Sustainable Ownership Client Forum (SOCF): Consisting of eight to 10 members drawn from a pool of pension committee representatives who have a particular interest in sustainable ownership issues.

Although the Trustee retains primacy over investment decisions – as does Railpen, where the Trustee has delegated this responsibility – the member perspective is explicitly considered as a criterion that helps shape how Railpen engages on thematic issues such as climate change or executive remuneration quantum (both of which matter to the membership).

Providing members with regular and up-to-date information about Railpen's sustainable ownership work also helps raise awareness among members, ensuring they can provide Railpen with more targeted feedback. Although Railpen has always taken member communication on sustainable ownership seriously, believing that accessible and engaging disclosures can have benefits for member engagement with pension savings more generally, the UK has seen several regulatory or industry developments aimed at encouraging disclosures from pension schemes on, or incorporation of, the member perspective in sustainable ownership activities.[2]

This section has demonstrated how Railpen's approach to active ownership has changed – and its emphasis on different activities shifted in response to changes in the regulatory environment – the way it runs its assets and strategic asset allocation across different jurisdictions and asset classes. The next section offers insights into the impact of Railpen's engagement, voting and public policy activities on outcomes for key portfolio holdings.

ACTIVE OWNERSHIP CASE STUDIES

The sustainable ownership team undertakes active ownership activities all year round and with hundreds of companies each year, prioritised for materiality to the portfolio and potential impact on member outcomes. The following case studies are a small sample of the work Railpen undertakes, but are considered representative of its approach to active ownership and demonstrate the efforts to achieve impact on members' behalf.

Engagement (direct)

Typically, the team will write to the company seeking either an in-person meeting or a phone call with management or the board. The annual update of the public-facing voting policy is an opportunity to continue dialogues, outlining expectations on key issues for the year ahead and how Railpen will vote where the expectations are not met.

Each target company – often in the internally and actively managed fundamental and quantitative equities portfolio – will have a series of short- and long-term engagement objectives against which progress is monitored. Short-term targets usually aim at relatively straightforward changes, such as disclosure or simple governance or remuneration changes centred around voting decisions. Medium- or long-term targets will seek a substantive change in practice: meaningful change does not happen overnight, and neither does the building of the effective relationships required to achieve positive impact.

Table 10.1 Case study: Direct engagement

Case study	Direct engagement: Company A
Issue	Company A is a technology company and is held in Railpen's Fundamental Equities strategy. Ahead of the May 2020 AGM, concerns were identified around the company's compensation report and the board's approach to Covid-19. The company had also been repeatedly criticised for unsafe working conditions, linked to the inadequate provision of personal protective equipment (PPE) and lack of transparency around the number of employees who have contracted Covid-19.

Initiative and role	Members of the sustainable ownership team and the investment management team engaged with the company, aiming to highlight concerns and understand company A's perspective.
Outcome and next steps	Discussions confirmed that the multi-million dollar bonus reported for a long-standing named executive officer primarily related to the accounting effects of an amendment to their previously awarded restricted stock units. Therefore, the Railpen team felt comfortable supporting the compensation report in line with 97.5% of votes cast. It became evident that company A's efforts to protect its workforce were evolving, and there had been multiple learning points. For example, company representatives noted that questions were sent to subsections of the workforce daily via the employee connection programme, with real-time responses reported to management. Despite this, Railpen continued to feel that there was disparity between the views expressed by management and those "on the ground". Railpen also felt that disclosure on the impact of company A's efforts to protect its workforce, alongside the effectiveness of board-level oversight, would provide better insight to shareholders and reinforce accountability for worker safety. Therefore, a vote was cast in favour of those 2020 shareholder resolutions aimed at improving disclosure on these issues. Railpen used its 2021 voting policy update – with its new lines on the importance of treating the workforce fairly during Covid-19 and beyond – to prompt further dialogue with senior company executives in early 2021. Intelligence from this meeting will inform the vote in the 2021 AGM.

Engagement (collective)

Railpen recognises that combining its voice, influence and expertise with those of other investors and stakeholders – where interests and objectives are aligned – can make engagement efforts more effective. This is particularly, although not exclusively, the case for thematic issues or system-wide risks.

Railpen participates in collective engagement activities, subject to any applicable laws and regulations in relevant jurisdictions, where:

- the issue aligns with core thematic engagement priorities;
- the objectives of the collective engagement participants are aligned with its own;

Table 10.2 Case study: Collective engagement

Case study	**Collective engagement: Cybersecurity**
Issue	Railpen and National Employment Savings Trust (NEST) report (2019) highlighted the materiality of cyber breaches and the importance of investor engagement on this issue. Since the report's publication, the global pandemic has contributed to shifts in the threat landscape and exacerbated the risk that cyber breaches pose. The majority of companies publish limited information on cybersecurity management as they do not wish to disclose unnecessary details to potential adversaries. While the need for caution is recognised, shareholders benefit when companies are able to provide clear information on their oversight and mitigation of cybersecurity risks.
Initiative and role	Since 2021, Railpen has worked alongside the Brunel Pension Pool, NEST, Border to Coast and the Universities Superannuation Scheme (USS) in a collective cybersecurity engagement led by Royal London Asset Management (RLAM). During the first phase of the engagement, 25 companies were selected and contacted by the group due to their high-risk exposure. Subsequent discussions highlighted previously underexplored third-party vulnerabilities, and enabled the group to refine its existing expectations on cybersecurity. Railpen led one engagement with a high-profile sportswear company and supported discussions with five smaller holdings within the portfolio.
Outcome	Companies were rated post-engagement according to the strength of their board oversight, risk management, disclosure and performance. The group has since followed up with companies that received a negative rating or did not respond to initial letters. The second phase of the engagement was also initiated, partly triggered by and focused on the global pandemic's unprecedented effect on corporate activity, alongside investigations into significant cyber-attacks on US companies.
Next steps	The group continues to engage, update company ratings and develop its understanding of this increasingly complex risk. With this knowledge, it is intended that the group develops a best practice framework and encourages the adoption of these practices. From 2021, a key thematic engagement priority will be "responsible technology", given the impact of Covid-19 on remote working and the rapid expansion of digitalisation across major sectors. This will broaden Railpen's focus beyond cybersecurity and privacy to look at content moderation, content governance and the corporate governance arrangements of technology firms.

- there are clear targets, roles and responsibilities;
- there is a clear and well-defined process for escalation; and
- it is believed that more impact will be achieved as part of a bigger group.

Voting

Railpen believes in exercising its ownership and voting rights as far as possible, and considers thoughtful voting, in a way that is aligned with engagement, to be a powerful tool for achieving impact. Each year it publishes a global voting policy that allows it to exercise voting rights systematically, consistently, and in a way that responds to thematic and stock-specific engagement priorities in members' best interests. The voting policy reflects key corporate governance and sustainability themes in a way that is accessible to portfolio companies, external managers and members.

Railpen also retains control of its voting policy including, where possible, its underlying beneficial interests in pooled funds and has

Table 10.3 Directing the vote on remuneration at a 2020 AGM

Case study	Directing the vote on remuneration at a 2020 AGM
Issue	A key holding in Railpen's fundamental equities strategy is a UK-based intellectual property commercialisation company. At the May 2019 AGM, Railpen voted against the company's remuneration policy and report, as the exceptional limit on the long-term incentive plan (LTIP) for executives was considered to be excessive at 400% of base salary. In addition, Railpen voted against the chair due to low gender diversity on the board.
Approach	As the company's largest shareholder, Railpen seeks to engage with board members on corporate governance and sustainability topics. It has been in dialogue with board members to encourage remuneration practices and director appointments that it can support. The company was open to Railpen's views, and resolution was achieved.
Outcome and next steps	Since 2021, Railpen was pleased to see the introduction of a 300% cap on the LTIP and the appointment of two highly skilled female directors to the board. Following the company's implementation of these positive changes, Railpen was able to support all resolutions on the agenda at the June 2020 AGM. This example demonstrates the effectiveness of voting sanctions and constructive engagement when combined.

Table 10.4 Voting in private matters

Case study	Voting in private markets
Issue	One of Railpen's private markets holdings, an investment company and operator of sustainable infrastructure, proposed candidates for election to the board to be voted on by at-large shareholders in October 2020.
Approach	Railpen has a nominated individual from the private markets team that sits on the company's board as an observer. The sustainable ownership and private markets teams worked together to ask the firm's leadership further questions around which of the core designed competency gaps it was felt that one of the proposed candidates filled. This was in line with Railpen's core 2020 voting policy theme of "board composition and oversight".
Outcome and next steps	Following its engagement, Railpen felt comfortable with the proposed candidates in question, and understood that their experience in social infrastructure and strategy would be valuable to the board. Railpen also felt comfortable that the board evaluation had identified the appropriate gaps, and that the process to do so had been robust. Railpen was therefore able to support all the proposed candidates.

centralised vote execution. The sustainable ownership team undertakes all voting and engagement activities, including monitoring of the activities in portfolios. In contrast, the global voting policy is reviewed every year in a discussion between the sustainable ownership team, the CIO and the investment management team.

Public policy

Railpen's work on public policy advocacy is aimed at supporting active ownership work to tackle market-wide risk and those systemic governance and sustainability issues, such as climate change and Covid-19, that require system-level change.

Table 10.5 Climate change and public policy

Case study	Climate change and public policy | TCFD reporting
Railpen responded to the Department for Work and Pensions' (DWPs) consultation "Taking Action on Climate Risk: Improving Governance and Reporting by Occupational Pension Schemes" in Autumn 2020. Railpen produced its own written response, and fed into the response produced by the Pensions and Lifetime Savings Association (PLSA) in its role on the PLSA's Stewardship Advisory Group. Railpen also played a significant role in reviewing the accompanying final (voluntary) guidance for asset owners	

on Task Force on Climate-Related Disclosures (TCFD) reporting as part of the Pensions Climate Risk Industry Group (PCRIG), and had informal conversations with relevant government officials during this consultation.

Railpen agreed to participate for these reasons:

- it aligns with the core engagement theme of "the climate transition";
- Railpen considers climate change to be material to nearly every holding across every part of its portfolio;
- it is a key consideration and issue for the Trustee;
- the way in which the requirement is placed upon the Trustee board would have implications for how Railpen undertakes sustainable ownership work; and
- it complements work as a lead investor on certain company engagements as part of Climate Action 100+ (CA100+).

The government published its response to this consultation and the next set of consultations in early 2021. Railpen was pleased to note that all its suggestions around moving to a more pragmatic frequency for undertaking scenario analysis and the particular situation for multi-employer (section) schemes were recognised.

Railpen decided not to produce a formal written response to the next stage of TCFD consultations (draft regulations and draft statutory guidance). Instead, it fed through specific comments and thoughts on the draft responses produced by the UK Sustainable Investment and Finance Association (UKSIF) and the PLSA.

Public policy is a core part of Railpen's activity as an engaged owner of its assets, and it will seek to influence the policy debate where doing so would have an impact either on a core thematic priority or on the ease with which Railpen can do impactful, sustainable ownership work.

CONCLUSION

Investors need to understand the theory and academic evidence base of active ownership. However, putting this theory into practice in an impactful way requires an approach that reflects the particularities of an investor's governance arrangements, culture, how investments are structured and the (now rapidly evolving) regulatory framework within which it operates.

Railpen's active ownership work aligns with the philosophy of the Trustee, builds upon its heritage as a corporate governance and voting pioneer, and is tailored to maximise impact across a portfolio that is often internally managed, with a significant allocation to growth assets and active equities and with large holdings in the UK, the US and Europe. The increased focus on thematic or system-wide risks reflects a growing recognition of the risks that face Railpen as a universal owner while improving the dialogue with members, which is at least in part a response to regulatory developments.

APPENDIX 10.1 TOP TIPS FOR PENSION SCHEMES

- A clear mandate on active ownership from the Trustee board (or equivalent governance body) is vital. Regulatory developments have led to most UK trustee boards sharpening their focus on active ownership. This should not be seen as a "once and done" activity. Instead, scheme stewardship professionals – or those responsible for scrutinising the stewardship activities of asset managers – should engage with the Trustee board alongside the board's legal and investment advisers (where relevant) on an ongoing basis to ensure a clear and up-to-date understanding of the Trustee's investment beliefs and stewardship priorities.
- Consider the parameters and structures of your investment arrangements, and focus your active ownership priorities accordingly. Railpen is unusual in managing a significant proportion of its assets internally. If your scheme delegates the majority or all of the day-to-day investment activities to external managers, your priorities should shift to considering how to work with any investment consultants and lawyers to hold these managers to account and scrutinise effectively (through drafting of legal contracts, specific review meetings, etc).
- If you are invested in pooled arrangements, you may wish to consider pressing your manager for ways to influence their voting approach, or asking more questions about client consultation on stewardship issues during the manager selection process. Similarly, you should consider your allocation across jurisdictions, asset class and sectors, as well as the concentration or otherwise of your portfolio when deciding which ESG issues are most material to the portfolio and the mechanisms for influence.
- Good governance and documentation around active ownership are becoming ever more important. Regulators and other stakeholders increasingly expect scheme investment decision-makers (and scheme managers) to be able to articulate a clear rationale for their chosen approach to active ownership. You should ensure you have a secure database or way of storing the

information you used to support your decisions on active ownership, as well as accurately minuting the decisions made and any relevant points from the discussion.

- Effective active ownership – particularly if you are doing any of this in-house – also requires a structured approach to tracking and monitoring the progress of engagements, and any outcomes. Ideally, escalation "triggers" should be decided and documented before the engagement starts. This will be important for providing relevant information should your scheme decide to sign up to reporting against voluntary codes such as the UK Stewardship Code, or for any member-focused responsible investment reports.

My thanks go to my colleagues Michael Marshall, Jessica Cassey, Sophie Harris and Helen Smith for their contributions to the 2020 Stewardship Report, the material for which underlies parts of this chapter.

1 The SIP is a written statement that governs decisions about investments for the purposes of an occupational pension scheme. Trustees of most UK occupational pension schemes are required to prepare, maintain and periodically revise the SIP.

2 These include the 2018 and 2019 UK government amendments to the "Occupational Pension Schemes (Investment) Regulations 2005" to encourage pension scheme trustees to consider including an "optional policy on member views" in their SIP, and requiring new disclosures such as the "implementation statement". Saver-focused campaigns such as Make My Money Matter, or the publication "Understanding and Aligning with Beneficiaries' Sustainability Preferences (UN PRI, 2021) have also helped shift the mood music on engagement with members.

REFERENCES

Barko, T., M. Cremers and L. Renneboog, 2017, "Shareholder Engagement on Environmental, Social and Governance Performance", European Corporate Governance Institute, Finance Working Paper No. 509/2017

Dimson, E., O. Karakas and X. Li, 2015, "Active Ownership", *The Review of Financial Studies*, 28(12), December, pp. 3,225–68.

Dimson, E., O. Karakas and X. Li, 2018, "Co-ordinated Engagements", European Corporate Governance Institute, Finance Working Paper No. 721/2021.

Dyck, A., K. V. Lins, L. Roth and H. F. Wagner, 2019, "Do Institutional Investors Drive Corporate Social Responsibility? International Evidence", *Journal of Financial Economics*, 131(3), March, pp. 693–714.

Hoepner, A. G. F., I. Oikonomou, Z. Sautner, L. T. Starks and X. Zhou, 2018, "ESG Shareholder Engagement and Downside Risk", European Corporate Governance Institute, Finance Working Paper No. 671/2020.

Railpen and NEST, 2019, "Why UK Pension Funds should Consider Cyber and Data Security in their Investment Approach", November.

UN-backed PRI, 2021, "Understanding and Aligning with Beneficiaries' Sustainability Preferences", April 21.

PART V

ALTERNATIVES

11

Identifying ESG risks and opportunities in alternative investments

Joachim Merten and Callum Macpherson

Alternatives cover a very wide array of assets. More or less anything that is not a direct investment in bonds or stocks in the public market has been classified under this broad term. In this chapter we will not, and cannot, cover all the different aspects of ESG in alternative assets as the topic would require a book in itself to do it justice. Instead, we will try to give a glimpse of the importance of ESG for many of these types of investments. The chapter is split into two parts. The first covers equity and debt investments into unlisted businesses, while the second deals with expressing ESG themed views on traded commodities and considers the ESG implications of the emerging field of cryptocurrencies.

PART 1: PRIVATE EQUITY/DEBT, FUNDS

Joachim Merten

ESG have been a dominant theme in alternative assets since the early 2010s. From real estate to buyout investments, asset managers were challenged to adhere to increasingly stringent standards by regulators as various jurisdictions started to introduce mandatory ESG disclosures for asset managers (Benson *et al*, 2021). There was also growing demand by the investor community, such as the formalisation of requirements in their internal guidelines (Zeisberger, Prahl and White, 2017), to comply and fulfil given standards with regards to environmental, social and regulatory/ compliance topics.

Considering the strong growth of alternative assets, strongly fuelled by investors' hunt for return in times of low to zero interest rates, gives this asset class additional importance in creating a more sustainable society. Ever more sophisticated investors will demand closer relationships: with fund managers; product innovation; and improvements in reporting, transparency and ESG standards. Research has shown that the alternative industry could represent US$17.2 trillion by the end of 2025 (Prequin, 2020).

The most prominent alternative asset classes are real estate, commodities (or natural resources), private equity, private debt and infrastructure (see Figure 11.1). Each of those asset classes is confronted with their own challenges towards ESG. Real estate is faced with increasing rent prices and their effect on low income households, and the resulting increased regulatory pressure in this segment (PWC, 2020). Large infrastructure projects need to consider bureaucratic involvement, corruption and money laundering (OECD, 2019). All in all, different sub-asset classes of the alternative space need to be looked at differently, and require their own specific strategy to consider ESG impacts, especially during portfolio construction.

Another key aspect is the form of trading of certain assets. While many alternative assets are held privately and are often traded directly between parties, such as private equity or most other

Figure 11.1 Development of alternative assets under management

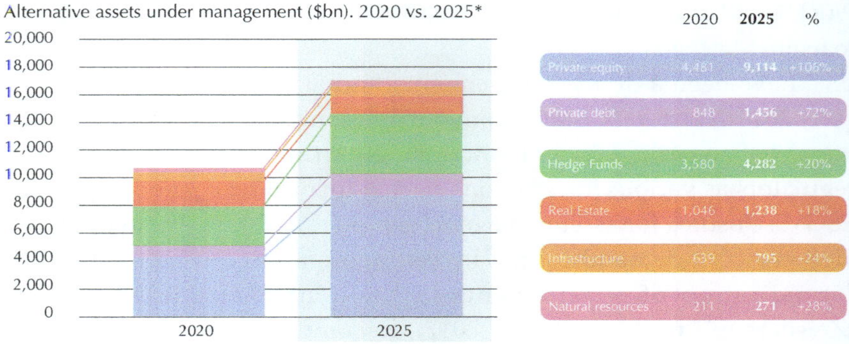

* 2020 figure is annualised based on data to October. 2021–2025 are Preqin's forecasted figures.
Source: Prequin (2020)

illiquid alternative assets, some assets also have a strong public touch, such as publicly traded real estate portfolios.

In this part of the chapter we will only look at privately held assets, covering real estate, private equity, infrastructure and private debt. Since some alternative assets, such as hedge funds, commodities and cryptocurrencies, are traded mainly or solely publicly, they will be considered in the second part of the chapter.

Private assets

This section will look at the four key segments of private investment classes: private equity; real estate; infrastructure; and debt. All these asset segments face their own particular challenges under the consideration of ESG. While assessing the different assets for portfolio construction, it is important to consider how different aspects of environmental regulation, labour laws and reporting obligations could affect the underlying assets. A negative ruling on an environmental case of a private equity asset could taint an entire portfolio and cause massive financial, reputational and ethical damages.

Some of the main challenges in the private asset class arise from a lack of comparable data. As most private companies do not publicly report their ESG data, or most of their data in general, it is really hard to assess their performance compared to other market participants. This might not be a strong consideration for larger buyouts, which are typically closely comparable to publicly traded companies, but for the vast majority of deals in the small to medium enterprise segment, this poses a significant challenge.

There are increasing demands from regulators and investors for ESG compliance with norms, standards and frameworks. This is also putting more pressure on asset managers to comply with regulation and standards while leveraging positive ESG benefits.

The asset manager

Almost all these assets are usually managed by an independent asset manager, which usually holds the assets via a standard limited partnership structure. At this point, it is important to consider how the asset manager approaches the topic of ESG. Typically, the following three layers of engagement are paramount.

- Asset manager ESG compliance: The absolute minimum an asset manager should offer is its own compliance. This would require the asset manager to have proper policies in place to cover the different areas of risk exposure, and being a signatory to one of the major reporting frameworks. An overview should be taken as to how the asset manager runs its ESG compliance, and at least annually, preferably quarterly, an ESG assessment should be carried out by a dedicated resource.
- Portfolio ESG compliance: In a second step, it should be considered whether the portfolio companies or invested managed assets are subject to an ESG-compliant policy. This would require active engagement of the asset manager with its asset to confirm and monitor that all requirements and standards are adhered by portfolio companies, or in the case of breach there is a process in place to avoid spill-over effects throughout the portfolio. An advanced asset manager would have systems in place to ring-fence potential threats and risks.
- Portfolio ESG alpha: So far, we have only considered the risk management side in looking at ESG compliance. The far more interesting element in ESG portfolio construction is ESG alpha. Here, an asset manager actively uses the tools of ESG monitoring and improvement to create additional value in portfolio companies. The proper implementation of a sustainable reporting framework demands the company to have a well-managed reporting system, giving a detailed insight on the key performance indicators (KPIs) and development mechanism of its value chain. It should be obvious that a well-managed reporting system would also benefit the analysis strength of the portfolio company. The reporting system should have an impact on the company's overall performance (Sheu and Lo, 2005). Additionally a company with a sustainable business model will more likely attract highly motivated employees, grow revenues by adding sustainable focused customers and reduce costs by reducing waste (Henisz, Koller and Nuttall, 2019). Paying attention to ESG topics will, in 63% of cases, cause a positive return effect for the underlying asset (Friede, Busch and Bassen, 2015).

Of course, every asset manager has to approach the topic differently in consideration of its underlying assets. A private equity investor that holds majority in a company has a very different way to deal with a potential conflicting situation than a debt fund that is merely providing a loan. Therefore, the next section will examine the different asset managers and potential requirements they face under successful implementation of ESG procedures and policies.

Private equity

The private equity segment is diverse in itself. The standard private equity fund would be a buyout fund with a majority stake in a company and would wield significant influence over its management. Next, a minority growth investor would have a lower level of influence, as the manager would need to agree with its co-investors on certain measures. Last but not least, the segment of venture capital would also be addressed within private equity. Here, a split can be seen between early stage and growth stage investors. While the former face companies with very limited resources, they have the opportunity to influence the management positively early on the topics of ESG, although their influence would be more limited. Growth stage investors would join at a much later stage, when the company had already achieved a certain maturity and might be set in some ways; nonetheless, they tend to provide far larger amounts of investment, and therefore might carry a stronger influence in pushing for ESG integration in the company's policies and processes.

Buyout

The buyout asset class is by far the largest in private equity. It typically involves the acquisition of a company or a spin-out of a corporate unit financed by a private equity fund together with the management. The private equity fund would usually retain a controlling stake of over 75%. From an ESG perspective, these asset managers are very interesting as they can actively pursue an improvement in the asset via the selection of the management (Hawker, 2021). By setting targets and goals for the management team, the asset manager can incentivise them to implement a strategy that improves the company's ESG scoring.

While investing into a fund focused on buyout, the investor should consider the ESG compliance and focus set-up of the manager.

- ❑ Does the manager have a proper ESG policy in place?
- ❑ Does the manager track ESG KPIs on a regular basis?
- ❑ How often does the manager report on ESG performance?
- ❑ Does the manager consider ESG a value driver?
- ❑ Has the manager dedicated resources to address ESG topics in its firm and/or portfolio companies?
- ❑ Is the manager actively trying to improve its ESG efforts?

These are only examples of questions that should be considered when investing with a private equity buyout manager.[1] If a manager takes the topic of ESG seriously, they will bring up the topic themselves and engage with an investor on its importance for their daily operations and performance improvement.

There is no particular focus on segments for buyout on what topic might be the most important during the assessment. An investor considering manufacturing companies with high potential environmental impact would face different challenges than a financial company focused investor more strongly exposed to governmental risk. An assessment of focus should be taken while considering the particular investment strategy of the asset manager.

However, there are some areas that are important for the entire range of buyout investments.

- ❑ Climate impact: All companies should consider their impact on the environment in terms of CO_2 emissions. A sustainable company will at least have considered this in their activities in some way. Although it might not have been able to implement efficient processes or procedures, it should have been aware of the importance of the topic. An investment manager that is not checking this during a due diligence process is most likely not deeply considerate of sustainability topics (Coppola and Blohmke, 2019).
- ❑ Workers' rights and child labour: These are key issues that should be looked into by every company before investing. As these topics carry substantial financial risk for the investor, an asset manager that has no consideration of these topics may not have sufficient risk management procedures in place to cover large-scale black swan events (Crawford, 2021).
- ❑ Regulatory requirements and financial monitoring: Almost all

industries are subject to some industry standards and regulatory requirements. While some companies have self-certification and self-governing ruling in place that do not require regular governmental oversight, best practice (or even decent practice) would demand some focus on those topics in their daily business. The same holds for financial monitoring and regular reporting on performance. If an investment manager is rather lax on testing the portfolio companies for such issues, there is an increased chance they might not have the oversight of the portfolio company that would be required to effectively take a reasonable investment decision.

In addition, there are some quick standard questions that explore the ability of the investment manager to engage with ESG topics in their portfolio companies.

- ❏ For highly regulated businesses: Do you know how often the policies are updated in your portfolio company? If this is more than one year, the topic is probably handled too lightly, particularly for highly regulated industries such as financial services.
- ❏ For early stage manufacturing companies: Do you consider the recycling activities of your portfolio company? Companies in the production of pre-products, such as steel or plastics, typically have an increased output of waste and waste water, and recycling offers additional value enhancement potential. An investment manager not exploring this will usually not explore other value addition potentials either.
- ❏ For trading companies producing abroad: Do you take a deeper look into the supply chain of the products of your company and their origins? Investment managers without a detailed interest in the supply chain of their companies run the major risk of spill-over effects, and might not consider them in other scenarios either.

It should be stressed that all of these are very simple examples. The full due diligence is, as any investor knows, far more complex. The core focus here is to raise awareness of the inclusion of these checks into the process, and their wider implications for the overall investment activity of the manager.

Growth investment

Growth investments are typically the provision of additional capital for a minority stake in a silent partnership in a company that needs additional equity for an expansion or acquisition strategy. The key difference between buyout and growth is the influence the investment manager can wield over a company. In a growth scenario, the investor rarely ever holds a controlling majority and can have extensive influence on the portfolio company beyond advice and board representation. Those influences tend to be limited to blocking certain activities and actions, and therefore an investment activity should be valued on the process of exclusion and divestment.

The most common approach is an exclusion strategy of the investment manager in having a clear process to avoid investing in companies that pose an extensive ESG risk and the potentially inflicted return effects they carry. The most common way to achieve this is through an exclusion list. An investment manager's ESG policy should clearly indicate which businesses they will not invest in, and how they are ensuring this alongside their investment process.

This could be extended for the investment manager to demand exclusion of certain activities by the underlying business, but this is usually a given as in the investment agreements a change of business model (that could breach this exclusion) would need common consensus among investors in the company. Nonetheless, this should be challenged and, depending on the industry the investment manager is actively involved with, the exclusion lists could be sizable, which increases the demand for due diligence. Of course, it should not be forgotten that we are talking about a minority investor here. A too-demanding exclusion list could render their business model obsolete, although this would only be for rare cases.

A second alternative to influence the portfolio company could come via the "threat" of divestment or refusing to follow-on investing in later rounds. This is more important for venture capital investment, but could also play a role in growth investment.

Good ESG practice of a growth investor should include the regular review of ESG KPIs provided by the portfolio company, and understanding their efforts and path of compliance and improvement. This should then also provoke the investment manager to re-evaluate their investment on a regular basis to ensure it is still in line with its investment requirements and if the manager would still invest today.

If an investment manager comes to the conclusion that the ESG risks and performance of the portfolio company are not sufficiently transparent and decides against the inclusion of the investee company in the portfolio, divestment scenarios could be considered. Good practice is to determine a process that also includes the legal documentation.

This of course does not mean that every investment the investment manager might not choose today should be directly considered for divestment, but they should demand the manager engages into dialogue with the portfolio company about the relevant developments. An investment manager should be able to provide information or material on this, when challenged by the limited partnership (LP) community.

Growth investment remains a challenging field for ESG portfolio construction. Many investment managers might consider several aspects of ESG, but are not able to properly reflect or report on them due to their size. In particular, smaller managers might be challenged by the amount of reporting required to fully explain their approach to sustainable investment. This would increase if the investment tickets those investment managers provide are rather small. However, those small ticket investments are becoming more important from an ESG perspective as they allow smaller companies broader access to capital and improve the imbalance in the financial market.

Therefore, when considering smaller funds and growth funds, an LP might consider taking the time to engage in a deeper conversation with the investment manager without solely relying on their documentation. In the end, many of them are also learning about this topic.

Venture capital late stage

Late stage venture capital would typically get involved with investment in investment rounds for Series C and beyond. The ticket sizes here can be extensive, being more comparable with large buyout investments than traditional venture capital investments.

Single investment rounds of above US$100 million are no longer a rarity.

This also leads us to a key difference in the influence and demands of an investment manager of a larger venture capital investment compared to a smaller one that potentially only provides seed investment. When providing such a large amount of capital, a company can demand certain standards and procedures. After all, this company wants to become (or is already) a billion dollar company. If it wants plays in the big league, compliance to ESG standards should not be a challenge but a welcome development on the path to an initial public offering (IPO).

One other aspect that becomes more and more important in this field of investment are the partners in these rounds. Foreign state funds and national banks, as well as oligarchs and rich individuals from Asia and the Middle East, are discovering this is a highly interesting field. While this is of course great news for the industry overall, there would need to be considerations made as to how these investors might affect the portfolio company – particularly for the cooperation with investors where the source of money is questionable from an ESG perspective.

Venture capital early stage

Early stage venture capital is focused on seed funding up to Series B or even C. The companies invested at this stage are rather small, and typically consist of a core team of founders and some first employees. Here lies the challenge of ESG investing in this field – these companies are so small that they will find it difficult to adhere to standards beyond their minimum requirement, as their focus is typically on a market-changing technology, for instance, that demands all their attention. In this case, the work of the investment manager should again concentrate on an exclusion list and the potential refusal to provide further follow-on investments if certain issues are not addressed and solved until the next funding round.

There is also the wide field of impact investing, which is particularly strong in this segment. However, as this is addressed in another chapter of this book, we will omit further discussion here. On the whole, private equity is a challenging asset class to analyse. An in-depth knowledge of the different types of investment is required to fully understand the impact of ESG on the different key value drivers.

As a general note, a good investment manager will have an appropriate ESG policy in place covering their particular investment class, and are engaging with their portfolio companies on this topic on a regular basis, including regular reporting on KPIs as well.

Real estate

Real estate is by far the largest asset class in alternative investments. They are formed of publicly traded real estate funds, as well as privately held closed-end funds. As they provide a steady form of revenue over an extensive length of time, they are particularly interesting for pension funds.

Latterly, with the inflationary monetary policy the market has seen a massive boom in valuation and return. Therefore, even more money is provided into this market, which of course has both positive and negative implications from an ESG perspective.

Environmental issues

Environmental issues arise during the real estate building process. For instance, the much-used building material concrete is one of the largest contributors to CO_2 emissions. Therefore, a sustainable building approach by an investor would be a strong indication of their seriousness on this topic. The inclusion of regenerative building materials such as wood would show that the impact is understood. Alternatively, a gold standard offset of the CO_2 costs in the pricing of the property would display an awareness of the issue.

Another important factor is urbanisation and mobility, which plays an increasingly important role when planning and building real estate, particularly in densely populated areas. An investment manager that understands the importance of this will not just make sure enough parking spots are available, but will also consider cargo bike stands, connectivity to public transport and the creation of green spaces. There are several approaches that can measure the approach of investment managers on this topic. The reduction of parking spots for the provision of spaces for bikes and other means of transportation is only one example.

Another factor of increasing importance is style of living. While the single family home is still propagated as the optimal life choice, multi-family homes are far better from an environmental perspective. An investor providing more focused financing in this field and stating this as their motivation, and potentially even trying to transform areas under this agenda, clearly shows an understanding of the impact of investment (CBRE, 2021).

Last but not least, an investment manager should consider the inclusion of renewable energy sources and energy reduction measures during the investment process. Although this has developed far in recent years, driven by regulatory standards and financial incentivisation, it should be seen as a must-have rather than a should-have. An investment manager not considering these aspects during investment decisions might lose out on significant upside potential.

Social issues

Social issues have become more of a focus in real estate, something that is also pushing up the cost of housing. The increased valuations of property make it simply impossible for many families to obtain ownership and are forced to consider renting. Therefore, an investor focused on providing residential real estate in particularly challenged areas to help with this issue does not only see the return potential, but also the importance of generating additional living space.

Another element is the factor of gentrification. The increased refurbishment of existing low rent housing into luxury apartments is not helping the housing situation, but rather cause increased pressure as these properties usually house less people per square metre. Ever-rising house prices have led to a situation where housing affordability has become a major political issue, a central area of conflict in the inequality wars (Desmyter, 2021).

This does not mean that an investment manager shouldn't be investing in these properties and trying to promote the improvement of residential areas, but rather it would be a question if this topic is considered, and compensated – for example, by building sufficient additional low rent homes to compensate (or better overcompensate) for the impact.

A final aspect here are living conditions. An investment manager should always understand the conditions the tenants of the property are exposed to. This counts for commercial as well as residential real estate. It is simply good human nature to ensure that one is not exposing others to conditions that oneself would not deem acceptable in any circumstance. A good investment manager will have this in their monitoring procedures.

Governance

The real estate market is highly regulated in most countries. Regulatory topics span a broad universe of their own and commonly include "governance" areas such as building standards or "social" criteria related to tenant rights and responsibilities.

However, the framework has become more challenging, caused by the rise in short-term lettings, the gentrification process and more recently by Covid-19 measures. Although most of these risks are outside the control of the investment manager, the investment manager should have processes and procedures in place to cope with the ever-changing environment.

In conclusion, when deciding to include real estate investments in a portfolio, the key aspects of ESG review should be environmental and social topics. Governance is such a standard factor, and an investment manager not able to provide detailed understanding of this clearly shows a lack of competence in this field.

Infrastructure

Infrastructure investments have several touch points with real estate investments, but face their own challenges with regard to ESG. From an investment perspective, they are again highly interesting for pension funds, as they provide a very stable cashflow over a long period of time.

Again, a differentiation must be made between impact-driven investment, such as the investment in renewable energy, and the ESG efforts of classical infrastructure investments. However, investments in wind and solar power have become so standard that they can be seen as almost classical investments since these types of investment themselves face their own ESG issues aside from the positive CO_2 impact they generate. To ensure consistency, this chapter will solely focus on the ESG considerations for the classical investments an investment manager might face.

Environmental

When investing in infrastructure, there is almost always a strong impact on the environment. Infrastructure investment typically demands a lot of space and is implemented over a whole region or even country. By creating such a significant investment, an impact on the environment is unavoidable.

The key aspect here is how this impact is considered, tracked and mitigated by the investment manager. Good practice would demand extensive understanding of the long-term effects of the investment, and how these can be compensated.

In addition, scenario modelling and impact analysis should be detailed and extensive. As many projects have very large investment volumes, such expenditures are more than justified. In particular, any negative long-term impact that could disrupt the operation would have far more severe financial consequences (eg, a wind power plant that has to be moved as it could be endangering a bird species).

An investment manager should be able to provide information on these analyses quickly and completely. Although a study of such material might be not fruitful for a general investor, the assurance that these topics are considered would be essential.

Social

Many infrastructure investments provide a public service, such as energy, water, transportation and telecommunications. Numerous services are also offered for free or are highly subsidised to the public (eg, transportation). Therefore, a key question here is about access and fairness in distribution.

An investment manager should consider how the provision of a public service would affect different social groups, in particular minorities and low income households. Providing a train connection between two cities that is only affordable for high income households would surely not serve the purpose of improving transportation in most cases.

Although it is not the task of the investment manager to create a socially justified investment, as this would again rather fill the corner of impact investment, good practice would be considering the wider implication as infrastructure investments are also often subject to public acceptance and approval.

Governance

The aspect of governance is a key element of infrastructure investment. As the investment partner, or at least customer, is the public in form a city, state or nation, considerations on clear governmental regulations and stability are essential.

Investments in emerging markets with a less than an optimal legal structure, for instance, could provide difficulty for investors, especially for situations that result in conflict with the partner. There have been several cases where the partner used their power to limit the profitability and value of the investment.

Another element is bribery and fraud. Large-scale projects, especially with a public partner, attract those involved in such activities. An investment manager should have a clear policy in place to address this, as just one case could put all the value of the investment at jeopardy.

Private debt

Private debt has been emerging as a strongly growing asset class in the space of alternatives alongside the retreat of banks from many financing activities, particularly in the smaller ticket size. The increased regulatory pressure on banks means it is no longer of interest for them to serve this market. New lending partners have therefore emerged and offer products in this field.

A lender effectively has no control over the ESG activity of the borrower. However, a lender should also consider ESG risk and the activities of the borrower. A good investment manager would also work here with exclusion lists and a divestment policy. In strong cases, covenants could also be defined on ESG parameters if they are an existential risk to the business model.

Of all the alternative asset classes, private debt is probably the least affected by ESG risk and value improvement, as the upside is limited and the downside would be carried more by black swan events. Nonetheless, depending on the lender, certain key events need to be analysed and policy put in place to avoid loss of investment.

CONCLUSION

The topic of ESG in alternatives is so broad that it could cover several books on its own. Key themes for ESG within alternative

Table 11.1 Summary of the key implications of each private asset class

Asset class	General	Environmental	Social	Governance
Private equity buyout	The control of the asset holder allows for true impact on the portfolio company by setting incentives and goals to the management.	Depends on industry key topics relating to waste reduction, water preservation and CO_2 reduction.	Supply chain topics and workers' rights are key elements for consideration, including the risk of child labour. An understanding of the risk chain is important.	Regulatory and financial risks need to be covered. A sustainable company will have a working reporting framework that is resilient to crisis.
Private equity growth investment/ venture capital late stage/private debt	The limited power of control gives less strength to actively impact a portfolio company. However, guidelines can be set at the time of investment or incentives given by set investment requirements.	Key elements would be CO_2 reduction and waste reduction. These capital investments are often for certain measures, and could be connected to environmental goals.	In the case of violation of certain social standards, the investment manager should always consider divestment. They should demand reporting rights at time of investment.	Governance remains a key part for investors. Information rights need to be clearly set and the articles should clearly state the adherence to certain reporting standards.
Venture capital early stage	Those companies usually lack the resources to fulfil complicated reporting requirements.	The investment manager can try to set base rules, such as CO2 measuring.	There is limited ability to have social impact, although workers' rights are already a topic for some companies.	As the reporting is still rather "light", it is important to continuously demand improvements as the company grows.
Real estate	The boom in the real estate market impacts all aspects of ESG. Increasing demand and urbanisation will need to be met with sustainable investment strategies.	Construction is one of the largest contributors to CO_2 emissions, but aspects such as mobility, housing style and renewable energy also play a role.	This is the most important factor for real estate. Increasing housing prices can weigh heavily on lower income groups. Pricing and gentrification impacts need to be considered.	The market is highly regulated. It is important that investors are aware of the legislation and their impact on the investment. Government intervention in case of negligence can have a strong performance impact.
Infrastructure	As a highly attractive asset class for pension funds, there is increasing demand for sustainable investment opportunities in this segment.	Considering their typical strong impact on their environment, larger infrastructure projects should only be conducted after sufficient environment impact analysis.	Considering their importance to society, infrastructure projects need to consider the broader public, particularly the more vulnerable members of society.	The close interaction with politically exposed people in these projects demands extra diligence and the clear avoidance of bribery and fraud.

assets and portfolio construction are ESG risk and opportunities identification at the portfolio and the firm level. ESG statements made by investment managers need to be put to the test more frequently. A good indication of an alternative asset manager with a good ESG practice in place is their reporting effort. Membership of the Principles for Responsible Investment (PRI) should be considered as a minimum commitment for reflection and consideration but increasingly additional information available about this manager via sources such as Preqin, Cambridge Associates and PitchBook will give some indication about the sustainability profile, philosophy, and portfolio activity. ESG statements and proclamations on their own can indeed sometimes be perceived as misleading as (alternative) asset managers commonly try to promote their efforts in the context of good governance and sustainability (see Table 11.1).

PART 2: COMMODITIES AND CRYPTOCURRENCIES

Callum Macpherson

Commodities

In its broadest sense, the term "commodity" covers produce that is sufficiently elementary in nature and is available in such bulk that its properties have been standardised to enable efficient markets in such produce, to satisfy the need of those using them to produce (or drive in the case of energy commodities) other things. The production and use of commodities inevitably has some environmental impact and can have a social one too. Consequently, commodities tend to be viewed as inherently challenging from an ESG point of view. However, given that raw materials, energy and agricultural produce all fall under the umbrella of commodities, we need to be realistic. They are essential for modern life as it is lived in much of the world today. In other words, the ESG challenges associated with commodities are in fact the ultimate expression of modern human impact on the world, and so commodities necessarily need to be at the forefront of global strategies to lessen that impact.

For the purposes of this chapter, we limit ourselves to those commodities that have tradable markets, typically in the form of futures, with some reasonable level of liquidity. This spans oil and refined products, gas, electricity, petrochemicals, agriculture, industrial metals and precious metals.

Expressing views on ESG through commodity markets

If there were separate futures for commodities produced via supply chains with high ESG standards and those without specific standards, then it would be interesting to buy one and sell the other, thus expressing a view on the ESG premium. For example, if there were a green aluminium future that related only to aluminium produced using renewable energy, it could be traded against the standard aluminium futures. The premium of one over the other could provide price discovery for the benefit of producing green aluminium and incentivise its production.

There has been discussion about this concept, but no liquid futures of this type have yet emerged. For example, the London Metal Exchange (LME) launched a consultation on a low carbon aluminium future, but decided not to proceed with it to avoid splitting liquidity in the aluminium market between two contracts. The desire for consumers to improve the ESG credentials of their raw materials is instead satisfied by systems of certificates, or simply bilateral arrangements between producers and consumers that allow consumers to demonstrate the origin and production methods of the materials they are using.

There are efforts being made by some exchanges to improve the sustainability of futures trading on them through product specifications and membership requirements. The work of the Sustainable Stock Exchanges initiative is an example of that (SSE and WFE, 2021). Where we do have some price discovery, connected with climate change at least, is via emissions allowances and offsets. Aside from that there are great opportunities to use commodities to express views on ESG themes, such as the energy transition that is forecast to lead to demand for particular metals to increase.

Supercycles and the risk of hubris

Since the end of 2020, there have been strong rallies across a broad range of commodities leading to stories of a commodity supercycle that many commentators associated with the energy transition. However, it is all too easy to fit stories to price trends without proper analysis of the situation of particular commodities. The idea that the whole commodity complex can be reduced to a single seemingly simple story is particularly seductive as it holds the tantalising promise of understanding all commodities without the need to look into the details of any of them! This all sounds too similar to the relatively short-lived price booms ahead of the financial crisis in 2008 (remember peak oil?) and on Brazil, Russia, India and China (BRIC) demand in (copper in 2011). Those were cycles, but not super, just the usual interplay of production, consumption and inventories that have been driving commodity prices up and down for millennia. Indeed, while energy and agricultural commodity prices have been super-charged by the war in Ukraine, industrial metals prices have fallen as the inflationary impact of higher fuel and food costs points to reduced economic activity and lower metal demand – the correlation between energy and metals has turned negative.

A supercycle is different altogether, as it involves a step change in demand from some kind of industrial, technological or societal revolution that unfolds over decades (Raskopf, 2021). Typical commodity business cycles will be superimposed upon it. The push to drive down global carbon emissions, with the aim of achieving net zero emissions in a few decades, has a potential impact on demand that could meet the condition of a supercycle. However, understanding how and when this will affect particular commodities and their relationship to others requires detailed study and careful consideration. The remainder of this section aims to give a starting point in forming ideas on taking views about ESG via commodity markets. It does not aim to be comprehensive and is certainly not offering any recommendations.

The cost of living crisis that has arisen out of the inflationary impact of some commodity price rises highlights a social dimension to commodity markets, which adds to the more obvious environmental ones. In using commodity markets to express an ESG view, investors may wish to consider whether their positions could aggravate social problems by, for example, bidding up the price of wheat.

Accessing exposure to listed commodities

Price exposure to futures can be obtained by trading actual futures on exchange (either directly or via a broker) and via exchange-traded funds (ETFs), and derivative products that are linked to them, often via indexes. Most tradable commodities have futures with a string of monthly expiries stretching a few years into the future. The forward curve can be downward sloping (known as backwardation) as with Brent in August 2022, or upward sloping (contango) as Brent was in August 2020 (see Figure 11.2). Commodity forwards can also be seasonal, such as natural gas, where the curve shape reflects higher demand in the winter than the summer (see Figure 11.3).

One of the challenges of maintaining an ongoing long or short position in a commodity is that futures expire, and so prior to expiry a given future must be sold and another, with a latter expiry, purchased. This process of rolling futures is complicated by the shape of the curve. A backwardated curve involves buying a cheaper contract than that being sold, resulting in a gain: a positive roll yield. The opposite is true when the curve is in contango. The roll yield (whether positive or negative) can make up a significant component of the economics of holding commodities (Fama and

Figure 11.2 Brent's changing curve shape

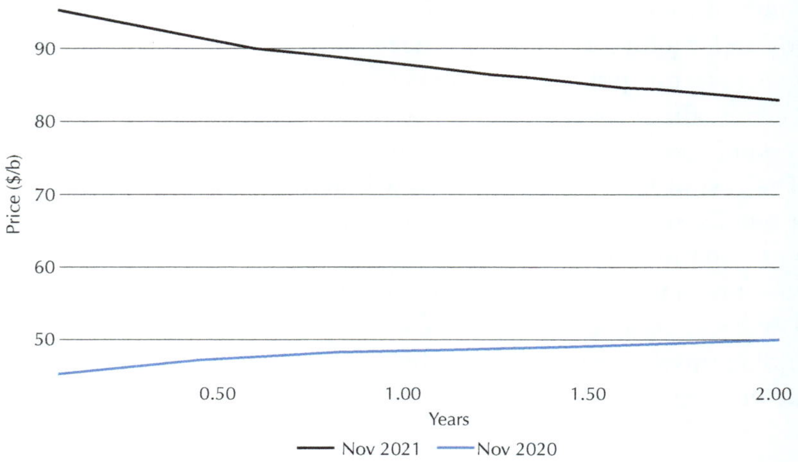

Source: Investec, Bloomberg

Figure 11.3 Seasonality in US natural gas forwards

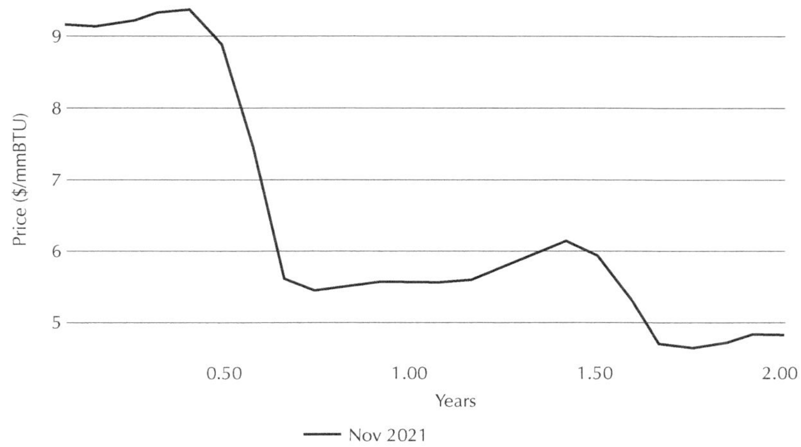

Source: Investec, Bloomberg

French, 1987), and can lead to investors in ETFs that follow a strategy of rolling the front contract, experiencing very different economics to what they expected.

It is also possible to trade spreads consisting of a long position in one future and a short in another. The two futures can be different futures on the same commodity forward curve (a time spread), thus taking a view that the curve will get steeper or flatter, or on different commodities – expressing the view that one commodity will perform better than another.

The cost of storing and financing physical commodities suggests that forward curves should always be upward sloping (to charge for those costs), but a tight supply situation can lead to consumers paying a premium to get hold of the commodity immediately, which leads to backwardation. Consequently, investors holding long positions by rolling short-dated futures contracts tend to have a double benefit when markets are tight as they get the positive roll yields as well as rising prices.

Having covered some of the principles of commodity investing, we now move onto ESG themes and consider how views can be taken via commodities.

Table 11.2 The uses of some metals traded on the LME

Metal	Exchange	Use
Copper	LME	Electric motors/dynamos, wiring
Aluminium	LME	Lightweight vehicle bodies, high voltage power lines
Nickel	LME	Batteries
Cobalt*	LME	Batteries
Lithium*	LME	Batteries

* these metals have very limited liquidity and are challenging to trade
Source: IEA (2022)

Metals and electrification

Electrification is a central theme in the energy transition. Switching from fossil fuels to electrical energy leads to zero emissions at the point of energy use. Grid networks enable optimisation of energy supply and demand over great distances, while renewable and other low carbon sources of electricity decarbonise the whole system. Considerable investment in supply and transmission infrastructure, as well as electric vehicles, heating systems, etc, are necessary to achieve this, and metals are critically important to that transformation (see Table 11.2).

Carbon markets

There is growing interest in carbon markets as a policy tool for governments, as a means for corporations to offset exposure, and of course from investors. They are two main types of carbon market.

- Cap and trade: This involves a government agency issuing legal entitlements to emit carbon.
- Offsetting schemes: Here, either a carbon sequestration project generates credits from stored carbon or a project leads to an emission reduction in an existing industrial or power generation process, which can then be used to offset emissions elsewhere.

As both approaches seem to be putting a price on carbon, it is tempting to assume they are comparable, but they are actually very different. The EU emissions allowances are probably the best known and most widely traded of the cap and trade systems. The

EU Commission issues allowances each year, and EU carbon emitters are compelled by law to have a sufficient number of allowances at the end of each compliance year to be able to surrender an amount equal to their emissions over that year. By controlling the flow of emission allowances into the system, the Commission is able to control and reduce actual carbon emissions. The crucial difference between this and offsetting schemes is that there is no carbon sequestration involved. The commission is issuing legal rights to emit carbon; it does not have a means of sequestering that carbon.

As carbon offsets are connected with carbon sequestration or emission reduction projects, they can in principle be used to offset emissions rather than merely to charge for them. However, verifying that the project is of genuinely incremental benefit can be very challenging. Imagine that a farmer owns a 100 acres of arable land and a 100 acres of forest. The farmer could start a rewilding project to turn the arable land into forest and thereby sequester carbon, generating a stream of offset credits to be sold. What if the farmer also cuts down the existing forest and turns this into arable land? If this was allowed, the farmer would have generated emissions credits without sequestering any carbon.

This rather simplistic example illustrates the challenges in creating systems with sufficient integrity that companies could use them to offset emissions and to make credible claims they are carbon-neutral. Figure 11.4 shows how different the prices of EU Allowances (EUAs) and offsets are. Buying land to carry out rewilding projects in developing countries to sequester carbon is relatively cheap compared to EUAs. However, if the EU were to allow emitters to buy offsets to reduce their emissions, hence reducing the amount of EUAs they would need to buy, it is likely that the price of offsets and EUAs would converge. A plausible spread trade would be to buy offset futures and sell EUA futures.

Market prices for commodities are driven by the interplay of supply, demand and storage. The same is true of carbon markets. Early in 2022, EUAs traded up towards €100/MT – around three times the highest levels seen historically. Some have celebrated this as a sign that carbon prices are heading towards charging for the damage that emissions of greenhouse gases (GHGs) bring about,

Figure 11.4 EUAs and CME global emission offset futures

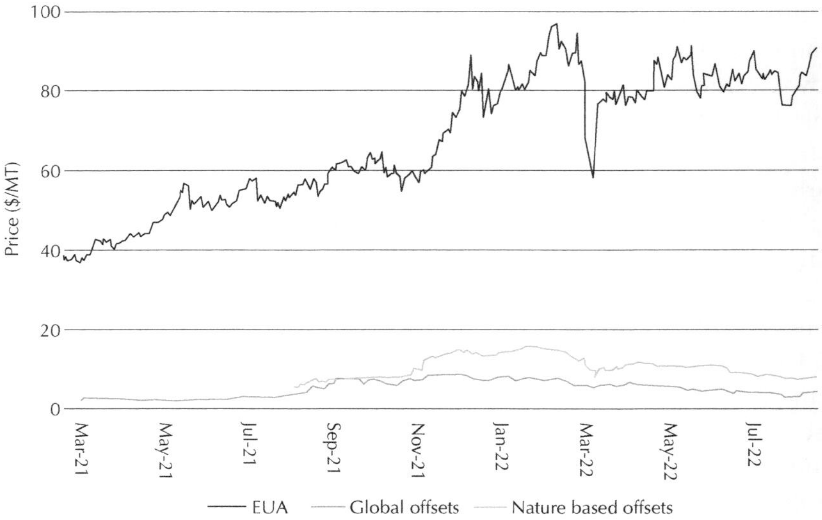

Source: Investec, Bloomberg

but it is important to understand that this surge was driven by increased carbon emissions in the EU, driving up demand for EUAs. Record high gas prices led to increased use of coal in power generation.

Figure 11.5 shows that, until late 2021, EUA prices tended to track the price of carbon that leads a coal-fired power plant in Germany breaking even based on the forward coal and electricity prices. In 2022, however, the high price of gas and low electricity output in France led to this relationship breaking down. The EUA market is wary that the EU Commission would not tolerate EUA prices accelerating with coal prices given how high energy prices are. The Commission can easily print more EUA's but not more gas!

Energy

Tradable energy products can be split broadly into three categories:

- ❑ oil and refined products, for conventional transportation (internal combustion and jet engines);

Figure 11.5 2023 EUA forwards and German coal-fired power

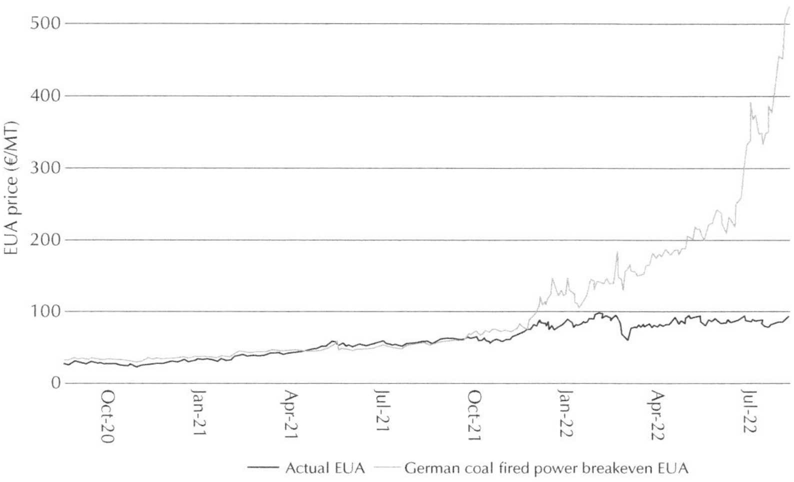

Source: Investec, Bloomberg

- gas and coal, for power for generation, industry and space heating; and
- electricity, increasingly used for just about everything.

Figure 11.6 compares the history of the price of different energy sources on an energy equivalent basis.

Why are the prices so different? These sources of energy are consumed by a particular selection of cars, aeroplanes, blast furnaces, power stations, home heating systems, etc. It is not possible to switch to running aeroplanes on coal, nor can a gas boiler run on diesel. Therefore, the fact that those sources of energy might be cheaper at a particular time is irrelevant. Supply/demand mismatches in particular forms of energy can drive significant differences in energy equivalent prices in the short term. Over long time periods (many years and decades), the energy demand mix can change significantly as the mix of consuming technologies changes. An obvious example is electric vehicles, which may disrupt the energy mix significantly in the coming years. The high energy density of oil, combined with relatively easy storage and combustion, has traditionally made it ideal to power transportation where space in vehicles is limited and mass needs to be

Figure 11.6 Global energy prices (in barrels of oil equivalent)

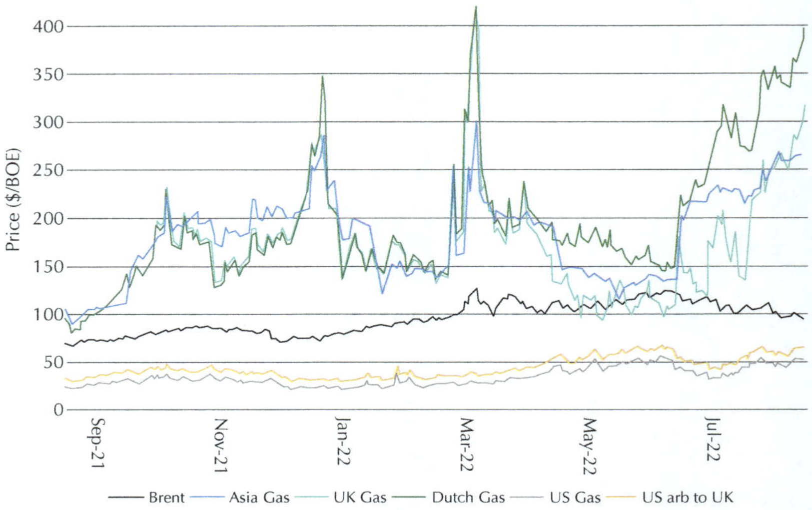

Source: Investec, Bloomberg

minimised. However, improvements in the storage capacity of batteries, together with the greater efficiency and simplicity of electric drive trains, is now challenging oil's traditional dominance in transportation – at least for cars and light goods vehicles.

ESG-themed trade ideas

- Long CME offset credits: Corporations are under growing pressure from shareholders and clients to decarbonise. This is not always possible in the short to medium term, creating demand for offsets. The cost of projects may rise once the cheapest options for sequestration have been used up.
- Oil product mix trades: Crude oil contains a mixture of hydrocarbons, and the refining industry has the challenge of matching the composition inherent in the input crude oil with the mixture required by end-user demand. As well as oil demand tailing off in the long term, it is likely that the demand mix will change. Electrification will likely impact diesel and gasoline demand first.
  - Short gasoline versus WTI futures in the US.
  - Long European jet fuel swaps versus diesel.

- The rise of gas: Switching from coal to gas for power generation can be an attractive means of reducing carbon emissions from the power sector. In addition, electrification of transport and other sectors will increase power demand. For both of these reasons, gas demand is likely to remain strong.
  - Long Nymex gas (avoiding the front end of the curve where contango can lead to roll losses).
  - Long TTF gas versus API2 coal.
  - Long TTF versus Brent.

  Of course, European gas prices are already at extraordinary levels because of the impact of strongly reduced Russian supplies, so it may make sense to express these views at the long end of the curve where the current crisis has less effect.
- Energy transition metals.
  - Long a portfolio of copper, aluminium and nickel.
- Synthetic green metals: Separating metals from the oxygen with which they are chemically combined is an energy-intensive process. Aluminium in particular requires a significant electricity input. 1MT of aluminium requires about 15 MWh of electricity, assuming this has been produced from coal-fired generation with a carbon intensity of 0.76 MT per MWh (S&P Global, 2022).
  - Long LME and $15 \times 0.76 = 11.4$ MT of CME offset credits per MT of aluminium.

CONCLUDING REMARKS ON COMMODITIES AND ESG THEMES

Commodities are an integral part of the energy transition. The economics of replacing infrastructure and switching between different fuels are determined by the prices of raw materials and energy. The rich variety of tradable futures that are available can enable investors to take all manner of views on the energy transition and other ESG themes.

Cryptocurrencies: An environmental curse or social liberator?

Cryptocurrencies have gone from being a fringe interest to being seen as a new asset class, worthy of inclusion in a portfolio as a diversifier, much like gold. How should they be viewed from an ESG point of view? There is an increasing (and belated) awareness of the extraordinary amount of energy employed in the process of crypto mining. There are also obvious social and governance issues connected with the ability of cryptocurrencies to enable transactions for nefarious purposes between parties without the inconvenience of intervening banks and anti-money laundering policies, or the cumbersome process of physically exchanging cash.

At a much broader level, some proponents of cryptocurrencies seem excited by the prospect of undermining traditional currencies, and at the same time the governments and countries that issue them. In countries where the probity of the banking system and public intuitions is in question, and this lack of trust undermines economic activity, cryptocurrencies might provide a more reliable alternative. In this case, they could provide a useful social function in enabling economic activity (Holtmeier and Sandner, 2019). However, this must be weighed against the disadvantages, including the very considerable energy consumption connected with Bitcoin mining. We shall focus on understanding the energy consumption of Bitcoin mining, and to consider comparisons with the carbon footprint of carrying out transactions via traditional centralised banking.

A very brief introduction

To understand the cause of the energy consumption, it is essential to understand how cryptocurrencies really work. Most laymen's introductions describe them as being a decentralised ledger, and have a rather loose description of the mining process that underpins its value. These explanations leave us feeling we have not really got to the nub of the concept, but people are disinclined to admit they don't understand it. On the other hand, many take the view that some very clever people are behind this new form of value – who must know what they are doing – and those that criticise it for being opaque or illusory simply have an axe to grind. We need to do better than this.

"Bitcoin: A Peer-to-peer Electronic Cash System" is a paper by Satoshi Nakamoto (Nakamoto, 2008), which sets out the principles of the blockchain, whose code to enable Bitcoin was published in the same year. The actual identity of Nakamoto remains unknown, but this has not stopped Bitcoin developing into a multi-billion dollar mainstream asset.

One of the key components of the blockchain is a hash function, which takes some input data and generates a string of characters. Unlike many mathematical functions where a small change in the input leads to a small change in the output, the output of the hash function can change dramatically. So much so in fact, that the change is statistically random. This means that, when given the output of a hash function, it is incredibly hard to work out what input could have generated it. Indeed, there is no better approach than to laboriously work through all possible inputs in turn and run the hash function on each to see if the desired output is produced. However, if the input is known, it is very easy to run the function and check that it does correspond with the desired output.

The blockchain consists of an evolving history of transactions. The records of this do not sit on any one central computer. Rather, copies are held on many servers around the world. Any new transactions are published to this network, and any members of the network are able to add new transitions into the blockchain by publishing a new block. However, for this new block to be accepted by the network, the infamous proof of work must have been carried out. This involves finding a string of characters (known as the nonce) that, when added to data representing the proposed block, produces an output with a specific number of leading "0"s when the combined input is put through the hash function. Due to the nature of hash functions mentioned above, there is no better way of finding the appropriate nonce than working through all values in turn. The new block and the nonce are broadcast to the network. Other members of the network can easily run the hash function on the nonce and proposed block – verifying that the proof of work has been performed correctly. The new block is accepted and the account that submitted it receives payment in Bitcoin.

Energy consumption

To be successful as a Bitcoin miner, vast computational resources must be thrown at the problem, consuming tremendous amounts of energy. *Miner Daily* estimates that, as of August 2021, on average 143 MWhrs were needed to mine one coin (Ling, 2021), while the Cambridge Centre for Alternative Finance estimates current global power consumption by Bitcoin mining to be 13.19 GW,[2] putting it between Holland and Argentina in terms of electricity consumption.

Investors in Bitcoins do not need to get involved in mining, they can simply buy Bitcoins in the hope that the prices rise – but, in doing so, they are relying on constant energy consumption to maintain the value of their investment. It has been argued that the use of renewable energy could green Bitcoin; indeed, it has been estimated that the power usage for mining is 39% renewable already (Blandin *et al*, 2020). However, in view of the enormity of the challenges of achieving net zero, and given that the energy system is still very largely dependent on fossil fuels, there is a need to use energy sparingly, and it is legitimate to question whether greening crypto mining is a good use of renewable energy.

How does the energy involved in Bitcoin mining compare to traditional financial systems based around banking? The comparison is a challenging one and there are limited examples of studies on this subject. One that is widely cited was conducted by Galaxy Digital Mining (Rybarczyk, Armstrong and Fabiano, 2021), which concluded that the banking system consumed 263.72 TWh in 2019, compared to Bitcoin usage at 113.89 TWh. The report claims that most banking power consumption is expended in data centres, and estimates this consumption to be 238.92 TWh. However, the International Energy Agency estimated that total global data centre power demand was only 200 TWh in 2019 (IEA, 2021). Whatever the actual power consumption connected with banks using data centres actually is, it does not seem credible that the energy intensity of transaction data (which is very simple in terms of the information required) could be comparable with, for example, streaming videos. This raises questions over the estimated power consumption of traditional transaction processing.

The incredible increases in Bitcoin prices clearly make them interesting, as does statistical evidence suggesting that a small Bitcoin allocation may improve portfolio diversification (Bakri *et al*, 2021). However, for an ESG-conscious investor there are some complex issues to consider where Bitcoin is concerned. The energy consumption has a significant environmental impact and diverts energy from other needs, potentially exacerbating the cost of living crisis.

The views and opinions expressed in Part 2 are those of the author and do not necessarily represent or reflect the position of Investec.

1 A useful guide to this has been produced by Invest Europe (n.d.).
2 See https://ccaf.io/cbeci/index.

REFERENCES

Bakri, W., A. Rashid, S. Al-Mohamad and N. El-Kanj, 2021, "Bitcoin and Portfolio Diversification: A Portfolio Optimization Approach", *Journal of Risk and Financial Management,* 14(282) (available at https://www.mdpi.com/1911–8074/14/7/282/pdf).

Benson, N., D. Berman, P. A. Davies, L. N. Ferrell, S. Hawkins, N. Higgs, F. Sharmeen, A. Mainwaring, D. Schoeneberger, S. Wong and C. Collins, 2021, "ESG in Asset Management: A Global Perspective", Latham & Watkins, October 1 (available at https://www.globalelr.com/2021/10/esg-in-asset-management-a-global-perspective/).

Blandin, A., G. Pieters, Y. Wu, T. Eisermann, A. Dek, S. Taylor and D. Njoki, 2020, "3rd Global Cryptoasset Benchmarking Study", Cambridge Centre for Alternative Finance, September (available at https://www.jbs.cam.ac.uk/wp-content/uploads/2021/01/2021-ccaf-3rd-global-cryptoasset-benchmarking-study.pdf).

CBRE, 2021, "The Role of ESG in the Multifamily Property Market: Considerations for the Irish Market", June (available at https://www.cbre.ie/en/research-and-reports/Ireland--The-Role-of-ESG-in-the-Multifamily-Property-Market--Considerations-for-the-Irish-Property-M).

Coppola, M. and J. Blohmke, 2019, "Feeling the Heat? Companies are Under Pressure to Act on Climate Change and Need to Do More", Deloitte Insights, December 12 (available at https://www2.deloitte.com/us/en/insights/topics/strategy/impact-and-opportunities-of-climate-change-on-business.html).

Crawford, B., 2021, "Private Equity, Labour Rights and the New Corporate Debt Economy", Institute of Employment Rights, November 29 (available at https://www.ier.org.uk/comments/private-equity-labour-rights-and-the-new-corporate-debt-economy/).

Desmyter, S., 2021, "What if ESG Could Solve the Global Housing Crisis?", *Forbes,* May 25 (available at https://www.forbes.com/sites/stevendesmyter/2021/05/25/what-if-esg-could-solve-the-global-housing-crisis/?sh=e8de7d912010).

Fama, E. and K. French, 1987, "Commodity Futures Prices: Some Evidence on Forecast Power, Premiums, and the Theory of Storage," *Journal of Business,* 60(1), pp. 55–73.

Friede, G., T. Busch and A. Bassen, 2015, "ESG and Financial Performance: Aggregated Evidence from More Than 2000 Empirical Studies," *Journal of Sustainable Finance & Investment,* 5(4), October (available at https://www.tandfonline.com/doi/full/10.1080/20430795.2015.1118917).

Hawker, E., 2021, "Private vs Public: The Renewables Balancing Act", ESG Investor, August 4 (available at https://www.esginvestor.net/private-vs-public-the-renewables-balancing-act/).

Henisz, W., T. Koller and R. Nuttall, 2019, "Five Ways that ESG Creates Value", *McKinsey Quarterly,* November (available at https://www.mckinsey.com/~/media/McKinsey/Business%20Functions/Strategy%20and%20Corporate%20Finance/Our%20Insights/Five%20ways%20that%20ESG%20creates%20value/Five-ways-that-ESG-creates-value.ashx).

Holtmeier, M. and P. Sandner, 2019, "The Impact of Crypto Currencies on Developing Countries", FSBC Working Paper, December (available at http://explore-ip.com/2019_The-Impact-of-Crypto-Currencies-on-Developing-Countries.pdf).

IEA, 2021, Data Centres and Data Transmission Networks", November (available at https://www.iea.org/reports/data-centres-and-data-transmission-networks).

IEA, 2022, "The Role of Critical Minerals in Clean Energy Transitions", World Energy Outlook Special Report (available at https://iea.blob.core.windows.net/assets/ffd2a83b-8c30-4e9d-980a-52b6d9a86fdc/TheRoleofCriticalMineralsinCleanEnergyTransitions.pdf).

Invest Europe, n.d., "ESG Due Diligence Questionnaire for Private Equity Investors and their Portfolio Companies" (available at https://www.investeurope.eu/media/1777/invest-europe_esg_dd_questionnaire.pdf).

Ling, S., 2021, "How Much Power Does it Take to Mine a Bitcoin", *Miner Daily,* August 19 (available at https://minerdaily.com/2021/how-much-power-does-it-take-to-mine-a-bitcoin/).

Nakamoto, S., 2008, "Bitcoin: A Peer-to-peer Electronic Cash System", March.

OECD, 2019, "Fraud and Corruption in European Structural and Investment Funds: A Spotlight on Common Scheme and Preventive Actions" (available at https://www.oecd.org/gov/ethics/prevention-fraud-corruption-european-funds.pdf).

Prequin, 2020, "The Future of Alternatives 2025", Special Report, November (available at https://www.preqin.com/insights/research/reports/preqin-special-report-the-future-of-alternatives-2025).

PWC, 2020, "Emerging Trends in Real Estate: Europe 2020" (available at https://www.pwc.com/gx/en/industries/financial-services/asset-management/emerging-trends-real-estate/europe-2020.html).

Raskopf, M., 2021, "Does ESG Spell the End for Commodities? We Don't Think So", Russell Investments, Special Report, September 15 (available at https://russellinvestments.com/us/blog/esg-investing-commodities-outlook).

Rybarczyk, R., D. Armstrong and A. Fabiano, 2021, "On Bitcoin's Energy Consumption: A Quantitative Approach to a Subjective Question", Galaxy Digital, May (available at https://www.lopp.net/pdf/On_Bitcoin_Energy_Consumption.pdf).

S&P Global, 2022, "Specifications Guide European Electricity", July (available at https://www.spglobal.com/commodityinsights/en/our-methodology/methodology-specifications/electric-power/european-electricity-assessments-and-indices).

Sheu, H.-J., and S.-F. Lo, 2005, "A New Conceptual Framework Integrating Environment into Corporate Performance Evaluation", *Sustainable Development,* 13(2), pp. 79–90 (available at https://onlinelibrary.wiley.com/doi/abs/10.1002/sd.247).

SSE and WFE, 2021, "How Derivatives Exchanges Can Promote Sustainable Development: An Action Menu", April (available at https://sseinitiative.org/wp-content/uploads/2021/04/SSE-WFE-Derivatives-Exchanges-Guidance.pdf).

Zeisberger, C., M. Prahl and B. White, 2017, *Mastering Private Equity: Transformation via Venture Capital, Minority Investments and Buyouts* (Hoboken, NJ: Wiley).

PART VI

DATA, TAXONOMIES AND REGULATION

12

Reviewing the EU regulatory framework for ESG investors

Arthur Carabia and Anne Schoemaker

Morningstar Sustainalytics

As inflows into sustainable investment funds continue to grow exponentially, policymakers around the globe are reviewing and enhancing rules applicable to these products, and those who manage or distribute them. As Europe concentrates the large bulk of sustainable investment funds (in terms of both number of funds and assets under management, AuM) and has been at the forefront of this new wave of regulation, this chapter will mainly focus on the European region (see Table 12.1).

To date, the EU's approach, underpinned by its sustainable finance strategy (European Commission, 2021a), could be mainly characterised by a will to tackle greenwashing by requiring enhanced disclosures (the Sustainable Finance Disclosure Regulation, SFDR), and to channel further investments into sustainable assets by developing a common language (the EU Taxonomy and amendments to the Markets in Financial Instruments Directive,

Table 12.1 Global sustainable fund universe

Region	AuM (US$bn)	Number of funds
Europe	2,276	4,958
US	343	555
Rest of the world	159	939

Source: Morningstar, "Global Sustainable Fund Flows – Q1 2022" (May 2022)
Note: This table does not contain "ESG integrated funds" nor funds that employ limited exclusionary screens

Figure 12.1 Main developments and interactions under the EU sustainable finance strategy

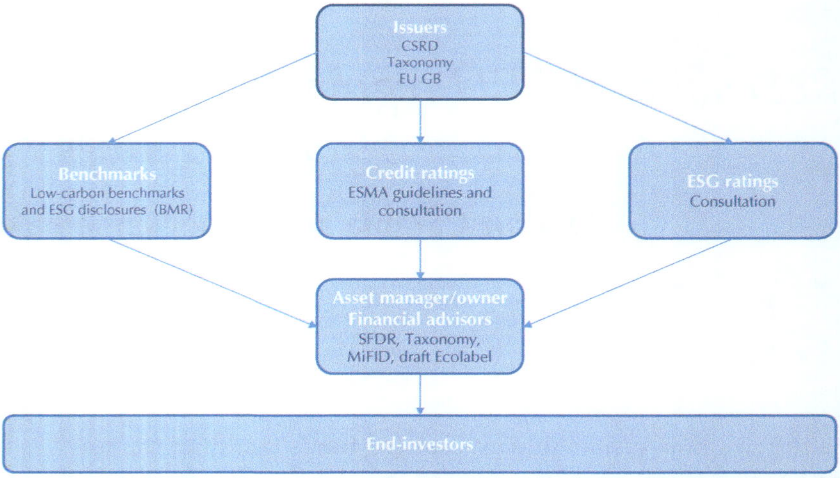

MiFID) and optional labels (eg, EU green bond regulation and the EU Ecolabel for investment funds).

Financial product providers with investment products for sale in the EU need to pay close attention to these new developments as they may impact: (i) the way products are labelled and marketed; (ii) the information asset managers need to publish and provide to clients; and (iii) the eligible investment universe of these products (see Figure 12.1).

This new EU regulatory regime, which co-exists with national rules, and normative ESG labels are sometimes completed by national supplementary rules and best practices, with France and Germany creating separate fund classification, exclusion thresholds and disclosure rules. This creates a confusion of provisions that is sometimes complex to navigate, but which this chapter will attempt to summarise.

NEWLY INTRODUCED EU RULES AND THEIR IMPACT ON ESG INVESTING

Newly introduced EU rules potentially impacting ESG investors covered under this section are the SFDR, the Taxonomy regulation, and the amendments to MiFID related to the consideration of potential sustainability preferences of clients.

SFDR[1]

Introduction to SFDR

SFDR is one of the first initiatives launched under the EU Sustainable Finance Action Plan, and is a key regulatory development for investors. While financial market participants were required to apply most of the high-level, entity-level and product-level provisions as of March 10, 2021, the application of the more granular implementation and reporting measures are due on January 1, 2023.

The regulation introduces three key definitions: sustainable investment; sustainability risk; and principal adverse impacts, which are defined as follows.

- Sustainable investment is an investment in an economic activity that: (i) contributes to either an environmental or social objective; (ii) does not significantly harm any environmental or social objectives; and (iii) where the investee company follows good governance practices.
- Sustainability risk is an environmental, social or governance (ESG) event or condition that, if it occurs, could cause a material negative impact on the value of an investment.
- Principal adverse impacts (PAIs) on sustainability factors are the investment's impact when considering environmental, social and employee, human rights, anti-corruption and anti-bribery matters.

Using these three concepts, SFDR mainly intends to enhance sustainability transparency of financial products (such as investment funds, mandates, pension funds/products and certain insurance products) and that of the financial market participants who issue/sell them (eg, asset managers, asset owners and financial advisers), through website and pre-contractual disclosures as well as periodic reports.

Firm disclosure

At the entity-level, financial market participants (FMPs) must disclose on their website: (i) how they integrate sustainability risks regarding investment decisions, or advice and remuneration, and engagement policies; and (ii) how they consider PAIs looking at all their investments.

Table 12.2 List of mandatory KPIs under entity disclosure requirement

Environment	1. GHG emissions	Scope 1 GHG emissions
		Scope 2 GHG emissions
		Scope 3 GHG emissions
		Total GHG emissions
	2. Carbon footprint	Carbon footprint
	3. GHG intensity of investee companies	GHG intensity of investee companies
	4. Exposure to companies active in the fossil fuel sector	Share of investments in companies active in the fossil fuel sector
	5. Share of non-renewable energy consumption and production	Share of non-renewable energy consumption and non-renewable energy production of investee companies from non-renewable energy sources compared to renewable energy sources, expressed as a percentage
	6. Energy consumption intensity perhigh impact climate sector	Energy consumption in GWh per million euros of revenue of investee companies, per high impact climate sector
	7. Activities negatively affecting biodiversity-sensitive areas	Share of investments in investee companies with sites/operations located in or near to biodiversity-sensitive areas where activities of those investee companies negatively affect those areas
	8. Emissions to water	Tonnes of emissions to water generated by investee companies per million euros invested, expressed as a weighted average
	9. Hazardous waste ratio	Tonnes of hazardous waste generated by investee companies per million euros invested, expressed as a weighted average

Social	10. Violations of UN Global Compact (UNGC) principles and Organisation for Economic Co-operation and Development (OECD) Guidelines for Multinational Enterprises	Share of investments in investee companies that have been involved in violations of the UNGC principles or OECD Guidelines for Multinational Enterprises
	11. Lack of processes and compliance mechanisms to monitor compliance with UNGC principles and OECD Guidelines for Multinational Enterprises	Share of investments in investee companies without policies to monitor compliance with the UNGC principles or OECD Guidelines for Multinational Enterprises or grievance/complaints-handling mechanisms to address violations of the UNGC principles or OECD Guidelines for Multinational Enterprises
	12. Unadjusted gender pay gap	Average unadjusted gender pay gap of investee companies
	13. Board gender diversity	Average ratio of female to male board members in investee companies
	14. Exposure to controversial weapons (anti-personnel mines, cluster munitions, chemical weapons and biological weapons)	Share of investments in investee companies involved in the manufacture or selling of controversial weapons
Indicators applicable to investments in sovereigns and supranationals		
Environment	15. GHG intensity	GHG intensity of investee countries
Social	16. Investee countries subject to social violations	Number of investee countries subject to social violations (absolute number and relative number divided by all investee countries), as referred to in international treaties and conventions, United Nations principles and, where applicable, national law
Indicators applicable to investments in real estate assets		
Environment	17. Exposure to fossil fuels through real estate assets	Share of investments in real estate assets involved in the extraction, storage, transport or manufacture of fossil fuels
	18. Exposure to energy-inefficient real estate assets	Share of investments in energy-inefficient real estate assets

In practice, these disclosure requirements at the firm level have so far led to the publication of a series of qualitative yet comprehensive statements. However, when it comes to the consideration of PAIs, the provisions are expected to become quantitative and more challenging with the application of the implementation measures on June 30, 2023.

FMPs will have to report at the entity level their ESG footprint by assessing all their investments against 18 mandatory environmental and social key performance indicators (KPIs) and two others chosen from a list of 46 optional indicators. They will have to disclose the impact against these indicators for year *n* and year *n*–1, provide an explanation, and if they have any actions or targets planned for the next reporting period.

These KPIs listed in the annex 1 of the delegated regulation[2] relate to climate and social aspects such as greenhouse gas (GHG) emissions, biodiversity, water, waste, and social and employee matters (see Table 12.2). Separate indicators applicable to investments in sovereigns and supranationals, as well as real estate assets, are proposed.

Many data providers are already providing PAI data solutions to assist FMPs in complying with this SFDR requirement. For illustration, Sustainalytics' PAI coverage includes 13 000 companies for corporate KPIs, 172 countries for sovereign KPIs, 100% of mandatory and soon 95% of optional KPIs.[3]

However, reporting against this granular regime will be particularly challenging for FMPs that are exposed to specific asset classes and investee companies – eg, when considering commodities, ABS, non-EU and private companies – so much so that SFDR has contributed to triggering the review of the Non-Financial Reporting Directive (NFRD)[3] and other sectorial regulation, such as the STS securitisation regulation (ESA, 2022), which could lead to the adoption of enhanced sustainability disclosures for issuers/originators, including KPIs aligned with SFDR.

Although SFDR entity disclosures bring many challenges (ie, data availability, reconciliation, relevance), this new regime could lead asset managers to review their ESG filters when selecting securities as they may be inclined to paint a positive sustainability footprint for clients and other observers.

Product disclosure and features

SFDR also sets specific transparency requirements at the product level. The regulation makes a distinction between products that "promote ESG characteristics" (article 8) and products with "a core sustainable investment objective" (article 9).

Article 8 products

SFDR is not prescriptive when it comes to the consideration of environmental and social characteristics in the context of article 8:

> Article 8 of Regulation (EU) 2019/2088 remains neutral in terms of design of financial products. It does not prescribe certain elements such as the composition of investments or minimum investment thresholds, the eligible investment targets, and neither does it determine eligible investing styles, investment tools, strategies or methodologies to be employed. Therefore, nothing prevents financial products subject to Article 8 of Regulation (EU) 2019/2088 not to continue applying various current market practises, tools and strategies and a combination thereof such as screening, exclusion strategies, best-in-class/universe, thematic investing, certain redistribution of profits or fees.[5]

In that context, asset managers were forced to develop their own definition/methodology to meet the classification and disclosure requirements. This has led to diverging classifications of similar strategies.

Definition of a sustainable investment and article 9 products

An article 9 product is a product that has a sustainable investment as its objective. A sustainable investment is an investment in an economic activity that: (i) contributes either to an environmental or a social objective; (ii) does not significantly harm any environmental or social objectives; and (iii) where the investee company follows good governance practices.

However, SFDR does not provide for a minimum proportion of sustainable investments to be classified as article 9. It only requires that article 9 products: (i) comply with the definition of a sustainable investment objective that contains the Do No Significant Harm (DNSH) requirement; and (ii) also (according to the Q&A published by the EC),[6] that "other" assets – eg, for hedging and liquidity purposes – must be in line with the sustainable investment objective of the product and therefore meet the minimum safeguards.

The conditions by which the DNSH and minimum safeguards tests could be considered positive/negative are not defined, and they are currently left at the discretion of asset managers. The list of mandatory PAIs cited in the entity disclosure above and 46 other optional PAIs have to be considered for the purpose of the DNH, but there are no thresholds specified by regulators. Safeguards as defined by the Taxonomy are rather high level (referring to widely accepted global norms and standards) and also refer to the SFDR DNSH (see Panel 12.1).

PANEL 12.1 ARTICLE 18 EU TAXONOMY REGULATION: MINIMUM SAFEGUARDS

1. The minimum safeguards referred to in point (c) of Article 3 shall be procedures implemented by an undertaking that is carrying out an economic activity to ensure the alignment with the OECD Guidelines for Multinational Enterprises and the UN Guiding Principles on Business and Human Rights, including the principles and rights set out in the eight fundamental conventions identified in the Declaration of the International Labour Organisation on Fundamental Principles and Rights at Work and the International Bill of Human Rights.
2. When implementing the procedures referred to in paragraph 1 of this Article, undertakings shall adhere to the principle of "do no significant harm" referred to in point (17) of Article 2 of Regulation (EU) 2019/2088.

Classification

To date, asset managers have had to disclose in prospectuses (in a non-prescriptive way) how a given product is classified between these two categories, and how the ESG characteristics and/or the sustainable investment objective are met. According to one report (Morningstar, 2022), article 8 and 9 funds account for 37.7% and 4.7%, respectively, of reviewed fund assets, and amounted to €4.05 trillion in total at the end of December 2021.

As noted in the report, "Fund companies have taken different approaches to product classification based on their own interpretation of the regulation, resulting in a wide range of ESG approaches represented in Articles 8 and 9 funds, with similar strategies featuring in both categories" (see Figure 12.2).

The diverging classification of similar strategies is not entirely surprising, and can be explained by the fact that: (i) SFDR is subject

Figure 12.2 Examples of ESG investment strategies according to SFDR classifications

Article 8 funds
Promoting environmental or social characteristics

- Values-based exclusions
- Material ESG considerations + engagement
- Portfolio-level ESG KPIs
- Min 50% of sustainable assets
- Exclusion of 20% worst-in-universe
- Best-in-class
- Thematic

Article 9 funds
With a sustainable investment objective

- Values-based + fossil-fuel exclusions
- Portfolio-level ESG KPIs
- Best-in-class
- Thematic
- Impact

Light green → Dark green

to interpretation, and this dual categorisation exercise (ie, article 8 versus article 9) does not always allow fund managers to capture all the nuances of products and strategies; and (ii) given these legal uncertainties, some fund managers may have opted for a prudent classification while waiting for the finalisation of the implementation measures.

It looks like there are several funds that on paper could qualify as article 9 – such as a fund with a minimum 50% of green bond exposure that ended up opting for an article 8 classification. This could also happen for compliance reasons and notably for the lack of appropriate benchmarks to be able to classify as article 9.

Under SFDR, financial market participants are required to disclose how their benchmarks are material and consistent with the characteristics or objectives of their products, yet index providers are not in the scope of SFDR, and their ESG disclosure obligations under the Benchmark Regulation (BMR) are different. For instance, BMR requires administrators to disclose ESG features for their ESG indexes, but not for "broad market indexes".

SFDR, on the other hand, goes further in that it requires for article 9 products "a comparison between the overall sustainability-related impact of the financial product with the impacts of the designated index and of a broad market index through sustainability indicators". This leads to situations where fund managers cannot find a suitable benchmark for article 9 products, forcing them to requalify them as article 8 products (see Panel 12.2).

PANEL 12.2 THE CLASSIFICATION OF BEST IN CLASS STRATEGIES CONSTITUTE AN INTERESTING CASE STUDY HIGHLIGHTING THE CHALLENGES AROUND THE SFDR CLASSIFICATION

According to Morningstar (Bioy, 2021), a large number of funds using best in class strategies have opted to classify their funds as article 8. This would seem to be in line with what is assumed by the European Supervisory Authorities (ESAs, recital 18 of its draft RTS): "financial products that promote, among other characteristics, environmental or social characteristics, or a combination of those characteristics (environmental or social characteristics) cover various investment approaches and strategies, from best in class to specific sectoral exclusions".

Nevertheless, in some cases funds using best in class strategies have opted to classify as article 9 because, on top of selecting the best-issuers, they have a measurable sustainable objective – eg, a GHG reduction target against their benchmark. This would appear to be in line with the definition of a sustainable investment: "an investment in an economic activity that contributes to an environmental objective, as measured, for example, by key resource efficiency indicators on the use of energy, renewable energy, raw materials, water and land, on the production of waste, and greenhouse gas emissions (…)".

There are also cases where best in class funds using a binding selectivity approach and with a clear environmental focus (eg, investment universe narrowed by at least 20% based on climate change scores on top of firm-wide ESG criteria and exclusions) have been classified as article 9. However, it is unclear under what conditions the use of binding selective processes could be considered to lead to a sustainable investment, and therefore an article 9 classification of a product.

The Q&A published by the EC on July 14, 2021[7] regarding the interpretation of the level 1 regulation seems to suggest that best in class strategies could potentially be used in the context of both article 8 and article 9:

> Therefore, nothing prevents financial products subject to Article 8 of Regulation (EU) 2019/2088 not to continue applying various current market practises, tools and strategies and a combination thereof such as screening, exclusion strategies, best in class/universe, thematic investing, certain redistribution of profits or fees. Certainly, many of those market practises, tools and strategies are also available to financial products subject to Article 9 of Regulation (EU) 2019/2088, provided the investments qualify as "sustainable investments", as defined in point 17 of Article 2 of Regulation (EU) 2019/2088.

We therefore argue that the classification of products based on best in class strategies are very much at the discretion of fund managers and local regulators, who will need to approve, for the second time, the classification and the new pre-contractual documents to be issued to comply with the second implementation deadline on the January 1, 2023.

Underlying investments of article 8 and article 9 products

There is no evidence at this stage that application of SFDR (without technical measures) has drastically changed the investment choices made by ESG/sustainable product managers. However, in aggregate, article 8 and article 9 funds continue to perform better on ESG metrics than article 6 products. For instance, 52% of article 8 funds and 70.4% of article 9 funds received the highest ratings, four or five globes, compared with 34.6% of article 6 funds. We also note that they apply more exclusions, and article 9 funds also typically have lower involvement in controversial weapons, tobacco, fossil fuel and severe controversies (see Tables 12.3 and 12.4, and Figure 12.3).

Upcoming and upgraded transparency measures under SFDR

On October 22, 2021, the SFDR delegated regulation containing detailed implementation measures was adopted by the European Commission. One could wonder if the granular measures, which are expected to raise the level of transparency of products (eg, the percentage of Taxonomy alignment, performance against chosen sustainability indicators) and may require further efforts from asset managers to justify their product classification, could potentially impact their investment decisions made under article 8 and article 9 products.

Product disclosure requirements are indeed expected to become more stringent with the entry of mandatory templates for article 8 and article 9 products to be provided with pre-contractual documents and periodic reports. Four templates are being proposed in total.

Although there are some specificities, the fields under the four templates largely overlap and can be summarised as follows.

- ❑ Type of product: ESG characteristics versus sustainable investment objective.
- ❑ Actual ESG characteristics promoting the product's sustainable investment objective, its investment strategy, how it considers good governance practices and sustainability indicators, and any binding ESG/sustainability elements to attain characteristics/objectives.
- ❑ The share of assets that contribute to ESG characteristics/sustainable investment objective versus others.

Table 12.3 Most commonly held stocks in article 8 funds (June 30, 2022)

Stock	Sector	Number of funds owning the stock	Average portfolio weight	% of Article 9 funds owning the stock	Equity style box	ESG risk rating assessment
Alphabet Inc	Communication services	485	2.8%	29%	Large growth	OOO
Microsoft Corp	Technology	439	4.2%	26%	Large growth	OOOO
Novo Nordisk A/S	Healthcare	384	2.5%	23%	Large growth	OOO
Roche Holding AG	Healthcare	384	1.9%	23%	Large blend	OOO
ASML Holding NV	Technology	377	3.0%	22%	Large growth	OOOO
Schneider Electric SE	Industrials	358	1.7%	21%	Large blend	OOOO
Taiwan Semiconductor Manufacturing Co Ltd	Technology	345	4.4%	20%	Large blend	OOOO
Alibaba Group Holding Ltd	Consumer cyclical	327	3.3%	19%	Large blend	OOO
SAP SE	Technology	324	1.9%	19%	Large blend	OOOO
Sanoñ SA	Healthcare	313	1.9%	19%	Large blend	OOO
Astrazeneca PLC	Healthcare	312	2.1%	18%	Large growth	OOO
Samsung Electronics Co Ltd	Technology	310	3.2%	18%	Large value	OOO
Atlas Copco AB	Industrials	301	1.8%	18%	Large blend	OOOO
Unilever PLC	Consumer defensive	300	1.7%	18%	Large blend	OOO
Tencent Holdings Ltd	Communication services	292	4.3%	17%	Large growth	OOO
Amazon.com Inc	Consumer cyclical	292	3.2%	17%	Large growth	OO
Allianz SE	Financial services	283	1.7%	17%	Large value	OOOO
L'Oreal SA	Consumer defensive	278	1.8%	16%	Large blend	OOO
Nestle SA	Consumer defensive	275	2.4%	16%	Large blend	OOO
LVMH Moet Hennessy Vuitton SE	Consumer cyclical	271	2.7%	16%	Large growth	OOOO

Table 12.4 Most commonly held stocks in article 9 funds (June 30, 2022)

Stock	Sector	Number of funds owning the stock	Average portfolio weight	% of Article 9 funds owning the stock	Equity style box	ESG risk rating assessment
Schneider Electric SE	Industrials	123	2.3%	45%	Large blend	OOOO
ASML Holding NV	Technology	100	2.9%	37%	Large growth	OOOO
Vestas Wind Systems A/S	Industrials	99	1.8%	37%	Large growth	OOOO
Microsoft Corp	Technology	80	3.6%	30%	Large growth	OOOO
Novo Nordisk A/S	Healthcare	79	1.9%	29%	Large growth	OOO
Roche Holding AG	Healthcare	74	1.8%	27%	Large blend	OOO
Unilever PLC	Consumer defensive	71	1.8%	26%	Large blend	OOO
Koninklijke DSM NV	Basic materials	71	1.6%	26%	Large blend	OOOO
SAP SE	Technology	70	1.8%	26%	Large blend	OOOO
Thermo Fisher Scientific Inc	Healthcare	67	2.1%	25%	Large growth	OOOO
Siemens Gamesa Renewable Energy SA	Industrials	65	1.3%	24%	Large growth	OOOO
Koninklijke Philips NV	Healthcare	65	1.7%	24%	Large blend	OOO
L'Oreal SA	Consumer defensive	64	1.9%	24%	Large blend	OOO
Xylem Inc	Industrials	63	1.4%	23%	Mid blend	OOOO
Allianz SE	Financial services	63	1.8%	23%	Large value	OOOO
Alphabet Inc	Communication services	63	2.5%	23%	Large growth	OOO
Air Liquide SA	Basic materials	63	1.6%	23%	Large blend	OOOO
Umicore SA	Industrials	62	1.1%	23%	Large blend	OOO
Siemens AG	Industrials	62	1.7%	23%	Large blend	OOO
Infineon Technologies AG	Technology	60	1.7%	22%	Large growth	OOOO

Figure 12.3 Article 8 and article 9 funds tend to be less exposed to controversial activities

- The performance over several years against sustainability indicators (KPIs at the discretion of asset managers) that ensure the ESG characteristics are met.
- The top investments.
- The share of assets that contribute to an ESG characteristics/sustainable investment objective versus others, and whether other assets observe minimum environmental and social safeguards.
- The sustainable investment that the product may have and how it complies with the DNSH objective and consideration of PAIs (ie, 64 KPIs).
- The share of investments aligned with the EU Taxonomy, the eventual use of an external review, the methodology used, and the share between transitional and enabling activities.
- The share of sustainable investment alignment not aligned with the EU Taxonomy.
- Actions taken to meet the ESG characteristics/sustainable investment during the reference period.
- ESG characteristics/sustainable investment of the reference benchmark, and how the product and its performance are differentiated against it and the broad market index.

EU Taxonomy alignment at the product and entity level

The EU Taxonomy regulation requires FMPs to report on the extent to which investments are aligned with "sustainable objectives".

In the regulation, an activity is aligned if:

- it contributes to one or more of the sustainable objectives defined in the EU Taxonomy for sustainable activities;
- it does not do significant harm to any other sustainable objective; and
- passes separate minimum safeguards (eg, related to human rights).

In the context of an individual company, Taxonomy alignment is defined as the proportion of a company's revenue that comes from activities that meet the above alignment criteria. In the context of an individual fund or portfolio, alignment is defined as the portfolio-weight weighted average Taxonomy alignment of included companies.

FMPs are required to disclose the Taxonomy alignment of their products, and financial advisors are required to report the Taxonomy alignment of managed portfolios of their private wealth management customers. According to the Q&A published by the EC,[8] products with environmental characteristics or an environmental objective should be subject to the Taxonomy alignment reporting requirement (see Figure 12.4). Additionally, amendments to MiFID require asset managers and financial advisors to allow customers to define binding sustainability targets based on Taxonomy alignment (or, alternatively, SFDR PAI indicators).

Taxonomy alignment at product level should be calculated as follows.

- A first KPI is calculated establishing the weighted average Taxonomy-aligned activity contribution of investments in the numerator and using all investments as the denominator.
- A second KPI should be included in the same way but excluding all sovereign exposures (which includes any investment that results in an exposure to central governments, central banks and supranational issuers) from the numerator and the denominator.
- The numerator should further be broken down into Taxonomy-contributing assets by differentiating between green bonds under the future EU Green Bond Standard, other green bonds, and investments in non-financial and financial undertakings.
- Green bonds issued under the future EU Green Bond Standard should count for 100% of their value in the numerator as such bonds must use 100% of their proceeds towards environmentally sustainable economic activities.
- For green bonds issued under other green bond frameworks, the proportion of their value that corresponds to the share of the proceeds of those bonds used for environmentally sustainable economic activities should be included.
- For non-financial investee companies, the value in the numerator should correspond to the value of the securities invested by the financial product in those companies weighted by the share of turnover or, where relevant, capital expenditure or operational expenditure contributed to environmentally sustainable economic activities.

Figure 12.4 Mandatory graphs to be used in pre-contractual and periodic reporting documents to disclose a product's percentage of investments aligned with the EU Taxonomy

Pre-contractual disclosure

The two graphs below show in green the minimum percentage of investments that are aligned with the EU Taxonomy. As there is no appropriate methodology to determine the Taxonomy-alignment of sovereign bonds*, the first graph shows the Taxonomy-alignment in relation to all the investments of the financial product including sovereign bonds, while the second graph shows the Taxonomy-alignment only in relation to the investments of the financial product other than sovereign bonds.

* For the purpose of these graphs, 'sovereign bonds' consist of all sovereign exposures

Periodic disclosure

The graphs below show in green the percentage of investments that were aligned with the EU Taxonomy. As there is no appropriate methodology to determine the Taxonomy-alignment of sovereign bonds*, the first graph shows the Taxonomy-alignment in relation to all the investments of the financial product including sovereign bonds, while the second graph shows the Taxonomy-alignment only in relation to the investments of the financial product other than sovereign bonds.

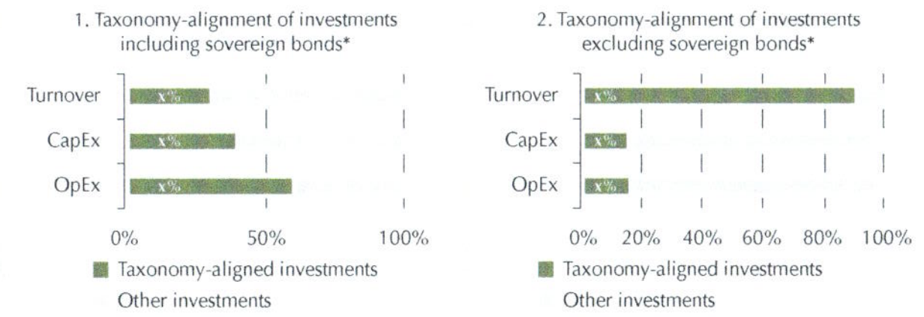

* For the purpose of these graphs, 'sovereign bonds' consist of all sovereign exposures

- For pre-contractual documents, FMPs must choose one of the three types of calculation basis for all non-financial undertaking investee companies the product invests in and explain the reasons for that choice, including how that choice is appropriate for the investors in the product. For periodic disclosures, FMPs need to show their Taxonomy alignment against all three KPIs on non-financial investee companies.
- The calculation should be netted for the purposes of reporting the share of investments in Taxonomy-aligned economic activities by applying the methodology used to calculate net short positions laid down in article 3, paragraphs 4 and 5, of Regulation (EU) No 236/2012 of the European Parliament and of the Council.
- For financial undertaking investee companies, the value in the numerator should correspond to the share of activities associated with environmentally sustainable activities disclosed by those companies under their article 8 TR disclosures.
- The disclosure should be accompanied by narrative explanations, including a breakdown of investments by enabling and transitional activities.

Challenges linked to Taxonomy disclosure

Although all investments are to be accounted for, it does not mean that all investments can be assessed against the EU Taxonomy. At the outset, "non-climate-related green bonds" will not be able to contribute to the EU Taxonomy ratio given that the EC has yet to finalise the technical criteria for the four other objectives of the taxonomy (ie, water, circular economy, pollution prevention and biodiversity). These complementary measures were supposed to be adopted in the first half of 2022 but were delayed, and instead will start to be applied from 2023. Likewise, social bonds will not contribute for the EU Taxonomy ratio until the EC proposes a specific methodology.

Another challenge for the buy side is that under article 8 of the Taxonomy regulation: (i) some issuers will not have to report on their level of Taxonomy alignment in the foreseeable future (non--EU companies, small and medium-sized enterprises, SMEs, sovereign and supranational issuers); and (ii) issuers in scope are only going to have to start reporting on Taxonomy alignment as of

2023. Although exposure to these types of issuers can be reflected in the Taxonomy alignment at the product level, this means that the buy side will not be able to rely on public information made available by these issuers, and instead will need to rely on estimates.

To date, this had led asset managers to opt for a prudent approach when updating their prospectus with the use of a disclaimer on the current level of data availability regarding Taxonomy alignment (when allowed by their national competent authority, NCA) or by reporting data in a very conservative (0%) or approximate way (brackets).

The inability to report on current Taxonomy alignment is also explained by the strict approach taken so far on the use of estimates. In that respect, it is worth noting that on June 2, 2022, the EC published a Q&A document[9] indicating the possibility to use estimates when assessing companies outside, not subject to, taxonomy reporting requirement, and for which investors cannot obtain the relevant information to reliably determine the alignment:

> In such exceptional cases and only for those economic activities for which complete, reliable and timely information could not be obtained, financial market participants are allowed to make complementary assessments and estimates on the basis of information from other sources. Such assessments and estimates should only compensate for limited and specific parts of the desired data elements and produce a prudent outcome. Financial market participants should clearly explain the basis for their conclusions as well as the reasons for having to make such complementary assessments and estimates for the purposes of disclosure to end investors.

This departs from the strict approach suggested so far by the ESAs, which ruled out all sort of estimates.

For companies in scope of the Taxonomy regulation, only information made available by issuers or "equivalent information" made available by data providers could be used by investors for their own reporting obligation. The notion of equivalence is not further defined, but our interpretation is that the use of proxy methodologies – notably for the purpose of the DNSH and minimum safeguards (eg, controversy tools) – are not recognised as producing "equivalent information".

In this context, data providers such as Sustainalytics decided to offer via its EU Taxonomy Solution a clear breakdown between estimated and reported data (see Figure 12.5 for an example).

Figure 12.5 IBM example

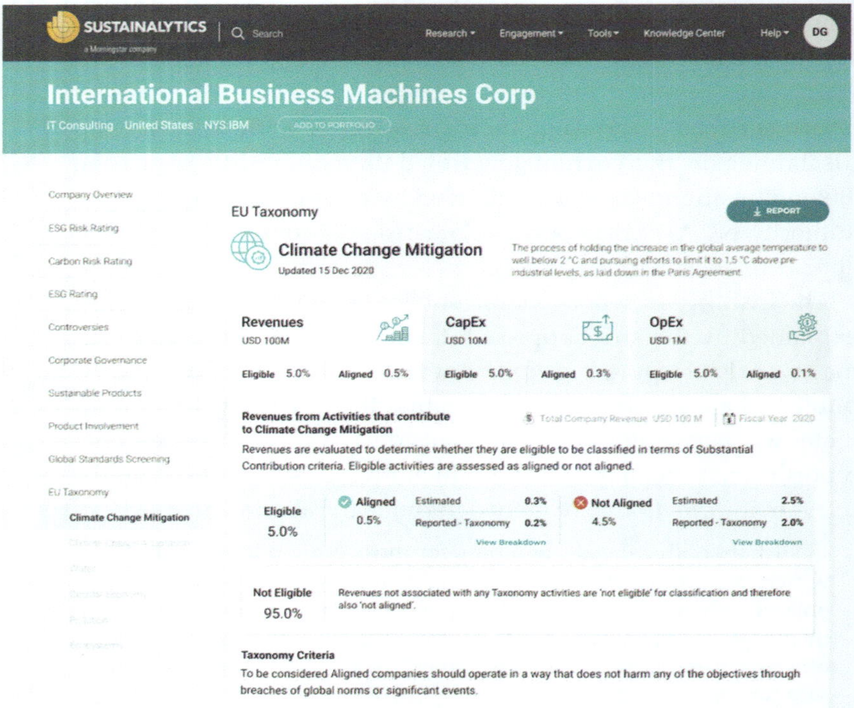

Sustainable investment disclosure

According to the draft implementation, fund managers will also need to indicate "the minimum share of sustainable investments that are not aligned with the EU Taxonomy" – ie, the share of investments that satisfy the SFDR's definition of a sustainable investment but not the EU Taxonomy. There is no prescriptive methodology beyond the sustainable investment definition of SFDR. It should allow accounting for assets for which the EU Taxonomy methodology is not yet available, as mentioned previously (eg, for social bonds, non-climate-related green bonds, green sovereign bonds).

Below are some options that may be considered by investors to determine the minimum proportion of sustainable investment that will need to be disclosed to investors as of August 2, 2022 (see also the later section on MiFID).

- A Taxonomy-like approach: Percentage of revenue from sustainable economic activities (eg, aligned with Sustainable Development Goals, SDGs) of companies with the DNSH test performed at the activity level (eg, sectorial materiality thresholds defined for PAIs). The main difficulty with this approach is the data gap to assess PAIs at the activity level.
- A more stringent approach: Percentage of revenue from sustainable economic activities but with the DNSH at the company level instead of the activity level. Although this simplifies the DNSH assessment, it also contributes to lower alignment. For instance, it would most likely lead to excluding the revenue from renewal energy of utility companies that also generate electricity through fossil fuel as they are unlikely to pass the DNSH test.
- The threshold approach: An investment is considered sustainable if a company's portfolio generates above a certain threshold of revenue aligned with a sustainable objective (SDGs) and Does Not Significantly Harm the objective. This approach would allow disclosure of the highest proportion of sustainable investment in funds.

MiFID and the need to meet potential sustainability preferences of clients[10]

In addition to SFDR and the EU Taxonomy disclosure, the targeted review of MiFID to include the obligation to consider a client's sustainability preferences when a financial adviser assesses a client's suitability for an investment is one important development to bear in mind.

To avoid mis-selling or misrepresentations, investment advisers should first assess the investor's investment objectives, time horizon and individual circumstances before asking for the client's potential sustainability preferences. Financial instruments will need to have specific features to be able to meet the client's potential sustainability preferences. They will need either to have a minimum proportion of investments in sustainable investments as defined under the EU Taxonomy or SFDR, or consider PAIs on sustainability factors as defined under SFDR on a quantitative or a qualitative basis – ie, a list of ESG KPIs. The proportion of investments in sustainable investments or the consideration given to adverse impacts will need to be determined by the client, and the products identified accordingly.

These new measures, applied from August 2, 2022, present several challenges. They crystallise all the difficulties highlighted above. The short-term unavailability of taxonomy data and the uncertainty around the use of estimates put asset managers and distributors in a difficult position. At the same time, the void left by SFDR regarding the sustainable investment definition makes the comparison of products almost meaningless. The consideration of PAI is also subject to data gaps and aggregation challenges, as explained above.

There are also inherent challenges to the new MiFID requirements. Asset managers and distributors will need to guide clients through the different product types and new concepts introduced by these new rules, and achieving this in clear, concise and simple terms may prove difficult – for example, the distinction between the sustainable investments under SFDR and the EU Taxonomy. Distributors may therefore have to depart from the regulatory categories (taxonomy, sustainable investments, PAIs) to consider the different investment solutions available. There might be a discrepancy between the minimum level of sustainable investments required and the level that can be achieved by certain products – eg, owing to the diversification pocket, lack of sustainable investment opportunities, lack of legal certainty around the implementation of a certain concept and the reversibility of sustainable investments. Another difficulty will be to understand what the consideration of PAIs actually means, and if some strategies or types of product can or cannot qualify (eg, exclusion-only products, engagement strategy) to this new MiFID suitability assessment.

The European Securities and Markets Authority (ESMA) has also launched a consultation to update its suitability guidelines following amendments to MiFID II relating to sustainability preferences. ESMA will consider the feedback it receives to the consultation in Q2 2022 and expects to publish a final report in Q3 2022.

Finally, it is important to note that FinDatEx, a joint structure established by industry representatives of the European financial services sector, is working on an ESG template for fund reporting for the purpose of the MiFID sustainability preferences requirements. This European ESG Template (EET) contains 578 data fields (including the regulatory data mentioned in this chapter) and was available from June 1, 2022.

According to a survey run by Morningstar with 68 asset managers, 62% of them were expecting to produce their EET report by June 2022. 38% of manufacturers are leaning towards populating the EET with their full range of funds in applicable domiciles. As of June 16, 2022, reporting 37,310 share classes have some EET data corresponding to around 22% of the European open fund universe, less than 2% of article 9, 12% of article 8 and 8% of article 6 products. Morningstar has also published a guide to support financial advisors when assessing the sustainability preferences of clients, which highlights the different solutions it provides via Morningstar Direct to meet this new requirement.

NATIONAL MEASURES COMING ON TOP OF SFDR AND MIFID

The fact that, under SFDR, there is no minimum investments or binding elements to meet the ESG characteristics or sustainable objective of a product, has led national regulators to issue or consider local rules to fill this void. Below are a few examples.

In France, the Autorité des Marchés Financiers' (AMF) position/recommendation DOC-2020–03,[11] which has applied since March 2020 to all funds that consider non-financial criteria and which are marketed to non-professional investors in France, makes a distinction between funds: (i) with significantly engaging approaches; (ii) with non-significantly engaging approaches; and (iii) with an approach not meeting central or limited communication standards. These categories dictate the ability to put forward a product's sustainability characteristics/objectives via the name of the product, pre-contractual documents and marketing materials.

Under the non-significant approach, communication on products' sustainability characteristics/objectives is restricted to pre-contractual documents and marketing materials, and needs to be done in a proportionate, concise and balanced way. Funds also need to have measurable objectives regarding non-financial criteria, and the non-financial coverage must be greater than 75%/90%.[12]

Under the significant approach communication on products' sustainability characteristics/objectives via the name of the product, pre-contractual documents and marketing materials are not limited. Funds need to have measurable objectives regarding non-financial criteria, and the non-financial coverage must be greater than 75%/90%. Additionally, best in class strategies will have to comply with minimum standards – ie, a minimum 20% reduction of the investment universe or average rating/extra-financial indicator must be higher than the average of the investment universe after reduction. Other types of strategies (eg, thematic and impact funds) will also have to demonstrate to the AMF that their approach is "significant". For green bond funds, "the significance may, for example, be assessed based on the requirement of 75% of the assets required by the reference document for the Greenfin label".

In terms of interaction with SFDR, to be able to present non-financial criteria as a key aspect of product communication, article 8 and article 9 products sold in France must meet the significant approach minimum standards defined by the position/recommendation DOC-2020–03. Given the definitions and provisions contained in the SFDR, the AMF anticipates that products presenting themselves as "having as their objective sustainable investment", as described in article 9 of the said regulation, will implement "significantly binding" approaches within the meaning of AMF position/recommendation DOC-2020-03. However, it is specified that the AMF considers an approach based on a significant commitment of the managed assets is not sufficient to comply with the provisions of article 9 of the SFDR regulation. Alternatively, non-French article 8 or article 9 funds that do not meet the minimum investment (and other) criteria under the AMF doctrine have to include the following disclaimer in their marketing materials ("marketing materials" does not include the key investor information document, KIID, or prospectus) according to the following timeline to be in compliance with the AMF doctrine: "Investors should note that, relative to the expectations of the Autorité des Marchés Financiers, this [Undertakings for the Collective Investment in Transferable Securities, UCITS] presents disproportionate communication on the consideration of non-financial criteria in its investment policy".[13]

In Spain, the National Securities Market Commission (CNMV) published on June 1, 2021, a Q&A on SFDR[14] setting local expectations for article 8 products going beyond SFDR:

> [collective investment schemes] CISs that were registered as Socially Responsible Investments (SRIs) before the entry into force of Regulation 2019/2088 (SFDR) may continue to use the SRI features that they promote in their commercial name. All other CISs that, after the entry into force of the Regulation, wish to be classified as a financial product pursuant to Article 8, may include ESG elements in their name only if the minimum amount of investments indicated in their prospectus to achieve the environmental or social characteristics that they promote is greater than 50%.

In Germany, the Federal Financial Supervisory Authority (Bafin)[15] launched in August 2021 a consultation on the possibility to require, among others, that funds labelled or marketed as sustainable investment products are at least 75% invested in "sustainable assets". Furthermore, the fund's investment strategy shall ensure, such as through investment restrictions or additional sustainability criteria, that: (i) a significant contribution is made to the realisation of one or more environmental or social objectives; (ii) other environmental or social objectives are not significantly harmed; and (iii) good governance aspects are taken into account. Finally, portfolio companies may not generate revenue from energy production from fossil fuels (excluding gas) or nuclear power exceeding 10% of their total revenue; exploration for, or extraction of, oil or coal exceeding 5% of their total revenue; and extraction of, and services for, oil sands and oil shale. As an alternative to the minimum investment quota, funds can also pursue a sustainable investment strategy – for example, in the form of a best in class approach. From an investment universe, for instance, the assets that are particularly advantageous from a sustainability point of view are selected or weighted more heavily. Finally, a sustainable investment fund can also be created by replicating a sustainable index. It remains to be seen in the end if these rules will be adopted or amended.

However, in May 2022 Bafin announced that it would not finalise the guidelines while indicating their intention to apply some of the principles that they have consulted on: "Against the backdrop of the dynamic situation in regulation, energy and geopolitics, we have decided to put our planned directive for sustainable investment funds on hold... The environment isn't stable enough for permanent regulation".

Fondsverband BVI, der Deutsche Derivate Verband (DDV) and the Bankendachverband Deutsche Kreditwirtschaft (DK) have

Figure 12.6 Basic concept: Product-independent definitions[1]

Other products – Not part of the MiFID target market			Products which may be addressed to customers with sustainability-related objectives pursuant to Art. 9 No 9 subpara. 1 MiFID II Delegated Directive[2]		
Non-ESG	Basic	ESG strategy product	PAIs (consideration of significant adverse impacts, Art. 2 No. 7 lit. c) MiFID II regulation)[5]	Sustainable investments as defined by the SFDR (ES, Art. 2 No. 7 lit. b MiFID II regulation	Ecologically sustainable investments within the meaning of the Taxonomy (Art. 2 No. 7 lit. a) MiFID II regulation)
No data or declared as non-sustainable	Consideration and transparency of sustainability risks and chances + Product manufacturer takes into account a recognised industry standard	Product pursues dedicated ESG strategy + Product manufacturer takes into account recognised industry standard	Dedicated ESG strategy with consideration of standard PAIs on environmental and/or social issues[3] + Minimum exclusions[4] + Product manufacturer takes into account a recognised industry standard	ESG strategy with a proportion of sustainable investments pursuant to SFDR: specific percentages[5] + No serious violations of the UN Global Compact and democracy/human rights[4] + Product manufacturer takes into account a recognised industry standard	ESG strategy with a proportion of sustainable investments pursuant to the Taxonomy Regulation: specific percentages[6] + No serious violations of the UN Global Compact and democracy/human rights[4] + Product manufacturer takes into account a recognised industry standard

1 For product-specific details, see the following slides.
2 Multiple answers are possible; if the product can be addressed to customers with sustainability-related objectives, no entry should be made for "other products".
3 Standard PAIs according to Annex 1 Table 1 RTS-E to the SFDR.
4 See slide 3.
5 For a possible differentiation, see slide 7.
6 Percentage enables distributors to allocate to standardised or individual clusters (optional implementation, eg, ambitious, moderate, leader).

Source: BVI; DDV; Deutsche Kreditwirtschaft (2021)

been developing a new "Zielmarktkonzept" to include "Guidelines for Responsible Investment". Their concept is also instrumental in shaping ESG funds registered for distribution in Germany in line with MiFID II, and aims to align the specifications of sustainable investment classifications under SFDR and ecologically sustainable investments under the EU Taxonomy (see Figure 12.6). A range of minimum sector-specific and normative exclusion thresholds are being defined by this new rulebook.

The UK has decided not to onshore SFDR. The Financial Conduct Authority (FCA) has announced new measures to improve the climate-related financial disclosure rules of product and firms who

Table 12.5 Metrics per proposal

Metric	Proposal
Scope 1 and 2 Grrenhouse gas (GHG) emissions	The metrics are widely used in the market, including as part of disclosure regimes in the UK and internationally. We propose to mandate this metric from when our proposal rules intered into force.
Scope 3 GHG emissions	Although this is a widely recognised metric, we acknowledge that methodologies differ and there may be significant data gaps among investee companies, at least in the short term until the implementation of further disclosure requirements in the UK and internationally. We are therefore proposing that firms should disclose Scope 3 emissions from no later than 30 June 2024. This is 1 year later than the deadline for the first disclosures in accordance with the rest of our proposals.
*Total carbon emissions	As total carbon emissions are the sum of the GHG emissions referenced above, we consider it appropriate to mandate that this metric be disclosed to the same timeframes. Scope 3 emissions would therefore need to be included in the total figure from 30 June 2024.
*Carbon footprint	This is a widely used metric in the market. We propose that this be disclosed on a mandatory basis from when our proposed rules enter into force.
*Weighted average carbon intensity (WACI)	In its final report, the TCFD acknowledged limitations with this form of carbon footprinting due to data availability. As such the TCFD is currently proposing that asset managers and owners should disclose a financed-emissions metric based on WACI and the *Partnership for Carbon Accounting Financials* (PCAF) methodology. The PCAF provides methodologies for asset managers, asset owners and banks to measure or estimate financed emissions for different asset classes. It also provides for alternative solutions when data is not available.

issue them (FCA, 2021). It is worth noting that, compared to SFDR, firm disclosures would be qualitative. Firms would be required to publish, annually, an entity-level report aligned with the recommendations of the Task Force on Climate-Related Financial Disclosures (TCFD, 2021), and considering how they take climate-related physical and transition risks[16] and opportunities into account in managing or administering investments on behalf of clients and consumers. Product level disclosures would be both qualitative and quantitative. Firms would be required to produce, annually, a baseline set of consistent, comparable disclosures in respect to their products and portfolios, including a core set of metrics (see Table 12.5).

Beyond the climate-related disclosure, the FCA is also considering broader Sustainability Disclosure Requirements (SDR) and investment labels. Under SDR, companies, including listed issuers, and asset managers and asset owners, will be required to report on their sustainability risks, opportunities and impacts. The regime will build on measures already taken or underway to implement disclosure rules aligned with the recommendations of the TCFD across the economy, expanding the scope to cover wider sustainability topics beyond climate change. SDR will also include disclosure requirements relating to the forthcoming UK Green Taxonomy. Sustainability reporting standards to be developed by the International Financial Reporting Standards (IFRS) Foundation's International Sustainability Standards Board (ISSB) will form a core component of the SDR framework, and the backbone of its corporate reporting element. Regarding investment labels, certain investment products will be required to display a label reflecting their sustainability characteristics.

The approach proposed by the FCA to a sustainable product classification and labelling system is composed of five categories (see Figure 12.7).

These diverging approaches are a great source of concern for asset managers as they could fragment the European market for funds. It seems like ESMA is attempting to better coordinate and converge these approaches in 2022 (ESMA, 2021):

> Extensive work will be required in relation to supervisory convergence to build consistent application of rules and effective approaches for incorporating ESG factors in national supervisory practices.

Figure 12.7 FCA's sustainable product classification and labelling system

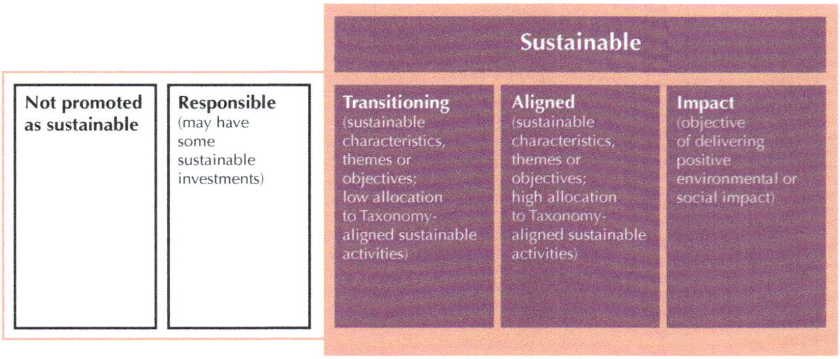

Note: The five blocks in this figure represent potential categories of product in the classification and labelling system. Each would be supported by clear definitions and criteria.

ESMA will therefore implement a roadmap for supervisory convergence in the area of sustainable finance, covering a number of priority sectors such as asset management and issuer disclosure, as well as gaining a better understanding of 10 transversal themes like data availability and quality and greenwashing. In relation to the latter, ESMA will undertake work to better understand the risk of greenwashing and the main forms it takes to address this consumer detriment in a coordinated way across NCAs, as well as across ESAs for areas of common interests.

VOLUNTARY NATIONAL AND EUROPEAN LABELS

It is important to also remember that on top of these mandatory EU and national rules, funds may also want to apply for other, national labels as these are being mandated increasingly by investors. Funds using these ESG labels manage approximatively €633 billion (Megaeva, Engelen and Van Liedekerke, 2021), whereas funds classified under articles 8 and 9 manage approximatively €3,000 billion (Bioy, 2021).

In Europe, there are a variety of voluntary labels for ESG and impact-focused funds. While some of these are market-led initiatives (eg, FNG-Label for sustainable investment funds), others are based on cooperation between the policymakers and market participants (eg, LuxFLAG) or developed solely by the official sector (eg, SRI Label or GreenFin). Novethic reported in January 2020 that there are nine dedicated labels launched since 2011 in Europe (see Table 12.6).

Table 12.6 Simplified overview of green/impact voluntary labels versus the draft EU Ecolabel

Labels	ESG coverage -green ratio	Exclusions
LuxFLAG Environment	24,75%* (FTSE classification system)	At the discretion of fund manager
LuxFLAG Climate Finance	Equity: 37,5%* (IDFC) Bond: 75% in green bonds (International Capital Market Association, ICMA, Green Bond Principles, GBP, or Climate Bonds Initiative, CBI, standard)	Coal (partial), fossil fuels (partial), nuclear (partial) Hydro-electric projects with a capacity above 20MW (partial) Geothermal plants (partial) Biofuel projects (biodiesel and ethanol), certain biomass and organic waste projects (partial)
Greenfin Label (France)	Equity: 15,5%* (CBI) Bond: 75% in green bonds (ICMA GBP)	Coal, fossil fuels, nuclear (5% max) Companies generating 33% or more of their turnover from forest exploitation, except if sustainably managed, and peatland agriculture are excluded (Greenfin) Issuers contravening the conventions on the prohibition of the use, storage, production and relocation of anti-personnel mines and their destruction (known as the 1997 Ottawa Convention) and concerning cluster munitions (known as the 2008 Oslo Convention) are excluded (Greenfin) Firm subject to repeated and serious ESG controversies (Greenfin)
Draft EU Ecolabel	Equity: 50% (EU Taxonomy) Bonds: 70% in green bonds (EU taxonomy or EU green bonds regulation)	Exclusions applying to all issuers (including issuers of green bonds): Specific environmental exclusion/requirements for activities involving production/use pesticides, fertilisers, timber, coal, fossil fuels, hazardous waste, certain chemicals (POP), passenger and commercial vehicles Exclusion of sovereign with no trajectory to reach Paris goal and other international environmental agreements Social exclusions based on human rights, freedom of association and collective bargaining, compulsory/child labour, corruption, bribery, minorities and indigenous communities (International Labour Organization, ILO, Convention, UN Global Compact, OECD Guidelines for Multinational Enterprises, UN Guiding Principles on Business and Human Rights, International Humanitarian Law) Sectorial exclusion: tobacco, controversial weapons Exclusion of sovereigns that have not ratified ILO conventions, core human right treaties, subject to EU/UN sanctions, low corruption perception index, applying death penalty, produce/trade/possess controversial weapons

* aggregating company and portfolio thresholds
Source: Novethic (2020)

With respect to ESG-focused funds, despite some degree of differences in implementation and stringency, all these labels require ESG screening of portfolios, and some combine those with exclusion criteria that may apply to specific business sectors (such as weapons and tobacco) or limit the exposure of eligible assets to fossil fuel-related activities, or require the conformity with international safeguards related to social rights, notably with references to the UN Global Compact. The differences around exclusion criteria and thresholds adds to the complexity for fund managers that aim to apply for more than one label, and that already have to comply with regulatory requirements at the EU or national level.

For impact-focused funds, labels may also require adherence to internationally accepted standards and/or market-based taxonomies. For example, LuxFLAG's Green Bond Label requires that applicants follow the ICMA Green Bond Principles (ICMA, 2021)[17] or the Climate Bond Initiative[18] standard, while its Climate Finance Label refers to the multilateral development banks (MDBs) and the International Development Finance Club (IDFC) Taxonomy[19] as part of its assets selection criteria. Either for ESG or impact-focused fund labels, transparency measures are common although they vary in the frequency of reporting requirements and scope.

More generally, there are market-led initiatives such as the European SRI Transparency Code led by Eurosif. The key motivation of the Transparency Code is to provide further clarity to investors of notably retail SRI funds in an easily accessible and comparable format, as well as setting a common framework for transparency best practices and self-regulation.

Draft EU Ecolabel

It is worth noting that the EU is expected to propose in 2022 a voluntary label called the "EU Ecolabel for Financial Products". This label is likely to be niche and could be a missed opportunity to alleviate some of the market fragmentation issues mentioned previously. Under the last draft published in 2021 (European Commission, 2021b), funds would need to comply with a significant level of green ratio, a comprehensive list of environmental and social exclusions, and a demanding engagement strategy. For instance, in the latest draft version 50% (UCTIS equity funds) to

70% (eg, UCITS bonds funds) of the AuM should be invested in economic activities aligned with the EU Taxonomy.

Not only does the minimum Green Ratio under the EU Ecolabel go far beyond those currently required by national labels, it is also based on a much more stringent definition of green investments – ie, the EU Taxonomy. Indeed, data seems to indicate it is not possible for some of the "greenest" investment funds to comply with the EU Ecolabel portfolio thresholds even though these case studies only focus on meeting part of the EU Taxonomy (ie, the significant contribution to an environmental objective), but not the other steps required under the EU Taxonomy (ie, technical screening criteria do no significant harm against other environmental objectives, minimum social safeguards).

An additional challenge is that under the current draft Ecolabel the sustainable portion of the portfolio (ie, 50% or 70%) would be subject to both the Taxonomy safeguards (technical screening criteria, DNSH and minimum social safeguards) and environmental and social exclusion criteria applicable to the entire portfolio. This means that issuers will need to pass these two tests to be eligible for an EU Ecolabelled fund. This could be problematic for issuers of use-of-proceed green bonds, and in particular two important sectors for this market: transport and energy. The partial exclusion criteria for these two sectors (which represent more than 50% of the GB market) are very stringent.

Finally, one last hurdle worth mentioning is that there are refinancing conditions for use-of-proceed GBs to be eligible for the EU Ecolabel. The value of refinanced projects within a green bond issue may only contribute to portfolio greenness if the issuer can demonstrate that the refinancing supports the creation of asset-backed securities or the recycling of funds for lending to new green projects. Under current market practice, but also the EU GB regulation[20] as proposed by the EC, green bond issuers are not obliged to use the freed-up capital to fund another green project as required by the current draft EU Ecolabel.

It is very common for corporate issuers to fund green projects via syndicated loans, for example, which are then refinanced by green bonds issued by corporate issuers. This standard financing structure would not meet the refinancing requirement set under the Ecolabel. As a result, many green bonds issued by corporate issuers (under ICMA GBP or the EU GB regulation) would not be eligible, leaving bond funds with a narrower eligible investment universe. This highlights the need for the EC to recalibrate the EU Ecolabel proposal and, more broadly speaking, to issue pragmatic recommendations to facilitate the usability of the EU Taxonomy.

CONCLUSION

Existing normative and regulatory rules for ESG fund classifications and disclosures aim to increase transparency and address greenwashing to meet the requirements set out by the EU Sustainable Finance Action Plan. However, the pluralism of these rules and the lack of harmonisation of the rules at EU, national and label level may ultimately lead to significant implementation issues for investment product providers and advisers in Europe.

Policymakers will almost inevitably have to alleviate some of the following challenges.

- Addressing the data gap: Disclosures by issuers will need to be enhanced swiftly to allow the buy side to comply with their own transparency requirements. The work undertaken by the ISSB at international and the European Financial Reporting Advisory Group (EFRAG) at the EU level will be instrumental, but is unlikely to be able to produce the desired results in the short term. The necessity to use estimates may need to be further recognised.
- Usability of the Taxonomy: The fact that the green bonds issued under the EU Green deal do not refer to the EU Taxonomy but instead the ICMA GBP highlights the usability issue and the need to find a pragmatic approach (in particular when it comes to the use of estimates and proxy methodologies for the purpose of the DNSH and the minimum safeguards). This is all the more needed now the EU taxonomy underpins many other rules (EU GB regulation, Ecolabel, MiFID sustainability preferences, SFDR product disclosure).
- Usability of the disclosures by end-investors: The complexity of the ESG disclosures required, combined with the data gaps and ambiguity in certain definitions, might make it very difficult for end-investors without ESG experience to interpret and compare the disclosures.

- Avoiding market fragmentation: The proliferation of national rules (despite SFDR and the EU Taxonomy) and labels in the EU may push regulators to address potential risks of market fragmentation via the development of pan-European labels or amendments to existing rules.
- Transition versus divestment: The energy crisis may incentivise policymakers to focus on transition rather than divestment. The most controversial yet illustrative example of this is the proposal by the EC to integrate certain activities related to nuclear and gas in complementation delegated act to the EU Taxonomy.

The opinions and views expressed or reflected within this chapter pertain to its authors and do not represent the official position of Sustainalytics, a Morningstar company. Where referenced as such, information and data contained herein are proprietary of Sustainalytics/Morningstar. These are intended for informational, non-commercial use only and may be made available to third parties provided that appropriate citation and acknowledgement is ensured. They do not constitute an endorsement of any product or project, nor an investment advice and are not warranted to be complete, timely, accurate or suitable for a particular purpose. Neither Sustainalytics, Morningstar nor its content providers are responsible for any damages or losses arising from any use of this information and use is subject to conditions available at https://www.sustainalytics.com/legal-disclaimers/.

1 See https://eur-lex.europa.eu/legal-content/EN/TXT/PDF/?uri=CELEX:32019R2088&from=EN.
2 See Annex 1, Commission delegated regulation of 6.4.2022 supplementing Regulation (EU) 2019/2088.
3 Excluding real estate KPIs due to a lack of the required asset level data.
4 EU Council press release following agreement on the review of NFRD (CSRD), (June 21, 2022).
5 See "Question Related to Regulation (EU) 2019/2088 of the European Parliament and of the Council of 27 November 2019 on Sustainability-related Disclosures in the Financial Services Sector, 14/07/2021, EC (available at https://www.esma.europa.eu/sites/default/files/library/sfdr_ec_qa_1313978.pdf).
6 ibid.
7 See https://www.esma.europa.eu/sites/default/files/library/sfdr_ec_qa_1313978.pdf.
8 See https://www.esma.europa.eu/document/questions-related-regulation-eu-2019 2088-sfdr.
9 ibid.
10 See https://eur-lex.europa.eu/legal-content/EN/TXT/PDF/?uri=CELEX:32021R1253&from=EN.
11 See https://www.amf-france.org/sites/default/files/doctrine/Position/Information%20to%20be%20provided%20by%20collective%20investment%20schemes%20incorporating%20non-financial%20approaches.pdf

12 The percentage of ESG-analysed issuers in the fund must be above 90%. It concerns equities issued by large capitalisation companies whose registered office is located in "developed" countries, debt securities and money market instruments with an investment-grade credit rating, sovereign debt issued by developed countries excludes the cash portion held by the fund. For equities issued by large capitalisations whose registered office is located in "emerging" countries, it concerns equities issued by small and medium capitalisations, debt securities and money market instruments with a high-yield credit rating and sovereign debt issued by "emerging" countries. The ESG coverage must be above 75% for equities issued by large capitalisations whose registered office is located in "emerging" countries, equities issued by small and medium capitalisations, debt securities and money market instruments with a high-yield credit rating and sovereign debt issued by "emerging" countries. These rates may be expressed either in terms of the number of issuers or the capitalisation of the net assets of the collective investment. In the event of investment in several categories by the same fund, the above-mentioned rates apply transparently to each category. For the purposes of this position, it is considered that small caps are those below €5 billion, mid caps are those between €5 billion and €10 billion, and large caps are those above €10 billion.

13 See https://www.amf-france.org/en/news-publications/news/implementation-sfdr-regulation-asset-management-companies-march-10–2021.

14 See http://cnmv.es/docportal/Legislacion/FAQ/PyR_Sostenibilidad_pdtos_finan_en.pdf.

15 See https://www.bafin.de/SharedDocs/Veroeffentlichungen/DE/Konsultation/2021/kon_13_21_WA4_Leitlinien_nachhaltige_Investmentvermoegen.html.

16 Climate-related risks, including: (i) transition risks such as policy constraints on emissions, imposition of carbon tax, water restrictions, land use restrictions or incentives, and market demand and supply shifts; and (ii) physical risks such as the disruption of operations or destruction of property.

17 The Green Bond Principles (GBP) seek to support issuers in financing environmentally sound and sustainable projects that foster a net zero emissions economy and protect the environment. GBP-aligned issuance should provide transparent green credentials alongside an investment opportunity. By recommending that issuers report on the use of green bond proceeds, the GBP promote a step change in transparency that facilitates the tracking of funds to environmental projects, while simultaneously aiming to improve insight into their estimated impact.

18 The Climate Bonds Standard (V3.0, December 2019) provides clear, sector-specific eligibility criteria for assets and projects that can be used for climate bonds and green bonds.

19 IDFC (2021) consist of a set of definitions and guidelines and a list of eligible activities that allow for consistent accounting and reporting of financial flows for climate change mitigation finance.

20 See https://www.icmagroup.org/assets/documents/Sustainable-finance/Responses/ICMA-analysis-of-the-EuGB-Regulation-080721v2.pdf.

REFERENCES

Bioy, H., 2021, "SFDR Four Months On", Morningstar, August 3 (available at https://www.morningstar.co.uk/uk/news/214207/sfdr-four-months-on.aspx).

Deutsche Kreditwirtschaft, 2021, "Supplement to the Target Market to Include Information on Sustainability-related Objectives and Sustainability Factors", December 13 (available at https://www.derivateverband.de/EN/MediaLibrary/Document/Zielmarktkonzept/22%200325%20ESG_VerbändekonzeptENG_final.pdf).

ESA, 2022, "Joint Consultation Paper on Sustainability Disclosures for STS Securitisations", ESMA, May 2 (available at https://www.esma.europa.eu/press-news/consultations/joint-consultation-paper-sustainability-disclosures-sts-securitisations).

ESMA, 2021, "2022 Annual Work Programme", September 27 (available at https://www.esma.europa.eu/sites/default/files/library/esma20–95–1430_2022_annual_work_programme.pdf).

European Commission, 2021a, "Strategy for Financing the Transition to a Sustainable Economy", Communication from The Commission to the European Parliament, the Council, the European Economic and Social Committee and the Committee of the Regions", July 6 (available at https://eur-lex.europa.eu/resource.html?uri=cellar:9f5e7e95-df06-11eb-895a-01aa75ed71a1.0001.02/DOC_1&format=PDF).

European Commission, 2021b, "Development of EU Ecolabel Criteria for Retail Financial Products", JRC Technical Report, March (available at https://susproc.jrc.ec.europa.eu/product-bureau/sites/default/files/2021–03/2021.03.05%20-%20EUEL%20financial%20products%20-%20Technical%20Report%204%20FINAL.pdf).

FCA, 2021, "FCA's New Rules on Climate-related Disclosures to Help Investors, Clients and Consumers", December 17 (available at https://www.fca.org.uk/news/news-stories/new-rules-climate-related-disclosures-help-investors-clients-consumers#:~:text=FCA%2Dregulated%20asset%20managers%20and,related%20attributes%20of%20their%20products).

ICMA, 2021, "Green Bond Principles: Voluntary Process Guidelines for Issuing Green Bonds", June.

IDFC, 2021, "Common Principles for Climate Mitigation Finance Tracking", Version 3, October 18 (available at https://www.eib.org/attachments/documents/mdb_idfc_mitigation_common_principles_en.pdf.

Megaeva, K., P.-J. Engelen and L. Van Liedekerke, 2021, "A Comparative Study of European Sustainable Finance Labels", SSRN, January 1 (available at https://papers.ssrn.com/sol3/papers.cfm?abstract_id=3790435).

Morningstar, 2022, "SFDR Article 8 and Article 9 Funds: Q1 2022 in Review", February (available at https://www.morningstar.com/en-uk/lp/sfdr-article8-article9).

Novethic, 2020, "Overview of European Sustainable Finance Labels", January (available at https://www.novethic.com/fileadmin/user_upload/tx_ausynovethicetudes/pdf_complets/Novethic_Overview-European-Sustainable-Finance-Labels_2020.pdf).

TCFD, 2021, "Implementing the Recommendations of the Task Force on Climate-related Financial Disclosures", October (available at https://assets.bbhub.io/company/sites/60/2021/07/2021-TCFD-Implementing_Guidance.pdf).

13

Assessing data and disclosure challenges in ESG investing

Marie Lehmann and Beate van Loo-Born

This chapter focusses on the role data management plays in ESG investment decision-making. Naturally, data sits at the source of the investment community's decision-making processes, not only when it comes to risk versus return predictions and the constant search for alpha, but also when and where decisions are being made to integrate ESG into investment decision-making.

For instance, investment management companies invest in bonds issued by companies and governments that wish to finance their environmental and social projects. Meanwhile, global assets under management also continue to grow. The AUMs of the world's largest 500 asset managers have reached US$119.5 trillion (Willis Towers Watson, 2017).

Moreover, in its 2020 Global Sustainable Investment Review (2020), the GSIA found that sustainable investment assets in the five major markets on which its study focused (Australasia, Canada, Europe, Japan and the US) had witnessed a 15% increase within two years, reaching US$35.3 trillion as at the beginning of 2020, equal to 36% of all professionally managed assets across the regions covered in this report. Global interest in ESG investing from institutional investors has also significantly increased since the early 2000s with investment managers encountering growing pressure from various stakeholder groups to implement social responsibility. The investment community increasingly recognises the importance of ESG and considers ESG factors as "material" in investment portfolios. As of 2021, over 3,800 organisations with total assets under management of about US$121.3 trillion had signed the United Nations Principles for Responsible Investment (UNPRI) and committed to incorporate ESG considerations into their investment and ownership decisions.

Additionally, the "Financing our Future" report published by the Accounting for Sustainability (A4S) project and Aviva Investors (2018) explains that institutional investors need to have the knowledge to integrate ESG into investment decisions. ESG ratings constitute an important element of that knowledge since they help investors make more informed decisions when trying to incorporate ESG factors into their investment processes.

Table 13.1 Continued consolidation among ESG data providers

Buyer (ticker)	Target (percent acquired, if not 100%)	Target country	Announce date
Institutional Shareholder Services Inc.	CAER	Australia	02/19/19
	Oekon Research AG	Germany	03/15/18
	IW Financial Inc.	US	01/05/17
	Ethix SRI Advisors AB	Sweden	09/15/15
Moody's Corp. (MCO)	Syn Tao Green Finance Co. Ltd (minority stake)	China	10/28/19
	Four Twenty Seven Inc.	US	07/22/19
	Vigeo Eiris	France	04/11/19
	Vigeo SAS	France	10/12/15
	Conflict Risk Network	US	05/15/13
Morningstar Inc. (MORN)	Systainanalytics BV (60)	Netherlands	04/21/20
	Systainanalytics BV (40)	Netherlands	07/24/17
	Responsible Research Pte Ltd	Singapore	09/15/15
	ESG Analytics AG	Switzerland	09/08/15
MSCI Inc. (MSCI)	Carbon Delta AG	Switzerland	09/09/19
	GMI Rating Inc.	US	06/27/14
S&P Global Inc. (SPGI)	RobescoSAM AG's ESG rating business	Switzerland	11/21/19
	Trucost PLC	UK	08/12/16
Spread Research SAS	EthiFinance	France	03/06/17
StatPro Group PLC	ECPI Group Srl's ESG research and index business	Italy	06/12/19
Techedge SpA (EDGE)	ESGeo Drl	Italy	12/09/19

Source: S&P Global; ODDO BHF AM, 2021

Investors' interest in ESG investing and more particularly in ESG data, ratings and metrics disclosed by corporations on the one hand and analysed and aggregated by data providers on the other[1] has increased significantly. At the same time, the number of providers who produce ESG data and ratings has grown rapidly. Over the years, multiple data providers have merged or been bought by global exchanges, index or credit rating institutions (see Table 13.1).

However, issues surrounding ESG ratings related to diverging methodologies and data quality have continued to increase. In this chapter, we assess the impact of ESG and carbon data discrepancies, diverging methodologies and challenges related to the disclosure of ESG/carbon information.

ISSUES SURROUNDING ESG RATINGS ACROSS ASSET CLASSES

ESG ratings context

ESG rating agencies commonly provide investor-solicited and company-solicited rating services for a range of asset classes. In their approach towards specific ratings criteria and key performance indicators (KPIs), these assessments are similar to those offered by credit rating agencies but with an emphasis on sustainability criteria. ESG ratings follow a different methodology and scope, and often provide a sector-specific approach and coverage. Meanwhile, credit ratings focus more on the creditworthiness of a specific financial instrument or entity.

ESG ratings are an evaluation and rating by various third-party providers of reports and ratings of the environmental, social and governance performance of international and domestic public (and many private) companies. Financial institutions, institutional investors, asset managers and other stakeholders are increasingly relying on these reports and ratings to assess and measure a company's ESG performance over time and in comparison to peers.

Studies, such as by MIT Sloan Business School (2019), have shown that ESG ratings are just correlated at 61%, versus credit ratings which have shown a correlation of 99% when comparing assessments by S&P Global and Moody's credit ratings (see Figure 13.1).

ESG ratings play a considerable role in investment managers' decision-making processes. In 2018, ESG data was being used to

Figure 13.1 Challenges: ESG ratings' divergence

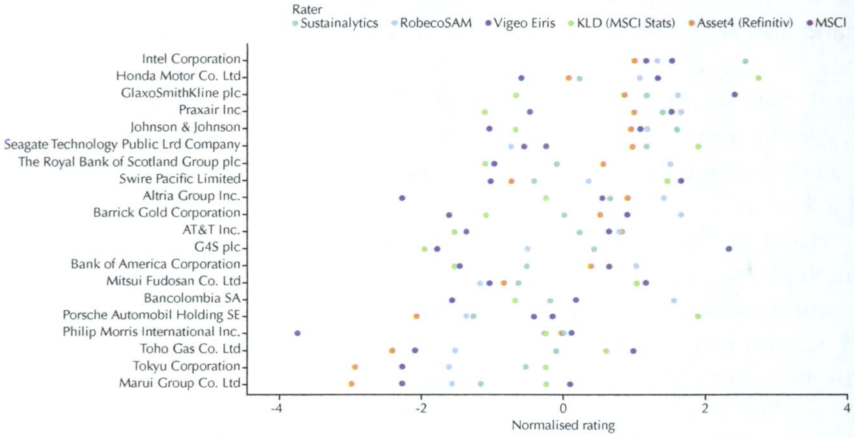

Three main sources of divergence:		
50.1%	36.7%	13.2%
Measurements divergence	Scope divergence	Weight divergence

Source: MIT Sloan, 2019

inform investment decisions of one-third of all professionally run assets across the globe. This is the equivalent to US$30 trillion and this figure keeps growing (Global Sustainable Investment Alliance, 2020).

So far, many ESG ratings business models are offering both solicited and non-solicited ratings, paid for by the users (ie, companies or investors). Some have warned against ESG ratings providers charging companies for obtaining ESG ratings (similar to credit ratings agencies' models involving the organisations being analysed paying for the service along with the users of the ratings). Indeed, this "company pays" model could lead to a conflict of interest with companies being able to influence their ESG rating since they are paying for it, thereby resulting in misinformed investment decisions by investment managers. Another cause for concern is the conflict of interest that may arise when ESG ratings providers, or one of their affiliated companies, offer consulting services to the companies that are being rated by them.

Issues with ESG ratings within equity markets

While ratings have grown in popularity and become an important part of the assessment of corporate sustainability, they have been criticised by some researchers and practitioners. We will now look at the various criticisms about ESG ratings within equity capital markets that have arisen to date:

- plethora of ESG ratings offerings and the complexity of surveys;
- lack of transparency of ESG ratings methodologies;
- lack of standardisation of ESG ratings, resulting in a lack of comparability;
- lack of independence of ESG raters;
- poor quality and credibility of data sources;
- lack of materiality of issues considered in ESG ratings;
- biases;
- trade-offs;
- cost of ESG ratings; and
- insufficient engagement from ESG raters with the companies they rate.

Plethora of ESG rating offerings and complexity of surveys

The plethora of ESG rating offerings and the complexity of surveys submitted to companies seems to constitute a major issue with investors regarding whether they are obtaining the right information, something that could lead to poor investment decisions. As some ESG providers may be stronger than others in some areas of sustainability, investment companies and consultancies must be clear on the strengths and weaknesses of a provider if they have chosen to work with only one.

Lack of transparency of methodologies

Lack of transparency is another major criticism of ESG ratings. Rating agencies use different types of data, assumptions, standards, measurements and weightings, and according to users of these ratings there is hence a lack of transparency, clarity, comparability and consistency (Sadowski, Whitaker and Buckingham, 2010;

Stubbs and Rogers, 2013; The SustainAbility Institute, 2018). This lack of transparency is mainly explained by the fact that the providers of these ratings consider their methodologies and the data used as proprietary and confidential information. Research organisations do not always disclose the methodologies, collection methods, assumptions, calculations and weightings used to create a rating in detail, leading to doubts about their reliability. Increasing the degree of transparency of ESG ratings would be one way to address the lack of uniformity that makes it difficult for investors to discriminate among ratings. If rating agencies were more transparent and had convergent standards over time, this would help investment managers make more informed investment decisions.

Lack of standardisation of ESG ratings

Another major concern among users of ESG ratings is the lack of standardisation of ESG ratings due to providers using different/ varying methodologies. Standardisation is impeded by the fact that firms do not collect or communicate corporate sustainability information in a similar way, leading to a lack of comparability and poor quality of ratings. Others arguethat a lack of standardised rules for environmental and social disclosures, and the absence of a disclosure auditing process to verify the data reported by firms, leads agencies to make assumptions which, in turn, also adds to the subjective nature of ESG ratings (Doyle, 2018). The lack of uniformity of rating scales, criteria and objectives that currently characterises the ESG rating industry impedes investors' ability to compare ratings across agencies. This view is shared by several academics and practitioners who also argue that this lack of uniformity affects the ability of investors to differentiate between ratings (Scalet and Kelly, 2010).

Lack of independence of ESG raters

The lack of independence of ESG ratings can often be another source of criticism. The different methodologies of rating agencies (irrespective of whether they provide credit, sustainability or other types of ratings) affect the level of independence of an agency's opinion. These methodologies can be "solicited", where ratings are requested by companies and some rating agencies may receive a payment for their ratings services, or "unsolicited". This affects the level of independence agencies have in forming an unbiased opinion and, ultimately, the degree of reliability of the rating. Furthermore, conflicts of interest can arise when companies are already engaged, or are planning to engage, in a commercial relationship with rating providers for other services (such as consulting services). The personal relationships between rating agencies' researchers and companies' staff may also affect the independence of the ratings (Beloe, Scherer and Knoepfel, 2004).

Poor quality and credibility of data sources

The quality and credibility of data sources used for ESG ratings are also perceived as an issue among users (SICM, 2016). Poor quality of data sources results in low quality of ESG ratings, potentially leading portfolio managers to make wrong investment decisions. Some believe that the data sources used by some ESG providers are of questionable quality and suggest the creation of quality standards for ESG ratings (ESMA, 2020). Another issue is "questionnaire fatigue" among companies, which can result in lower levels of disclosure, ultimately adversely impacting on the quality of ratings. Many industry experts believe that quality is an issue and there is a risk of oversimplification (The SustainAbility Institute, 2018). Indeed, sustainability issues are very complex. ESG ratings reduce the analysis of these issues to a single number or score, which could be very misleading. Examining ESG issues within their context is hence paramount (The SustainAbility Institute, 2018).

Lack of materiality

The lack and different uses of materiality concepts for sustainability issues considered in ESG ratings is another major area of criticism (LaBella *et al*, 2019). Corporates believe that they are too often assessed and rated on issues that are not material to their business activity and sustainability performance. This causes some frustration since, while they believe that ratings do help raise new issues within corporations, the gap in agreement is too great and leaves them feeling frustrated when they see issues they consider as immaterial affecting overall rating scores. In addition, firms feel punished for being different and innovative when raters do not benchmark the unique or evolving nature of their business models.

Biases

Subjectivity has been flagged as a concern with numerous researchers accusing rating agencies of bias in the methods they employ due to the assumptions they make and the different weightings they assign to the components of various ratings. Some argue that ESG rating agencies' lack of objectivity resulting from their reliance on analyst interpretation is a real issue for investors (Stubbs and Rogers, 2013). For some, one cannot rely on the judgement of trained ESG experts using publicly available information and without access to information provided by companies themselves.

Institutional bias is also a major concern (Beloe, 2016). Various types of institutional bias have been identified, such as market cap size, location and industry sector, which are rooted in the absence of uniform disclosure and can lead to significant disparities in the value, accuracy and importance of ratings. Company size bias is an issue since firms with larger market capitalisation can obtain higher ESG ratings than smaller peers (Doyle, 2018). Other types of bias are, for instance, a geographic bias towards companies located in regions with high regulatory reporting requirements and an industry sector bias with ESG rating agencies assigning weightings to the E, S and G without taking sector- and company-specific risks and differences in business models into consideration. All these biases can mislead investors about the reality of companies' ESG practices and drive them to make ill-informed investment decisions.

Trade-offs

Trade-offs also constitute another issue for ESG ratings. The main objective of the vast majority of ratings is to produce one single score in the form of a letter (eg, MSCI's "AAA"–"CCC") or a number. However, while this facilitates the expression of a company's performance and allows easy comparisons of companies, such a simplification of the performance of firms with a single score means that rating providers imply that values can be reduced to one dimension. This simplification can result in a score that is not representative of the actual sustainability performance of an organisation. There is also a trade-off between what can be measured and what should be measured due to a lack of publicly available data, reporting fatigue or a reluctance of companies to disclose information, for example, about their environmental emissions (Chatterji and Levine, 2006).

Cost of ESG ratings

Concerns about the cost of ESG data are growing among investors. A survey carried out by BNP Paribas (2017), found that 16% of institutional investors consider cost as a barrier to further incorporating ESG factors into investment decision-making, with this percentage due to rise to 27% in 2019. Almost a third of asset managers expect cost to be a significant barrier in the short term. More particularly, some wonder who will foot this cost and whether this will become an additional expenditure for asset managers, or whether this incremental fee could be reclaimed from asset owners.

Insufficient engagement from raters with companies

Many investors argue that the levels of engagement of ESG rating providers with the firms they assess are far too low (The SustainAbility Institute, 2018). Engagement of raters with companies is important to differentiate between leaders and laggards in the field. Rating providers also need to engage more with firms since all too often they fail to update a company's ESG score even though the company already took steps to improve its ESG processes and performance since the last assessment period.

ESG ratings in fixed income investments

Increasing integration of ESG factors into investment decisions by fixed income investors

ESG investing has traditionally been more predominant in equity markets. Since fixed income investment focuses mainly on quantitative aspects such as interest rates, inflation, credit quality and liquidity risks, the inclusion of ESG factors is more arduous for fixed income portfolio managers who may be, as a result, more resistant to change related to ESG. However, with bonds increasingly constituting a substantial percentage of institutional investors' portfolios, ESG has spread out to other asset classes, including fixed income (Inderst and Stewart, 2018; Baker, 2017). It has also been demonstrated that the incorporation of ESG factors in fixed income investments does not impact the spread and performance of bonds negatively, but rather translates into modest incremental returns in corporate bond portfolios (Polbennikov *et al*, 2016).

Bond holders have less direct influence over an issuer's strategy and governance than equity investors. Therefore, the use of ESG analysis by fixed income investors to manage the risk of default is fundamental. In addition to this, while equity investors have been well-served by providers in terms of ESG analysis, fixed income investors have not received the same level of support.

However, there have been positive developments with 28 credit rating agencies joining the ESG in credit ratings initiative led by the UNPRI and backed by 170 institutional investors with US$40 trillion of assets under management in 2020 (UNPRI, 2020a). This initiative aims to enhance the transparent and systematic integration of ESG factors in credit risk analysis. The aim of the PRI is to facilitate a dialogue between credit rating agencies (CRAs) and investors to cultivate a common language, discuss ESG risks to creditworthiness and bridge investor/CRA disconnects.

Many challenges surround ESG ratings in fixed income markets (LM Capital Group Advisor Perspectives, 2018).

- Until recently, many ESG ratings were mainly focused on equity investors' concerns. ESG data providers generally did not cover firms that do not have publicly listed shares. This resulted in the exclusion of large parts of the fixed income market. This means that rating providers may have inadequately addressed the perspectives and concerns of fixed income investors and of investments in alternative asset classes, as highlighted in other parts of this book.
- The following issues are specific to fixed income providers: a lack of ESG information on numerous issuers; different maturities resulting in different time horizons; ESG scores too focused on equity markets; and the role of the issuer's capital structure on the assessment of material risk.
- Another issue mentioned by fixed income investors is the non-exclusion in current ESG integration practices of firms based on attributes that are not considered as material investment risks.

In fixed income credit ratings are routinely used to establish the creditworthiness of companies. The major credit rating agencies, such as Moody's Investors Service, S&P Global Ratings and Fitch Ratings, have started to engage more actively with the ESG agenda. They have expanded their internal expertise by hiring experts in this field, acquiring specialist service providers and training analysts on ESG factors. However, a number of issues remain with the inclusion of ESG criteria in credit ratings. UNPRI (2018a) identified four main investor/CRA disconnects that need to be addressed: "(i) materiality of ESG factors to credit risk; (ii) relevant time horizons to consider; (iii) organisational approaches to ESG consideration; and (iv) communication and transparency".

Other criticisms of ESG ratings in fixed income markets include: (i) the increase in the oligopolistic role of rating providers; (ii) the prices charged by ESG data providers; (iii) the lack of transparency of ESG methodologies and scores; (iv) the lack of ESG research coverage for some instruments, market segments and regions (eg, for high yield, emerging markets and private debt); (v) timeliness; (vi) the lack of available data; and (vii) the poor quality of data (Inderst and Stewart, 2018).

To conclude, there are many issues surrounding ESG ratings in equity and fixed income markets that can lead to poor investment decision-making by investment professionals and ultimately hinder sustainable investments. Although the issues surrounding ESG ratings in equity and fixed income markets are broadly the same, there are some specific issues with ESG ratings in fixed income markets, and there is still some way to go until these issues have been resolved. However, it is felt in the market that the solutions will mainly come from investors, standard-setters and regulators, and that increased collaboration with ESG ratings agencies, credit rating agencies and companies should help improve current methodologies and reach a certain degree of standardisation, leading to more sustainable investment decisions by investors.

To highlight the impact of these data and disclosure challenges in more detail, we now provide an example that highlights the key carbon data and disclosures challenges.

ESG DATA CHALLENGES FOR CARBON DISCLOSURES

This section explores the state of carbon disclosure standard setting and addresses the shortcomings of the existing landscape. It sheds light on what a carbon disclosure standard can accomplish in the context of mitigating and adapting to climate change through influencing investment decision-making, and concludes with the result of an academic study concerning the EU ESG regulatory regime at the University of Cambridge.

As outlined above, there is much condemnation of the lack of transparency in ESG data in general. With considerable media attention on COP26 in 2021, more vocalised corporate commitments to net zero than ever, and EU regulations setting a clear focus on climate change mitigation and adaptation, it seems as though the focus on carbon or greenhouse gas (GHG) emissions is a recent phenomenon. In reality, the focus on carbon was set in the early 1990s with climate change becoming a widely acknowledged scientifically proven fact and the United Nations Environment Programme (UNEP) and the World Meteorological Organization (WMO) establishing the Intergovernmental Panel on Climate Change (IPCC). Yet, the global community struggles with mitigating and adapting to climate change, which is often blamed on confusion around the transparency of carbon emission data and the lack of standardisation thereof.

Where do we stand with carbon disclosures?

We have lots of carbon data, and arguably high transparency but equally low comparability. For decades, GHG emission disclosure was meant to support the global community in reaching its climate targets (UNFCCC, 2008). Today, the "how" is still a frequently debated issue among standard setters, reporting specialists, data professionals, climate interest groups and especially financial services regulatory bodies such as the US Securities and Exchange Commission (SEC), the International Organization of Securities Commissions (IOSCO) and the European Securities and Markets Authority (ESMA) (Barker and Eccles, 2020; ESMA, 2020; UNEP, 2020a; IFRS, 2021; IOSCO, 2021a; Segal, 2021). Considerable time and resources are being allocated to perfecting a single, generally accepted standard with the result that we have a large selection of voluntary carbon disclosure standards, none of which are widely accepted (the EU taxonomy is an exception in the sense that it is a mandatory (regulatory) standard that will have to be followed, at least in the European jurisdiction). We are left with increasing volumes of data being disclosed along different standards, which has a detrimental effect on the comparability of the disclosed data.

How did we get here?

Years of hard work in global alignments and agreements have created little more than awareness. The global community has, except for some temporary outliers such as the US under the Trump administration (Popovich, Albeck-Ripka and Pierre-Louis, 2021), agreed that global warming is a reality, that it is largely caused by GHG[2] emissions created by human activity, and that it is accelerating at a rate that will make our planet unable to sustain human life (IPCC, 2019). One of the first major markers kicking off attempts to mitigate this phenomenon was the Kyoto Protocol in 1997 (Gerden, 2018),[3] where 192 parties acknowledged man-made climate change as a fact and agreed to reduce GHG emissions on average by 5%[4] by 2021. This percentage was later revised to more ambitious temperature targets at the 2015 United Nations Framework Convention on Climate Change, where 195 nations signed the Paris Agreement (UNFCCC, 2015).[5] In the same year, at the 2030 United Nations Sustainable Agenda, 193 UN member states endorsed 17 Sustainability Development Goals (SDGs) (World Bank Group, 2019), one of which, SDG 13, sets a focus on the "integration of climate change measures into national policies, the improvement of education, awareness-raising and institutional capacity on climate change mitigation, adaptation, impact reduction and early warnings" (Sustainable Development Goals Knowledge Platform, 2021).

Despite the above-mentioned and various other agreements,[6] the prognosis is dire as explained by the WMO Secretary-General, Professor Petteri Taalas in the "United in Science Report 2020": "Greenhouse gas concentrations – which are at their highest levels in three million years – have continued to rise. [...] And now 2016–2020 is set to be the warmest five-year period on record" (WMO, 2020). A 2021 IPCC report confirms "Each of the last four decades has been successively warmer than any decade that preceded it since 1850" (IPCC, 2021). The global community is struggling to accelerate climate change mitigation. Integrating existing disclosures and calculations of GHG into supplementary financial services regulations is one prominent avenue of exploration by the EU (European Commission, 2018a).

Reporting frameworks and standards

Can reporting frameworks and standards solve the comparability problem?

The existing standards and frameworks allow for too much flexibility to foster full comparability, even if only one single disclosure standards was adhered to by disclosing entity. Despite the ever-increasing demand (Eccles *et al*, 2012; Eccles, Lee and Stroehle, 2019), disclosed carbon data is not delivering on its promise of providing comparability. There is an intolerable level of confusion with regard to what and how to disclose "among producers and users of sustainability information" (IMP, 2020), leading to a lack of comparability (Wegener, Labelle and Jerman, 2019) between organisations, countries and individual activities. Hence, there is a general divergence of the various ESG and climate performance assessments (Berg, Kölbel and Rigobon, 2019; Eccles, Lee and Stroehle, 2019). The EU Commission (2019), the WEF (Deloitte *et al*, 2020), the Institute of International Finance (IIF) (Portilla, Gibbs and Rismanchi, 2020) and IOSCO are also flagging the ineffectiveness of available carbon disclosures due to the lack of comparability. The data currently fails to facilitate meaningful investment decision-making for investors (Vesty, Telgenkamp and Roscoe, 2015; IOSCO, 2020).

Reporting frameworks such as the Global Reporting Initiative (GRI), the Task Force on Climate-Related Disclosures (TCFD) and the International Integrated Reporting Council (IIRC) provide important tools to organisations to measure performance in sustainability matters and quantify impacts and risks in relation to sustainability topics (Whitfield and McNett, 2013; Deloitte, 2016; Barker and Eccles, 2018, 2020). However, while reporting frameworks are often useful to the organisations themselves, they do not allow for comparability between organisations from an investor perspective because they merely provide loose guidelines of what to consider when managing the organisation – a description of the interpretation of those guidelines is then published. Those frameworks lack a clear definition of how to report for comparability (as opposed to what disclosure standards require, for example). Therefore, despite the overall increase in carbon reporting (Tempero, 2019; King, 2019), it remains difficult to compare the published information across different organisations (Vesty, Telgenkamp and Roscoe, 2015; Chatterji *et al*, 2016; Esty and Cort, 2017; Allini, Giner and Caldarelli, 2018; Zsóka and Vajkai, 2018; Wegener, Labelle and Jerman, 2019). One could argue that this specificity gap could be filled by a carbon disclosure standard that provides more specific metrics.

However, where carbon disclosure standards exist with specific metrics, the comparability of reports is still equivocal (Zsóka and Vajkai, 2018; Berg, Kölbel and Rigobon, 2019), which is often attributed to a lack of a common definition between competing standards (Stechemesser and Guenther, 2012). Nevertheless, even when applying the widely accepted GHG Protocol (World Economic Forum, 2020),[7] the lack of comparability persists, as pointed out by the World Business Council for Sustainable Development and World Resources Institute (WBCSD and WRI, 2004; Wegener, Labelle and Jerman, 2019). Wegener *et al* (2019) agree with Depoers (Depoers, Jeanjean and Jérôme, 2016), stating that "comparability issues related to using multiple methods would still exist if the GHG Protocol [...] were to be followed by all firms" because it "allows for discretion in the choice of collection and reporting methods".

In conclusion, the current carbon disclosure standards and frameworks allow for too much flexibility within themselves and among each other to achieve appropriate comparability that can sufficiently inform climate-friendly investment decision-making. Hence, climate change mitigation and adaptation cannot be sufficiently fostered by investment decision-making.

Where does the divergence come from?

While there is a common goal on a high level, frameworks and standards differ in target users, metrics, materiality concepts, scope, depth and methods. Some of the most prominent organisations providing guidelines for carbon disclosure are frameworks (eg, the TCFD), others are standards (eg, the Climate Disclosure Standards Board, CDSB, or the Sustainability Accounting Standards

Table 13.2 Scope 1–3 carbon disclosure discrepancies between the main disclosure standards

	Metric required	Disclosures comparable to TCFD?	Greenhouse Gas Protocol used?	Disclosures comparable between organisations?	Explanation
			TCFD		
	Disclose Scope 1, Scope 2, and, if appropriate, Scope 3 greenhouse gas (GHG) emissions, and the related risks.				
Scope 1	Yes	Comparable to TCFD	Yes	Yes	
Scope 2	Yes	Comparable to TCFD	Yes	Yes	
Scope 3	Yes	Comparable to TCFD	Yes	Yes	
			SASB		
	– Inclusion of industries for disclosure of carbon is based on the level of financial materiality to the company – Energy consumption replaces "Scope 2"				
Scope 1	Partially	No	Possible, not required	Yes	Scope 1 only required for 22 out of 77 industries 55
Scope 2	Partially	No	No	Yes	Scope 2 not included, however, 35 of 77 industries are asked to disclose a metric for direct energy consumption
Scope 3	No	No	No	Yes	Scope 3 not included, however indirect impacts are disclosed via other general issue categories
			IR		
	– IR recommends disclosure of anything that affects the organisation's ability to create value without specific metrics				
Scope 1	No	No	No	Partially	
Scope 2	No	No	No	Partially	Scope 1–3 potentially indirectly included
Scope 3	No	No	No	Partially	

GRI					
	– GRI asks for the potential impact of climate-related risks & opportunities on the organisation's markets, businesses, corporate or investment strategy, financial statements, and future cash flows (Principle 1) – Without clear required metrics, overlap to scope 1–3 disclosure is likely, identical reporting is unlikely				
Scope 1	Partially	No	Possible, not required	Partially	Scope 1–3 emissions are not required but climate-related risks and opportunities are to be reported
Scope 2	Partially	No	No	Partially	
Scope 3	No	No	No	Partially	
CDSB					
	– CDSB considers green house gas emissions as material to all companies and suggests reporting of measures, indicators and other information – CDSB does not enforce the use of the GHG protocol				
Scope 1	Partially	No	Suggested, not required	Partially	Scope 1–3 emissions are not required but disclosures shall report quantitative and qualitative results
Scope 2	Partially	No	Suggested, not required	Partially	
Scope 3	Partially	No	Suggested, not required	Partially	
CDP					
	– CDP requires carbon disclosure, recommends the GHG Protocol without enforcing it – Scope 1 & 2 require historical data, scope 3 does not (TCFD does)				
Scope 1	Yes	Yes	Suggested, not required	Yes	Scope 1–3 emissions are not required but disclosures shall report quantitative and qualitative results
Scope 2	Yes	Yes	Suggested, not required	Yes	
Scope 3	Yes (not historical)	Yes	Suggested, not required	Yes	

Board, SASB), which partially explains the issue of diverging carbon disclosures.

Despite extensive alignment efforts (IMP, 2020), data professionals are struggling to achieve carbon disclosure comparability (Chatterji *et al*, 2016; Esty and Cort, 2017; Berg, Kölbel and Rigobon, 2019; IIF, 2019; Cort and Esty, 2020). The TCFD, the Value Reporting Foundation (VRF), GRI, Carbon Disclosure Project (CDP) and CDSB are aligned in the general purpose of increasing transparency around carbon emissions, but they focus on different disclosure users (shareholders versus stakeholders), have different approaches to materiality (environmental, financial or double) and ask for different disclosure methods and metrics (descriptive versus numeric, historic versus forward-looking) (Corporate Reporting Dialogue, 2019). While the Better Alignment Project claims that there is a "strong alignment between the frameworks and standards and the TCFD as well as between each other [meaning the five frameworks]" (Corporate Reporting Dialogue, 2019), a comparison of how scope 1–3 emissions[8] are disclosed in each of the frameworks indicates that the existing level of alignment does not achieve comparability. Table 13.2 illustrates this by comparing how carbon is disclosed under the TCFD, (formerly) SASB and IIRC, GRI, CDSB and CDP.

Do we need an alignment of voluntary standards or mandatory regulations?

Standards are merging and regulations are being passed, but it is yet unclear which path will bring comparability. The multitude of voluntary disclosure frameworks is often seen as the reason that transparency efforts of the last decades have failed, because it creates a lack of data comparability leaving investors confused while providing ample scope for greenwashing (Berg, Kölbel and Rigobon, 2019; Cort and Esty, 2020; Ingman, 2020; Portilla, Gibbs and Rismanchi, 2020; European Financial Reporting Advisory Group, 2021).

Acknowledging this issue, the main players in voluntary ESG reporting have repeatedly stated their intention of alignment to simplify disclosure and increase data comparability (Corporate Reporting Dialogue, 2019; IMP, 2020; World Economic Forum, 2020; European Financial Reporting Advisory Group, 2021; IFRS, 2021;

IOSCO, 2021). Members of this group are the IFRS Foundation, the European Financial Reporting Advisory Group (EFRAG), the World Economic Forum International Business Council (WEF-IBC) and the "five framework- and standard-setting institutions of international significance" (IMP, 2020), namely the CDP, the CDSB, the GRI, the IIRC and the SASB. To further these efforts, the SASB and IIRC have merged into the VRF (IIRC and SASB, 2020. While acknowledging existing frameworks, the EU is enacting its own disclosure framework into law (EU taxonomy supported by the CSRD and the SFDR) to eliminate the confusion and provide comparable data for climate mitigating investment decision-making (UNEP, 2020). They jury is still out on the success of this endeavour.

Disclosing on what is important: Why understanding materiality is crucial

Different definitions of materiality will considerably skew data analysis results. The carbon data is provided to capital markets either directly via voluntary company reports or indirectly via rating agencies (Berg, Kölbel and Rigobon, 2019; Lopez, Contreras and Bendix, 2020). The reasons for the previously discussed discrepancies within those disclosures are: (i) the difference in definitions of "what is sustainable"; and (ii) the viewpoints of "what is important" that are specified in different ways by the various standard setters, regulators, rating agencies, disclosure creators and data users.

For example, the understanding of materiality in a climate context has been debated extensively (Corporate Reporting Dialogue, 2019), and only latterly has the difference between financial materiality and environmental materiality been sufficiently recognised (Eccles *et al*, 2012; European Commission, 2018b; Cort and Esty, 2020; UNEP, 2020). For the purpose of this section, environmental materiality also includes the social and governmental aspects summarised under ESG.[9] Figure 13.2 shows that many disclosure standards are based on the notion that what is financially material to the organisation is also material to be disclosed. This works if the climate risks encountered by the organisation are also climate risks encountered by the environment (or stakeholder base). As soon as those interests no longer overlap, climate disclosure solely satisfies the needs of the shareholder (assuming the

Figure 13.2 Financial versus stakeholder and double materiality

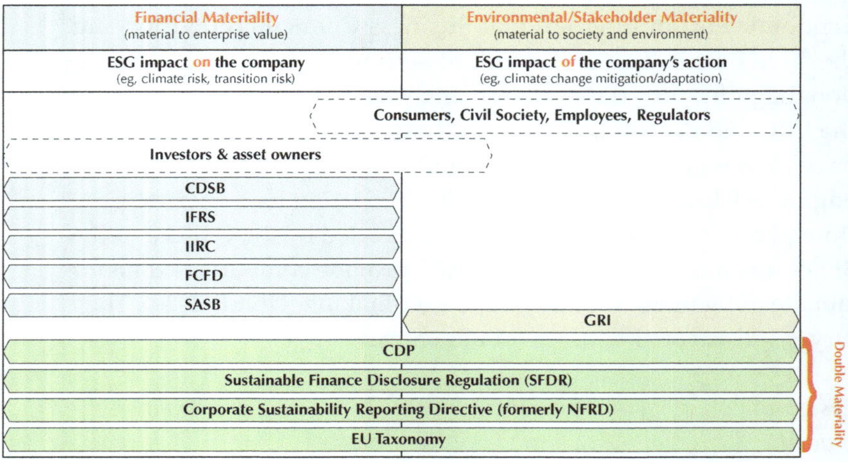

Source: Created by the author based on regulatory text as well as framework-, and standard setter documentation

shareholder is mostly interested in financial risk mitigation and return) rather than the stakeholder. The EU Commission has hence implemented the concept of "double materiality"[10] (European Commission, 2020), under which the impact on the value of the organisation as well as the impact on the stakeholder base is reported. As Barker and Eccles (2020) state, this "includes information that simultaneously serves the needs of both investors and other stakeholders".

Academic study: Is a mandatory regulation the solution to the comparability problem?

The research

Thus far, a considerable body of research has focused on specific characteristics of disclosure standards. The author of this section has undertaken further research to assess whether the approach of the EU regulator in creating a mandatory standard for carbon disclosure has the potential to improve efforts to mitigate and adapt to climate change through influencing the behaviour of capital markets.

The aim of the research was to identify the crucial success factors or downfalls of mandatory carbon disclosure standards by using the EU taxonomy (which serves as the basis for EU carbon disclosure regulations) as an example. It evaluated the EU taxonomy in combination with the situation and environment it is set in. Applying a systems approach, characteristics of the EU carbon disclosure standard were set in context with external enablers and inhibitors such as incentives of investment decision-makers, their understanding of materiality concepts in carbon disclosure, and the existence of accountability mechanisms for carbon reporting. 38 semi-structured interviews were conducted and 67 surveys completed by ESG reporting experts with a financial services, regulatory, academic or consulting background.

The respondents are clearly divided about the potential effectiveness of integrating the EU taxonomy into the EU ESG regulatory regime and articulate the following limitations and utility:

- incomplete scope in geography (only EU), content (not all economic activities in all industries) and disclosing entities (only larger organisations);
- difficulties in enforcement caused by enormous complexity, constant need for revision due to its rules-based nature and limited regulator resources;
- lack of third-party assurance and therefore accountability; and
- competition with other (voluntary, but often widely accepted) standards.

More importantly, a large number of respondents explain that the main reason the EU carbon disclosure standard might not change investment behaviour and therefore help to mitigate and adapt to climate change is a mindset misalignment in the users and creators of reports. Some have a financial risk mitigation mindset while others display a climate change mitigation mindset. This often leads to disclosures geared towards the mitigation of financial and reputational risks rather than the mitigation of climate risk, and therefore does not foster increased asset flow into climate-friendly investments. This could be mitigated by enforcing mandatory third-party assurance of disclosures and, additionally, a maturing implementation of EU disclosure regulations.

The utility of the EU carbon disclosure standard is based on the fact that it is both specific and mandatory. Respondents welcome thresholds for carbon emissions based on economic activities within a specific industry that define whether those activities can be considered sustainable. Many believe that enacting a rules-based standard into law will force the creators and users of carbon disclosure data to use only that standard, which will increase the comparability of disclosures. By making it a law, it would automatically become widely accepted.

Findings

An improved carbon disclosure standard could engender better transparency and comparability, but that alone would not push assets towards climate-friendly investments. Rather, what alters investment behaviour is a change in the goals and mindset of investors with regard to climate change. Once that mindset has shifted, a disclosure standard can then provide the necessary information for investors to make climate-friendly investment decisions. There was no clear preference among respondents for the taxonomy over any other standard, however, meaning that there is no consensus as to whether its utility outweighs its limitations.

It can be concluded that the main utility of the mandatory EU carbon disclosure standard is the role it can play in developing the conditions for its own effectiveness by causing system change (ie, clear materiality concepts and carbon threshold definitions, third-party assurance, a mature regulatory regime and dominance of a single standard). However, to be effective it must go hand-in-hand with a change in EU mindset, which must ultimately adopt the importance of mitigating and adapting to climate change as its first principle.

CONCLUSION

With shifting demographic trends, increasing awareness of sustainability issues (whether social or environmental) and a rapidly growing interest in sustainable practices, responsible investing is here to stay. Also, numerous studies have shown that investments in companies that score high on ESG metrics are less risky – something which will in turn drive further integration of ESG factors into investment analysis (Clubb, Takahashi and Tiburzio, 2016). However, more than ever, the need for investment professionals to understand ESG data providers' various methodologies and how these can impact investment decisions will be crucial.

Until now, ESG data providers have been mainly unregulated. However, because of the risks that the lack of transparency of their methodologies, their uneven coverage and potential conflicts of interest pose to the protection of investors, asset allocation and efficiency of markets, the need for regulation of ESG data providers has been highlighted by many organisations.

IOSCO (2021b) has highlighted the lack of transparency of methodologies used by ESG raters, and the lack of standards that could lead to assets misallocation or greenwashing and ultimately a lack of trust of investors in the reliability of ESG data. It has issued 10 recommendations to its members, ESG ratings and data products providers, ESG ratings and data products users, as well as entities assessed by these providers.

Other institutions that are calling for ESG data providers to be regulated are the European Commission (2021), which plans to introduce rules to increase the comparability, transparency and reliability of ESG data, and regulators in a number of countries – such the UK (eg, the Financial Conduct Authority (FCA, 2021), France (Autorité des Marchés Financiers, 2020) and the Netherlands.

Time is not on our side when it comes to the global climate crisis and action by regulators is urgently needed. Therefore, it will be interesting to see how regulators address these data and related disclosure challenges in the coming months and years.

1 For an overview and analysis of ESG data and metrics complexity management issues, see Macpherson and Schmid (2021).
2 GHG is used interchangeably with carbon in this chapter.
3 The Kyoto Protocol was adopted in 1997 but came into force in 2005.
4 The 5% reduction was to be achieved between 2008 and 2021, with 1990 emissions being the benchmark.
5 In December 2012, the DohaAamendment inaugurated the second commitment period of the protocol running until 2020.
6 Other agreements/conferences include: Agenda 21 – Climate Change and the United Nations Framework Convention of Climate Change (UNFCCC) in 1992; the Cancun Agreements in 2010; the Durban Climate Change Conference in 2011; the Warsaw Climate Change Conference in 2013; and the SIDS Accelerated Modalities of Action (SAMOA) Pathway in 2014 (Sustainable Development Goals Knowledge Platform, 2021).
7 "More than 9 out of 10 Fortune 500 companies reporting to CDP use GHG Protocol. It is also recommended [...] by GRI" (CDP, 2021).

8 Scope 1–3 as used by the GHG Protocol and in accordance with Annex III of Regulation (EU) 2016/1011 of the European Parliament and of the Council of 8 June 2016 (Benchmark Regulation).

9 Barker and Eccles (2020) call it "societal materiality".

10 It is sometimes referred to as "dynamic or dual materiality".

REFERENCES

Accounting for Sustainability and Aviva Investors, 2018, "Financing our Future" (available at https://www.accountingforsustainability.org/financing-our-future.html).

Aggarwal, P. and A. Kadyan, 2014, "Greenwashing: The Darker Side of CSR", *Indian Journal of Applied Research*, 4(3), pp. 61–6.

Allini, A., B. Giner and A. Caldarelli, 2018, "Opening the Black Box of Accounting for Greenhouse Gas Emissions: The Different Views of Institutional Bodies and Firms", *Journal of Cleaner Production*, 172, pp. 2,195–205.

Amel-Zadeh, A. and G. Serafeim, 2018, "Why and How Investors Use ESG Information: Evidence from a Global Survey", *Financial Analysts Journal*, 74(3), pp. 87–103.

Autorité des Marchés Financiers, 2020, "French and Dutch Financial Markets Authorities Call for a European Regulation of ESG Data, Ratings and Related Services", December 15 (available at https://www.amf-france.org/en/news-publications/news-releases/amf-news-releases/french-and-dutch-financial-market-authorities-call-european-regulation-esg-data-ratings-and-related).

Avetisyan, E. and K. Hockerts, 2017, "The Consolidation of the ESG Rating Industry as an Enactment of Institutional Retrogression", *Business Strategy and the Environment*, 26(3), pp. 316–30.

Bailey, J., S. Flaherty, C. Kocinski and K. Nazli, 2017, "Rating the Raters on ESG", Neuberger Berman, December (available at https://www.nb.com/documents/public/global/s0314_rating_the_raters_on_esg.pdf).

Baker, S., 2017, "ESG Factors Making Gains in Fixed-income Portfolios", *Pensions & Investments*, 45(1).

Ball, R., 2006, "International Financial Reporting Standards (IFRS): Pros and Cons for Investors", *Accounting and Business Research*, 36, pp. 5–27.

Barker, R. and R. G. Eccles, 2018, "Should FASB and IASB be Responsible for Setting Standards for Nonfinancial Information?", *SSRN Electronic Journal*, October.

Barker, R. and R. G. Eccles, 2020, "Comment Letter in Response to the IFRS Foundation Consultation Paper on Sustainability Reporting", Oxford, pp. 1–32.

Beloe, S., 2016, "What do ESG Ratings Actually Tell Us?", WHEB Commentary, London (available at http://www.whebgroup.com/what-do-esg-ratings-actually-tell-us/).

Beloe, S., J. Scherer and I. Knoepfel, 2004, *Value for Money: Reviewing the Quality of SRI Research* (London: SustainAbility).

Berg, F., J. Kölbel and R. Rigobon, 2019, "Aggregate Confusion: The Divergence of ESG Ratings", *SSRN Electronic Journal*, August 20.

BNP Paribas, 2017 "Great Expectations for ESG: What's Next for Asset Managers and Asset Owners?".

CDP, 2021, "Climate Change Report" (available at https://www.snclavalin.com/~/media/Files/S/SNC-Lavalin/download-centre/en/report/cdp-report-2021.pdf).

Chatterji, A., R. Durand, D. Levine and S. Touboul, 2016, "Do Ratings of Firms Converge? Implications for Managers, Investors and Strategy Researchers", *Strategic Management Journal,* 37(8), pp. 1,597–614.

Chatterji, A. K. and D. I. Levine, 2006, "Irresponsibility in Measuring Corporate Responsibility", working paper, University of California at Berkeley.

Chatterji, A., D. Levine and M. Toffel, 2009, "How Well Do Social Ratings Actually Measure Corporate Social Responsibility?", *Journal of Economics & Management Strategy,* 18(1), pp. 125–69.

Chatterji, A. and M. Toffel, 2010, "How Firms Respond to Being Rated", *Strategic Management Journal,* 31(9), pp. 917–45.

Chava, S., 2014, "Environmental Externalities and Cost of Capital", *Management Science,* 60(9), pp. 2,223–47.

Clubb, R., Y. Takahashi and P. Tiburzio, 2016, "Evaluating the Relationship between ESG and Corporate Fixed Income", Breckinridge Capital Advisors and MIT Sloan Business School (available at https://mitsloan.mit.edu/sites/default/files/2018-10/Breckinridge_Capital-Report-2016.pdf).

Collison, D., G. Cobb, D. Power and L. Stevenson, 2009, "FTSE4Good: Exploring its Implications for Corporate Conduct", *Accounting, Auditing & Accountability Journal,* 22(1), pp. 35–58.

Corporate Reporting Dialogue, 2019, "Driving Assignment in Climate-related Reporting", in M. Blumberg (Ed), *Startup CEO: A Field Guide to Scaling Up Your Business* (Hoboken, NJ: Wiley).

Cort, T. and D. Esty, 2020, "ESG Standards: Looming Challenges and Pathways Forward", *Organization & Environment,* 33(4), pp. 491–510.

Crabtree, E., 2017, "Taking ESG to the Next Level", BNP Paribas.

De, I. and M. Clayman, 2015, "The Benefits of Socially Responsible Investing: An Active Manager's Perspective", *Journal of Investing,* 24(4), pp. 49–72.

Delmas, M. and V. D. Blass, 2010, "Measuring Corporate Environmental Performance: The Trade-offs of Sustainability Ratings", *Business Strategy and the Environment,* 19(4), pp. 245–60.

Deloitte, 2016, "Sustainability Disclosure: Getting Ahead of the Curve".

Deloitte, EY, KPMG and PwC, 2020, "Toward Common Metrics and Consistent Reporting of Sustainable Value Creation", World Economic Forum, January (available at https://www3.weforum.org/docs/WEF_IBC_ESG_Metrics_Discussion_Paper.pdf).

Depoers, F., T. Jeanjean and T. Jérôme, 2016, "Voluntary Disclosure of Greenhouse Gas Emissions: Contrasting the Carbon Disclosure Project and Corporate Reports", *Journal of Business Ethics,* 134(3), pp. 445–61.

Dorfleitner, G., G. Halbritter and M. Nguyen, 2015, Measuring the Level and Risk of Corporate Responsibility – An Empirical Comparison of Different ESG Rating Approaches", *Journal of Asset Management*, 16(7), pp. 450–66.

Doyle, T. M., 2018, "Ratings that Don't Rate: The Subjective World of ESG Ratings Agencies", American Council for Capital Formation, July (available at https://accf-corpgov.org/wp-content/uploads/2018/07/ACCF_RatingsESGReport.pdf).

Eccles, R. G., M. P. Krzus, J. Rogers and G. Serafeim, 2012, "The Need for Sector-specific Materiality and Sustainability Reporting Statndards", *Journal of Applied Corporate Finance*, 24(2), Spring, pp. 65–71.

Eccles, R. G., L.-E. Lee and J. C. Stroehle, 2020, "The Social Origins of ESG: An Analysis of Innovest and KLD", *Organization & Environment*, 33(4), November.

El Ghoul, S., O. Guedhami, C. C. Kwok, and D. R. Mishra, 2011, "Does Corporate Social Responsibility Affect the Cost of Capital?", *Journal of Banking and Finance*, 35(9), pp. 2,388–406.

ESMA, 2020, "E144HD Response to your Consultation Paper on Sustainable Reporting", 33, December.

Esty, D. C. and T. Cort, 2017, "Corporate Sustainability Metrics: What Investors Need and Don't Get", corporate-sustainability.org.

European Commission, 2018a, "Action Plan: Financing Sustainable Growth", EUR-Lex.

European Commission, 2018b, "Regulation of the European Parliament and of the Council Amending Regulation (EU) 2016/1011 on Low Carbon Benchmarks and Positive Carbon Impact Benchmarks", Brussels.

European Commission, 2019, "Questions and Answers: Political Agreement on an EU-wide Classification System for Sustainable Investments (Taxonomy)", December.

European Commission, 2020, "Summary Report on the Public Consultation on the Evaluation and Review of the ePrivacy Directive", February.

European Commission, 2021, "Sustainable Finance and EU Taxonomy: Commission Takes Further Steps to Channel Money Towards Sustainable Activities", press release, April 21 (available at https://ec.europa.eu/commission/presscorner/detail/en/ip_21_1804).

European Financial Reporting Advisory Group, 2021, "Final Report: Proposals for a Relevant and Dynamic EU Sustainability Reporting Standard", February.

FCA, 2021, "A Strategy for Positive Change: Our ESG Priorities", November 3 (available at https://www.fca.org.uk/publications/corporate-documents/strategy-positive-change-our-esg-priorities).

Ferri, G. and L. Liu, 2005, "Assessing the Effort of Rating Agencies in Emerging Economies: Some Empirical Evidence", *The European Journal of Finance*, 11(3), pp. 283–95.

Finch, N., 2004, "International Rating Agencies and Sustainability", *SSRN Electronic Journal* (available at https://papers.ssrn.com/sol3/papers.cfm?abstract_id=658082).

Gerden, T., 2018, "The Adoption of the Kyoto Protocol of the United Nations Framework Convention on Climate Change", United Nations, *Prispevki za Novejso Zgodovino*, 58(2).

Global Sustainable Investment Alliance, 2020, "2020 Global Sustainable Investment Review" (available at http://www.gsi-alliance.org/wp-content/uploads/2021/08/GSIR-20201.pdf).

Graafland, J. J., S. C. W. Eijffinger and H. SmidJohan, 2004, "Benchmarking of Corporate Social Responsibility: Methodological Problems and Robustness", *Journal of Business Ethics,* 53(1), pp. 137–52.

Greenhouse Gas Protocol, 2020, "We Set the Standards to Measure and Manage Emissions".

GSIA, 2016, "2016 Global Sustainable Investment Review" (available at http://www.gsi-alliance.org/wp-content/uploads/2017/03/GSIR_Review2016.F.pdf).

GSIA, 2019, "2018 Global Sustainable Investment Review" (available at http://www.gsi-alliance.org/wp-content/uploads/2019/03/GSIR_Review2018.3.28.pdf).

Hower, M., 2015, "Could Sustainability 'Survey Fatigue' Launch a $1 Billion Industry?", *GreenBiz.*

Huber, B. and M. Comstock, 2017, "ESG Reports and Ratings: What They Are, Why They Matter?", *The Corporate Governance Advisor,* 25(5), pp. 1–12.

IFRS, 2021, "IFRS Foundation Trustees Announce Next Steps in Response to Broad Demand for Global Sustainability Standards", February 2.

IIF, 2019, "The Case for Simplifying Sustainable Investment Technology", IIF Sustainable Finance Working Group Report, October.

IIRC and SASB, 2020, "IIRC and SASB Announce Intent to Merge in Major Step Towards Simplifying the Corporate Reporting System", November 25.

IMP, 2020, "Statement of Intent to Work Together Towards Comprehensive Corporate Reportng", September.

Inderst, G. and F. Stewart, 2018, "Incorporating Environmental, Social and Governance Factors into Fixed Income Investment", World Bank Group (available at https://documents1.worldbank.org/curated/en/913961524150628959/pdf/Incorporating-environmental-social-and-governance-factors-into-fixed-income-investment.pdf).

Ingman, B. C., 2020, "EU Environmental Social Governance (ESG) Regulations Guide".

IOSCO, 2020, "IOSCO Media Release 34/2020.

IOSCO, 2021a, "IOSCO Media Release 05/2021.

IOSCO, 2021b, Recommendations on Sustainability-related Practices, Policies, Procedures and Disclosure in Asset Management", Consultation Report CR01/21, June (available at https://www.iosco.org/library/pubdocs/pdf/IOSCOPD679.pdf).

IPCC, 2019, "IPC Report 15: Global Warming of 1.5^{0}C", *Journal of the International Commission on Radiation Units and Measurements.*

IPCC, 2021, "Climate Change 2021: The Physical Science Basis Summary for Policymakers"

Kendall, J., 2016, "Why ESG Matters in Fixed Income", *Professional Pensions,* September 26 (available at https://www.professionalpensions.com/feature/2471992/-esg-matters-fixed-income).

King, A., 2019, "Towards Net Zero: How the World's Largest Companies Report on Climate Risk and Net Zero Transition", KPMG.

LaBella, M. J., L. Sullivan, J. Russell and D. Novikov, 2019, "Values to Value-based Investing: The Evolution of Sustainability", QS Investors, September (available at https://qsinvestorsproduction.blob.core.windows.net/media/Default/PDF/Values%20to%20Value-Based%20Investing_The%20Evolution%20of%20Sustainability.pdf).

Lai, A., G. Melloni and R. Stacchezzini, 2016, "Corporate Sustainable Development: Is 'Integrated Reporting' a Legitimation Strategy?", *Business Strategy and the Environment,* 25(3), pp. 165–77.

Linnenluecke, M., S. Russell and A. Griffiths, 2009, "Subcultures and Sustainability Practices: The Impact on Understanding Corporate Sustainability", *Business Strategy and the Environment,* 18(7), pp. 432–52.

LM Capital Group Advisor Perspectives, 2018, "The ESG Conundrum: Environmental, Social and Governance Factors for the Fixed Income Investor", *Advisor Perspectives,* April 4 (available at https://www.advisorperspectives.com/commentaries/2018/04/04/the-esg-conundrum-environmental-social-and-governance-factors-for-the-fixed-income-investor).

Lopez, C., O. Contreras and J. Bendix, 2020, 'Disagreement Among ESG Rating Agencies: Shall we be Worried?".

Macpherson, M. and S. Schmid, 2021, "Erfolgsfaktoren der Integration von KI in der ESG-Analyse", Börsen-Zeitung Nr. 175, Special Supplement, September 11 (available at https://daten.boersen-zeitung.de/bzpro/sonderbeilage/2021/BZ_210911.pdf).

MIT Sloan Business School, 2019, "The Aggregate Confusion Project" (available at https://mitsloan.mit.edu/sustainability-initiative/aggregate-confusion-project).

Mooij, S., 2017, "The ESG Rating and Ranking Industry: Vice or Virtue in the Adoption of Responsible Investment", *Journal of Environmental Investing, State of ESG Data and Metrics,* 8, pp. 331–67.

Partnership for Carbon Accounting Financials, 2020, "The Global GHG Accounting & Reporting Standard for the Financial Industry", November 18

Peiró-Signes, A., M. Segarra-Oña, J. Mondéjar-Jiménez and M. Vargas-Vargas, 2013, "Influence of the Environmental, Social and Corporate Governance Ratings on the Economic Performance of Companies: An Overview", *International Journal of Environmental Research,* 7(1), pp. 105–12.

Polbennikov, S., A. Desclée, L. Dynkin and A. Maitra, 2016, "ESG Ratings and Performance of Corporate Bonds", *The Journal of Fixed Income,* 26(1), pp. 21–41.

Popovich, N., L. Albeck-Ripka and K. Pierre-Louis, 2021, "The Trump Administration Rolled Back More Than 100 Environmental Rules. Here's the Full List", *The New York Times,* January 20.

Porter, M. E. and M. R. Kramer, 2019, "Creating Shared Value", in G. Lenssen and N. Smith (Eds), *Managing Sustainable Business* (Dordrecht, Netherlands: Springer).

Portilla, A., S. Gibbs and K. Rismanchi, 2020, "Sustainable Finance Policy & Regulation: The Case for Greater International Alignment", IIF, March.

Rajgopal, S. and R. Foster, 2018, "ABCs of ESG", *Breakingviews*, Reuters, August 10 (available at https://www.breakingviews.com/features/guest-view-esg-ratings-arent-reliable-enough/).

Sadowski, M., 2012, "What is the Value of Corporate Sustainability Ratings?", *The Guardian*, September 11 (available at https://www.theguardian.com/sustainable-business/blog/value-corporate-sustainability-ratings-rankings).

Sadowski, M., K. Whitaker and F. Buckingham, 2010, "Rate the Raters: Phase Two: Taking Inventory of the Ratings Universe", SustainAbility, February 23.

Sadowski, M., K. Whitaker, M. Lee and A. Ayars, 2010, "Rate the Raters Phase Four: The Necessary Future of Ratings", SustainAbility.

Scalet, S. and T. Kelly, 2010, "CSR Rating Agencies: What is their Global Impact?", *Journal of Business Ethics*, 94(1), pp. 69–88.

Schäfer, H., J. Beer, J. Zenker and P. Fernandes, 2006, "Who is Who in Corporate Social Responsibility Rating? A Survey of Internationally Established Rating Systems that Measure Corporate Responsibility", Bertelsmann Foundation.=

Seelos, C., 2004, "Finding a Path in the Sustainability Jungle", occasional paper, IESE Business School University of Navarra.

Segal, M., 2021, "SEC Launches Climate and ESG Enforcement Task Force".

SICM, 2016, "Who are the ESG Rating Agencies?", February (available at https://www.sicm.com/docs/who-rates.pdf).

Spencer, J., 2020, "The Sustainable Development Goals", in E. Tsekleves, R. Cooper and J. Spencer (Eds), *Design for Global Challenges and Goals* (Abingdon, England: Routledge).

Stechemesser, K. and E. Guenther, 2012, "Carbon Accounting: A Systematic Literature Review", *Journal of Cleaner Production*, 36, pp. 17–38.

Stern, N., 2016, "The Roles of Financial Institutions and Finance Ministries in Delivering the Paris Agreement on Climate Change", LSE, November 29 (available at https://www.lse.ac.uk/GranthamInstitute/news/the-roles-of-financial-institutions-and-finance-ministries-in-delivering-the-paris-agreement-on-climate-change/).

Stubbs, W. and P. Rogers, 2013, "Lifting the Veil on Environment-social-governance Rating Methods", *Social Responsibility Journal*, 9(4), pp. 622–40.

Sunder, S., 2010, "Adverse Effects of Uniform Written Reporting Standards on Accounting Practice, Education, and Research", *Journal of Accounting and Public Policy*, 29(2), pp. 99–114.

Sustainable Development Goals Knowledge Platform, 2021, "Climate Change" (available at https://sustainabledevelopment.un.org/topics/climatechange).

Tempero, M., 2019, "The Time Has Come!", KPMG.

The SustainAbility Institute, 2018, "Rate the Raters 2018: Ratings Revisited".

UNEP, 2020a, "Carrots and Sticks 2020 – Sustainability Reporting Policy: Global Trends in Disclosure as the ESG Agenda Goes Mainstream".

UNEP, 2020b, "Task Force on Climate-related Financial Disclosures", Finance Initiative, June.

UNFCCC, 2008, "Kyoto Protocol Reference Manual".

UNFCCC, 2015, "Paris Agreement of the United Nations Framework Convention on Climate Change", United Nations.

UNPRI, 2017, "What Rating Agencies are Doing on ESG Factors", July 3 (available at https://www.unpri.org/credit-risk-and-ratings/what-rating-agencies-are-doing-on-esg-factors/81.article).

UNPRI, 2018a, "Credit Ratings Initiative" (available at https://www.unpri.org/investment-tools/fixed-income/credit-risk-and-ratings).

UNPRI, 2018b, "Shifting Perceptions: ESG, Credit Risk and Ratings – Part 2: Exploring the Disconnects" (available at https://www.unpri.org/download?ac=4944).

Van Marrewijk, M., 2003, "Concepts and Definitions of CSR and Corporate Sustainability: Between Agency and Communion", *Journal of Business Ethics*, 44(2), pp. 95–105.

Vesty, G. M., A. Telgenkamp and P. J. Roscoe, 2015, "Creating Numbers: Carbon and Capital Investment", *Accounting, Auditing and Accountability Journal*, 28(3), pp. 302–24.

WBCSD and WRI, 2004, "A Corporate Accounting and Reporting Standard", *Greenhouse Gas Protocol*.

Wegener, M., R. Labelle and L. Jerman, 2019, "Unpacking Carbon Accounting Numbers: A Study of the Commensurability and Comparability of Corporate Greenhouse Gas Emission Disclosures", *Journal of Cleaner Production*, 211, pp. 652–64.

White, A., 2013, "Swamped by Sustainability Indicators that Fail to Drive Transformation", *The Guardian*, August 7 (available at https://www.theguardian.com/sustainable-business/blog/sustainability-indicators-corporate-transformation).

Whitfield, R. and J. McNett, 2013, *A Primer on Sustainability: In the Business Environment* (New York, NY: Business Expert Press).

Willis Towers Watson, 2017, "Assets of World's Largest Fund Managers Passes US$80 Trillion for the First Time", press release, October 30 (available at https://www.wtwco.com/en-GB/News/2017/10/Assets-of-worlds-largest-fund-managers-passes-US-80-trillion-for-the-first-time).

WMO, 2020, "United in Science 2020".

World Bank Group, 2019, The 2030 Sustainable Development Agenda and the World Bank Group: Closing the SDGs Financing Gap", 2019 Update.

World Economic Forum, 2020, "Measuring Stakeholder Capitalism. Toward Common Metrics and Consistent Reporting of Sustainable Value Creation", January.

Zsóka, Á. and É. Vajkai, 2018, "Corporate Sustainability Reporting: Scrutinising the Requirements of Comparability, Transparency and Reflection of Sustainability Performance", *Society and Economy*, 40(1), pp. 19–44.

PART VII

PAST, PRESENT AND THE FUTURE IN ESG

14

Corporate social responsibility across industries: When and who can do well by doing good?

Andreas G. F. Hoepner and Pei-Shan Yu

University College Dublin and Mistra Financial Systems; ICMA Centre

While much of the literature considers whether corporate social responsibility (CSR) pays, this chapter takes a more nuanced perspective, theoretically and empirically, by investigating when CSR pays and for whom? Theoretically, we develop two contingency perspectives. First, we extend previous work to argue that CSR's impacts on corporate financial performance (CFP) are moderated by five factors: CSR form; firm characteristics; time; national framework; and industrial characteristics. Focusing on industrial characteristics, we theorise that differences in industries' dependency on certain stakeholder groups, their proximity to the end-consumer, their potential for social and environmental damages, and their level of product/service differentiation moderate CSR's value relevance.

Our second contingency perspective considers for whom CSR might pay. While previous research has almost exclusively viewed CSR's value from a corporate perspective, we argue that stakeholders, government and investor perspectives are also relevant. Empirically, we analyse CSR's value across 10 industry sectors from a corporate and investor aspect, respectively. We find that CSR has substantial value for corporations in the healthcare, industrials and consumer discretionary sectors, but not elsewhere. Publicly informed investors can exploit this positive CSR effect in the former two industries, which yields significantly abnormal excess returns of more than 6% and 8.5% per annum, respectively. Hence, we consider our results provide strong evidence to reject the implicit hypothesis that underpins much of the previous work that explores the homogeneous CSR/CFP relationship across industries. Our results suggest that many previous studies on CSR value that controlled for the industrial drivers of CFP but not for the industrial drivers of the CSR/CFP link, might need to be re-estimated. Furthermore, for practitioners our study implies that CSR value should be assessed in the context of the industrial business processes.

According to Barnett (2007):

> Whether corporations are "owned" by their shareholders or by society and whether they have any obligations [or ability] beyond becoming increasingly efficient at shareholder wealth production are topics that have long been fiercely debated. This debate…shows no signs of resolution and will surely remain a contentious topic for the foreseeable future. …As long as we desire capitalism with a safety net, this is a dialectic tension that our society must continuously manage, not resolve.

Doing well by doing good? Is doing good good for you? Does it pay to be good? Many papers that investigate the relationship between corporate social performance (CSP) and CFP start with such questions. Drawing on prior research that emphasises a contingency-based approach (Barnett, 2007; Rowley and Berman, 2000), we rephrase the question and ask: when and who can do well by doing good?

We investigate this question based on a theoretical elaboration of two contingency perspectives and a subsequent empirical investigation of the current implicit assumption that the CSP/CFP link across industries is homogeneous from the corporate and investor perspective. First, we extend Barnett's (2007) contingency perspective on CSR value relevance to include national framework and industrial characteristics as drivers in addition to CSR form, firm characteristics and time. Focusing on the industrial characteristics, we theorise based on a mosaic of previous suggestions and empirical observations that the CSP/CFP link is likely to be heterogeneous across industries due to industrial differences in four concepts: their dependence on individual stakeholder groups; their proximity to the end-consumers; their potential for social and environmental damage; and their level of product/service differentiation.

Second, beyond theorising a contingency perspective on when CSR might pay, we develop a second contingency perspective asking for whom CSR might pay. Although previous research almost exclusively views CSR value from the perspective of corporations, CSR might (or might not) pay for various stakeholder groups, governments or investors. While we consider various perspectives on CSR's financial impact relevant, we acknowledge that only a few perspectives can be investigated in any single empirical setting.

For a unique dataset, our empirical investigation allows us to investigate the CSP/CFP link across 10 industries from at least two perspectives: the corporate and the (publicly informed) investor perspective. We find that CSP has a significant positive effect on CFP of industries overall. However, at the industry level, we observe that CSP has at best a neutral relationship to CFP in five out of our 10 industries, while it significantly improves CFP in the industrials, healthcare and consumer discretionary sector. Moreover, we find that publicly informed investors can trade upon the positive CSR effect in the former two industries, and realise significant abnormal excess return of above 6% and above 8.5% per annum, respectively. In the third industry, however, the market appears to react to the publication of the CSP and thereby prevents investors from exploiting any positive effect. Hence, we consider our results a strong reason to reject the previously implicitly made hypothesis that the CSP/CFP link is homogeneous across industries.

Our results imply that many previous studies of the CSP/CFP link might need to be re-interpreted, as they are controlled for industrial drivers of CFP but not for industry effects on the CSP/CFP relationship. In this sense, our results open up a potential research agenda that would control for industrial heterogeneity in CSR's financial performance. Future research could also build on our study by analysing the potential heterogeneity of CSR sub-concepts (eg, employee relations, environment) across industries, exploring specific heterogeneity drivers of industrial differences in CSR value, or analysing the CSP/CFP link from new (stakeholder or government) perspectives.

This chapter is structured in six sections. The next section discusses conceptualisations of CSR, whereby we focus on its predominantly contextual and intangible nature. The second section develops our contingency perspective on when CSR pays with a specific focus on industrial characteristics as a driver. In the following section, we develop our second contingency perspective to ask for whom CSR pays. The fourth section then commences our empirical analysis by describing our datasets and methods, while the fifth section discusses our empirical results, followed by a section that reports on robustness tests.

CSR: A CONTEXTUAL, INTANGIBLE CONCEPT[1]

An agreement within a group of academics on a single precise, general definition of CSR is a very challenging and often unsuccessful task given that a wide range of views have been expressed on questions concerning the scope and priority ascribed to CSR. If one replaced the group of academics by groups of investors, corporate managers or corporate stakeholders, differences in national and industrial context would likely lead to similarly distinct views on the scope and priority of social responsibilities (Jaworski, 2007; Matten and Moon, 2008; Siegel and Vitaliano, 2007).

This contextuality of CSR has been recognised in a number of different ways. On the one extreme, writers such as van Marrewijk (2003) conclude that the search for "a 'one solution fits all' definition for CSR should be abandoned". On the other, Dahlsrud (2008), who examines 37 definitions of CSR, argues that a context specific definition of CSR would be "less useful". Between these two extreme views, for instance, lies the approach of the Global Reporting Initiative (GRI), the quasi-standard for CSR reporting worldwide. The GRI develops not only core guidelines for CSR reporting in any circumstance, but it also provides additional, complementing guidance for specific sectors and nations. Many researchers follow this intermediate position, as their definition of CSR explicitly or implicitly recognises its contextual nature (eg, Matten and Moon, 2008; Siegel and Vitaliano, 2007).

We also advocate a definition of CSR that recognises the contextuality of the concept. Inspired by Siegel and Vitaliano (2007), we define a corporation as displaying social responsibility when it engages in processes that appear to advance a general or contextual social or environmental agenda beyond legal requirements. Examples of processes advancing a general social agenda are work/life balance arrangements, supporting employee relations practices or corporate codes of ethics. These processes can be used by companies from any industry. By contrast, only car manufacturers have the context-specific opportunity to signal social responsibility through the production of hybrid vehicles. Similarly, only financial institutions have the resources to communicate social responsibility by engaging in microfinance activities.

Besides the contextuality of CSR, we emphasise that the outcomes of CSR processes are predominantly of an intangible nature. In most cases, CSR business processes aim to generate intangible assets such as reputational capital, corporate culture, legitimacy or loyalty. Only in a few cases do CSR business processes result in tangible assets – for instance, eco-efficient production technologies (Fombrun, Gardberg and Barnett, 2000; Gardberg and Fombrun, 2006; Godfrey, 2005). Notably, these intangible assets resulting from CSR are in the vast majority of cases not reflected on corporate balance sheets, as contemporary accounting standards tend not to recognise them (the main exception would be the incorporation of an acquired firm's intangible assets, such as goodwill). As a result, most corporate investments of (cash) resources in CSR are considered expenses by current accounting standards.

Hoepner (2010) argues that this expensing of corporate CSR investment could have created an accounting illusion of a positive link between corporate social and financial performance as found in the meta analyses (Allouche and Laroche, 2005; Margolis, Elfenbein and Walsh, 2007; Orlitzky, Schmidt and Rynes, 2003). He reasons that the expensing of most corporate CSR investments leads to *ad hoc* reductions in the book value of a corporation's equity and total assets. In contrast, the alternatives of not investing the respective corporate resources or investing them in tangible assets instead of CSR lead to no (immediate) expenses, and hence these alternatives have no effect on the book value of a corporation's equity and total assets (apart from minor depreciation expenses). Consequently, Hoepner argues that, even if a firm's investment in CSR has no effect on its earnings, it will increase its short-term return on equity (ROE) and return on assets (ROA), as it decreases denominators of these ratios.

ROE and ROA are the most common accounting measures applied in analyses of the link between corporate social and corporate finance performance, and an equivalent effect appears in the case of other (partially) accounting-based measures such as Tobin's q. Therefore, Hoepner (2010) suggests that the found positive link between CSP and CFP, which is mainly driven by accounting-based measures of financial performance, might represent an accounting illusion. Specifically, he writes that if a firm had the choice of investing in CSR, investing in tangible assets or not investing at all, the CSR investment would, *ceteris paribus*, lead to the highest short-term ROE or ROA.

WHEN DOES CSR PAY?

Hoepner's (2010) accounting illusion explanation is one reason why it appears premature to conclude "that there is a positive association between CSP and CFP across industries and across study contexts" (Orlitzky, Schmidt and Rynes, 2003). There are at least two other reasons.

First, if Orlitzky, Schmidt and Rynes' (2003) "universally positive relationship" between CSP and CFP were to exist, corporations could maximise their financial performance by investing unlimited resources in any CSR business process. However, it appears impossible that unlimited investments in (most) CSR business processes would increase corporate financial performance. For instance, if a corporation invested multiples of its revenue in charitable donations or corporate social reporting, contemporary market mechanisms would be virtually unable to sufficiently compensate it financially. Consequently, while the relationship between CSP and CFP might be positive within a certain range of observed CSP value, it seems unlikely that a positive relationship exists for any range of, especially very high, CSP value.

Second, Orlitzky, Schmidt and Rynes' (2003) attempt to identify one single type of relationship (positive, neutral or negative) between any CSP indicator and CFP in any industrial context fails to recognise any contextual nature of the CSR concept. It implies, for instance, that eco-efficiency projects in manufacturing industries, microfinance activities of financial institutions and donations of medicine supply in the healthcare sector are comparable activities with the same type of effect on CFP simply because they are conducted under the flag of CSR. In line with other contingency-based perspectives of CSR's impact on CFP (Barnett, 2007; Rowley and Berman, 2000), we see no theoretical reason to justify the *a priori* assumption that there is one type of relationship between CSP and CFP across industries and other analytical contexts. (We understand CSP here as the measured outcomes of CSR business processes.)

CSR's impact on CFP: A contingency perspective

Drawing on prior conceptualisations (Rowley and Berman, 2000; Ullmann, 1985), Barnett (2007) advocates a contingency perspective on the link between CSP and CFP, and calls for future research to determine the contextual circumstances in which CSR pays:

> I advocate ... a contingency perspective that affirms the payoffs to some forms of CSR for some firms at some points in time. CSR cannot financially please all of the corporations all of the time, but it can please some of the corporations some of the time. Researchers should try to figure out which ones and when.

Figure 14.1 Contingence perspective on the effect of CSR on CFP

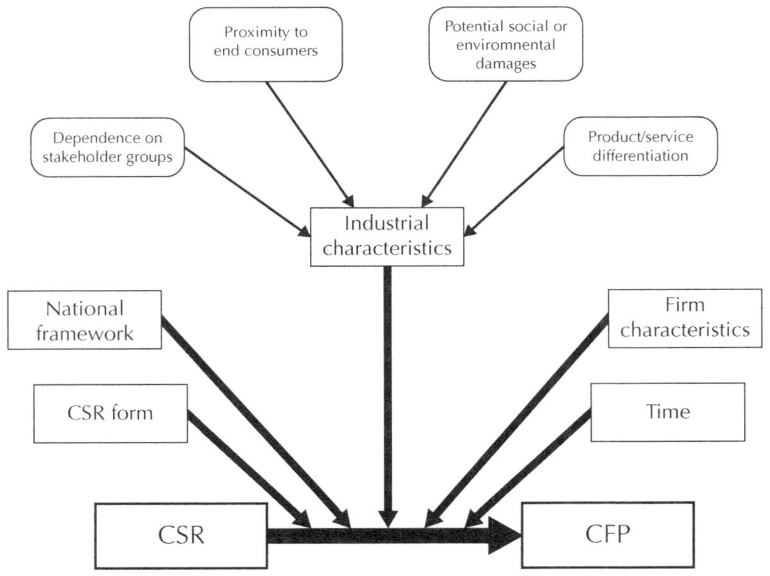

Barnett's contingency perspective is based on three main conditional dimensions: CSR form; firm characteristics; and time. Following previous studies (Matten and Moon, 2008; Rowley and Berman, 2000), we add national framework and industrial characteristics as the fourth and fifth dimension to our contingency perspective, which is illustrated in Figure 14.1.[2]

CSR form refers to specific CSR activities (eg, carbon neutrality, charitable donation, human rights policies). Since CSR represents a contextual concept, the relevance of individual CSR activities depends on its application context. For instance, while carbon neutrality is of very high relevance for stakeholders of firms in manufacturing industries or the fossil fuel sector, it is not a top priority of stakeholders of financial institutions. Consequentially, the adoption of different CSR activities across firms is in most cases not significantly correlated (Kempf and Osthoff, 2007). CSR activities also differ in how they affect CFP. Some CSR activities have a direct cost-saving effect (eg, eco-efficiency programmes); other CSR activities aim to improve employees' long-term performance (eg, employee relations); again other CSR activities attempt to build reputation capital, and so on. Therefore, different forms of CSR can fairly be expected to have non-identical effects on CFP in different application contexts.

Firm characteristics, especially firm size and the level of a firm's intangible assets, are thought of as factors that affect a firm's ability to profit from CSR activities. Stakeholder activism tends to focus on larger firms as these receive more public attention (Clark, Salo and Hebb, 2008). Similarly, CSR rating agencies tend to focus on a pool of largest companies (Schäfer *et al*, 2006). Hence, the opportunity of larger, more scrutinised firms to capitalise on CSR is likely to differ from the equivalent of smaller, less publicly watched companies. A firm's level of intangible assets has also been theorised to moderate a firm's ability to generate economic value from CSR processes. For instance, firms with a higher capacity to influence stakeholders, a better culture and working environment, or more human capital are considered to experience a greater ability to gain from CSR (Barnett, 2007; Surroca, Tribó and Waddock, 2010).

Time affects numerous variables that moderate the link between CSP and CFP, including the severity of problems deriving from accumulated corporate externalities, the speed and scope of information diffusion, consumer culture and investor culture. The more severe climate change, the quicker and more global the information diffusion about corporate irresponsibility scandals, the more value expressive consumer and investor culture, the higher should be the value relevance of CSR. For instance, it is highly unlikely that the effect of some CSR forms on CFP was the same in the post-war decade of the 1950s as in the Internet-age decade of the 2000s. Similarly, researchers would be naive to expect that the relationship between (forms of) CSP and CFP would remain constant over future decades.

National frameworks that consist of political, educational, legal and cultural systems are theorised to determine a firm's level of explicitly shown and implicitly practiced CSR activities. The reflection of national frameworks in firms' preferred CSR strategies and business processes implies that firms themselves believe national characteristics moderate the value relevance of CSR. This belief appears theoretically intuitive, since, for instance, subsidies for CSR business processes differ among political systems, fines for corporate irresponsibility differ among legal systems, or consumer and employee culture depends on a nation's cultural and educational system (Chih, Chih and Chen, 2010; Matten and Moon, 2008; Renneboog, ter Horst and Zhang, 2008b).

Industrial characteristics are the fifth condition in our contingency perspective. Since the first research question of our chapter focuses on which industries CSR pays, we conceptualise the moderating effects of industrial characteristics on the link between CSP and CFP in a separate section.

CSR's impact on CFP: Heterogeneity across industries?

Decades ago, Ullmann (1985) suggested that industries moderate the relationship between CSP and CFP. Subsequently, many researchers have reinforced calls for research on the potential heterogeneity of CSR's impact on CFP across industries (eg, Barnett, 2007; Godfrey and Hatch, 2007; Hart, 1995). However, they seem to have been nearly entirely ignored. To date, several studies into the link between CSP and CFP focus on one specific industry type (eg, Ogden and Watson, 1999; Simpson and Kohers, 2002), while a few studies investigate the moderating effects of a specific property of industries (eg, Baron, Harjoto and Jo, 2009; Hull and Rothenberg,

2008).[3] It seems, however, that no single paper analyses the effect of CSP on CFP across industries.

This lack of understanding of the CSP/CFP relationship across industries appears unfortunate for at least two reasons. First, managers, policymakers and other stakeholders would likely appreciate guidance from academia on how CSR impacts CFP in a specific industry of their interests. Particularly given the increasing public presence of corporations and consequently their occasional irresponsibility scandals, managers appear in a considerable need of knowing which CSR business processes they can implement without compromising CFP. Similarly, the crises caused by accumulated corporate externalities such as global climate change may present the question to policymakers – such as which industries can be expected to voluntarily improve their CSP and which would have to be regulated to mitigate the crises.

Second, evidence of heterogeneity of the CSP/CFP relationship across industries would have important implications for the interpretation of past and future academic research on this issue. Many previous studies have used the control variable "industry". In fact, industry is the number one control variable in Margolis and Walsh's (2001) analysis of 95 studies on the CSP/CFP relationship. However, the vast majority of these studies control only for industry drivers of CFP, but do not control for industry drivers of CSP's effect on CFP. These studies implicitly assume that the CSP/CFP relationship is homogeneous across industries. In the case of a cross-sectional or panel regression of a CFP measure on a CSP measure and a set of control variables, many studies include standalone industry dummies to capture industry effects. While industry dummies adjust industry drivers of CFP, they do not control for industry drivers of CSP's effects on CFP unless they are multiplied by the CSP variables. Therefore, if evidence would be found suggesting a heterogeneous effect of CSP on CFP across industries, the results of many previous empirical studies of multiple industry datasets should be interpreted with slightly more caution than is currently assumed. Such evidence would also imply that future research on the topic should control for the heterogeneity of the CSP/CFP relationship across industries, and that re-estimations of some previously influential studies with appropriate control variables could be fruitful.

Indeed, constructing a mosaic from many previously separated theoretical suggestions and empirical findings provides us with at least four reasons to assume that the CSP/CFP relationship is actually heterogeneous across industries. Generally, industries operate on heterogeneous business models. Business models differ in: (i) their dependence on individual stakeholder groups; (ii) their proximity to the end-consumer; (iii) their potential social or environmental damage to society or the natural environment; and (iv) their levels of product/service differentiation due to their diverse business models and different levels of competition.

Since industries differ in their dependence on various stakeholder groups, an individual stakeholder group's power, legitimacy and urgency differ in attempts to shape CSR policies and practices for various industries (Mitchell, Agle and Wood, 1997). In this sense, distinct industrial characteristics are major drivers of the outcomes and costs of CSR for companies that strategically integrate CSR into their business models (Siegel and Vitaliano, 2007). Following Porter and Kramer (2006), for instance, we argue that employee's healthcare benefits are less expensive and potentially more rewarding in industries with rather small and well-compensated workforces, such as software development, than in industries depending on large low-cost workforces such as retailing. Similarly, Padgett and Galan (2010) argue that environmental performance affects the CFP of manufacturing industries to a stronger (positive or negative) degree compared with the equivalent of other industries, since manufacturers' environmental responsibility experiences a much greater scrutiny from stakeholders. In line with these arguments, Salo (2008) finds that industries differ substantially in their environmental performance.

Industries' proximity to the end-consumers has been identified as moderating the impact of CSR on CFP. The underlying intuition of this moderator is that private end-consumers show more social concerns in their consumption than businesses in their procurement departments. Two studies seem to have empirically investigated this effect to date. Both find a positive effect of CSR on CFP in industries serving end-consumers and a negative effect in industries serving businesses (Baron, Harjoto and Jo, 2009; Curcio and Wolf, 1996). This result is supported by Lev, Petrovits and Radhakrishnan (2010), who find charitable contributions lead to a significant sales growth in consumer industries but not elsewhere. Siegel and Vitaliano's (2007) results imply that the positive effect of CSR on CFP on consumer industries could even be related to the type of consumer goods sold. They find firms that sell durable experience goods (eg, cars) or credence services (eg, financial services) display more CSR than firms selling non-durable experience goods, experience services or search goods. This implies that CSR might be most beneficial in the industries that depend heavily on the trust of end-consumers.

Industries' potential for social or environmental damage has also been suggested as a cause to heterogeneous CSP/CFP relationships across industries. On the environmental side, Derwall *et al* (2005) and Semenova and Hassel (2008) find positive effects of CSR on CFP are substantially less pronounced in environmentally problematic industries than elsewhere. Both studies explain their results as due to the higher cost of environmental performance in environmentally sensitive industries. Indeed, the results of Semenova and Hassel (2008) and Ziegler, Schroeder and Rennings (2007) suggest that the effect of an industry's environmental performance on the financial performance of a certain company might be stronger than the effect of the respective company's environmental performance itself. On the social side, a mirror effect seems to take place, since Herremans, Akathaporn and McInnes (1993) and Lee and Faff (2009) find a positive effect of CSR on CFP is more pronounced in socially problematic industries. Ziegler, Schroeder and Rennings (2007) again observe industry-level CSR dominates firm-level CSR in driving CFP. However, while they find environmentally problematic industries significantly underperform financially, they observe the opposite for socially problematic industries. All these empirical results strongly suggest that the effect of CSR on CFP could be heterogeneous across industries.

Industrial levels of product/service differentiation can be thought of as a factor that moderates the CSP/CFP link, as CSR can be viewed as a product/service differentiation strategy (McWilliams and Siegel, 2001). Indeed, empirical evidence suggests that CSR is employed to differentiate products or services (Chih, Chih and Chen, 2010; Fernández-Kranz and Santaló, 2007). However, evidence also implies that this strategy is financially more successful in industries with low levels of product/service differentiation than in highly differentiated industries (Hull and Rothenberg, 2008).

FOR WHOM DOES CSR PAY?

A vast majority of previous research on the question of whether CSR pays has taken the perspective of the corporation (Margolis, Elfenbein and Walsh, 2007; Orlitzky, Schmidt and Rynes, 2003). While the corporate view on this question is certainly important, it is not the only perspective that matters. Beyond the corporate perspective, researchers could analyse the financial performance impacts of CSR from the perspectives of various types of stakeholders, policymakers or investors. We illustrate our contingency perspective subject, for whom CSR might pay, in Figure 14.2.

Although many forms of CSR are meant to pay for the targeted stakeholder groups, they might be measured imprecisely, conducted inefficiently, or be subject to agency problems and eventually only (or predominantly) benefit CSR consultants. Empirical research on the question as to what degree various measures of corporate social performance actually translate into well-being for the targeted stakeholder seems relatively scarce in the CSR literature. For instance, Chatterjii, Levine and Toffel (2009) were the first to investigate if KLD's corporate environmental ratings have a

Figure 14.2 Contingence perspective on the subject, for whom CSR might pay

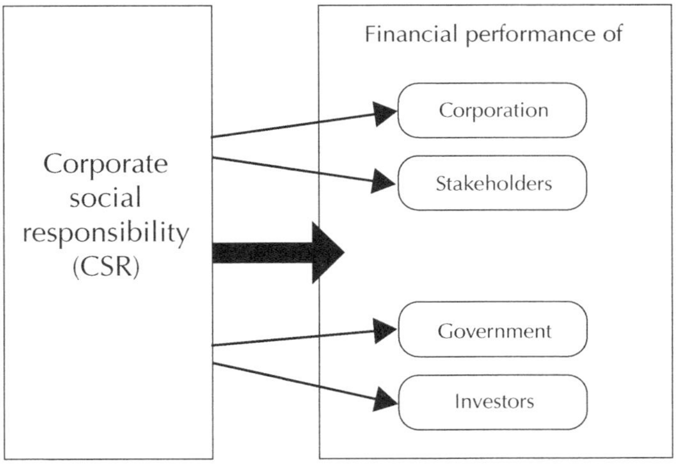

significantly positive impact on the subsequent well-being of the natural environment. While they find emissions ratings could predict future emissions, pollution prevention ratings have no significant relationship to subsequent pollution. Other interesting projects on the general question of whether CSR actually pays for certain stakeholder groups might include analyses of the degrees to which CSR budgets are spent on consultants or charitable donations arrive at the target groups.

Since CSR in many cases represents a private provision of a public good (Siegel and Vitaliano, 2007), many forms of CSR should pay from a governmental perspective. Indeed, many governments offer legislative support for social responsibility in markets (Renneboog, ter Horst and Zhang, 2008b; Riess and Welzel, 2006). However, we are not aware of any research that investigates the relationship between the degree of governmental CSR support, which is absorbed by corporations, and the degree to which policy supported CSR pays back for governments by improving national welfare levels. For instance, a promising research project could be an investigation of the relationship between employment legislation, corporate employee relations policies and national birth rates.

If CSR pays from a corporate perspective, it supposedly pays for the respective corporation's shareholders as well. However, this does not mean that CSR generally pays for investors, as the time gap between many CSR business processes and investors' awareness of these processes can be considerable. Therefore, only investors with a perfect ability to forecast CSR business processes could actually profit from each case of CSR that pays for respective corporations. As (nearly) all investors practically lack such a perfect ability for the vast majority of CSR processes, investors need to wait until specialised information providers recognise CSR business processes before they can act upon them.

Most investors acting upon CSR information are so-called responsible investors who consider the environmental or social criteria in their investment decision-making. The number and assets of these responsible investors appear important for CSR itself, since firms' CSR strategies are shown to be potentially reactive to the CSR demand from responsible investors (Mackey, Mackey and Barney, 2007), and hence a self-reinforcing process exists between responsible investment and CSR. The more responsible investors can benefit from investing in CSR, the more demand for CSR there will be. The number of responsible investors who can benefit from investing in CSR depends *inter alia* on the length of time during which a positive CSR effect allows investors to generate abnormally high returns. We differentiate among three different durations of positive CSR effects.

First, some forms of CSR might in a certain context improve CFP, but the positive effect vanishes before specialised CSR information providers can inform certain investors privately for a fee. This type of CSR effect is consistent with the strong form market efficiency hypothesis, as it implies that investors would not be able to outperform the market. Second, other contextually positive impacts of certain forms of CSR on CFP might be exploitable for investors based on private data provided by CSR information agencies. This type of CSR effect would imply temporary strong form market inefficiency, as investors could outperform the market based on private information. Third, some positive CSR effects might be so persistent that investors can still exploit them once the underlying CSR business processes are publicly announced. Such effects would imply temporary semi-strong form market inefficiency, as investors could outsmart the market based on publicly available information. Consequently, the occurrence of this third type of CSR effect is unlikely from a financial theory perspective. However, if the third type CSR effect appears, it can be expected to result in a considerable demand for CSR from investors in the respective context.

To conclude our theoretical elaborations, we advocate two contingency perspectives concerning the financial effects of CSR. First, building on previous lines of reasoning (Barnett, 2007; Rowley and Berman, 2000), we develop a contingency perspective related to when CSR pays. Our contingency perspective maintains that the form of CSR, firm characteristics, time, national framework and industrial characteristics, are the five main contextual variables moderating CSR value relevance. Our particular focus is the industrial characteristics. We argue that if the CSP/CFP relationship is heterogeneous across industries, as a mosaic composed of previous evidence on related questions indicates, the majority of previous studies of the CSP/CFP link might need to be reinterpreted as they did not control for this heterogeneity.

Second, we propose a separate contingency perspective for

research on the financial effect of CSR by asking for whom CSR pays. We very broadly distinguish among four potential beneficiaries of CSR (corporations, stakeholders, governments, investors), and briefly discuss ways in which CSR might pay for them. However, we acknowledge that it is highly unlikely, if not impossible, to find an empirical setting in which one single piece of empirical research can inform the perspectives of all four potential beneficiaries of CSR. Therefore, we encourage researchers to simply be aware of other potential beneficiaries of CSR other than the corporation itself, and suggest empirical research to focus on as many perspectives as possible if their empirical setting allows them. In this sense, our subsequent empirical analyses of when and who can do well while doing good through CSR engage in the corporate and the investor perspective.

RESEARCH DESIGN, DATA AND METHOD

Research design requirements

Based on our two research questions – (i) when does CSR pay? and (ii) for whom does CSR pay? – and our theoretical elaborations, we specify four requirements for our empirical setting. First, we aim to test the previously implicit hypothesis that the impact of CSR on financial performance is homogeneous across industries, and hence we require a dataset of CSR performance across various industries. Second, CSR represents a contextual concept. While some forms of CSR have a similar relevance to all industries (eg, codes of ethics), other forms are of high priority only for certain industries (eg, microfinance). Thus, if we adopt an unconditional measure of CSR that weights its sub-indicators identically in any industrial context, we will likely find differences in the CSP/CFP relationship among industries simply because some indicators matter more to certain industries. A robust research design, by contrast, would test the hypothesis of homogeneous CSP/CSP relationships in a setting that is least likely falsified. To generate such a setting, we need a conditional measure of CSR that weights its sub-indicators conditionally on their relevance to each industry.

Third, we aim to investigate the impact of CSR on financial performance for different industries from the corporate and the investor perspective. Therefore, our results should be able to display all three types of positive CSR effects discussed in the previous section, if in addition to a certain corporation, privately informed investors and perhaps even publicly informed investors would be able to benefit from CSR business processes. To enable us to examine all three types of positive CSR effects, we require an empirical setting in which CSR business processes are publicly announced at certain point after they are known to privately informed investors. Fourth, as we want to engage in the investor perspective, and as Hoepner (2010) has shown that the common accounting-based measures of CFP are substantially biased upwardly when related to the predominantly intangible concept CSR, we aim to use financial market-based measures of financial performance.

CSR data

To the best of our knowledge, only one unique Innovest-based data sample fulfils our first three requirements when we commenced this study. Innovest Strategic Value Advisors is one of the few CSR rating institutions that employ a conditional definition of CSR and weight their CSR sub-indicators conditionally on their relevance in an industrial setting. In contrast to the few other CSR rating agencies with conditional CSR definitions (eg, SAM, Sarasin), a specific part of Innovest's data is disclosed about one month after its availability to privately informed investors at a very high-profile event: the World Economic Forum at the end of January each year in Davos (Schäfer *et al*, 2006).

This annual publication has been offered since 2005 by Corporate Knights, a Canadian CSR-focused media company that signed Innovest to provide the CSR rating underlying its announcement of its annual list of the "Global 100 Most Sustainable Companies in the World". The 100 companies in this list are selected from the MSCI World universe based on Innovest's rating of their social performance at the end of each year. Despite the list being labelled most sustainable by Corporate Knights, it effectively displays the MSCI-listed companies with the highest CSR scores in Innovest's database whose four main criteria represent a relatively balanced set of CSR sub-areas (environment, human capital, stakeholder capital and strategic governance). The Global 100 list almost ideally meets our research design requirements, as it represents an annual rating of CSR leaders per industry, which is known to privately informed investors about one month before publicly informed investors could utilise this information. As a result, we can investigate the effect of CSR on the financial returns of corporations' privately informed investors and publicly informed investors. We analyse the effect of CSR on CFP during the year in which a firm's CSR business processes have resulted in its exceptional Innovest rating. In case Innovest's CSR rating have a significant positive effect on CFP, we can further study whether privately informed investors could exploit this in January, and if publicly informed investors could gain in the remaining months of the year.

Innovest's substantial commitment to industry-specific CSR assessments is manifested in its four-step rating process underlying the Global 100 list. First, it generates a shortlist of all MSCI World listed stocks in its large rating universe, which includes 1,800 companies whose overall CSR rating is AAA on December 31. AAA is the highest of Innovest's seven letter grades (AAA, AA, A, BBB, BB, B, C), and signals that a company is leading in its industry. Second, as Innovest is convinced that firms from different industries cannot fairly be compared in their CSR performance, it does not compare CSR performance across industries but only within industries. In line with this philosophy, Innovest calculates the Global 100 list's industry weights based on the MSCI World's industry weights in respective years. Third, Innovest analysts fill each industry's available places on the Global 100 list with those AAA-rated stocks from the shortlist that they consider the very best in the industry worldwide. Fourth, the first draft of the Global 100 list is reviewed by Innovest's director of research to ensure consistency. Following Innovest's philosophy of industry-specific CSR assessments, the companies on the Global 100 list are not ranked. Instead, the companies are presented in alphabetical order, whereby each corporation's country of jurisdiction and two-digit Global Industry Classification Standard (GICS) are displayed (Corporate Knights, 2009; Schäfer *et al*, 2006).

Following the original list, we also structure our sample according to nationality and two-digit GICS code. As 10 different two-digit GICS codes exist, we are hence investigating 10 industrial sectors: energy (GICS sector code: 10); materials (15); industrials (20); consumer discretionary (25); consumer staples (30); healthcare (35); financials (40); information technology (45); telecommunication services (50); and utilities (55).

Financial data

To assess the shareholder value and investor value of CSR, we employ financial market-based measures of financial performance (Hoepner, 2010; Mackey, Mackey and Barney, 2007; Margolis, Elfenbein and Walsh, 2007). More specifically, we aim to compare the performance of portfolios of CSR leaders in an industry with the average industrial performance while controlling for common share price drivers. At the economy-wide level, the cutting edge measure for assessing the relative stock performance is the Carhart (1997) model (eg, Edmans, 2009; Hong and Kacperczyk, 2009).

Like its origin, the capital asset pricing model (Lintner, 1965; Mossin, 1966; Sharpe, 1964), and virtually all other common financial market performance measures (eg, information ratio, Sharpe ratio), the applicability of the Carhart model is restricted to normal market conditions that offer a return premium for risk (Israelsen, 2005; Jobson and Korkie, 1981). During irregular market conditions, which exist when the equity market offers on average less return than the risk-free alternatives, the Carhart model could, for instance, display a positive financial performance for an insolvent fund. Unfortunately, the credit crisis led to such irregular market conditions that forces us to end our sample period in May 2008.[4] Therefore, we investigate the effect of CSR on CFP during the year in which a firm's CSR business processes have resulted in its exceptional Innovest rating from January 2004 to May 2008. We analyse if informed investors can benefit from potentially positive CSR effects from January 2005 to May 2008.

After cleaning our total sample from 16 companies that were acquired, merged or split during our sample period, the sample reaches 196 companies from 16 countries and all 10 GICS industry sectors, and any of which has been listed at least once on the Global 100 list announced at the World Economic Forum between 2005 and 2009.[5] Our descriptive sample statistics are displayed in Table 14.1, and show that consumer discretionary, financial and industrials are the dominant industries in the MSCI World and consequentially in our sample. The remaining industries have a similar presence, with only telecommunication services lagging somewhat behind. The most common countries in our sample are UK, US, Japan and Germany. Our 196 sample companies aggregate jointly 478 data points (individual year selection in the Global 100 list).

Table 14.1 Descriptive sample statistics

Country	Industry (GICS 2 digit code)										All industries
	Consumer discret. (25)	Consumer staples (30)	Energy (10)	Financials (40)	Health care (35)	Industrials (20)	IT (45)	Materials (15)	Telecom. services (50)	Utilities (56)	
Australia				6				3			**9**
Austria			1					1			**2**
Belgium				1							**1**
Canada			4	4					1	1	**10**
China						1					**1**
Denmark					1	1		1			**3**
Finland	1	1	1			1	2	1		1	**8**
France	3	2		2		2		1			**10**
Germany	2	1		3	1	4	1	1	1		**14**
Italy			1			1					**2**
Japan	6	1		3		6	3	1	1		**21**
Netherlands	2			2		1					**5**
Norway			1	1		1					**3**
Spain	1					3	1			1	**6**
Sweden	2			2		4	1	2			**11**
Switzerland	1	1		1	2	2	1				**8**
UK	8	5	4	12	2	5		2	3	3	**44**
US	6	2	1	6	4	6	6	3	1	3	**38**
All countries	**32**	**13**	**13**	**43**	**10**	**38**	**15**	**16**	**7**	**9**	**196**

Year of list											
2005 list	16	8	5	16	6	14	9	7	4	6	**91**
2006 list	15	9	3	15	7	14	9	9	4	7	**92**
2007 list	19	7	5	18	6	14	9	9	3	6	**96**
2008 list	18	7	6	21	6	17	8	8	3	5	**99**
2009 list	16	9	7	16	7	18	9	10	3	5	**100**
Total list memberships	**84**	**40**	**26**	**86**	**32**	**77**	**44**	**43**	**17**	**29**	**478**

Note: This table displays descriptive statistics of our sample of all companies with at least a one listing in the Global 100 list between 2005 and 2009. The columns display all 10 GICS industries with a two-digit code. The rows show how many companies in our sample from a respective country or from a respective annual list can be assigned to the respective industries. The total number of all list memberships is 478 and not 500, since companies that merged, have been acquired or split are excluded from our sample.

For all 196 companies, we downloaded monthly share prices inclusive of distributions and denoted in US dollar from Datastream. After calculating simple return for each company, we constructed two equal-weighted portfolios for each industry, which we updated on December 31st every year. The first portfolio is constructed with hindsight to analyse from the corporate perspective if CSR business processes have had a positive effect on CFP while they are conducted. This corporate perspective portfolio includes the companies that Innovest rates as top 100 CSR companies at the end of any respective year. The second portfolio takes the investor perspective. This investor perspective portfolio comprises in any year the companies that Innovest rated on December 31st of the previous year as in the top 100 CSR firms. After constructing all industrial CSR leader portfolios, we calculated their continuously compounded returns.

Estimation models

Despite the Carhart (1997) model appearing to only have previously been employed at country, region or global level, it is not limited in its applicability to geographical areas. Thus, we employ a Carhart model at the industry level, which is shown in equation 14.1.

$$r_{xp,t} = \alpha_p + \beta_p r_{xind,t} + \gamma_p SMB_{ind,t} + \delta_p HML_{ind,t} + \lambda_p MOM_{ind,t} + \varepsilon_{p,t} \quad (14.1)$$

$r_{xp,t}$, and $r_{xind,t}$, denote the continuously compounded return of portfolio *p* and industry *ind* in excess of the continuously compounded return of the risk-free asset at time *t*, respectively.[6] $SMB_{ind,t}$, $HML_{ind,t}$ and $MOM_{ind,t}$ are independent variables controlling for a firm's size, degree of intangible assets and recent share price momentum, respectively. The construction is described in Appendix 14.1. α_p represents the systematic return difference between the portfolio and its benchmark factors. Alpha's significance and magnitude determine if and how much a industrial CSR leader portfolio out/underperforms, respectively. β_p, γ_p, δ_p and λ_p are coefficients to the respective independent variables, and $\varepsilon_{p,t}$ is a random disturbance term.[7] We use this industry-level Carhart model as the baseline model for our corporate perspective portfolio.

To assess our investor perspective portfolio from the privately and publicly informed investor perspective, we add a dummy variable ($PRIV_t$) to our baseline model, which is set to one in January and to zero otherwise. In the resulting model displayed in equation 14.2, alpha informs us if and how strong publicly informed investors benefit from a potentially positive CSR effect, while the coefficient of the dummy variable (φ_p) determines if and how strong privately informed investors can exploit a potentially positive CSR effect better than publicly informed investors.

$$r_{xp,t} = \alpha_p + a_p PRIV_t + \beta_p r_{xind,t} + \gamma_p SMB_{ind,t} + \delta_p HML_{ind,t} + \lambda_p MOM_{ind,t} + \varepsilon_{p,t} \quad (14.2)$$

While our two baseline models control for all firm-specific characteristics within a national economy that are commonly known to influence stock returns, they do not control for portfolio exposure to national economies. This means that if a national equity market has performed particularly well (bad) during our sample period, an industrial CSR leader portfolio that is overexposed to this equity market will have upwards (downwards) biased financial performance estimations, and vice versa. To control for the potential impact of strong or weak performing national equity markets, we add an independent variable (R_{ortnat}) to both baseline models. It represents a column vector of all national MSCI equity market indexes in our sample, which significantly out- or underperformed the MSCI World during the respective sample period. To avoid multicollinearity problems, each national equity market control variable has been orthogonalised from the MSCI World using Elton *et al*'s (1993) orthogonalisation procedure. The resulting two models are displayed in equations 14.3 and 14.4, where θ'_p is a row vector of coefficients attached to the national control variables.

$$r_{xp,t} = \alpha_p + \beta_p r_{xind,t} + \gamma_p SMB_{ind,t} + \delta_p HML_{ind,t} + \lambda_p MOM_{ind,t} + \theta'_p R_{ortnat} + \varepsilon_{p,t} \quad (14.3)$$

$$r_{xp,t} = \alpha_p + \varphi_p PRIV_t + \beta_p r_{xind,t} + \gamma_p SMB_{ind,t} + \delta_p HML_{ind,t} + \lambda_p MOM_{ind,t} + \theta'_p R_{ortnat} + \varepsilon_{p,t} \quad (14.4)$$

DISCUSSION OF RESULTS

In which industry does CSR pay for corporations?

The results displayed in Table 14.2 clearly signal that the effect of CSR on CFP is heterogeneous across industries. Our all industry portfolio results in a Carhart model alpha of 0.26% per month, which is significant at the 5% level. If we had ignored the potential heterogeneity of CSR across industries, we could have concluded based on this all-industry estimation that our results substantially support Orlitzky, Schmidt and Rynes' (2003) "universally positive relationship" between CSP and CFP. However, as we theoretically conceptualise the heterogeneity of the CSP/CFP relationship across industries and empirically disaggregate our estimations to an industry level, we can see beyond Orlitzky, Schmidt and Rynes' general relationship between CSP and CFP.

Indeed, our results support our and other contingency perspectives on the CSP/CFP relationship (Barnett, 2007; Rowley and Berman, 2000) that suggest no general relationship between CSP and CFP exists. Despite our all-industry portfolio convincingly outperforming the MSCI World, seven (eight) out of our 10 industrial CSR leader portfolios do not outperform their industry benchmarks (when we control for country effects). Even if we consider that the energy portfolio and perhaps also the consumer staples portfolio more likely out- than underperform their benchmarks, we still find that CSR clearly does not have a positive effect on CFP in five industries, despite it clearly showing positive effects in two other industries. We interpret this discrepancy as a strong sign of the heterogeneity of the CSP/CFP relationship across industries.

The two industries with a significantly positive CSR effect on CFP are consumer discretionary and healthcare. Both fit our theoretical elaborations as they have a relatively high proximity to the end-consumer. Furthermore, both industries comprise many firms that sell durable experience goods and credence services, which Siegel and Vitaliano (2007) find display substantially more CSR than other companies in consumer industries. This implies that dependence on consumer trust might be a highly relevant moderator of the CSP/CFP relationship across industries.

The characteristics of the firms in our sample of the 100 best CSR-rated companies per year become a further indicator of the CSP/CFP link of heterogeneity across industries. While top CSR firms in the healthcare and utilities industry have substantially more intangible assets than their industry peers (as signalled by the significant negative exposure to the high minus low, HML, factor),

Table 14.2 Financial performance estimations (corporate perspective portfolios)

Industry	Alpha (in %)	βeta	γ(SMB)	δ(HML)	λ(MOM)	Country controls	Adj. R^2
All industries	0.26**	1.02***	-0.03	0.01	-0.01	No	0.92
Consumer discretionary	0.60*** 0.41**	0.96*** 0.95***	-0.05 0.00	-0.06 -0.31*	0.08 -0.11	No Yes	0.80 0.85
Consumer staples	0.29 0.29	1.40*** 1.33***	-0.26 -0.42**	0.05 0.07	0.05 0.10	No Yes	0.74 0.76
Energy	0.60 0.58	0.71*** 0.71***	-0.46*** -0.46***	0.07 0.14	-0.21 -0.22	No Yes	0.71 0.70
Financials	-0.06 -0.17	1.02*** 1.03***	-0.20 -0.22	0.38* 0.31	0.29*** 0.24**	No Yes	0.85 0.86
Health care	0.75*** 0.56**	0.80*** 0.75***	-0.34** -0.38**	-0.44*** -0.36**	-0.23 -0.22	No Yes	0.47 0.46
Industrials	0.63** 0.41	1.00*** 0.99***	-0.20 -0.22	-0.26 -0.23	0.13 0.17	No Yes	0.83 0.77
IT	0.03 -0.03	1.09*** 1.10***	-0.09 -0.03	0.28*** 0.27**	-0.08 -0.11	No Yes	0.78 0.83
Materials	-0.29 -0.34	0.88*** 0.87***	-0.28 -0.31*	-0.02 -0.03	-0.02 0.03	No Yes	0.76 0.75
Telecom. services	-0.18 -0.30	0.83*** 0.89***	0.06 0.14	-0.12 -0.12	-0.11 -0.13	No Yes	0.36 0.36
Utilities	0.03 -0.05	0.99*** 0.96***	-0.08 -0.14	-0.39* -0.45*	-0.40** -0.39*	No Yes	0.64 0.64

Note: This table reports the financial performance of an equal-weighted all-industry portfolio and our 10 corporate perspective industry CSR leader portfolios, which are displayed in the respective rows. The first estimation displayed in each row is based on equation 14.1, and the second estimation uses equation 14.3. The second column displays the alpha of a portfolio. If it is positive and significant, the respective portfolio significantly outperformed its benchmarks, and vice versa. A portfolio's exposure to the respective benchmarks is displayed in columns three to six. The seventh column indicates if country controls were employed in the regression model, and the eighth column displays the adjusted R-squared. *, ** and *** attached to a coefficient indicate significance at the 10%, 5% and 1% level, respectively. Standard errors and coefficient covariances are made heteroscedasticity- and autocorrelation-consistent based on the approach of Newey and West (1987).

Table 14.3 Financial performance estimations (investor perspective portfolios)

Industry	Alpha (in %)	βeta	γ(SMB)	δ(HML)	δ(HML)	λ(MOM)	Country controls	Adj. R^2
All industries	0.17		1.01***	-0.04	0.23**	0.03	No	0.90
Consumer discretionary	0.34		1.09***	-0.30	0.17	0.18*	No	0.81
	0.41	-0.007	1.09***	-0.33*	0.18	0.16	no	0.81
	0.22	-0.003	1.05***	-0.12	-0.21	-0.09	Yes	0.84
Consumer staples	-0.07		1.29***	-0.19	0.27	0.18**	No	0.69
	-0.21	0.01	1.34***	-0.21	0.24	0.16*	No	0.69
	-0.28	0.008	1.10***	-0.35***	0.26**	0.28***	Yes	0.76
Energy	0.15		0.84***	-0.24***	-0.22*	-0.28***	No	0.90
	0.20	-0.005	0.84***	-0.25**	-0.24*	-0.28***	No	0.89
	-0.03	-0.003	0.85***	-0.29***	-0.15	-0.26**	Yes	0.89
Financials	0.08		0.97***	0.17	0.07	0.17**	No	0.78
	0.07	0.002	0.97***	0.18	0.06	0.17**	No	0.78
	-0.20	0.004	1.01***	0.10	-0.03	0.04	Yes	0.80
Health care	0.90**		0.73***	-0.45***	-0.47***	-0.57***	No	0.48
	0.90***	-0.001	0.73***	-0.46***	-0.47***	-0.57***	No	0.47
	0.74*	0.00	0.74***	-0.47***	-0.41**	-0.54***	Yes	0.50
Industrials	0.54**		1.17***	-0.47***	-0.09	-0.03	No	0.83
	0.66***	-0.01***	1.14***	-0.54***	-0.02	-0.03	No	0.83
	0.63**	-0.012**	1.10***	-0.59***	-0.25	-0.04	Yes	0.84
IT	0.26	0.95***	0.95***	0.01	0.18*	0.10	No	0.78
	0.59	0.89***	0.89***	-0.08	0.12	0.02	No	0.80
	0.42	0.94***	0.94***	-0.04	0.16	0.00	Yes	0.79

Materials	0.32 0.58 -0.06	0.78*** 0.76*** 0.74***	0.78*** 0.76*** 0.74***	-0.75*** -0.78*** -0.73***	-0.01 -0.01 -0.05	-0.06 -0.05 -0.02	No No Yes	0.63 0.65 0.76
Telecom. services	-0.32 -0.18 -0.40	0.87*** 0.83*** 0.85***	-0.12 -0.13 -0.14	-0.12 -0.13 -0.14	0.15 0.15 0.06	-0.04 -0.03 0.01	No No Yes	0.50 0.49 0.50
Utilities	-0.06 0.05 0.01	1.04*** 1.03*** 0.97***	0.11 0.09 0.24	0.11 0.09 0.24	0.03 0.01 -0.06	-0.14 -0.17 -0.14	No No Yes	0.78 0.78 0.85

Note: This table reports the financial performance of an equal-weighted all-industry portfolio and our 10 corporate perspective industry CSR leader portfolios, which are displayed in the respective rows. The first estimation displayed in each row is based on equation 14.1, and the second estimation uses equation 14.3. The second column displays the alpha of a portfolio. If it is positive and significant, the respective portfolio significantly outperformed its benchmarks, and vice versa. A portfolio's exposure to the respective benchmarks is displayed in columns three to six. The seventh column indicates if country controls were employed in the regression model, and the eighth column displays the adjusted R-squared. *, ** and *** attached to a coefficient indicate significance at the 10%, 5% and 1% level, respectively. Standard errors and coefficient covariances are made heteroscedasticity- and autocorrelation-consistent based on the approach of Newey and West (1987).

IT firms leading in CSR have significantly under-proportional intangible assets. This implies that the suggested effect of intangible assets on the CSP/CFP link might itself be heterogeneous across industries (Barnett, 2007).

In summary, our results provide strong supports for a rejection on the implicit hypothesis that the CSP/CFP relationship is homogeneous across industries. This implies that future research on this issue might consider controlling for this heterogeneity as past research has usually controlled for the difference in industrial CFP. Furthermore, future research might find interesting research questions in a deeper exploration of the drivers of the heterogeneity of CSR impacts on CFP across industries.

In which industry does CSR pay, and for what kind of investors?

Our results from the investor perspective portfolios displayed in Table 14.3 show that the heterogeneity of the CSP/CFP relationship across industries also holds from the investor perspective during our sample period. These results are striking, as they imply at least temporary semi-strong form market inefficiency.

While investors cannot benefit from the positive CSR effect on CFP in our all-industries portfolio and in the industrial CSR leader portfolio in the consumer discretionary industry, they can exploit the positive CSR effects in the healthcare and industrials sectors. In the industrials sector, investors can achieve a significant abnormal excess return of more than 6% per annum by trading on CSR leaders. In the healthcare industry, they can even realise a significant abnormal return of above 8.5% per year. Interestingly, privately informed investors cannot exploit this effect any better in our sample than publicly informed investors in both industries.

However, this result is most likely to derive from the fact that privately informed investors have only one month per year to use their information advantages in our empirical setting instead of from a general uselessness of private information. Much to the contrary, if the top 100 CSR companies were not announced at the end of January but the end of June, private investors would probably have substantially benefited from their information advantage, since the market does not appear to react to the announcements of the top CSR companies in the healthcare and industrials sectors. In contrast, the market seems to react somewhat to the announcement of the top CSR companies in general and strongly to the announcement of the top CSR companies in the consumer discretionary sector, in which the positive CSR effect vanishes shortly after Innovest's rating. This implies that while financial markets recognise the value of CSR in some industries, such as consumer discretionary, which analysts might link to high-profile CSR advertisement, financial markets do not recognise positive CSR effects in other industries such as healthcare or industrials. Hence, our results not only support the heterogeneity of the CSP/CFP link across industries, but also imply a perceived heterogeneity of CSR value by financial market participants.

ROBUSTNESS TESTS[8]

We pursue two robustness tests. First, we estimate our portfolios value-weighted instead of equal-weighted. We select equal weighted for our main models as we aim to investigate the effect of CSR on CFP per company, not mainly in the largest companies. Moreover, some of our industrial CSR leader portfolios comprise only a few companies. Therefore, value weighting could result in some cases virtually estimating the value of CSR for one or two large companies instead of the average CSR leaders in an industry. Consequently, we consider the results of our value-weighted portfolios more erratic and less relevant than the results of our equal-weighted portfolios. However, when we estimate the value-weighted portfolios, we find the results consistent with our equal-weighted portfolios with the exception that the outperformance of the industrials portfolio vanishes.

Second, it could be that the CSP/CFP relationship is not only heterogeneous across industries but also within industries. In such a case, a few specific companies within the consumer discretionary, industrials and healthcare sector might drive the positive CSR effect, and a few specific companies in other industries might hinder a positive CSR effect. To investigate this possibility, we estimate a variation of each of our four models for each of our 196 companies. The variation of each model includes an additional dummy variable that is set to zero for years during which a company was on the Global 100 list, and set to one otherwise. This dummy variable ensures that our financial performance estimations are not systematically biased by the performance of companies during periods for which they did not receive a top 100 CSR rating. The results of these robustness tests show distributions of CSR leader performance within an industry, which does not indicate the CSP/CFP relationship is heterogeneous within industries.

CONCLUSION

Based on previous contingency perspectives (Barnett, 2007; Rowley and Berman, 2000), we presume the effect of CSR on CFP to be heterogeneous across industries. We consider the main reasons for this heterogeneity as stemming from differences among industries' dependency on certain stakeholder groups, their proximity to the end-consumer, their potential for social and environmental damage, and their degree of product/service differentiation. We advocate a second contingency perspective beyond the question concerning when CSR pays, as we also ask for whom does CSR pay? Despite previous research nearly exclusively taking the perspective of the corporations, CSR might also pay or not for stakeholders, governments or investors.

A unique empirical setting allows us to analyse the question of which industries CSR pays from the corporate and the investor perspective, whereby we can distinguish between privately informed and publicly informed investors. Our results strongly reject previously implicitly made hypothesis that the CSP/CFP link is homogeneous across industries. Of the 10 GICS sectors with a two-digit code, we find five sectors clearly display an at best neutral relationship between CSP and CFP, while the healthcare, industrials and consumer discretionary sectors display a significantly positive relationship. Moreover, investors could exploit CSR value in the former two industries, which implies at least a temporary semi-strong form inefficiency of capital markets.

Our results signal to professionals that CSR is a contextual concept whose value has to be assessed in relation to industrial business processes. For future research, our results have at least four implications. First, while past studies of the CSP/CFP relationship usually control for industry-specific drivers of CFP, they rarely control for a potential heterogeneity of the CSP/CFP relationship across industries. This implies that previous results might have to be re-interpreted and future interesting research projects might be found in re-estimating a few relevant questions.

Second, while we theoretically conceptualise drivers of the heterogeneity CSR value across industries, it is beyond the scope of this chapter to empirically test these drivers. Therefore, it might be interesting for future research to explore the sources of industrial heterogeneity. Third, our unique empirical setting provides us with the opportunity to assess the CSP/CFP link from the corporation and investor perspectives. However, this opportunity comes at the cost of only having a conditional aggregate measure of CSR. Future research might want to investigate industrial differences using conditional measures of CSR sub-constructs (eg, employee relations, environment) or even individual indicators (eg, carbon emissions, female on board). Fourth, some future research might want to challenge our and other contingency perspectives, and continue the quest for one general relationship between CSP and CFP. Such future research might consider controlling for a potential heterogeneity of CSR value at the industry level to sharpen estimations and avoid bias. In this sense, we hope that this chapter can bring the potential heterogeneity of CSR impacts on CFP into the attention span of researchers in this field.

APPENDIX 14.1

We construct our control factors $SMB_{ind,t}$, $HML_{ind,t}$ and $MOM_{ind,t}$ for each of our 10 GICS sectors with the online research tool of Style Research Ltd, which is based on the Worldscope database. Our factor construction follows previous studies (Bauer, Koedijk and Otten, 2005; Renneboog, Ter Horst and Zhang, 2008a) that constructed the same factors using Style Research Ltd at the national level.

The size factor SMB (small minus big) is constructed as the return difference between the stocks in the lower half of a market capitalisation-ranked industry stock universe and the stocks in the upper half of the same universe. The intangible assets factor HML (high minus low) is based on an industry stock universe ranked according to book value to market value ratio, which can be viewed as the inverse of a company's intangible assets (Lev, 2003). HML represents the return of the top 30% minus that of the bottom 30% of this universe ranked according to book to market value ratios. The momentum factor MOM is based on an industry stock universe ranked according to each stock's return over the previous 12 months. It represents the return difference between the top 30% (previous winners) and the bottom 30% (previous losers). The MOM factor is updated monthly, while the SMB and HML factor are updated annually at the end of June in line with Fama and French (1993). All portfolios are value-weighted and based on one-month lagged information.[9]

We would like to thank Toby Heaps, Matthew Kiernan, Michael Rezec, John Wilson and seminar participants at the Universities of Dundee, the University of St. Andrews and the Corporate Responsibility Research conference in Belfast for their comments. We are indebted to Robert Schwob of Style Research Ltd for data provision. Any remaining errors or omissions are our sole responsibility.

1 Some professionals and academics have begun to rename the concept of corporate social responsibility with the maybe slightly more precise term "corporate sustainability". We recognise this development and understand both terms as synonyms. We use the traditional term – corporate social responsibility – here, as it is still more common (Salzmann, Ionescu-Somers and Steger, 2005; van Marrewijk, 2003).

2 We consider our fourth and fifth condition (national framework and industry characteristics) to jointly comprise Rowley and Berman's (2000) institutional environment and stakeholder environment concept.

3 In addition to these two types of studies relating industries to the CSP/CFP link, Heinze, Sibary and Sikula, Sr. (1999) analyse the effect of Fortune's financial soundness and long-term investment value rating on its CSR rating using the largest eight to 10 companies in each of 22 manufacturing industries. As their findings are neither based on more than a single year of perceptional Fortune ratings nor controlled for potential multicollinearity of the two independent CFP variables, their information value regarding CFP's effect on CSP appears inconsequential.

4 Unfortunately, we cannot extend our sample period substantially beyond the credit crisis, since Innovest and Corporate Knights abandoned their collaboration when Innovest was acquired by RiskMetrics in February 2009. Subsequently, both partners separately continued to publish a list of 100 companies with highest CSR ratings, but both new lists are incompatible with the previous list. RiskMetrics uses the Innovest ratings and a slightly modified method to announce a Global ESG 100 list at the end of January. However, while Innovest and Corporate Knights joint venture was announced publicly at the high profile World Economic Forum, RiskMetrics new list is announced on its website and only available to registered users. Hence, even if the RiskMetrics list would have a compatible method to the previous list, the communication to the publicly informed investor is incompatible. Corporate Knights continues its World Economic Forum announcements its Global 100 list at the World Economic Forum in Davos, but they have worked with different CSR rating agencies since 2010.

5 A list of sample companies and a list of excluded companies is available upon request.

6 The return for each GICS industry sector represents the respective MSCI Industry index retrieved from Datastream inclusive of distributions. To arrive at our risk-free asset return, we transform the investment yield of the four weeks US Treasury bill stated as arithmetically calculated per annum return in a monthly risk-free return in a two-step process. First, we arithmetically transform the annual figure in a 28-days return using 365.25 days per year. Second, we geometrically transform the 28-days return in a monthly (30.4375 day) risk-free return.

7 The random disturbance term captures all of a portfolio's return variation that cannot be systematically related to the regression equation's independent variables or its constant.
8 The results of our robustness tests are available upon request.
9 As Style Research Ltd does not offer the construction of the size and book to market factor precisely according to Fama and French (1993), we follow Renneboog, ter Horst and Zhang's (2008a) slightly amended procedure. Renneboog, ter Horst and Zhang (2008a) find that their "factors are virtually identical" to that of Fama and French (1993).

REFERENCES

Allouche, J. and P. Laroche, 2005, "A Meta-analytical Investigation of the Relationship Between Corporate Social and Financial Performance", *Revue de Gestion des Ressources Humaines,* 57(3), pp. 18–41.

Barnett, M. L., 2007, "Stakeholder Influence Capacity and the Variability of Financial Returns to Corporate Social Responsibility", *Academy of Management Review,* 32(3), pp. 794–816.

Baron, D. P., M. A. Harjoto and H. Jo, 2009, "The Economics and Politics of Corporate Social Performance", Stanford University Graduate School of Business Research Paper No. 1993 (available at http://papers.ssrn.com/sol3/papers.cfm?abstract_id=1202390).

Bauer, R., K. G. Koedijk and R. Otten, 2005, "International Evidence on Ethical Mutual Fund Performance and Investment Style", *Journal of Banking & Finance,* 29, pp. 1,751–67.

Carhart, M. M., 1997, "On Persistence in Mutual Fund Performance", *Journal of Finance,* 52(1), pp. 57–82.

Chatterjii, A. K., D. L. Levine and M. W. Toffel, 2009, "How Well Do Social Ratings Actually Measure Corporate Social Responsibility?', *Journal of Economics and Management Strategy,* 18(1), pp. 125–69.

Chih, H.-L., H.-H. Chih and T.-Y. Chen, 2010, "On the Determinants of Corporate Responsibility: International Evidence on the Financial Industry", *Journal of Business Ethics,* 93(1), pp. 115–35.

Clark, G. L., J. Salo and T. Hebb, 2008, "Social and Environmental Shareholder Activism in the Public Spotlight: US Corporate Annual Meetings, Campaign Strategies, and Environmental Performance, 2001–2004", *Environment and Planning A,* 40(6), pp. 1,370–90.

Corporate Knights, 2009, "The Global 100 Methodology".

Curcio, R. J. and F. M. Wolf, 1996, "Corporate Environmental Strategy: Impact on Firm Value", *Journal of Financial and Strategic Decisions,* 9(2), pp. 21–31.

Dahlsrud, A., 2008, "How Corporate Social Responsibility is Defined: An Analysis of 37 Definitions", *Corporate Social Responsibility and Environmental Management,* 15(1), pp. 1–13.

Derwall, J., N. Guenster, R. Bauer and K. G. Koedijk, 2005, "The Eco-efficiency Premium Puzzle", *Financial Analysts Journal,* 61(2), pp. 51–63.

Edmans, A., 2009, "Does the Stock Market Fully Value Intangibles? Employee Satisfaction and Equity Prices", *Journal of Financial Economics,* **101**(3), pp. 621–40 (available at http://papers.ssrn.com/sol3/papers.cfm?abstract_id=985735#PaperDownload).

Elton, E. J., M. J. Gruber, S. Das and M. Hlavka, 1993, "Efficiency with Costly Information: A Reinterpretation of Evidence from Managed Portfolios", *Review of Financial Studies,* 6(1), pp. 1–22.

Fama, E. F. and K. R. French, 1993, "Common Risk Factors in the Returns on Stocks and Bonds", *Journal of Financial Economics,* 33(1), pp. 3–53.

Fernández-Kranz, D. and J. Santaló, 2007, "When Necessity Becomes Virtue: The Effect of Product Market Competition on Corporate Social Responsibility", working paper, Instituto de Empresa Business School (available at http://papers.ssrn.com/sol3/papers.cfm?abstract_id=997007).

Fombrun, C. J., N. A. Gardberg and M. L. Barnett, 2000, "Opportunity Platforms and Safety Nets: Corporate Citizenship and Reputational Risk", *Business and Society Review,* 105(1), pp. 85–106.

Gardberg, N. A. and C. J. Fombrun, 2006, "Corporate Citizenship: Creating Intangible Assets Across Institutional Environments", *Academy of Management Review,* 31(2), pp. 329–46.

Godfrey, P. C., 2005, "The Relationship Between Corporate Philanthropy and Shareholder Wealth: A Risk Management Perspective", *Academy of Management Review,* 30(4), pp. 777–98.

Godfrey, P. C. and N. W. Hatch, 2007, "Researching Corporate Social Responsibility: An Agenda for the 21st Century", *Journal of Business Ethics,* 70(1), pp. 87–98.

Hart, S. L., 1995, "A Natural-resource-based View of the Firm", *Academy of Management Review,* 20(4), pp. 986–1,014.

Heinze, D., S. Sibary and A. Sikula, Sr., 1999, "Relations Among Corporate Social Responsibility, Financial Soundness and Investment Value in 22 Manufacturing Industry Groups", *Ethics & Behaviour,* 9(4), pp. 331–47.

Herremans, I. M., P. Akathaporn and M. McInnes, 1993, "An Investigation of Corporate Social Responsibility Reputation and Economic Performance", *Accounting, Organizations and Society,* 18(7/8), pp. 587–604.

Hoepner, A. G. F., 2010, "Corporate Social vs. Financial Performance Research: Could the Positive Link be an Accounting Illusion?", working paper, School of Management, University of St. Andrews.

Hong, H. and M. Kacperczyk, 2009, "The Price of Sin: The Effects of Social Norms on Markets", *Journal of Financial Economics,* 93(1), pp. 15–36.

Hull, C. E. and S. Rothenberg, 2008, "Firm Performance: The Interactions of Corporate Social Performance with Innovation and Industry Differentiation", *Strategic Management Journal,* 29, pp. 781–89.

Israelsen, C. L., 2005, "A Refinement to the Sharpe Ratio and Information Ratio", *Journal of Asset Management,* 5(6), pp. 423–27.

Jaworski, W., 2007, "Use of Extra-financial Information by Research Analysts and Investment Managers", European Center for Corporate Engagement.

Jobson, J. D. and B. M. Korkie, 1981, "Performance Hypothesis Testing with the Sharpe and Treynor Measures", *Journal of Finance,* 36(3), pp. 889–908.

Kempf, A. and P. Osthoff, 2007, "The Effect of Socially Responsible Investing on Portfolio Performance", *European Financial Management,* 13(5), pp. 908–22.

Lee, D. D. and R. W. Faff, 2009, "Corporate Sustainability Performance and Idiosyncratic Risk: A Global Perspective", *The Financial Review,* 44(2), pp. 213–37.

Lev, B., 2003, "Remarks on the Measurement, Valuation, and Reporting of Intangible Assets", *Economic Policy Review,* 9, pp. 17–22.

Lev, B., C. Petrovits and S. Radhakrishnan, 2010, "Is Doing Good Good For You? How Corporate Charitable Contributions Enhance Revenue Growth", *Strategic Management Journal,* 31(2), pp. 182–200.

Lintner, J., 1965, "The Valuation of Risk Assets and the Selection of Risky Investments in Stock Portfolios and Capital Budgets", *Review of Economics and Statistics,* 47(1), pp. 13–37.

Mackey, A., T. Mackey and J. Barney, 2007, "Corporate Social Responsibility and Firm Performance: Investor Preferences and Corporate Strategies", *Academy of Management Review,* 32(3), pp. 817–35.

Margolis, J. D., H. A. Elfenbein and J. P. Walsh, 2007, "Does it Pay to be Good? An Analysis and Redirection of Research on the Relationship Between Corporate Social and Financial Performance", working paper, Harvard University.

Margolis, J. D. and J. P. Walsh, 2001, "People and Profits? The Search for a Link Between a Company's Social and Financial Performance", Lawrence Erlbaum Associates.

Matten, D. and J. Moon, 2008, "'Implicit' and 'Explicit' CSR: A Conceptual Framework for a Comparative Understanding of Corporate Social Responsibility", *Academy of Management Review,* 33(2), pp. 404–24.

McWilliams, A. and D. Siegel, 2001, "Corporate Social Responsibility: Theory of the Firm Perspective", *Academy of Management Review,* 26(1), pp. 117–27.

Mitchell, R. K., B. R. Agle and D. J. Wood, 1997, "Toward a Theory of Stakeholder Identification and Salience: Defining the Principle of Who and What Really Counts", *Academy of Management Review,* 22(4), pp. 853–86.

Mossin, J., 1966, "Equilibrium in a Capital Asset Market", *Econometrica,* 34(4), pp. 768–83.

Newey, W. K. and K. D. West, 1987, "A Simple, Positive Semi-definite, Heteroskedasticity and Autocorrelation Consistent Covariance Matrix", *Econometrica,* 55(3), pp. 703–8.

Ogden, S. and R. Watson, 1999, "Corporate Performance and Stakeholder Management: Balancing Shareholder and Consumer Interests in the UK Privatized Water Industry", *Academy of Management Journal,* 42(5), pp. 526–38.

Orlitzky, M., F. L. Schmidt and S. L. Rynes, 2003, "Corporate Social and Financial Performance: A Meta-analysis", *Organization Studies,* 24(3), pp. 403–41.

Padgett, R. C. and J. I. Galan, 2010, "The Effect of R&D Intensity on Corporate Social Responsibility", *Journal of Business Ethics,* 93, pp. 407–18.

Porter, M. E. and M. R. Kramer, 2006, "Strategy & Society: The Link Between Competitive Advantage and Corporate Social Responsibility", *Harvard Business Review,* 84(12), pp. 78–92.

Renneboog, L., J. ter Horst and C. Zhang, 2008a, "The Price of Ethics and Stakeholder Governance: The Performance of Socially Responsible Mutual Funds", *Journal of Corporate Finance,* 14(3), pp. 302–22.

Renneboog, L., J. ter Horst and C. Zhang, 2008b, "Socially Responsible Investments: Institutional Aspects, Performance, and Investor Behaviour", *Journal of Banking & Finance,* 32(9), pp. 1,723–42.

Riess, B. and C. Welzel, 2006, "Partner Staat? CSR-Politik in Europa", Bertelsmann Stiftung.

Rowley, T. and S. Berman, 2000, "A Brand New Brand of Corporate Social Performance", *Business & Society,* 39(4), pp. 397–418.

Salo, J., 2008, "Corporate Governance and Environmental Performance: Industry and Country Effects", *Competition and Change,* 12(4), pp. 328–54.

Salzmann, O., A. Ionescu-Somers and U. Steger, 2005, "The Business Case for Corporate Sustainability: Literature Review and Research Options", *European Management Journal,* 23(1), pp. 27–36.

Schäfer, H., J. Beer, J. Zenker and P. Fernandes, 2006, "Who is Who in Corporate Social Responsibility Rating? A Survey of Internationally Established Rating Systems that Measure Corporate Responsibility", Bertelsmann Foundation.

Semenova, N. and L. G. Hassel, 2008, "Industry Risk Moderates the Relation between Environmental and Financial Performance", Sustainable Investment Research Platform Working Papers, 08–02, September (available at http://web.abo.fi/fak/esf/fei/redovisa/kurser/Lasse/Mistra%20wp/sirp%20wp%2008–02%20Semenova%20and%20Hassel.pdf).

Sharpe, W. F., 1964, "Capital Asset Prices: A Theory of Market Equilibrium under Conditions of Risk", *Journal of Finance,* 19(3), pp. 425–42.

Siegel, D. S. and D. F. Vitaliano, 2007, "An Empirical Analysis of Strategic Use of Corporate Social Responsibility", *Journal of Economics & Management Strategy,* 16(3), pp. 773–92.

Simpson, W. G. and T. Kohers, 2002, "The Link Between Corporate Social and Financial Performance: Evidence from the Banking Industry", *Journal of Business Ethics,* 35(2), pp. 97–109.

Surroca, J., J. A. Tribó and S. Waddock, 2010, "Corporate Responsibility and Financial Performance: The Role of Intangible Resources", *Strategic Management Journal,* 31(5), pp. 463–90.

Ullmann, A. A., 1985, "Data in Search of a Theory: A Critical Examination of the Relationships Among Social Performance, Social Disclosure, and Economic Performance of U.S. Firms", *Academy of Management Review,* 10(3), pp. 540–57.

van Marrewijk, M., 2003, "Concepts and Definitions of CSR and Corporate Sustainability: Between Agency and Communion", *Journal of Business Ethics,* 44(2–3), pp. 95–105.

Ziegler, A., M. Schroeder and K. Rennings, 2007, "The Effect of Environmental and Social Performance on the Stock Performance of European Corporations", *Environmental and Resource Economics,* 37(4), pp. 661–80.

15

Reflecting on how ESG investing, accounting and governance have evolved over time

Jill Frances Atkins

Cardiff Business School

This chapter reflects on the past, present and future of ESG investment, with a personal academic perspective on changes in the investment industry, predominantly in a UK context. As an academic researcher for around 30 years, I have been fortunate enough to be able to explore, track and assess the evolution of the ESG movement in the investment industry, but also more recently in the accounting sphere. When I was asked to contribute a chapter for this important new book, I decided to provide something quite unusual for an academic: a personal reflection. It seems an appropriate moment in time, from a personal point of view, but also in terms of contributing to practitioner developments as well as to academic research, to reflect on the ways in which the ESG "movement" has grown from its early roots in the UK, and through pockets of activity in other parts of the world, to a global phenomenon and a worldwide agenda for action, advocacy and emancipation in finance, accounting and governance. Another reason for adopting an autobiographical approach is to demonstrate the perennial close relationship between academia and practice in the accounting and finance discipline.

It may be obvious to many that academics in accounting and finance research practice, and in so doing "track" developments in practice, researching new developments through the gathering of data, and develop models and theoretical frameworks that seek to "explain" practice. However, less well acknowledged in my view is the influence of academic research on the industry. The relatively recent focus in the UK academic environment on the "impact" of research demonstrates the need for academics to be able to show the influence their work has on practice. This evolving emphasis in academic performance management is seen by some as suggesting that academic research "impact" is a new idea.

Certainly, the need to be able to demonstrate the social, environmental and economic impact of academic research on practice, on the "real world", through the composition of detailed impact case studies that include evidence of impact, is a relatively new, and clearly important, phenomenon. However, the actual impact of academic research on practice has always been there. Dialogic, two-way relationships between academic accounting research, for example, and practice are not a 21st Century phenomenon. Accounting academics have helped to shape the development of the accounting profession, of financial reporting and financial accounting, for decades. This is also clearly the case in the area of socially responsible investment (SRI). This chapter seeks to reflect on the ways in which ongoing dialogue between academics and practitioners in the ESG investment and accounting area has led to mutually beneficial relationships and positive outcomes for both practice and research.

My personal "story" *per se* may not be of particular interest to readers, but in this chapter I intend to demonstrate the growth and evolution of ESG through my own experiences of researching this evolution, as well as commenting on people and events that I feel have been most influential in the development of the ESG global phenomenon.

A RESEARCH STORY

Starting with a little autobiographical information, I received my PhD in finance in 1996 and the thesis focused on foreign currency exposure and foreign exchange risk management. In 1998, I worked on the first of many funded research projects that focused on the broad and newly evolving area of corporate governance, but specifically on the emerging practice of institutional investor engagement and dialogue, as well as the emergence of SRI. Funding from the Nuffield Foundation allowed several colleagues and I to start working in this fascinating new area. This first project saw the start of my long-term interest in the evolution of responsible investment. The research initially involved distributing a postal questionnaire to an extensive sample of UK unit trusts, pension funds and investment trusts. The study was the first to examine the impact of the 1992 Cadbury Report's recommendations to the institutional investment community to take a more active role in corporate governance through engagement and dialogue. The findings resulted in some of the first publications to address shareholder engagement activity (Solomon and Solomon, 1999; Solomon *et al*, 2000), as well as an influential paper on institutional investors views on corporate risk disclosure in *British Accounting Review* (Solomon, 1999).

From our research, we realised that the nascent practice of institutional investor engagement and dialogue recommended in the initial Cadbury Report seemed to be transforming the investment industry in the UK, and then gradually elsewhere from the mid-1990s. I found the whole emergence of this new "relationship investing" absolutely fascinating: an acknowledgment that people, psychology and one-on-one relationships were becoming seen as crucial to corporate behaviour due to the potential influence of large-scale investors on their investee companies. More than this, the idea that institutional investors could act as a "force for good" in the world, driving companies towards more positive societal and environmental outcomes, intrigued me.

Although there was some existing research into "ethical investment" by the end of the 1990s, it was largely restricted to quantitative studies that sought to compare the financial returns of dedicated "ethical portfolios" with those of "unethical portfolios" and funds – in other words, those that did not screen on an ethical basis ("ethically neutral" may be a more appropriate term). Results were mixed and there was very little evidence that an ethical investment approach could lead to enhanced financial returns from investment. However, as anyone with basic knowledge of finance knows, reducing a portfolio's scope and limiting the number of industries that an investor includes in their portfolio is accompanied by a reduction in return. Early negative screening approaches, where consumer-led ethical investors bought into portfolios that excluded, for example, companies in the energy industry, or companies involved in alcohol production, immediately limited the potential returns to their investment. The potential for these early forms of ethical investment to grow was also therefore delimited by these basic financial facts. Negative screening also led to a societal negative impression of ethical investment associated with making a choice between profit and ethics; it has taken a long time for responsible investment to shake off this characterisation.

It was only around the turn of the century that the true potential for investment to court higher financial returns from investment, leading to the widely celebrated "win–win" scenario, began to become a reality. The shift from ethical investment to SRI strategies based on a "best of sector" approach meant that whole industries would not be excluded, and investors could focus on best performers across social, environmental and ethical (SEE) outcomes. Of course, the measurement of these outcomes was then, as it is now, difficult. This is where accounting started to play a significant role in the evolution of the ESG phenomenon. Social and environmental accounting practices at the beginning of the 21st century represented really the only information available to investors and analysts for discerning between companies and identifying those with better social and environmental practices.

Just after the turn of the century, the UK's Association of British Insurers (ABI) began to provide guidelines on the type of information they wanted companies to disclose on SEE issues. Over time, the focus moved towards accounting for ESG issues.

The growth in what we now call ESG accounting has followed, indeed arisen from, the growing demand from the institutional investment industry for this type of information for investor decision-making purposes. Of course, there have been other well-documented drivers of social and environmental accounting, including corporate attempts to gain and maintain a social licence to operate (a legitimacy theory approach), reputational risk management, societal shifts in attitude, legislation. However, the investment industry has acted, and still acts, as one of the most, if not the most, significant drivers of ESG accounting.

Returning to the late 1990s, the funding provided by the Nuffield Foundation gave me and my co-authors the ability to travel to London on a weekly basis and interview the pioneers of the SRI movement. We were fortunate enough to meet some of the first "movers and shakers" in the industry,[1] discussing SEE issues with them, their engagement practices, as well as asking them where they thought the SRI movement would go in the future. The interviews were so informative, and the interviewees were keen to speak to us and to talk about their experiences and ideas. At that time, research always involved some wonderful lunches in London that provided the potential for some life-long friendships and collaborations.

I have to admit that my preconceptions as a "hard" finance academic, coming from an econometrics-based, positivist and economics background, were extremely sceptical. I expected to meet people who were at best "doing" SRI for reputational and impression management purposes, or at worst pretending to do SRI as a simple box-ticking exercise, with absolutely no interest in people or the planet. However, I was completely wrong – with every interview it became increasingly obvious that the people at the vanguard of this growing SRI movement were not just interested in and committed to SRI, but were passionate and deeply personally motivated. This was also the point when, as an academic I began my own transformational journey towards becoming an interpretive researcher, who shifted to qualitative research methods and ultimately moved completely away from econometrics and statistical approaches.

On the basis of the findings from our first research project, we applied for more funding and were awarded a further grant from the Nuffield Foundation for a project entitled "An Investigation into Institutional Investors' Attitudes towards Socially Responsible Investment (SRI)" in 2000. This project, for which I was the principal investigator (PI), built on the research conducted for the earlier Nuffield Foundation research grant. We interviewed 20 senior members of the UK institutional investment industry who were involved in SRI and SEE engagement, as well as 19 representatives from UK listed companies in the FTSE 100. Using the funds, we employed a research assistant to carry out some of the interviews and to transcribe them. The project resulted in several publications in leading academic journals, including one on impression management on SRI engagement (termed "private social and environmental reporting" in the accounting literature; Solomon *et al*, 2013), a theoretical paper (Solomon and Darby, 2005) and a paper focusing on institutional investor engagement on climate change risk (Solomon *et al*, 2011).

Again, these findings provided the underpinning for further research funding, this time from the Association of Chartered Certified Accountants (ACCA, 2009), to explore pension fund trustees and climate change. I was invited to propose (as chair of a forum) and run this project for the ACCA with Economic and Social Research Council (ESRC) funds, awarded to investigate a relevant issue in the accountability of the financial services industry. The project involved 40 interviews with trustees from the pension funds of leading UK companies to ascertain their awareness and knowledge base regarding climate change issues, as well as their understanding of their fiduciary duty in this area.

This research led to two research monographs published by ACCA, the second being a series of interviews with trustees one year on to evaluate progress. The report, "Pension Funds and Climate Change" (Solomon, 2009), had considerable impact through a variety of media. ACCA held a launch for the two research reports in September 2009 that was attended by a large number of practitioners. For example, its findings were summarised in Business Green, a website dedicated to environmental issues in business with a broad readership. This summary of the reports argues that trustees were guilty of ignoring the benefits associated with ethical investment. There was also coverage of this research at the time by Manifest, the City voting agency. In addition, the paper was discussed in an article in *Accountancy Futures* in 2010. This in itself demonstrates the strong ties between accounting and finance academia and practice in the past.

In 2013, I started working with a South African colleague from the University of the Witwatersrand, Warren Maroun, and we were awarded funding from ACCA to explore institutional investors' perceptions of integrated reporting. This meant extending earlier work into institutional investor engagement as well as investors' demand for social and environmental information into a South African context, given the then-emergence of integrated reporting within the South African governance environment. The funding allowed us to conduct a series of interviews with institutional investors in South Africa to gauge their reactions to the introduction of integrated reporting in South Africa, resulting in an ACCA research report (Solomon and Maroun, 2012).

Reflecting on shifts in the industry, it is fair to say that ESG emerged around 2006, mainly as a result of the United Nations Principles for Responsible Investment (UNPRI) initiative and the associated Principles. The language changed across the investment industry from "socially responsible investment" to "responsible investment", with the issues addressed shifting from SEE to ESG around this time. However, ESG as a terminology was couched primarily within the investment industry and applied to investor engagement. It is only latterly, really during the global pandemic, that we have seen ESG move into the accounting field. Integrated reporting from its earliest framework integrates social, environmental and economic issues, so the now global shift to adopting the ESG terminology across accounting and finance denotes the way in which practitioners are beginning to see governance as being inextricably linked with social and environmental factors. Or that they are now adopting a holistic view of governance and accountability that brings social and environmental issues into the heart of corporate behaviour, corporate disclosure and institutional investor engagement. Table 15.1 tracks various influences on the growth of ESG investment, focusing on the UK context. This list is not meant to be exhaustive, but rather illustrative of some of the forces driving the shift in institutional investor practice.

One of the most significant influences is the publication of the 2020 Stewardship Code, where ESG issues can be seen to be increasingly integrated into the form of institutional investment engagement and action expected of signatories to the Code. For example, Principle 1 states: "Signatories' purpose, investment beliefs, strategy, and culture enable stewardship that creates long-term value for clients and beneficiaries leading to sustainable benefits for the economy, the environment and society". We take sustainable here to imply the integration of social and environmental issues, as well as financial and economic. Indeed, an integrated ESG approach is made far more explicit in Principle 7, which specifies: "Signatories systematically integrate stewardship and investment, including material environmental, social and governance issues, and climate change, to fulfil their responsibilities". An ESG approach is no longer an add-on but is an expected and desirable part of institutional

Table 15.1 Tracking influences on the growth of ESG investment in the UK[2]

1992	Cadbury Report published the first policy document to stress the importance of institutional investor engagement with investee companies
1997	Huntingdon Life Science UK – institutional investors and later US investors pulled out over animal rights' abuses
2000	Global Reporting Initiative (GRI) guidelines launched, the first on sustainability reporting (they are now in their fourth generation)
2001	FTSE4Good Index Series launched – these UK SRI indexes include companies that are rated as performing well across ESG criteria
2001	Changes to the UK pension fund law made it a mandatory requirement for all institutional investors to disclose in the Statement of Investment Principles the extent to which, if at all, they consider social, ethical and environmental issues in their investment decision-making
2002	Institutional Shareholders' Committee (ISC) Code published – the Responsibilities of Institutional Shareholders and Agents: Statement of Principles established a benchmark for institutional investor practice in the areas of engagement and voting
2001	Association of British Insurers' (ABI) SEE reporting guidelines published, which indicate what SEE information institutional investors would like to see disclosed
2000	Carbon Disclosure Project (CDP) launched – this global institutional investors' collaborative group asks companies to complete an annual survey on carbon emissions and related information
2005	Freshfields Bruckhaus Derringer Report published, which specified that consideration of ESG issues be part of a pension fund's fiduciary duty where there was a consensus among pension fund members that ESG issues were deemed material
2006	Stern Review published, which stated scientific consensus on global warming and had an immediate impact on society
2006	Revision of UK company law that provided legal endorsement for companies to consider stakeholders in their decision-making
2006	UN endorsement of PRI, which provided them with greater international profile, and facilitated the introduction of the ESG concept into responsible investment
2007	ABI revised guidelines alter terminology from SEE to ESG disclosure
2009	King Code of Governance Principles (King III) embedded integrated reporting into corporate governance
2010	Stewardship Code published ISC Code, which was adopted by the Financial Reporting Council (FRC) as a code aimed at enhancing the quality of engagement between institutional investors and companies
2010	BP crisis: the high-profile oil spill in the Gulf of Mexico highlighted the financial nature of ESG risk
2010	PRI Clearinghouse's establishment of the Clearinghouse Engagement Platform marked a distinct step towards greater collaborative activism among global institutional investors on ESG issues

2011	Fair Pensions Report published, which specified the need for pension funds to redefine fiduciary duty to incorporate broader issues such as ESG
2015	Launch of the Sustainable Development Goals (SDGs)
2016	King IV Report on Corporate Governance enabled greater integration of ESG issues
2020	The start of the global pandemic shed light on poor social and environmental practices, and highlighted the interconnectedness between nature and business/investment
2020	Stewardship Code was updated with a greater focus on ESG
2021	EU's Sustainable Finance Disclosure Regulation (SFDR, EU Directive 2019/2088) required asset managers to report on the sustainability characteristics of their investments

investors' practice according to this Code, which lays the basis for good corporate governance for the investment industry.

Of course, we can only expect a strong focus on ESG by the latest PRI framework, and consideration of the six Principles demonstrates the critical importance of enshrining ESG at the heart of institutional investment for all PRI signatories.[3] The magnitude of the shift towards ESG investment is clear, as at the start of 2020 global responsible/sustainable investment had reached US$35.5 trillion across five major markets, representing a 15% increase in two years (GSIA, 2021). The latest statistics show that sustainable investment assets under management constitute a total of 35.9% of total global assets under management. These figures alone demonstrate the potential power of institutional investors to hold companies to account, and drive social and environmental accountability.

Our research focus has narrowed to exploring the ways in which the investment industry and accounting are addressing the crisis arising from biodiversity loss, species extinctions, and their financial and business ramifications. Again, the work involved raising funding, this time from the British Academy Research Funding Small Grants Scheme for a project entitled "Engaging Business on the State of Nature: Exploring the Implementation of an Extinction Accounting Framework for Integrated Reporting and Responsible Investment". This funding allowed us to develop further the extinction accounting framework that we had been working on, and to gauge the views of institutional investors on this framework. This research led to a book on *The Business of Bees* (Atkins and Atkins, 2016) that examined the financial and business risks arising from bee decline globally, and then a book on extinction accounting and investor engagement on species extinctions and biodiversity (Atkins and Atkins, 2019). The latest research in this area includes a new edited book *Extinction Governance, Finance and Accounting: Implementing a Species Protection Action Plan for the Financial Markets* (Atkins and Macpherson, 2022) that establishes the cutting edge of practice and research into the impact of species extinctions and biodiversity loss on investor engagement, banking practice, accounting, and governance more broadly. This work has produced a species protection action plan for the financial markets that makes detailed recommendations for every part of the finance industry and for the accounting profession.

FUTURE DIRECTIONS FOR ESG INVESTMENT

It is important to reflect on where ESG investment is likely to move over the next few years. We have seen a substantial focus on climate change in terms of the "E" of ESG investment in recent years. The focus thereby has shifted from carbon footprinting and intensity scoring to climate value-at-risk analysis and the assessment of implied temperature rise within portfolios. Meanwhile, traditional carbon credit and pricing models often remain fragmented and disconnected from the real economy when and where the green transition is concerned, not to mention the lack of relevant models to assess interrelated social issues, and the implications of a "just transition". Investors are taking a much broader view on the interconnectedness of other environmental and social issues. As can be seen from our discussion above and the emerging research and practitioner work enshrined in *Extinction Governance, Finance and Accounting*, the emphasis is already shifting to addressing biodiversity decline in tandem with climate change, given their increasingly obvious, linked financial impacts as well as their wider societal importance. In the "S" area, issues relating to human rights, and especially workers' rights and modern slavery, are receiving increasing attention, partly as a result of the growing awareness of these problems due to transparency around working conditions arising from the pandemic. Covid-19 has certainly acted as a catalyst for investors and businesses to tackle ESG issues given the light it has shone on inequalities, interconnectedness between nature and business, and poor working practices. In the "G" area, I would anticipate a continuing and deepening focus on boardroom diversity, and achieving control of excessive executive remuneration and business continuity issues. Moreover, systemic ESG risks will need to be assessed with an interconnected economic, financial and extra-financial impact lens, and a focus on real economy pathways, as outlined in the foreword of this book.

SOME FINAL ACADEMIC, METHODOLOGICAL AND THEORETICAL REFLECTIONS ON ESG ACCOUNTING, FINANCE AND GOVERNANCE

It is my hope that this chapter will also provide a benchmark, a model, for young researchers, for PhD students, to see how academic research can engage with practice and ultimately "make a difference". I also hope it illuminates the academic process in accounting and finance for practitioners, and maybe shows the usefulness, relevance and importance of academic findings to the industry. Further, I feel this "story" demonstrates the close linkages between accounting and finance disciplines, and how they should in my view be approached together.

There is a tendency in the academic community at times to treat them as separate disciplines and separate theoretical frameworks with separate journals, and to silo them rather than bring them together. The pioneering work of professors John Roberts and John Holland were inspirational to me as they brought accounting and finance research together with qualitative methods and approaches within an inductive methodology, inspiring further research of this kind. Finance research does not have to follow a positivist, quantitative route. Of course, my own work has developed from their approaches but in the SRI/RI/ESG areas. Again, what have been termed "soft" issues in accounting and finance are clearly now extremely "hard" and material. This increasing awareness of the financial materiality of environmental, ecological, social, community and other ESG issues is becoming firmly integrated, at last, into academic accounting and finance research.

A holistic governance model is becoming the dominant approach internationally, one that incorporates ESG issues into the heart of the governance framework. Today, it is so important to recognise that academic research is not confined to an ivory tower. Academics are passionate about ensuring that their research can make a difference and be transformational. Anyone who thinks academic accounting research must be a dull, dusty affair, with little or no significance to the real world, is gravely mistaken. I hope that these personal reflections and the story told by just one researcher opens the door to a different view of academia. However, this "story" also highlights the critical importance of collaboration between academics and practitioners, and the importance of teamwork and constructive, supportive academic and practitioner relationships.

I would like to dedicate this personal reflection to the late (Thomas) Jeremy Willoughby, former Group Compliance and Risk Director at Schroders, whose friendship and support of my research assisted my access into the early SRI industry for research purposes. He was a wonderful man and I miss our conversations and long lunches. I also would like to think that our conversations on SRI helped to influence developments in the industry.

1 I cannot name our interviewees here due to confidentiality and research ethics.
2 This is a development of a similar table in Atkins *et al* (2015) that tracks the evolution of a responsible investment "logic" using a theoretical framework of institutional logics.
3 See https://www.unpri.org/about-us/about-the-pri.

REFERENCES

Atkins, J., 2021, "Exploring the Business of Extinction", *Accountancy South Africa*, South African Institute of Chartered Accountants, July, pp. 54–55.

Atkins, J. and B. Atkins (Eds), 2019, *Around the World in 80 Species: Exploring the Business of Extinction* (London: Routledge).

Atkins, J. F. and B. C. Atkins (Eds), 2016, *The Business of Bees, An Integrated Approach to Bee Decline* (Greenleaf Publishing: Shipley, UK).

Atkins, J. F. and M. Macpherson (Eds), *Extinction Governance, Finance and Accounting: Implementing a Species Protection Action Plan for the Financial Markets* (London: Routledge).

Atkins, J. F. and W. Maroun, 2014, "South African Institutional Investors' Perceptions of Integrated Reporting", ACCA Research Report.

Atkins, J. F. and W. Maroun, 2015, "Integrated Reporting in South Africa in 2012: Perspectives from South African Institutional Investors", *Meditari Accountancy Research*, 23(2), pp. 197–221.

Atkins, J. F. and W. Maroun, 2018, "Integrated Extinction Accounting and Accountability: Building an Ark", *Accounting, Auditing & Accountability Journal*, 31(3), pp. 1–41.

Atkins, J. F., W. Maroun, B. C. Atkins and E. Barone, 2018, "From the Big Five to the Big Four? Exploring Extinction Accounting for the Rhinoceros?", *Accounting, Auditing & Accountability Journal*, 31(2), pp. 1–31.

Atkins, J. F., A. Solomon, S. D. Norton and J. L. Joseph, 2015, "The Emergence of Integrated Private Reporting", *Meditari Accountancy Research,* 23(1), pp. 28–61.

GSIA, 2021, "Global Sustainable Investment Review 2020" (available at http://www.gsi-alliance.org/wp-content/uploads/2021/08/GSIR-20201.pdf).

Hemmings, D. B. and J. F. Solomon, 1998, "Corporate Governance and Stock Market Duration for South Korea and the USA", *Global Economic Review,* 27(3), Autumn, pp. 76–92.

Houdet, J., P. Addison, P. Deshmukh, H. Ding, J. Finisdore, A. Grigg, M. O'Gorman, F. Quétier, J. Atkins, S. Sparg and R. Vincentz, 2021, "Biological Diversity Protocol (BD Protocol)", Endangered Wildlife Trust – Biodiversity Disclosure Project.

Jones, M. J. and J. F. Solomon, 2013, "Problematising Accounting for Biodiversity", *Accounting, Auditing & Accountability Journal,* 26(5).

Maroun, W. and J. F. Atkins, 2018, "The Emancipatory Potential of Extinction Accounting: Exploring Current Practice in Integrated Reports", *Accounting Forum,* 42, pp. 102–18.

McCann, L., A. Solomon and J. F. Solomon, 2003, "Explaining the Recent Growth in UK Socially Responsible Investment", *Journal of General Management,* 28(3), Summer, pp. 32–53.

Solomon, A. and J. F. Solomon, 1999, "Empirical Evidence of Long-termism and Shareholder Activism in UK Unit Trusts", *Corporate Governance: An International Review,* 7(3,) July, pp. 288–300.

Solomon, J., 2021, *Corporate Governance and Accountability (5e)* (New York, NY: John Wiley).

Solomon, J. and W. Maroun, 2012, "Integrated Reporting: The New Face of Social, Ethical and Environmental Reporting in South Africa?", ACCA, London.

Solomon, J. F., 1999, "Do UK Institutional Investors Adopt a Dual Strategy for Managing Foreign Exchange Risk?", *British Accounting Review,* 31(2), June.

Solomon, J. F., 2009, "Pension Fund Trustees and Climate Change", ACCA Research Report No.106.

Solomon, J. F. and L. Darby, 2005, "Is Private Social, Ethical and Environmental Disclosure Mythicizing or Demythologizing Reality?", *Accounting Forum,* 29, pp. 27–47.

Solomon, J. F., N. L. Joseph, S. D. Norton and A. Solomon, 2013, "Impression Management, Fabrication and Myth Creation in Private Social and Environmental Reporting: Insights from Erving Goffman", *Accounting, Organizations and Society,* 38, pp. 195–213.

Solomon, J. F. and A. Solomon, 2006, "Private Social, Ethical and Environmental Disclosure", *Accounting, Auditing & Accountability Journal,* 19(4), pp. 564–91.

Solomon, J. F., A. Solomon, N. L. Joseph and S. D. Norton, 2000, "Institutional Investors' Views on Corporate Governance Reform: Policy Recommendations for the 21st Century", *Corporate Governance: An International Review,* 8(3), July, pp. 217–26.

Solomon, J. F., A. Solomon, N. L. Joseph and S. D. Norton, 2011, "Private Climate Change Reporting: A Discourse of Risk and Opportunity?", *Accounting, Auditing & Accountability Journal,* 24(8), pp. 1,119–48.

Solomon, J. F., A. Solomon and S. D. Norton, 2002, "Socially Responsible Investment in the UK: Drivers and Current Issues", *Journal of General Management,* 27(3), Spring, pp. 1–13.

9781782724445
BVPRI - #0005 - 300922 - C56 - 234/156/25 - PB - 9781782724445 - Gloss Lamination